Also by Linda and Fred Griffith

The Best of the Midwest:
*Recipes from Thirty-two of America's
Finest Restaurants*

Linda and Fred Griffith

The New American Farm Cookbook

More Than 200 Recipes Featuring Today's Naturally and Organically Grown Foods

Illustrations by Stanka Kordic

Design by Francesca Belanger

VIKING
STUDIO
BOOKS

VIKING STUDIO BOOKS
Published by the Penguin Group
Penguin Books USA Inc., 375 Hudson Street,
New York, New York 10014, U.S.A.
Penguin Books Ltd, 27 Wrights Lane,
London W8 5TZ, England
Penguin Books Australia Ltd, Ringwood,
Victoria, Australia
Penguin Books Canada Ltd, 10 Alcorn Avenue,
Toronto, Ontario, Canada M4V 3B2
Penguin Books (N.Z.) Ltd, 182–190 Wairau Road,
Auckland 10, New Zealand

Penguin Books Ltd, Registered Offices:
Harmondsworth, Middlesex, England

First published in 1993 by Viking Penguin,
a division of Penguin Books USA Inc.

10 9 8 7 6 5 4 3 2 1

LIBRARY OF CONGRESS CATALOGING-IN-PUBLICATION DATA
Griffith, Linda.
The new American farm cookbook: more than 200 recipes featuring
today's naturally and organically grown foods / Linda and Fred Griffith;
illustrations by Stanka Kordic.
p. cm.
Includes index.
ISBN 0-670-84451-9
1. Cookery, American.   2. Farms—United States.   I. Griffith, Fred.   II. Title.
TX715.G84422   1993
641.5973—dc20   92-50406

Printed in the United States of America
Set in Stempel Garamond

To
MADISON NEWMAN MYERS
and
FORREST JENNINGS DRUCKER

*W*e pray that we will have many years to show you
what a great and glorious country we have . . .

*W*e hope that in the years to come you will look on some of
these recipes with the same warm feelings that we have
when we prepare wonderful things from *our*
grandparents' tables . . .

*F*inally, we hope you will have a great passion for life
and the courage and tenacity to follow
all your dreams.

Acknowledgments

This project has been a true labor of love. From the pristine lakes of northern Minnesota to the grain fields of the Texas panhandle, from the bayous of Louisiana to the far corners of Washington State, we visited parts of America rarely seen by tourists. And everywhere we went, we found people whose warm hospitality and generous hearts reached out to embrace us. It was a great journey, an intellectual and emotional adventure unlike any we have ever had before.

It is hard to adequately thank everyone who helped us. But as before, we begin with Donald Patz, Director of Sales and Marketing, Girard Winery, who has chosen American wines to accompany the recipes in this book. Like a musician with perfect pitch, Donald Patz has a God-given gift for matching food and wine.

A special blessing goes to Linda's cousin Susan Cavitch. Busy with four young children, a new home, two dozen egg-laying hens, three roosters, an organic garden, plus her various charitable projects, our Susan still found time to not only test recipes but even create them. We also bless our indomitable friend Sanford Herskovitz for forgiving us when we misspelled his name in our first book, for making certain that we used proper nomenclature for all cuts of meat, and for the encouragement he provided with the support of his wife, Frances.

We thank our new friend Jon Rowley, America's ultimate fish guru, for educating us, for introducing us to so many special people, and for opening our eyes to the challenges and perils facing our treasured waters.

We have driven thousands of miles for this project, all in Fords, thanks to

Pete Olson, Bill Carroll, Bob Horner, and Bob Bierman of the Ford Motor Company. Lucien Vendome and Joseph Reilly of Stouffer Hotels and Resorts watched over us where they could. Thanks also to Diane Hagen of Uniglobe Hagen Travel in Cleveland.

This project began to germinate as we interviewed chefs for *The Best of the Midwest.* Tim Anderson of Goodfellow's, Tejas's Mark Haugen, L'Etoile's Odessa Piper, and Pete Peterson at Tapawingo talked as much about their growers and suppliers as they did about their cooking. So did Clevelanders Zack Bruell, of Z Contemporary Cuisine, and Paul Minnillo, Baricelli Inn's creative force; Chicagoans Jean Joho, the creator of The Everest Room; Steve Lehaie, managing partner of Shaw's Crab House; and Rick and Deann Bayless, the geniuses behind Frontera Grill and Topolobampo—all had valuable suggestions, for which we send sincere thanks.

Chef Larry Vito and Craig Williams, vice president of Joseph Phelps Winery, helped us in California. In Washington, Schuyler Ingle, Mark Musik, and Le Gourmand's talented Bruce Naftaly sent us to great farmers. Thanks also to Tony Casad, executive chef at Elliott's Oyster House in Seattle. In New Mexico, the jump start came from Coyote Grill's Mark Miller; in Virginia, it came from Marcel Desaultniers, who holds court at The Trellis in Williamsburg. Johanne Killeen and George Germon, partners in life as well as in Lucky's and Al Forno, led us to wonderful people in Rhode Island and to Jamie Shannon, executive chef of Commander's Palace in New Orleans.

Then there are our friends Frank Ford, Boyd Foster, and Gary Brownd of Arrowhead Mills, who make the flours we use, and their friend Cliff Orr of Birkett Mills, whose buckwheat flour is the very best. Thanks also to Paul Hammersmidt of Texas State Coastal Fisheries, Virginia Marine Products' Shirley Berg, and Kevin Edberg of Minnesota's Department of Agriculture. And still more thanks to Connie Scheer, proprietor of the wonderful Sportsman's Paradise in Chauvin, Louisiana, and to her friend Sandy Pellegrin, owner of Cajun Tours in Houma. We also thank Michigan's Southmeadow Fruit Gardens for their able apple assistance.

Dear friends Rowena and Peter Fullenwider extended their Southern hospitality and introduced us to Sam Edwards. Hugs to Ingrid, Tom, and Patrick Flynn, who gave us a phenomenal introduction to Cuttyhunk Island. What a boat ride!

To Lisa and Lou Ekus, the ultimate public relations experts, special friends, and gracious hosts, go deep appreciation and admiration. To their courageous daughter Sally, our thanks for helping us to keep things in perspective.

Without Kathleen Crawford we would never have made it through the attendant paperwork. We must also thank Kathleen and her colleague, Mark Haynes, for encouraging Linda's sometimes flagging fitness activities, and for their tender loving care of our patient pets. And more thanks to Laura Stephens, who also loved our creatures while we were gone. And to our friends Deborah and David Klausner, Sandy and Peter Earl, and The Grapevine's Bob Fishman.

Hugs to Stanka Kordic for an even more gorgeous book than the last. To Viking's Michael Fragnito, our gratitude for your confidence; to our extraordinary dynamo editor, Barbara Williams, more appreciation for your encouragement. Thanks also to our outstanding copy editor, Toni Rachiele, and to Francesca Belanger for making this book more beautiful than *The Best of the Midwest.*

Once again, we must thank the great poodle, Dali, our loutish giant Schnauzer, Bacchus, and felines Rosebud, Mary Frances, Omar, Gingerpeachy, and Pooh Bear for loving us despite our absences, and to Pun'kin for watching over us.

Finally, we add our thanks to Andy Myers (Linda's son, the doctor); Rob and Tracy Myers, the parents of our first grandchild, Madison; to Wally Griffith; Gwen and Barry Drucker, the parents of our second grandchild, Forrest; and to Barbara Griffith and her husband, Rob Bialic—to all our children, for their patience and understanding.

For our new friends, the subjects of this work, our appreciation for your cooperation, your hospitality, your dedication, and your example. We wish you a lifetime of rain when you need it and sunshine when you wish it. We wish you supportive and agreeable governmental agencies, and consumers who appreciate quality and are willing to pay for it. We wish you good health and great happiness. And we hope that we will all enjoy the fruits of your labors for many years to come.

Contents

Introduction

Perhaps it was Odessa Piper who started us off on this journey. When we first met Odessa at her wonderful restaurant in Madison, Wisconsin, she said that the key to the quality of what she sent to the tables of her customers was the quality of what her suppliers sent to her. And her suppliers, it turned out, were farmers in her neighborhood, people she knew.

L'Etoile is a small second-floor restaurant overlooking the grounds of the Wisconsin state capitol, where every Saturday morning scores of farmers come to sell at the famous Dane County Market. Over the years Odessa and her chef have gone downstairs to the square to buy produce for the restaurant. Along the way she made many friends, and she found farmers who were excited by the prospect of growing food to her demanding standards of taste, quality, and freshness.

This important relationship between cook and grower, restaurant and farm, was crucial not only to Odessa Piper's success in Madison but also to the success of most of the fine restaurants that we wrote about in our earlier book. So we set off to learn how it worked. We went to see the farmers and fishermen, one by one, traveling more than forty thousand miles in sixteen months to every corner of the U.S.A.

Who are these elite farmers and fishermen who figure so importantly in the work of the great chefs? What are they like? How do they work? What drew them to the farm, to this demanding calling, to the uncertainties of its life? And what keeps them there?

What we found was that, first of all, they love what they do. They are dedicated to quality. Invariably, they are very smart. They think about what they do and why they do it.

Among them we found businessmen, some of them rich, looking for a new challenge, although any rich farmer we found was rich before he became one. On one farm, there was a novelist, the winner of a major literary prize. On others, Ph.D.s, one a professor of biomedical ethics, another a specialist in wild animal physiology. Some were people who were looking for a more tranquil existence than they had had in some busy city. Others included a factory worker whose dream it was to revive a long dormant family farm and a plain dirt farmer who had never left his land—both tending their farms with intelligence and skill and pulling from the land a fulfilling and rewarding living.

We met some polemicists who can tell you the life stories of the leaders of the organic movement; former dropouts, denizens of the counterculture who found meaning and salvation in growing things. There is a mathematician who is the curator of a living museum, an orchard that holds a collection of historic varieties of apple trees. We met fish farmers who know that for fish also, you are what they eat, and they will feed their stock only the best. We met raisers of chickens and turkeys and ducks and geese and pheasants who allow their birds to range freely and get strong and develop character; farmers who allow their sows to browse on the mast of the forest, farrow in the meadows, and suckle their piglets under the trees; people who as a matter of principle never give their livestock antibiotics or growth hormones; a woman who keeps horses and celebrates their ability to turn on a dime and never step on a cauliflower; wise, slow-talking middle-aged men of few words wearing gimme hats.*

---

*A baseball cap with a large bill, also known as a feed cap, that is universal in agriculture—even in Texas. A cowboy hat is fine if you're riding a horse all the time. It keeps the rain and the sun off your head. But unless you are uncommonly short, you just can't wear a cowboy hat in a pickup; there isn't enough headroom. So when a farmer goes into the seed or feed or equipment store he will say, "Gimme one of them hats." It will bear the logo and the name of the company that gave it to him.

On America's beautiful farms are people who like slower rhythms, who are fulfilled by observing the changing months, the passing seasons, or even the years that mark the cycles of the orchardist. There is a young couple who know the names of every one of their goats, milk them twice daily by hand, and from what they give, craft extraordinary cheeses for the kitchens of demanding chefs.

There are botanists who have fathomed the magic of mushrooms and who have learned to propagate these remarkable fungi efficiently and economically, and zoologists who have done the same thing with shellfish. We met a grain grower who flies an ultralight aircraft over his fields, sprinkling larvae of beneficial insects on his corn and wheat. Some of these farmers are tough-minded heroes who have confronted the agricultural establishment and the governmental bureaucracies, and won. Others have tilted with authority and lost but are glad, whatever the cost, that they fought the fight.

We encountered marketing wizards who were able to introduce high-quality, expensive produce to the public and teach them that it *is* better. There are daring, creative people in this book who handle adversity, drought, and the vagaries of the market with courage and dignity, people who celebrate life every day.

In 1975, F. J. Griffith, Fred's father, closed his little restaurant on Smith Street in Charleston, West Virginia. For forty-nine years he had been his own boss, setting up his first restaurant back in 1926. Part of his youth had been spent on his father's dairy farm. There were a couple of dozen Jersey cows, whose raw milk he delivered in glass bottles to residential, grocery, and restaurant customers.

As a boy he raised chickens, hatching the eggs in an old wooden gas-warmed incubator. He knew the taste of a fresh egg. He knew how good a roasted chicken could be. And when Fred would go to his paternal grandmother's house for Sunday dinner, the chicken had been killed just before it was fried, having inevitably eaten a bug or two—what we would today call free-range.

Diners at the McFarland Lunch thought the food was delicious. In that humble place Fred's father was, way back then, like today's finest chefs. He bought fresh. He tasted everything. He knew his farmers, his poultryman, the man who picked his Davis Creek strawberries.

In later years, driven by economic necessity, Fred's dad saw the death of the real connection between the farmer and the person who ate his food. Still, to the end, he could always tell you if a piece of pot roast was from a good steer, or whether a fast-food drumstick was from a chicken raised on three-quarters of a square foot of space in some chicken factory.

Today, 323,000 farmers, or about 1.5 percent of our population, produce 75 percent of our food and fiber. They are the most central but least rewarded component of a remarkable machine that feeds the people of the U.S.A. bounteously for just a fraction of the GNP. We are tempted to boast about that. Agribusiness, the commodities markets, the university–chemical-industry complex, the ag schools, the sophisticated handling and delivery system, and governmental agricultural bureaucracies all combine to make an engine of startling efficiency.

But there is some cost for all of this. In this system the farmer becomes ever more remote from the consumer and receives from his work hardly enough for a decent living. If he is to survive, he must understand this system and take advantage of every opportunity. The farmer must be a savvy business person, politically aware, up to date, competitive, sophisticated, in good financial shape without debt, and, most important, lucky. The farmer needs to pray for the market to be right when his crops come in, and he must not have suffered a drought or a flood, either one of which could cost him the whole place. If the commodities markets and the weather both stay good, the farmer has a chance to stay alive for another season.

There is, however, a slowly increasing number of farmers who have figured out a better way. They do not grow to a price. They are specialists in quality and taste and are directly involved in marketing what they grow. They are usually organic, or as close to it as possible. A weather disaster can still ruin the season; these farmers still have to be lucky. But it is a movement that is saving thousands of American farms.

Fred's maternal step-grandmother, Inez Burdick, was an organic gardener, although she had never heard the term. She had a "summer kitchen" at their home in

Ovapa, West Virginia—an auxiliary kitchen outside the main house, where she could stoke up the wood stove without getting too much heat in the house. In the late summer she would can in there, stuffing the produce from her garden into Ball jars and boiling and sealing them on top of the hot stove.

For kids, spending summers at Ovapa meant work. Everyone who came, even if it was just for a week, worked the garden patch. You carried wheelbarrows of manure out to the rows. You chopped the weeds with a hoe. You caught and killed the beetles that were eating the potato and  tomato plants. No sprays then—you painstakingly picked the bugs and their larvae off the leaves and pinched them with your fingers (the surest way) or crushed them into the dirt with a bare foot. And you knew not to kill the wasps and ladybugs.

The family had good potatoes and onions in the cellar, rows of green beans, peppers, and tomatoes from the garden, peaches, plums, pears, apples, and blackberries picked on the hillsides, all in neat rows of glass jars in the pantry, and crocks of pickles, vinegar, and lard rendered from the last hog killed in the fall. There were sides of bacon in salt and hams hanging in the shed. There was no electricity, no telephone—only the telegraph line, which Fred's grandfather operated at the oil pumping station that he managed. In World War II, the family ate well from their little farm, running it with none of the chemical agents that would soon change the face of American agriculture forever. Until 1950, when the oil ran out and they moved away, Inez and Archie Burdick were organic farmers.

Definitions of organic farming vary from state to state, but there are a number of basic principles. The soil should be free of chemical residues and be alive with organic material. It should be fertilized with natural substances. There should be a rotation plan designed to put nitrogen into the soil. Irrigation water must be free of contamination. Seeds and seedlings must be free of synthetic fungicides and pesticides. Weeds should be controlled by cultivation, rotation, and mulching. Insects should be managed by a complex system of predator insects, timely planting, trapping, and killing, and organic or natural insecticides. Nothing should be used that would leave a harmful residue in the soil or on the produce. Most states now have agencies to ensure that appropriate criteria are met by anyone claiming to be an organic grower.

We did not set out to write an apologia on organic farming. In some places it is not possible, and there are some crops for which it is not possible, at least in certain regions. In some fields of agriculture and aquaculture it is an irrelevant issue. We simply wanted to find men and women who were producing our best food, our most delicious food, our safest and cleanest food. And it turned out that most of them were practicing organic farming, or as close to it as possible.

If you are a farmer or a fisherman and your product is better, tastier, and cleaner than anything else around, you don't want to take it to a market that takes no note of your dedication to quality, that pays no premium for excellence.

Much of the success of the farmers in this book is based on their determination to get for their product what they think it is worth. Often just achieving an organic certification will open the doors to the better markets, attract the more discriminating buyers, and draw a better price. It may be something as simple as letting chickens run around in the barnyard, making them "free-range," packing dried tomatoes in a quality oil, packaging them attractively, and selling them to distributors at the specialty food industry show, or drying Anaheim peppers and stringing ristras for the Williams-Sonoma Christmas catalogue.

Finding the market, developing new customers, converting them to quality, and then getting the good stuff to them quickly and efficiently—these are the preoccupations of the specialist in freshness and taste. These farmers know about overnight air express. They know how to negotiate a contract that will guarantee a favorable price. Some sell shares in the crop—payable in advance—thereby spreading the risk. They have become entrepreneurs.

As backpackers, we often hike the woods of north central Pennsylvania. One week, we walked 88 miles on forest trails and saw only three people the whole time. On one trail, there was evidence that farmers had lived there. We saw the foundation of an old house, the wreckage of a barn, pastures grown over with scrub trees, and an occasional giant old apple tree, bent low by the ages but still with some apples on it, uncollected even by the backpackers and hunters passing by. Babies had been born and children raised on this abandoned farm and others like it.

This kind of emptiness is now a common sight in rural America. In a larger world, these small farms do not work. One cannot buy a pickup truck, a cultivator, or even a milking machine with the cash these marginal farms can generate. But some of the farmers we met have been able to return to places like this. They will succeed only if they can find in the market the customer support and the price they need. A tiny adversity ought not automatically to spell disaster.

It is hard to say that any recipe is your own. But most of the 230 in this book have been part of our repertoire for years. Others were given to us by the farmers and fishermen we visited, and still others were offered by the chefs who were so helpful in sending us to the right places. Friends and relatives have also contributed to this effort.

We have all understood that our mission is to produce recipes that showcase taste and texture, that enhance the quality of the wonderful products we are using. We have sought to avoid any gallimaufry in which the essence of a splendid morsel of meat might be lost.

Donald Patz, our wine maven, does not choose the wine for a dish by edict. He suggests, with his selections, ways to think about the marriage of the food on the plate and the wine in the glass. Appropriately, in this book, he recommends only American wines, the produce of another kind of American farmer.

We hope that we will help readers gain access to many organically grown products that may not be widely distributed in certain parts of the country. Once you have tasted the best, it's hard to go back. In our kitchen, for example, we work only with flours and meals from Arrowhead Mills, Hereford, Texas (page 67). Our jasmine rice is from Lowell Raun (page 90), and our wild rice is Manitok Wild Rice (page 97). When we call for vegetable oil in a recipe, we have tested it using TRISUN oil, sunflower oil high in monounsaturated fats that has been developed by the Lubrizol Corporation in Cleveland.

On a summer Sunday morning, after we had walked the dogs and read the papers, it was time for our bimonthly high-cholesterol breakfast. We sliced a fresh Big Rainbow tomato, one of dozens that would be produced by a little plant we bought from Molly Bartlett (page 297), and sprinkled on some of our own homemade vinegar. On a fresh black rye and buckwheat bread, made with flours from Arrowhead Mills (page 67), we spread some soft Hubbardston blue goat cheese (page 129). We cut a slice of a year-old smoked Edwards Wigwam ham (page 275) and fried some of Kip Rondy's pullet eggs (page 107), so fresh and strong that they snapped with life. We could not recall when it had been this good. It was stuff from people who are now our friends, people we celebrate in this book.

Vegetables

Richard de Wilde

Harmony Valley Farm
Route 2, Box 116
Viroqua, Wisconsin 54665
(608) 483-2143

*H*is grandfather farmed this way because there were no chemicals, and now Richard de Wilde farms this way because there are chemicals. He is a certified organic grower, who cultivates extraordinary vegetables and berries on 20 of the 40 tillable acres on his 200-acre farm in the hills and valleys of southwest Wisconsin. Geologists describe the region as a driftless area, a lush and beautiful patch of space that was missed by the glaciers eons ago.

The farm's wooded hillsides, in addition to protecting the crops from the wind, provide nourishment for forty ewes and fifty lambs. The flock is not large enough to be a source of profit, but Richard likes the lambs, because the babies keep him busy in the cold Wisconsin winters. He grows corn for their silage, has plenty of sweet hay, and supplements their diets with certified organic feed. Their manure thus becomes a truly organic fertilizer for the row crops. The sheep, a cross of Border Lester with Scottish Black Face (which have wonderful curled horns), also provide entertainment and activity for Jack, an energetic Border Collie who likes riding the wagon into the fields to supervise farm work.

Richard works closely with numerous restaurants; they have developed into good customers. Creative chefs understand the quality of his crops and are willing to pay the price. He produces so much, however, that he's able to sell half of what he grows at farmers' markets. It's important, he feels, to grow a wide variety of crops, as well as to make certain that the crops are not ordinary or commonplace. His potatoes are Yukon Golds and purples, not brown bakers. Celeriac and golden raspberries are there, along with rows of succulent strawberries and bicolor corn. There are also numerous rows of asparagus and rhubarb.

The variety of baby lettuces is extraordinary, and includes amaranth leaves, tatsoi, arugula, red and green mustard, mizuna, shungiku (an edible chrysanthemum leaf), red and yellow orach, red iceberg, and red shiso, a deep red leaf that looks like opal basil. Besides the usual popular herbs, there are anise, hyssop, and a wide variety of edible flowers, including a row of red runner beans, grown for their fabulous red-orange flowers. While he direct-sows as much as possible, he does begin summer squash, tomatoes, and cucumbers inside one of two greenhouses. His cash crops are limited only by seed sources. "To have this kind of diversity is ridiculous; it's a management nightmare," he commented with a smile.

The fields are impeccably neat. "It is best to raise your crops in a weed-free environment," he said. "If you keep at the weeds all the time, eventually it becomes a lot easier to have things look this way. Good weed management over the years pays off." He continued, "Flaming has been a big help, although I'm still not really good at it." Flaming, a technique in which a hot propane flame is used to kill weeds, is done when it's hot and sunny, between the time that you've planted the seeds and the time that they germinate. The flame doesn't char and burn the weeds; rather, it causes them to wilt in the sun and die. It saves hoeing and hand-weeding time. This method works well on slow-germinating crops, like many root vegetables and flowers. It's trickier with fast-germinating ones, such as lettuces. For these, Richard has learned to prepare the ground and delay planting just long enough to let the weeds sprout. Then he'll plant and zap the fields in a few days. Other crops, like corn and potatoes, can actually be flamed after they've sprouted.

"I think I'm best at growing cover crops," he said. "Green manure is an integral part of smart farming. It's foolish to not have a crop for the soil. Besides, you're growing your fertilizer right in place instead of hauling it all around; it just makes sense."

He plants a cash crop and a soil crop every year in every field. No field stands fallow. This kind of farming requires a carefully thought-out management program. His preferred cover crops are legumes, which are nitrogen fixers, and which have flowers that become breeding grounds for beneficial insects. He also likes hairy vetch, which is easy to till into the soil. His sweet clovers get 5–6 feet high and are filled with flowers. He plants cover crops along picking roads, spaced at 60-foot intervals, between the cash crops. The tractors can use these if needed. But mostly the cover crops are there so the blossoms can keep the beneficial insect populations very high, and rarely does Richard have to use any of the approved sprays. Some cover crops are cut, dried, and baled; then he has a good mulch for the tomatoes and strawberries. Mostly they are plowed into the soil.

Richard enjoys using a team of draft horses. "They're good with broccoli, but not with carrots," he commented dryly. Then he told us how important it is to know how and where to use all your equipment. "A plow is not just a plow." A moldboard plow, for example, digs down and flips the soil over; it's a good way to kill a cover crop when it has become too big, but it's wrong for everyday use. The chisel plow, however, is kind to the land, cutting things apart without changing the profile of the soil.

A covered wagon is used with a tractor at picking time. This important detail helps to enhance the quality of Richard's produce; the canopy protects the fruits and vegetables from the sun's heat. Things are quickly brought from the fields to a large packing and washing room, which even has a power washer for the root vegetables. Everything is washed with cool well water. There is also an ice machine and handsome boxes for each kind of crop. "It helps at market when things really glisten," he commented. Two huge walk-in coolers and a large refrigerated truck help enhance the packing process. As much care is given to planning his market stands. "Food should look good, too," he said. "Shape and color are as important as taste."

Many people still think that growing organically means simply doing nothing. "It's necessary to understand that a farm is not organic by neglect," he said. "Rather, organic is hard work. The farmer has to do lots of things to build the soil, especially to make better-tasting food. Certified Organic [certified by OCIA, the Organic Crop Improvement Association] is rapidly becoming understood as an important distinction. It rules out organic by neglect or fraud."

And then he reminded us, "Quality and cheap don't go together. My crops are not inexpensive, but they are the best; responsible persons should make an effort to seek out this kind of food. Our bird life is incredible, especially the songbirds. The trout stream is healthy. This system is the answer to environmental problems, not a contributor to them."

Richard takes great pleasure in showing guests around his farm, encouraging them to taste directly from the fields. There is no question that strawberries taste better when they are consumed as they are picked.

Richard's toddler son, Ari, visits the fields often. The best times are spent on the tractor, though acquiring a sticky, red face from the strawberry rows is great too. "Another generation organic farmer?" we asked. "It's possible," said the proud father.

And then he added, "For as long as I can remember, farming has been my first love, the most important thing in life to me. But that was before I had a child."

Algesa's Spinach and Feta Pie

Algesa O'Sickey is well known in northern Ohio for her vibrant paintings and soft sculptures; we who are lucky enough to be among her friends also know her to be a fine cook and elegant hostess. She often serves this as an appetizer, but it is also excellent for lunch with crusty bread and a splendid salad. And it's especially delicious when made with fresh ricotta and feta.

Makes 1 9-inch pie

- 1 tablespoon finely grated pecorino, dry Jack (see pages 139–141), or Parmesan cheese
- 1 pound fresh spinach, trimmed, cleaned, and drained
- 2 cups ricotta cheese
- 1 cup feta cheese
- 3 jumbo eggs, beaten
- 2 tablespoons olive oil
- ½ cup finely minced onion
- 2 cloves garlic, finely minced
- ½ cup finely diced zucchini
- ½ cup finely diced green bell pepper
- 2 teaspoons minced fresh oregano
- 2 teaspoons minced fresh basil
- 1 teaspoon kosher salt
- 1 teaspoon freshly ground black pepper
- 2 tablespoons grated pecorino or dry Jack cheese for garnish (optional)

Lightly butter a 9-inch pie plate or quiche pan. Add finely grated cheese and tilt to coat. Discard excess.

Preheat oven to 350°.

Add spinach to a pot of rapidly boiling salted water and cook for 3 minutes. Then drain, rinse with cold water, and press dry. Chop spinach and place it in a large mixing bowl. Add all other ingredients except the 2 tablespoons grated cheese. Mix thoroughly and spoon mixture into prepared baking dish. Sprinkle with grated cheese if you wish.

Bake pie for 40 minutes, or until pie is firm in the center and top is browned.

Wine: Handley Cellars Sauvignon Blanc (Mendocino County)

Fred's Fried Green Tomatoes

Generally, we have too many green tomatoes at our house because Linda invariably plants too many seedlings too close together, so they don't get enough sun. A benefit of writing this book, however, is that we have developed better gardening techniques ourselves!

Serves 4

- 1½ cups yellow cornmeal
- 3 tablespoons grated dry Jack (see pages 139–141) or Parmesan cheese

1 teaspoon kosher salt
1 teaspoon freshly ground black pepper
½ teaspoon freshly ground white pepper
½ teaspoon ground sage
½ teaspoon dried thyme, crushed
2 jumbo eggs
2 tablespoons milk
½ teaspoon Tabasco
4 very large green tomatoes
1 cup vegetable oil

Sour cream and minced fresh herbs for garnish

Combine first 7 ingredients in a shallow bowl and blend well. In another shallow bowl, combine the eggs, milk, and Tabasco. Beat vigorously.

Carefully remove the stem from the bottom of each tomato; slice off the tops as thinly as possible. Then cut each tomato into thick (⅜-inch) slices. Dip first into egg mixture, then into cornmeal mixture. Let coated slices rest on a cake rack for 30 minutes.

Heat the oil in a large cast-iron skillet. When very hot, add tomatoes. Fry until golden, about 3 minutes per side. Drain on paper towels. Keep each batch of fried tomatoes warm while you fry the rest. Garnish with a dollop of sour cream and sprinkle with herbs.

Couscous, Corn, and Grilled Chicken Salad with Tomatoes and Herbs

We make all kinds of variations on this, including one in which we substitute grilled shrimp for the chicken. It's a great addition to a summer picnic.

Serves 8 to 10

2¼ cups rich chicken stock
4 tablespoons unsalted butter or margarine
1½ cups uncooked couscous
3 ears grilled corn (kernels only)
1 cup shelled fresh peas
½ cup sliced scallions (white parts only)
½ cup diced celery
½ cup diced red bell pepper
1 cup peeled, seeded, and diced red and/or yellow tomato
1 small hot purple or red chile pepper, finely minced

DRESSING

4 tablespoons champagne vinegar
1 teaspoon Dijon mustard
½ cup walnut oil
1 clove garlic, finely minced
1 teaspoon minced fresh oregano
1 teaspoon minced fresh marjoram
Salt and freshly ground black pepper to taste

4–5 boneless, skinless chicken breasts, split, marinated in Basil Vinaigrette (see page 13), and grilled
½ cup walnuts, toasted and coarsely chopped

¼ cup minced fresh chives

Nasturtium flowers and leaves for garnish

Pour chicken stock into a heavy 2-quart pot and bring to a boil. Add butter and couscous. Stir well, cover, and remove from heat. Let stand for 15 minutes, then fluff with a fork and cool.

Combine cooled couscous with corn kernels, peas, scallions, celery, pepper, tomato, and chile. Toss gently.

To make the dressing, combine vinegar and mustard in a small bowl. Slowly add walnut oil, whisking constantly to form a thick emulsion. Add garlic, herbs, salt, and pepper. Combine all but two tablespoons of this dressing with the couscous mixture and blend gently. Distribute among 8–10 dinner plates.

Using a pastry brush, coat grilled chicken breasts with the remaining vinaigrette. Then slice breast halves across the grain, on the diagonal, into 5 or 6 slices. Fan slices over the couscous, a half breast to each plate. Sprinkle with nuts and chives and garnish with nasturtiums.

Wine: Farrari-Carano Fumé Blanc (Sonoma County)

Braised Leeks and Fennel in Mustard Sauce

This is just wonderful with a simple roasted chicken (page 287).

Serves 8

2 large fennel bulbs, trimmed
2 tablespoons unsalted butter
1 clove garlic, finely minced
8 small leeks, trimmed and well washed
1 bay leaf
Salt and freshly ground white pepper to taste
1¼ cups rich chicken stock
¼ cup minced fresh parsley
1 tablespoon minced fresh tarragon
½ cup Crème Fraîche (page 350)
¼ cup Pommery mustard

Fennel fronds for garnish

Cut fennel into eighths lengthwise.

Melt the butter in a large skillet over low heat. Add the garlic and sauté briefly. Add the leeks and fennel and toss to coat. Then add the bay leaf, salt, pepper, and chicken stock. Press a sheet of paper directly on the vegetables, then cover with a lid. Simmer over low heat until vegetables are nearly tender, about 15 minutes. Remove skillet from heat, discard the bay leaf, and, using a slotted spoon, carefully transfer vegetables to a heated platter. In the skillet, whisk the parsley, tarragon, crème fraîche, and mustard. Return the skillet to the stove and turn heat up to high for a moment or two to thicken the sauce. Adjust seasonings, return vegetables to skillet, lower the heat, and simmer until tender, about 2–3 minutes. Spoon into heated serving dish and garnish with fennel fronds.

Bob Cannard

1994 Sobre Vista Road

Glen Ellen, California 95476

(707) 938-8424

*T*here are 35 acres in Bob Cannard's main garden, which lies in a kind of natural amphitheater with higher ground all around it. Glen Ellen is in Sonoma County, far enough north that it gets cold in the winter, but not so cold as to keep things from growing in this rich soil even in December and January.

Cannard, one of the gurus of this organic gardening movement, had worked as a nurseryman in his family's business and had grown bored with it. He wanted to grow more than ornamental fir trees. In 1976, he left to start his own garden, and at about that time Alice Waters started Chez Panisse in Berkeley. She wanted more and better produce than she could get at the terminal. And she wanted it clean, organic, free of chemicals. They talked and struck a deal—he would grow good stuff and she would buy it, a relationship that drew the attention of the nation's food writers and a relationship that continues to this day. In fact, Bob and Alice and her chef, Paul Bertolli, still meet every week, to make their menu fit his garden.

As we walk we taste. We eat sprigs of rapini. We shell fava beans. Bob digs out a blood-red beet and slices it, pulls up an onion, and makes us an ambulatory garden salad, one leaf at a time. Radicchio, romaine, escarole, endive, mâche, oak-leaf lettuce. Sometimes it's hard to see the little lettuces peeping up between other crops. "I always do at least two crops at the same time on a patch of land. One for the garden," he said, "and one for the people." Cover crops, the ones for the garden, put nitrogen into the soil as other crops are simultaneously taking it out.

This is not one of your more manicured gardens. No machines run up and down these rows. Virtually everything is done by hand. Bob estimates that he goes to market with 250 different vegetables and fruits over the course of a year. Alice Waters has four different strains of zucchini to work with and half a dozen different small potatoes—yellow Finn, Yukon Gold, Ruby Crescents, purple, russets. Bob produced 200,000 pounds of potatoes from an astonishingly small part of the garden. "This soil," he said, "is great." He uses crushed basaltic rock and oyster shells to add minerals.

He showed us where he was setting in some alpine strawberries, which are so fragile that you have to eat them right after you pick them. He knows that in the summer, when the plants start to produce, he will have to stand by with a basket as they ripen, and then speed them to his restaurants. He wants them to sing with sweetness. Summer will bring great cherries, nectarines, plums, table grapes, raspberries, boysenberries, blood peaches, white peaches—never a down time.

Bob now has other restaurant clients. And he loves the society of the farmers' market. There he finds more and more people who understand the meaning of organic and they are willing to pay the price for this labor-intensive process, a farming approach that keeps Bob Cannard and his helpers in the field from before dawn until after sunset virtually every day of the year.

He is passionate about what he does, and fanatic about doing it organically. "Healthy plants," he said, "don't get sick."

It is dark by the time we walk back to the little house. Rabbits that have been out there since morning are still there, oblivious to us as we go by. It occurs to us to ask about them. Are they domestic? No, he said. They are wild.

"They are the spirits of the garden," he said. He watches them for a moment or two. "They don't eat anything I need."

Silky Carrot Soup with Tomatillo Salsa

While we know that the furry garden spirits of Bob Cannard's farm prefer to have their carrots uncooked, we're certain that even they would enjoy this delicious soup. If you want to serve this hot, zip it with curry and garnish it with watercress puree.

Serves 8

2 pounds young carrots, trimmed and well scrubbed
2 sprigs fresh thyme (lemon thyme, if possible)
6 cups rich chicken stock
1 1-inch knob fresh ginger, peeled
2 cups plain yogurt
1 cup buttermilk, or more if necessary
½ teaspoon kosher salt
1 teaspoon freshly ground white pepper

SALSA
3 tomatillos
1 tablespoon minced fresh cilantro
1 scallion, minced (white and tender green parts)
Juice of ½ lime
Freshly ground white pepper to taste

Sprigs of fresh thyme for garnish

Put the carrots, lemon thyme, chicken stock, and ginger in a large, heavy pot and bring to a boil. Cover, reduce heat to medium-low, and simmer briskly until the carrots are falling apart, about 30–40 minutes. Remove pot from the heat and let contents cool for 15 minutes. Remove thyme and ginger and discard.

In a food processor, puree the cooked carrots with part of the simmering liquid. Combine carrot puree and remaining liquid with the yogurt, buttermilk, salt, and pepper in a large mixing bowl. Whisk until well blended. Taste and adjust seasonings. Chill overnight.

To make the salsa, remove husks from tomatillos and combine with cilantro and scallion in a food processor. Pulse until finely chopped. Add the lime juice and blend. Add pepper to taste and keep chilled until needed.

Bring soup to room temperature before serving (about 30 minutes); thin with more buttermilk if necessary. Ladle soup into shallow soup plates and garnish with a dollop of salsa and a sprig of thyme on top of the salsa.

Wine: R. H. Phillips Night Harvest Sauvignon Blanc (Yolo County)

Beet Salad with Champagne-Tarragon Vinaigrette

If you cannot find champagne-tarragon vinegar, use white wine vinegar and some fresh tarragon.

Serves 4–6

> 1 pound beets, preferably several varieties, trimmed
> 6 small yellow potatoes
> 3 tablespoons champagne-tarragon vinegar
> ⅓ cup extra-virgin olive oil
> 1 tablespoon minced shallots
> 1 tablespoon minced fresh tarragon
> 1 tablespoon capers
> About ½ pound fresh baby greens, washed and drained
> ½ bulb fennel, trimmed and sliced into thin rings
> Kosher salt and freshly ground black pepper to taste

Preheat oven to 400°. Into a 9x13 baking dish, pour ¼ inch of water. Arrange beets in a single layer, cover pan tightly with foil, and bake until beets are tender when pierced with a fork. Remove beets from pan and allow to cool. Then carefully peel and discard skins. Slice beets into ¼-inch-thick rounds and reserve.

Place potatoes in a large pot filled with salted water. Bring to a boil and cook until tender when pierced with a fork, about 15 minutes. Drain and cool. Slice, unpeeled, into ¼-inch-thick rounds and set aside.

Pour vinegar into a small bowl. Slowly whisk in olive oil and beat until a thick emulsion is formed. Add shallots, tarragon, and capers. Chill.

Arrange greens among serving plates. Distribute beets and potatoes attractively on the greens. Scatter fennel slices over the plates and drizzle with vinaigrette. Sprinkle with salt and pepper and serve.

New Potato Salad with Basil Vinaigrette

This is superb when made with "marble" potatoes, those very small potatoes that slip through the sizing machines because they are the size of marbles. Just watch the cooking time.

Serves 8–10

> 3 pounds small red, yellow, or blue potatoes, scrubbed
> 4 peppercorns, crushed
> 4 cups rich chicken stock
> ¼ cup cider vinegar
> 1 red bell pepper, finely diced
> 1 green bell pepper, finely diced
> 4 ounces peeled jícama, finely diced
> ½ cup finely chopped scallions (white part only)
> 1 dried red chile pepper, crushed

BASIL VINAIGRETTE
> 4 tablespoons cider vinegar
> 1 tablespoon Dijon mustard
> ¼ cup vegetable oil
> ¼ cup extra-virgin olive oil
> ¼ cup minced fresh basil
> 2 teaspoons celery seed

Kosher salt and freshly ground black pepper to taste

Diced fresh peeled tomato and avocado for garnish

Combine potatoes, peppercorns, and stock in a heavy saucepan; bring to a boil, cover, and lower heat so potatoes just simmer. Cook until the potatoes are tender, about 15 minutes, depending on the size of the potatoes. Drain and save the liquid, if you wish, for a summer soup.

Carefully slice potatoes into thick slices, about ¼ to ½ inch thick. Put into a large bowl, sprinkle with ¼ cup cider vinegar, and cool. Then add the next five ingredients and toss well.

To make the vinaigrette, combine ¼ cup vinegar and mustard in a small bowl, whisking well. Slowly beat in oils to form a thick emulsion. Add the basil and celery seed.

Carefully combine the vinaigrette with the potatoes and vegetables. Toss and season with salt and pepper. This does best if it stands for a few hours. If you store it in the refrigerator, be sure to let it come to room temperature before serving. Divide among serving plates and garnish with tomatoes and avocado.

Sautéed Cabbage, Fava Beans, and Sage

We love the fragrance of this dish—it really smells like autumn. In fact, we frequently serve it as part of our Thanksgiving meal, since it goes so well with poultry.

Serves 6

½ cup unsalted butter or margarine
2 thick strips bacon, diced, or
   2 tablespoons olive oil
1 cup diced onion
1 small, firm head green cabbage, coarsely chopped
2 cups shelled fresh fava beans or lima beans
2 tablespoons minced fresh sage, or 1 tablespoon dried
   Kosher salt and freshly ground white pepper to taste

Melt butter (and olive oil if you are omitting the bacon) in a large, deep skillet. Add bacon and sauté until partially cooked. Add onion and cook over low heat until just transparent. Add cabbage and fava beans. Stir well to coat, then add sage. Cover and cook, stirring occasionally, over low heat until cabbage is tender, about 20 minutes. Add more butter or olive oil if mixture seems too dry. Add salt and pepper to taste.

D. L. "Mike" Michael

Ladybug Farm
Box 277, 8577 Richardson Road
Spring Grove, Illinois 60081
(815) 675-2463 or (708) 497-4603

"When you look at that," said Mike Michael, glancing ruefully at the weeds between his covered rows, "herbicide sounds awfully good. That natural way is a real pain when it comes to tomatoes."

But there will be no herbicides used at Ladybug Farm. No insecticides, either, or chemical fertilizers, or fungicides. Here, there is constant attention given to the weeds, and Mike is always trying to find new strategies for controlling them. "Here we're planting grass between rows," he said. "Grass tends to crowd out the weeds, and it makes it neater and cleaner for the people who work the rows." Also, on the rows themselves, he uses a lot of plastic—black photodegradable mulch with holes punched in it that allows the tomatoes to come through but holds back the weeds.

Mike Michael is at war with the weeds, but he fights fair—no poisons. And as tired as he sometimes gets, he is winning. "We raise the best tomatoes in Illinois," he said. "Maybe in the U.S.A." Things are under control; the tomatoes are off to a good start. "Can something still go wrong?" we asked. "Oh hell yes," he said. "But we'll just have to wait to see what it is."

Mike became a farmer after he retired. He had owned a company that published major trade journals, which caught the attention of a big media conglomerate and it made him an offer he couldn't refuse. So in 1983 he found himself looking for something new to do.

Mike and his wife enjoyed gardening and had bought some farmland a few years earlier. So, Mike added to his holdings and started raising vegetables. The farm, now 125 acres, is in Spring Grove, Illinois, about an hour's drive north of Chicago's Loop.

Mike had thought a lot about organic farming and he had the resources to give it a real try. He was not particularly attracted to the rhetoric of the organic farming movement, however. It was simply that he saw that "chemicals were ruining these lands." And he wanted to see if being organic would work and if it would make a difference. Would the land, in time, forgive us our abuse of it? And if so, could he find a niche in the market for his special tomatoes and lettuces?

At first Mike used fertilizer from a sewage-treatment plant. But in recent years he has leased some land to a dairy farmer who pays his rent in manure. Sometimes he is paid in horse manure, which may be why he has so many weeds. Weed seeds can sail through a horse's alimentary canal unharmed, ready to spring into action when the manure is deployed on the field.

Mike also makes good use of cover crops, plants that bring nitrogen to the soil and, when turned over, enrich it. He took us to see a planted field of clover. It was rich and thick. "This is the way to treat the land," he said. "This is the way it is supposed to be."

Early in his adventure, on a trip to London, Mike had a chance meeting with a Chicago restaurateur, who, when he learned that Mike was particularly interested in tomatoes, asked him if he could grow beefsteak tomatoes. Mike said yes and the deal was struck. The result of the collaboration was the famous beefsteak tomato salad at Morton's, one of Chicago's landmark steak houses.

Mike Michael learned that restaurants and supermarkets are two different animals. Markets generally want tomatoes that are hard and tough, easy to handle, with a lot of shelf life. Restaurants want them ripe, juicy, soft, delicious, and ready to eat. Mike knew that he had to grow the kind that gives you an immediate taste reward. Instead of buying his seed from a commercial seed house, he buys "garden" seed through catalogues. "If we bring the chefs ripe, home-garden tomatoes, they think it's wonderful," said Mike.

Here are a few of the varieties that Mike takes to the chefs, as listed on the farm's "menu": Lemon Boy, a yellow beefsteak; Golden Boy, a new tomato with a deep yellow flesh; Valencia, a bright orange fruit with a full rich taste; Pineapple, colored yellow and red with a vivid sunburst of those colors inside; Persimmon, another new variety, deep orange in color; Great White, a creamy white beefsteak; Evergreen, which, as you might expect, stays green even when it is ripe; Constuloto Genovese, which is red with a convoluted skin; Firebird, a garden classic, deep pink and rich; Purple Calabash, another new one, ruffled like the Constuloto and bronze in color; San Marzano plum, a classic Italian tomato; Giant Belgium, new and sweet and dark pink; and Oxheart, pink and heart-shaped and probably the biggest and best of the big ones.

At the other end of the size spectrum, there are cherry tomatoes, like Orange Sundrop; Ping Pong, a yellow tomato; Green Grape; and Red Pear, a teardrop variety.

This will always be a tomato farm. There are more than 10 acres of tomatoes. But there are also 3½ acres of asparagus. We ate it raw as we walked the fields, as delicious as we had ever tasted. And there are interesting varieties of peas, beets, carrots, eggplant, summer and winter squash, peppers, radishes, corn, and herbs. There are scores of varieties of greens—arugula, Dutch cress, peppergrass, Namfong Chinese mustard greens, komatsuma, mizuna, Tyfon Holland greens, Italian chicory, purple and red amaranth, red and yellow orach, lamb's quarters, shell-leaf mâche, Lolla Biondo, Lolla Rossa, and golden and green purslane ("Another weed we can sell").

Mike and his wife now stay up to four months at their place on Sanibel Island, Florida. But four months with no dirt to dig in is too much for Mike Michael. So he bought 30 acres on Pine Island and started an organic asparagus patch there. But the great chefs of Chicago need not despair. He'll be back in Illinois every spring. And if there has been a kitchen miscalculation and a chef really needs some baby lettuces, Mike will load them—organic, clean, chilled, and spun dry—into the back seat of his BMW and personally deliver them to the restaurant.

Fresh Golden Tomato Soup with White Beans

Linda happens to love yellow tomatoes. Thanks to Mollie Bartlett of nearby Silver Creek Farm, we enjoy an abundant and interesting variety. The first season we planted Mollie's seedlings, we had eight-foot tomato trees! We combine Yellow Marglobe and Yellow Plum for this soup.

Makes about 3 quarts

1 pound Great Northern beans
¼ cup olive oil
½ cup minced sweet onion
2 cloves garlic, minced

6 pounds garden-grown yellow tomatoes, stemmed and coarsely chopped
Sugar to taste
Kosher salt and freshly ground white pepper to taste
8 cups rich chicken stock
Bouquet garni, made by tying a sprig each of fresh parsley and thyme, a bay leaf, 1 clove, and a tablespoon of bruised white peppercorns together in cheesecloth

Fresh chives and shredded sharp cheese, such as aged Gouda or dry Jack (pages 139–141) for garnish

Place beans in a large mixing bowl and cover with plenty of water. Allow beans to soak overnight, then drain and set aside.

Heat olive oil over low heat in a heavy-bottomed 3-quart pot. Add onion and garlic and cook slowly, until onions become transparent. Then add tomatoes. After twenty minutes, taste mixture and add sugar, salt, and pepper. Cook over low heat for 40 minutes. Remove pot from heat and let cool for 15 minutes.

While tomatoes are cooking, place drained beans and chicken stock in a 5-quart soup pot. Bring to a boil over medium heat, then reduce heat to a slow simmer.

Purée tomatoes in a Foley food mill, then discard skin and seeds. Add puree and bouquet garni to stock-and-bean mixture. Simmer, partially covered, for 2 hours, or until beans are tender. If soup needs thickening, remove cover completely, increase heat, and cook at a low boil for 15 to 30 minutes more. Adjust seasonings.

To serve, ladle into flat soup plates and garnish with chives, a dollop of shredded cheese, and more freshly ground white pepper.

Shaw's Crab House Broiled Salmon with Teardrop Tomato Relish

The salmon comes by plane from Seattle; the tomatoes, peppers, and herbs are often driven to town by Ladybug's Mike Michael himself. You can always trust Chicago's Shaw's Crab House to serve only the very best.

Serves 4

> 1 pint teardrop tomatoes
> 1 small red bell pepper
> 1 small green bell pepper
> 10 fresh basil leaves
> 3 tablespoons olive oil
>   Salt and freshly ground black pepper to taste
> 4 8-ounce salmon fillets
>
>   Lemon wedges and fresh basil for garnish

Two hours before serving, remove stems from tomatoes, thinly slice peppers, and julienne basil leaves. Combine these in a small bowl with the olive oil. Season with salt and pepper and allow to marinate.

Heat broiler until hot. Arrange salmon on a lightly oiled broiling pan and place under broiler, 3½ inches from heat source, turning once, for 6–8 minutes, depending upon thickness of fillets.

Serve with tomato relish and garnish with lemon wedges and basil.

Wine: Chateau St. Jean Chardonnay "Robert Young Vineyard" (Alexander Valley)

Golden Gazpacho

Serves 6–8

> 2½ pounds ripe golden tomatoes, peeled and seeded
> 3 cloves garlic, minced
> 4 whole blanched almonds
> 1 English cucumber, peeled and diced
> ⅔ cup finely diced white onion
> 3 cups rich chicken stock
> 2 teaspoons sugar

1 teaspoon salt
3 drops Tabasco
1 teaspoon freshly ground white pepper
¼ cup extra-virgin olive oil
1 tablespoon cider vinegar

2 tablespoons minced chives for garnish

Combine tomatoes, garlic, almonds, half the cucumber, and ½ cup of the onion in the bowl of a food processor fitted with the metal blade. Pulse until mixture is puréed. Pour into a large bowl and whisk in chicken stock, sugar, salt, Tabasco, and white pepper. Blend well. Then vigorously whisk in olive oil and vinegar. Adjust seasonings and chill thoroughly.

Serve garnished with the remaining cucumber and onion and the minced chives.

Wine: St. Supery Sauvignon Blanc (Napa Valley)

Roasted Red Tomato Sauce

This sauce is splendid in combination with pizza or pasta. We especially enjoy it when made with heirloom-seed tomatoes, which have thinner skins and more flavor. This sauce also makes a superb base for fresh tomato soup.

Makes about 4 cups

4 pounds garden-grown red tomatoes
¼ cup olive oil
½ cup minced sweet onion
3 cloves garlic, minced
Sugar to taste

Salt and freshly ground black pepper to taste
Minced fresh basil, thyme, or rosemary to taste

Spray a well-scrubbed grill with Pam and heat until hot. (We like to add some hickory, apple, or cherrywood chips just before the food is placed on the grill.) Carefully arrange the tomatoes over the heat and turn often. The goal is to blister the tomatoes evenly, not to burn them. When they are well blistered, remove the tomatoes from the grill and let them sit until they are cool enough to handle. Remove stems and any burned skin areas, then coarsely chop the roasted tomatoes.

Heat olive oil over low heat in a heavy-bottomed 3-quart pot. Add onion and garlic and cook slowly until onion becomes transparent. Then add tomatoes. After 20 minutes, taste mixture and add sugar, salt, and pepper. Cook over low heat for 40 minutes. Remove pot from heat and let cool for 15 minutes.

Purée tomatoes in a Foley food mill and discard skin and seeds. Season with herbs according to your pleasure.

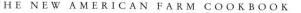

Carol Rees and Joseph Scanlon

Redwing Farm

RR #1, Box 2654

Townshend, Vermont 05353

(802) 365-4656

*I*s there a more beautiful place in all the earth than the mountains of Vermont on a sunny October day? Our hearts soared as we drove along the West River, the lovely stream that flows out of the Green Mountain National Forest, meanders through the countryside, and empties into the Connecticut River at Brattleboro. The mountains were exceptional, with their crackling shades of orange, scarlet, and gold. A brilliant blue sky completed the setting. But it became even more extraordinary as we left the main road and worked our way along the very narrow State Forest Road just outside of Newfane. Redwing Farm is nestled in a small valley within the state forest.

Carol Rees and Joseph Scanlon have 115 acres—30 are tillable, 45 are forest, and the balance is in hay. Half of the tillable acres are planted with what they call "green manure," a cover crop. Very little of the work in the fields is done with machine power. Carol, who grew up on the back of a horse, works several teams of gorgeous Amish-bred Percheron horses; she bought her first Percherons at auction in Ohio in the mid-eighties.

"Driving horses is very special," she said. "Also, they go between tight rows faster than a rototiller. And they turn in tight spots and sideways far better than a tractor. Finally, they require old equipment that is easily available here in Vermont, and it's cheap. They also provide a large supply of manure."

"We grow organic because we're trying to preserve the planet," Joe told us. "We're treading as lightly as possible on the earth. That the food tastes better is a nice benefit." Their early plan was to sell to farmers' markets and restaurants. But the need to have a huge variety of products, said Joe, "nearly drove us nuts."

They realized, finally, that to make organic growing work they would need a large grass-roots base. They found some other farmers who shared their concerns for the environment. They knew that there was a growing number of people who wanted organically grown products; the problem was to reach them in a way that was economically viable. Before the summer of 1984, they and four other farmers started Deep Root, a cooperative that, by the end of the season, had grown to eight member farms. Deep Root did between $50,000 and $60,000 worth of business that first summer. By 1989, Deep Root had grown to fourteen farms, including a few from Massachusetts and New Hampshire. And they did just about half a million dollars in business.

Planning and continuity are really important to the cooperative. Each farm has to do a production estimate each year. They plan by projecting their weekly output product by product. Where there are glaring voids or excesses, the farmers must negotiate with one another. Ultimately, each signs an agreement for the season. They also are committed to high quality and good appearance. In 1990, there were twenty-six farms in the group. By then, they also had a warehouse for storage, although their goal is to be sold out each year by Thanksgiving. Each member of the cooperative has its own label as well as that of Deep Root.

Each farm has different strengths and interests. Redwing's particular focus is on fall vegetables, although they also grow a variety of salad greens and carrots. They have 3½ acres of winter squash—sweet dumpling, butternut, buttercup, acorn, delicata, and Red Kuri (a Japanese soup squash that also makes a fine pie squash because of its rather dry texture). They plant one acre of cabbage and half an acre of Napa cabbage. They like peppers, too; there are about 6,000 plants on their own half-acre. Kale, green and red chard, Brussels sprouts, parsnips, some melons, and two acres of potatoes also keep them busy. In addition to Kennebec potatoes, they plant Red Morelands, an early potato, and Green Mountain, a smooth white that is especially popular with restaurants. In fact, they save all of the "marble" potatoes—the smallest potatoes—for Vermont's legendary Four Columns Restaurant. All of the potatoes are graded by an effective but old-fashioned machine—"a genuine antique," Carol boasted. The sweet and tasty Gilfeather turnip, an old variety currently enjoying a revival in New England, is also a favorite in Redwing's fields.

Neither Carol nor Joe can imagine working in an office; they both love being outside. "There's a nice rhythm to farming together," said Carol. They love what they do but worry that the farmer "may disappear into the realm of exotica. So many people see you as a hick, yet there is a very high level of education among the members of Deep Root." In order to encourage a better understanding of farming life, Carol and Joe operate a bed-and-breakfast at Redwing that specializes in giving guests a view of a real working farm. And while the theaters and night life of New York are very far away, Carol and Joe find that their own satisfactions are enormous.

But still, Carol looks at some of her contemporaries, caught up the business world, using their M.B.A.s, and she worries that "there are just too many people out there who still get an Incomplete in life."

Veal Breast Stuffed with Root Vegetables and Hazelnuts

This is wonderfully fragrant as it cooks. Start dinner with a nice fresh tomato soup and accompany the roast with Sautéed Cabbage and Fava Beans (page 14) and a toothsome bread. Then follow with a small green salad dressed with walnut oil and garnished with goat cheese.

Serves 8

- ½ pound turnips, trimmed and cleaned
- ½ pound parsnips, trimmed and cleaned
- 3 carrots, trimmed and scraped
- 1 very large onion, peeled
- 1 fennel bulb, trimmed and cleaned
- 6 ounces celeriac, trimmed and cleaned
- 3 large cloves garlic, minced
- 1½ tablespoons olive oil
- ¼ cup minced fresh parsley
- ¼ cup minced fresh chives
- 2 teaspoons minced fresh thyme
- 1 teaspoon minced fresh marjoram
- 2 jumbo eggs, beaten
- 3 tablespoons unbleached flour
- 6 ounces skinned hazelnuts, coarsely chopped

Salt and freshly ground black pepper to taste
- 3 tablespoons vegetable oil
- 1 veal breast, boned and with a pocket (about 6 pounds after boning)
- ½ cup unbleached flour
- 2 cups Cabernet Sauvignon or Syrah wine
- 1 cup rich beef stock
  Rich Wild and Shiitake Mushroom sauce (page 324)

Fresh herbs and edible flowers for garnish

In a food processor fitted with a fine shredding blade, carefully grate, in turn, the turnips, parsnips, carrots, onion, fennel, and celeriac. Combine vegetables in a large mixing bowl with the garlic, oil, herbs, eggs, 3 tablespoons flour, and nuts and mix well. Add salt and pepper to taste.

Preheat oven to 475°. Choose a large roasting pan that has a tight cover, coat the bottom with the vegetable oil, and set aside.

Open breast, pocket side up, on a large work surface. Pack entire pocket area with the vegetable mixture. Then roll the breast and carefully skewer it closed. Lace skewers tightly with string and secure.

Sprinkle roast with flour on all sides. Rub slightly to coat well, then season with salt and pepper. Place meat in pan, skewered side down. Roast, uncovered, in preheated oven for 1 hour. Add wine and stock to pan, reduce heat to 350°, and cover. Roast for 1½ hours more, basting several times. Transfer roast to a carving platter and let rest in a warm place for 10 minutes.

Meanwhile, pour Rich Wild Mushroom Sauce into roasting pan, place on the stove over medium heat, and deglaze pan, scraping until all particles adhering to the bottom have been loosened. This will make an extraordinary sauce. If necessary, simmer briskly until sauce is thickened.

Cut roast into half-inch-thick slices and garnish with sauce, herbs, and edible flowers.

Wine: Shafer Vineyards Merlot (Napa Valley)

Winter Squash Soup with Caramelized Garlic

Serves 8

- 3 pounds winter squash, such as delicata, butternut, or Red Kuri
- 6 cups rich chicken stock
- 2 teaspoons chopped fresh thyme
- 7 tablespoons unsalted butter or margarine
- 1 medium onion, chopped
- 1 stalk celery, finely chopped
- 2 cups plain yogurt
- 1 cup heavy cream
- ½ teaspoon kosher salt
- ½ teaspoon freshly ground white pepper

- 8 large cloves garlic, thinly sliced
- 3 tablespoons dark brown sugar, firmly packed

Fresh chives for garnish

Preheat oven to 425°. Cut squash in half, discard seeds, and place halves skin side up in a baking pan. Add water to a depth of ¼ inch. Bake squash in preheated oven until tender, about 45 minutes.

Meanwhile, in a large, heavy saucepan, heat stock with thyme to release the flavor of the herb and keep warm.

Melt 4 tablespoons butter in a skillet, add the onion and celery, place wax paper directly on the vegetables, and sweat over low heat until onions are translucent. Set aside.

When the squash is tender, scoop flesh into the bowl of a food processor fitted with the metal blade. Add onion mixture and purée until smooth.

Carefully stir the puree into the hot stock. Bring to a gentle boil, reduce heat, and whisk in the yogurt, then the cream. Allow mixture to simmer for at least 10 minutes. Do not bring to a boil. Taste and adjust seasonings.

Just before serving, melt the remaining 3 tablespoons butter in a small skillet. Add the garlic and sauté over low heat for 2 minutes. Add the brown sugar, turn heat up, and keep stirring until the mixture begins to caramelize.

Ladle soup into flat soup plates and add some caramelized garlic and a length of chive.

Wine: Folie à Deux Winery Chenin Blanc (Napa Valley)

Potato Pancakes

Although best when brought right from the skillet to the table, these can also be made ahead, frozen, and reheated in a hot oven. Besides being a terrific accompaniment for meat, they make a nifty cocktail nibble when garnished with sour cream and caviar.

Serves 4–6

> 6 large russet potatoes, peeled
> 1 large sweet onion
> 1 jumbo egg
> 2 tablespoons unbleached flour
> 1 tablespoon very finely minced chives
> Salt and freshly ground black pepper to taste
> Up to 1 cup vegetable oil for frying

Coarsely grate potatoes and onion by hand using the coarsest side of a four-sided grater. Alternate onion with potatoes (the onion keeps the potatoes from blackening) and keep gratings together in a large bowl. Squeeze the mixture with your hands against the inside of a colander until all liquid is gone. Combine with egg, flour, and chives and mix well. Season to taste.

Heat ½ cup oil in a large cast-iron skillet until smoking. Drop in pancake batter according to size preferred. Press lightly to keep thin. Do not crowd. Fry over medium-high heat until golden on the bottom, about 3 minutes. Turn and brown on other side. Remove with a slotted spatula and drain on paper towels. Keep warm in oven while you cook the remaining batter, adding more oil as necessary.

To reheat frozen pancakes, preheat oven to 500°. Place frozen pancakes on a cookie sheet; bake for 8–10 minutes, then serve.

Ruby Jones's Braised Red Cabbage

This recipe comes from Carol Rees's late grandmother. The sweet-sour sauce complements roast duck or pheasant to perfection.

Serves 6–8

> 1 head red cabbage, cored and chopped
> 4 tablespoons unsalted butter
> 1 tablespoon red wine vinegar
> 1 tablespoon sugar
> ½ cup apple cider
> ½ cup plum jelly
> 2 tart apples, peeled, cored, and chopped

Combine all ingredients in a large enameled saucepan. Place over medium-high heat and bring to a boil. Mix well, reduce heat, and cover. Simmer for 1½ hours, stirring from time to time.

Glen Lux

Willow River Farms
P.O. Box 450
San Felipe, Texas 77473
(409) 885-3614

Willow River Farms is 308 acres, certified organic by the Texas Department of Agriculture, and a member in good standing of TOGA, the Texas Organic Growers Association. In its first year, the farm sent 15 tons of scores of kinds of organically grown vegetables to market. The potential of this rich land is vastly higher than that, and the farm, its owners, its manager, and its dedicated workers are all focused on turning it into an agricultural showplace.

The owner of the farm is the Center for the Retarded of Houston, Texas. The manager is Glen Lux. The workers are retarded clients of the Center.

On the late-winter day when we arrived at the farm, the workers were taking a break after a morning in the fields. They were having their lunch at picnic tables they had set up near the craft shop. On this morning there were thirty of them—twenty who lived in handsome new cottages on the property and ten others who commuted from the city in the Center's van. They were delighted to have visitors, and one of the men went to fetch the manager.

Glen Lux grew up a farmer. But it was the oil patch that really attracted him, and for twenty years he was a welding contractor in oil fields all over Texas and the Southwest. But even in the salad days of Texas oil exploration, when he worked seven days a week, and sometimes around the clock, making quite a bit of money,

Glen always had farming on his mind. He knew it, understood it, and practiced it whenever he could.

The opportunity to become a full-time farmer again presented itself when his wife, Jane, a staff member of the Center for the Retarded, told him that the Center was planning to buy a farm as a residential center for some of its clients. Glen was ready for the change. He applied and got the job of farm manager. He thinks it is amusing that his wife, the professional in dealing with retarded people, works now in administration in Houston, while he, who knew nothing about it, is suddenly the one who deals with them all the time, teaching them, motivating them, caring for them.

There is a wonderful, comfortable, and easy rapport between Glen and the residents. They like him a lot and they always want to please him with their work. There is good-natured kidding and banter.

Eventually there will be twelve cottages to house ninety-six residents. Each house will have a house parent or parents. There is a new community center, which houses the craft activities, offices, and sales rooms. In it is a big kitchen where the residents can convert some of their abundant crops into salable sauces and other products.

To qualify for work on the farm, or to live there, the clients have to want to be there. They must have mastered self-care skills. They must be socialized enough so that they function well in a group setting. The family of the client is required to pay a few fees to cover the resident's costs, but they are not high, in part because so much of the food they eat is raised here. In effect, they earn part of their living by their work.

As we walked through the fields, we saw hardy arugula, parsley, and mint in raised beds that had grown all through the winter chill. Nearby rows were being prepared for four thousand broccoli plants. Two of the residents were laying the groundwork for a huge planting of hollyhocks around the administrator's cottage, not for the market but just because they are so beautiful.

Residents will set a thousand cherry tomato plants and a dozen other larger varieties, including Celebrity, Heat Wave and Lemon Boy, Roma and Summertime. Glen hopes to have tomatoes over several seasons, taking advantage of Texas's early spring and late fall. There will be gray and black zucchini and a score of other squashes, winter squashes, pumpkins, burgundy okra, eighty rows of cauliflower, both white and purple, jalapeños, habañeros, and bell peppers. They will grow cayenne peppers for drying, and White Greenwich, Burgundy Greenwich, and yellow onions, scallions, cantaloupe, and four kinds of watermelons.

Glen knows every detail about where everything will go. He shows us the patch for cucumbers, Texas Long, Straight Eight, and Texas Pickling. Potatoes do well here, and they are especially popular in the residential kitchens. As the crops grow, Glen works with restaurants and distributors to develop markets for this cornucopia of quality organic produce. He also consults with other experts to develop product ideas that will enable the farm to utilize their bounty long after the harvest is over.

As we drove past a field where several of the residents were at work, Peter, a fifty-five-year-old man with Down syndrome, waved at Glen and pointed at the row he was hoeing. "He likes me to see how well he is doing," said Glen. Peter had been given a job sorting garlic for planting. He liked that job, and when it was over he was reluctant to go back to the hoe. "Sometimes he will put down the hoe and go all the way back to the shed to see if there is any more garlic for him to sort." Glen was finally able to convince him that it is as important to plant the garlic as it is to prepare it.

Another middle-aged man was wielding a motorized weed cutter, doing solitary duty along the fence rows. "He doesn't like to work with a group," said Glen. "So we give him chores like that, which he does very well."

Without ever having been trained to work with the retarded, Glen does it with a natural patience and understanding. He seems instinctively to know how to motivate them. He likes these people who are with him on the farm, people whose toil could make Willow River Farms a model effort not only in agriculture but in human relations as well. His effort is one that would be of great interest to anyone concerned with and dedicated to helping the retarded have a better, happier, healthier, and more productive way of life. And it validates the idea that there is something inherently sustaining and health-giving in being close to the soil.

Cucumber Yogurt Soup

Serves 6

2 cups rich chicken stock
½ cup golden raisins
1 English cucumber (unpeeled), shredded and drained
⅓ cup minced scallion (white part only)
¼ cup minced red onion
2 tablespoons minced fresh parsley
2 teaspoons minced fresh dill or fennel
3 cups plain yogurt
½ cup buttermilk, or more if needed
Salt and freshly ground white pepper to taste
1 jumbo hardboiled egg, chopped

¼ cup chopped toasted pine nuts and dill leaves or fennel fronds for garnish

Combine stock and raisins in a large mixing bowl and let rest for 30 minutes. Add cucumber, scallions, onion, parsley, fennel, and yogurt. Mix until smooth. Add buttermilk, salt, and pepper; blend. If mixture is too thick, add more buttermilk. Taste and adjust seasonings. Fold in hard-boiled egg.

Chill and serve in flat soup plates, garnished with pine nuts and dill leaves or fennel fronds.

Cajun Smothered Chicken, Andouille Sausage, and Okra

Serves 8

1 pound andouille sausage, sliced into 1-inch pieces
1¼ teaspoons freshly ground black pepper
1¼ teaspoons freshly ground white pepper
1 teaspoon cayenne pepper
2¼ teaspoons kosher salt
1 teaspoon dried thyme
1 teaspoon dried basil
¼ teaspoon ground sage
1 bay leaf
½ cup onion, finely chopped
½ cup celery, finely chopped
1 medium green bell pepper, finely chopped
½ medium red bell pepper, finely chopped
1 jalapeño pepper, seeded and finely chopped

12 scallions (white part only), trimmed and finely chopped
1¼ cups unbleached flour
Up to 1 cup vegetable oil
2 3–4 pound frying chickens, cut into 8 pieces each
1 tablespoon finely minced garlic
½ pound fresh okra, trimmed and sliced into ½-inch rings
4 cups rich chicken stock
1 teaspoon Tabasco
3–4 cups hot cooked jasmine rice with butter and white pepper

2 tablespoons minced fresh chives for garnish

Place sausage in a 2-quart pot, cover with water, and bring to a boil; reduce heat and simmer for 5 minutes. Drain and reserve.

Combine next eight seasonings in a small bowl and set aside. Mix onion, celery, peppers, and scallions in another bowl and reserve.

Place flour in a plastic bag and add a few chicken pieces. Shake the bag to coat the pieces evenly with flour. Repeat until all meat is coated. Place chicken on a cake rack and reserve ¼ cup of the flour.

Pour about ¼ cup oil in a large deep skillet and heat over high heat until smoking. Brown chicken, adding more oil as needed. Set browned chicken aside and discard oil. Coat the bottom of the skillet with fresh oil and heat until hot. Add garlic, okra, and half of the vegetable mixture. Sauté over medium heat for 5–6 minutes, stirring often. Remove from heat, add chicken and sausage to the skillet, sprinkle with all the seasoning mixture, and set aside.

Pour stock into the 2-quart pot used for the sausage and bring to a simmer.

Meanwhile, make a roux by combining ¼ cup oil and the reserved flour in a small cast-iron skillet. Using a whisk, blend very well over medium-high heat until mixture is dark brown. Scrape the bottom of the skillet with a wooden spoon from time to time. Remove from heat and add remaining vegetables and Tabasco, whisking for at least a minute. Add this mixture to chicken stock and whisk over medium heat until mixture is nicely thickened. Pour sauce over chicken, cover skillet tightly, and simmer for 45 minutes. Remove bay leaf. Serve on a generous portion of seasoned rice and sprinkle with fresh chives.

Wine: Hidden Cellars Winery Zinfandel (Mendocino County)

Mr. Brisket's Veal Brisket

Our wonderful friend Sanford Herskovitz, a.k.a. Mr. Brisket, Cleveland's leading purveyor of the five major food groups—beef, veal, lamb, pork, and poultry—is more noted for eating than for cooking. Even so, we were very amused that when a version of this recipe was printed in a monthly column Linda writes for *Currents*, the typesetter goofed and wrote 203 pounds of onion. The mistake caused much laughter in Cleveland and was even noted in *The New Yorker*.

Serves 4–6

> 3 pounds sweet onions, thinly sliced
> 1 bay leaf
> 2 veal briskets, about 2½ pounds each

Salt and freshly ground black pepper to taste
Garlic powder to taste
Paprika to taste
1 teaspoon fresh thyme
1 tablespoon minced fresh parsley
2 cups rich chicken stock

The day before serving, preheat oven to 350°. In a heavy roasting pan with a cover or an ovenproof Dutch oven, combine onions and bay leaf. Arrange briskets, fat side up, on the onion bed. Season well with salt, pepper, garlic powder, and paprika. Add thyme, parsley, and stock, cover, and cook in oven for 2½ hours. Remove pan from oven and place briskets on a plate to cool. Then wrap them well in foil and refrigerate overnight. Remove onion and bay leaf from gravy and discard. Pour remaining gravy into a container, cover, and chill.

A few hours before serving, remove briskets and gravy from refrigerator and let come to room temperature.

Preheat oven to 350°. Slice the brisket thinly across the grain and arrange slices in an ovenproof dish. Remove congealed fat from surface of gravy. Pour gravy over sliced meat and cover with foil or a lid. Cook brisket for 45 minutes.

Wine: Nalle Winery Zinfandel (Sonoma County)

Orlando and JoAnn Casados

Ranch O Casados

P.O. Box 1149

San Juan Pueblo, New Mexico 87566

(505) 852-4482

There were chile peppers roasting on a huge charcoal grill (*horno*) when we arrived at Orlando and JoAnn Casados's New Mexico farm. You knew it even before you passed the entrance gate to the Casados compound, as the rich fragrance of smoky chiles wafted past the open car windows. In a long open shed, two men were tending the operation, turning the Numex Big Jim chiles with tongs.

These were destined for JoAnn Casados's restaurant, we later learned. They would become *chiles rellenos,* and some of them, to our delight, would be for our own dinner. JoAnn's Ranch O Casados Restaurant is in the town of Española, about seven miles from the farm.

Her customers come to feast bounteously on what JoAnn calls "new Mexican" dishes at startlingly reasonable prices. She prepares every tamale, every tortilla, every sopaipilla from scratch, by hand. There is *posole, chicos,* chiles, corn in every form, and special versions of virtually every well-known Mexican dish. Some sauces are rich in the flavor of good tomatoes. Others are made with a variety of lusty fresh peppers. This food is not bland, and some of it is so hot that it can make the unsuspecting diner cry. JoAnn is proud to state on her menu that almost everything they serve she and Orlando raise on their farm.

The restaurant became a logical extension of the family farm, which consists of 47 acres at El Guique, where Orlando Casados grew up and where he and

JoAnn are raising their family. The fields where they raise their corn, squash, and peppers are in easy view of the house. A big irrigation ditch runs through the property between the house and the farm itself. Water is a precious commodity in this arid climate, especially in the long, dry summers.

Orlando is an organic farmer who has a market for everything he grows. He laughs when you ask him how he came to the decision to give up chemical fertilizers, herbicides, and insecticides. "We never used chemicals," he said. "When my dad started farming we were just too poor to buy them. So we were organic because we had to be. Now we're in fashion."

Running an organic operation is not without its perils. He told us of losing fields to blight, rusts, insects, and other hazards that might easily have been handled with one chemical or another. He had just recently lost a field of bell pepper plants to a mold caused by some untimely spring wetness. So he just plowed them under and planted the field with corn, which tolerates almost anything. He said about such setbacks, "It's just the way it is."

While Orlando grows a lot of different vegetables, it is his chiles that have made him famous. He is an authority on the subject and is often consulted by agricultural experts. He shows us articles in magazines describing his operation and methods. Conventional wisdom holds that a cool-weather chile is a cool chile. But Orlando has worked with agronomists and geneticists at New Mexico State University to develop special varieties that are more suitable for the shorter growing season in his northern New Mexico region. Most of these have been derived from what Orlando calls the "native chiles of northern New Mexico." Perhaps the researchers' most important contribution is that they have developed chiles that still deliver substantial heat in spite of being grown in a cooler climate.

Numex Big Jim, Española Improved, Sandia (also called the Commercial Long Hot), Cuarteles Native, and Chimayo are just some of the varieties that have been developed for Orlando and others in cooler climates in recent years. The 14 acres that he plants every year yield what connoisseurs call some of the best chiles in the country.

Orlando does a lot of processing. His financial success has come from the value he adds to his crops on his farm before he ships them to market. He toasts corn for *chicos,* boils corn in lime for *posole,* and grinds and packages his own brand of cornmeal. He roasts chiles for canning and stuffing. And he grinds dried red chiles into wonderfully fragrant powder, makes flakes with others, and produces beautiful ristras. All these products are sold both retail and wholesale. JoAnn's restaurant is a big customer, of course, and he sells these products, as well as quantities of his fresh produce, at the Santa Fe Farmers' Market.

Over the years, when we have traveled to some place where we were not so sure whether the food would be tasty or bland, we have learned to take no chances. We always carry a bottle of Tabasco in our luggage. For Orlando Casados, it isn't Tabasco; it's cans of chiles. He always tucks a few into his suitcase as an antidote for whatever bland food he might encounter in his travels.

On the evening that we dined with the Casados family in the Ranch O Casados Restaurant in Española, we tried almost everything on the menu—and we did not miss our Tabasco!

While we were in the restaurant, a line of heavy thunderclouds had moved into the area. Lightning overpowered the sodium-vapor lights in the parking lot. We stood with Orlando and JoAnn in the doorway and watched the drenching rain come down.

Orlando Casados smiled. "Looks like we're living right," he said.

The Best Chili in the World

Everyone has an opinion about what is the best chili, but we know that this is the best. Because chiles vary, you will still have to adjust the seasonings according to your palate. We like our chili to be hot, but not so hot that one loses all ability to taste. We also feel that it is impossible to make a small quantity of chili. This freezes superbly. Serve it with some Country Cornbread (page 80).

Makes about 10 quarts

    2 dried ancho chiles
    2 dried pasilla chiles

2 dried mulato chiles
2 cups boiling water
2–3 fresh jalapeño peppers
1½ pounds mixed fresh mild chiles, such as Big Jim or Anaheim
1 green bell pepper
2 red bell peppers
2 tablespoons vegetable oil, or more if necessary
10 pounds beef brisket tops, trimmed of excess fat and cubed
1 bay leaf
2 teaspoons ground dried oregano
3 tablespoons ground cumin
2 tablespoons medium-hot chile powder
½ teaspoon ground allspice
12 cloves
1 tablespoon kosher salt
1 teaspoon cayenne pepper
1 tablespoon freshly ground black pepper
2 teaspoons freshly ground white pepper
2 pounds onions, thinly sliced
2 rounded tablespoons minced garlic
2 28-ounce cans crushed tomatoes
750 ml. R. H. Phillips Night Harvest Cuvée Rouge or a Côtes du Rhône
7 ounces unsweetened baking chocolate
2 27-ounce cans kidney beans, drained

Sour cream, chopped scallions, and grated sharp cheddar cheese for garnish

Break the 6 dried chiles in half and remove stems and seeds. In a small bowl, combine dried chiles with boiling water and soak for 30 minutes. Pour mixture into the bowl of a food processor fitted with the metal blade. Add jalapeños and pulse until mixture is well puréed; set aside. Stem, seed, and devein fresh chiles and peppers. Cut into ½-inch dice and set aside.

Heat 2 tablespoons vegetable oil in a large, heavy 12-quart pot. Brown meat, about a pound at a time. Remove browned cubes to a large bowl and add more oil to the pot if necessary. After all the meat is browned, sauté the next ten ingredients over medium-low heat for 2 minutes. Return browned meat to pot and mix well. Add chile puree, diced fresh peppers, and all remaining ingredients except kidney beans. Stir well, partially cover, and simmer briskly for 1 hour. Uncover and continue to simmer for another hour. Taste and adjust seasonings. Add beans and simmer 1 more hour. Skim and discard fat.

Serve in large bowls with a dollop of sour cream and a sprinkling of scallions and cheese.

Wine: R. H. Phillips Vineyard Night Harvest Cuvée Rouge (California) or Beer

Hot and Spicy Sauce

This sauce was inspired by Paul Prudhomme. Every time we make it, we seem to make more changes. It is wonderful with Hot and Spicy Meat Loaf (page 265) and terrific with grilled or roasted chicken.

Makes 4 cups

1 tablespoon minced garlic
1 teaspoon freshly ground black pepper

1 teaspoon freshly ground white pepper
½ teaspoon medium-hot chile powder
½ teaspoon freshly grated nutmeg
1 sprig fresh thyme
1 bay leaf
½ cup minced celery
½ cup minced onion
½ cup minced red bell pepper
½ cup minced scallion (white part only)
¼ cup minced fresh Big Jim or Anaheim chile pepper
1 tablespoon minced fresh cayenne chile
4 cups rich chicken stock
6 tablespoons vegetable oil
6 tablespoons flour
1 tablespoon Worcestershire sauce
1 teaspoon Tabasco, or more to taste
¼ cup minced fresh parsley

Combine the garlic, black pepper, white pepper, chile powder, nutmeg, thyme, and bay leaf in a small bowl. Combine the celery, onion, red pepper, and scallion and the two fresh chiles in another bowl. Pour stock into a heavy 2-quart saucepan and bring to a boil over medium heat, then lower heat to a simmer.

Combine oil and flour in a cast-iron skillet and whisk over medium heat until this roux becomes dark brown. Add reserved seasoning mixture and stir over heat for 30 seconds. Then remove pan from heat and stir in reserved minced vegetables. Continue to stir mixture for at least one more minute.

Gradually whisk this roux mixture into the simmering stock until mixture is evenly blended. Add Worcestershire and Tabasco and blend. Simmer this sauce very slowly for 30 minutes, or until it has lost its floury taste. Skim fat off top.

Adjust seasonings; you may wish to add more Tabasco. Just before serving, remove bay leaf and thyme sprig. Then add parsley, stir in, and serve.

Grits Soufflé

This dish is terrific with grilled skirt steaks and sautéed peppers. It is also wonderful with any kind of roasted chicken, meat loaf, or barbecue.

Serves 4–6

4 tablespoons unsalted butter
¾ cup hominy grits (not instant)
½ cup chopped scallions (white and tender part of green)

1 fresh red serrano or jalapeño chile pepper, finely minced
1 tablespoon minced green bell pepper
¼ teaspoon cayenne pepper
¼ teaspoon freshly ground white pepper
1 teaspoon salt
1 cup grated sharp cheddar cheese
3 jumbo eggs

Minced fresh parsley and cilantro for garnish

Preheat oven to 400°.

Butter a 1½-quart soufflé pan and set aside.

Cook grits according to the package directions. When done, remove from heat and add remaining butter and all other remaining ingredients except for eggs. Stir very well. Then whisk in eggs, one at a time. Pour into prepared soufflé pan and bake, uncovered, for 30–40 minutes, or until center is firm to the touch.

Southwest Sausage

If you have the equipment, then make links; otherwise, make sausage patties. We think they make great brunch food, along with Summer Salsa (page 43), spicy scrambled eggs, and Country Cornbread (page 80). The sausages freeze well, too.

Makes 3 pounds

1 dried ancho chile, seeded
1 dried pasilla chile, seeded

1 cup boiling water
2½ pounds boneless lean pork butt, ground
½ pound smoked bacon, ground
2 large shallots
3 cloves garlic
2 red jalapeño peppers
2 tablespoons red wine vinegar
3 tablespoons cilantro, chopped
2 teaspoons ground cumin
1 teaspoon ground cloves
1 teaspoon cinnamon
½ teaspoon dried oregano
   Salt and freshly ground black pepper to taste
   Vegetable oil
   Hog casings (optional)

Place ancho and pasilla chiles in a small bowl and cover with boiling water; soak for 30 minutes, then drain well. Purée in a food processor fitted with the metal blade.

Add all other ingredients except oil and casings to the food processor and process well. Quickly sauté a bit of the mixture in some of the vegetable oil for a taste test. Adjust seasonings accordingly.

Fill hog casings with the meat, or form mixture into 2-ounce patties. You can package and freeze either the patties or the links at this point.

To cook, brush a large cast-iron skillet with a light coating of vegetable oil and heat. When hot, add sausage and cook over moderate heat until brown on each side, about 4 minutes per side.

Wine: McDowell Valley Vineyards Les Vieux Cepages Grenache (McDowell Valley)

Elizabeth Berry

144 Camino Escondido
Santa Fe, New Mexico 87501
(505) 982-4149

*I*n the society of her dogs, half a dozen of them, including a Dalmatian, we explored Elizabeth Berry's remarkable farm.

We had made a date to meet her, but when we got there, after sixteen miles of four-wheel-drive territory, she wasn't. Truck trouble, we learned later. But since there is no electricity or telephone on the ranch, she couldn't let us know.

Those sixteen miles had taken us 1½ hours to traverse. Elizabeth Berry's farm is in high, dry country, spectacular for its starkness. In the distance, 1,000-foot-high rocky mesas, with their strata of oranges and greens, define the valley. Even when there is rain, the vegetation is sparse here. So we were not prepared, when we crested the final ridge, for the extraordinary lushness of the gardens around Berry's house. It was as green as Hawaii.

Her secret is in the highly efficient use of the meager water supply. There is a plastic-lined reservoir that holds the overflow from a small spring. This water is distributed to the rows of the garden by underground pipes that feed a drip irrigation system, which works best in arid climates. Often the ground around the growing crops is covered with cloth to inhibit evaporation. The farmers of Israel have designed comparable techniques to get the most out of every ounce of precious water.

Out of this sandy soil comes a profusion of flowers. Half a dozen varieties of sunflower look down on Berry's patio. Farther out, there are rows of various varieties of corn in different stages of development. There is a cornucopia of squash, beans, ornamental kales, eggplants, tomatoes, chiles, including some very special tiny purple ones, and in one large area, all kinds of delicate lettuces and herbs in sunken beds.

Elizabeth's house is fairly new, contemporary and open in design. We could see interesting art on the walls and a beautiful grand piano in the living room. How could she have gotten it here? Surely not over the road we used. There are various pieces of sculpture in the gardens among the flowers. And on the peak of the roof, as though it were the prow of a wooden sailing ship, there was a huge carved woman, bare-bosomed, looking out at the road that approaches the house.

Abiquiu, 55 miles north of Santa Fe, is well known as the home of the late artist Georgia O'Keeffe. It is also Elizabeth's mailing address. Elizabeth makes the 150-mile round trip from her garden to Santa Fe frequently, taking her produce to Mark Miller's Coyote Cafe and the city's other fine restaurants and markets.

At the Coyote Cafe, we met the farmer. For two hours we sat with her at the bar, eating squash blossoms stuffed with wild mushrooms. Elizabeth Berry is a strikingly attractive woman in early middle age. Her graying hair is long and straight. Her dress and jewelry are clearly a personal aesthetic statement. She is as fashionable as any affluent client in this fashionable and expensive restaurant.

Her husband is a retired geology professor from the University of California at Berkeley. It was he who designed and installed the efficient system of irrigation at the ranch. Their children are grown and on their own. The Berrys loved this area of New Mexico and found their ranch a number of years ago.

The garden started small. It was just something that Elizabeth loved to do, and when the restaurant scene started to develop in Santa Fe, and especially when Mark Miller started his famous Coyote Cafe, Elizabeth learned that she had a potential market. And she started working to develop it, researching the restaurants' needs and planting to answer them. Today she grows more than fifty varieties of tomatoes and almost as many varieties of squash and chiles. And there's a wide variety of corn as well.

Her seeds come from myriad sources. She might have as few as twelve seeds for one rare variety of tomato or chile. But her spring seedlings all together number close to ten thousand! We learned of a new plan to grow corn and flowers on a patch of land acquired in Abiquiu. This will enable her to plant more potatoes in the acreage near her home. With the long drive from one area to the other, how on earth will she manage to tend this new garden?

"I don't know," she answered, "but I'll figure it out when I have to."

It came time to find out what varieties of vegetables she has been growing on her farm.

"Not a chance," she laughed. "Trade secret."

And she meant it. "I don't want someone out there to grow what I'm growing and offer to sell it to Mark at a cheaper price."

It can sometimes be lonely out there so far away from everything. In the cold winter, when the gardens are covered with snow, Elizabeth attaches a stereo system to a car battery and listens to operas. That's also the time to catch up on reading and plan next year's gardens.

Any number of odd characters—hunters, hermits, renegades—have wandered through her property over the years. And one day, strangely, a piano tuner. Her workers live on the place these days, so when her husband is away there is at least someone she knows fairly close by.

We asked if the itinerant piano tuner tuned her piano. The answer was "Of course."

And finally, as we parted, we asked how she got the piano there. She had paid $5,000 for it after her first successful year of growing. A truck was able to bring it to within half a mile of her house, on the other side of the Chama River. The men brought it across on a raft and carried it the half mile from the river to her house.

"It makes beautiful music," she said.

Buster's Pickled Jalapeño Peppers

Buster Arnim gets his name on his mother-in-law's recipe because he swears that it is his hand that makes these for us every year. We love to visit The House on the Hill, Julie and Buster Arnim's wonderful bed-and-breakfast in Ellsworth, Michigan, because of their very special Texas hospitality. Even in the cold northern Michigan winter, the Lone Star will be fluttering on the flagpole and there will be some jalapeños to add a bit of warmth to the grilled Michigan whitefish or venison sausage.

Makes about 20 quarts

> ½ bushel jalapeño peppers
> 40–44 cloves garlic, peeled
> 2 very large dill bunches with seed heads (20–24 seed heads)
> Up to 4 cups kosher salt
> 3 quarts cider vinegar

Distribute peppers among hot, sterile jars. Take care not to force too many into each. Place two garlic cloves, a dill seed head, and a long stalk of dill cut into several pieces in each jar. Set aside.

To make brine, put 3 quarts of water in a large stockpot. Add 1 cup of salt and stir thoroughly, then let the water stand a minute. Try to float a whole egg in the water. If it doesn't float, gradually add more salt, stirring and letting it settle, until the egg will float. At that point, remove the egg, add 1½ quarts vinegar, and bring the mixture to a boil.

After brine has boiled for 2 minutes, remove from heat. Pour brine over prepared jars to fill. Seal jars and repeat brine-making process until all jars are filled.

Allow jalapeños to cure for several weeks before eating. Will keep for a month in refrigerator after opening.

Summer Salsa

Makes 3 cups

> 1 cup diced tomato, preferably yellow
> ¾ cup diced sweet onion
> ⅓ cup fresh lime juice
> ½ teaspoon kosher salt
> ½ teaspoon coarsely ground black pepper
> 1 small fresh chile pepper, minced
> 1–2 tablespoons minced cilantro
> 1 tablespoon minced fresh chives
> 1 avocado, diced

Combine all ingredients except avocado and blend. Let stand for several hours, if possible. Add avocado and blend well just before serving.

Fried Squash Blossoms

Squash blossoms are really quite versatile. They are delicious stuffed with sautéed wild mushrooms, cheese, or a shredded chicken or duck mixture.

Serves 15

> 1 cup dark beer, plus more if needed
> 1 teaspoon kosher salt
> 2 teaspoons ground cumin
> ¼ teaspoon ground allspice
> ½ teaspoon cayenne pepper
> 1 cup unbleached flour
> 6 ounces grated aged hard cheese, such as dry Jack (see pages 139–141), sheep's-milk, or dry goat

10 ounces young goat cheese, such as
   Capri
½ cup sour cream
¼ cup Crème Fraîche (page 350)
2 tablespoons minced cilantro
1 tablespoon medium-hot chile
   powder
1 tablespoon minced fresh chives
30 male squash blossoms, pistils
   removed
4 cups vegetable oil
   Summer Salsa (page 43)

   Cilantro and chives for garnish

Combine beer, salt, cumin, allspice, and cayenne in a mixing bowl and blend. Add flour all at one time and whisk vigorously until mixture is very smooth. Set aside to rest at least one hour.

In the bowl of a food processor fitted with the metal blade, combine cheeses, creams, cilantro, chile powder, and chives. Pulse until smooth. Scrape this mixture into a pastry bag fitted with a wide tip.

Spread open the leaves of one squash blossom, insert the tip of the tube, and fill. Carefully twist the ends of the petals to seal filling inside. Repeat until all the blossoms are stuffed.

Check reserved batter. If it is too thick, add more beer and whisk until smooth. Heat the oil in a deep fryer or wok to 350°. Dip blossoms in batter and fry, a few at a time, without crowding, turning once. They should be brown on both sides in about 2 minutes. Drain and serve with salsa and herbs.

Wine: Sanford Winery Sauvignon Blanc (Santa Barbara County)

Elizabeth's Squash Delight

Elizabeth Berry's little purple chiles are Aurora Chiles, from Southern Exposure Seed Exchange, Box 158, North Garden, Virginia 22959. In addition, Elizabeth likes the two squash varieties used below because they have large male blossoms, good for stuffing. The seeds are available from The Cook's Garden, Box 535, Londonderry, Vermont 05148.

Serves 4

2 tablespoons extra-virgin olive oil, or
   more if necessary
2 Aurora chiles or 1 serrano chile, cut
   in half lengthwise
2 cloves garlic, minced
6 baby Gold Rush squash, each about
   3 inches long, cut in half lengthwise
6 baby Ronde de Nice squash, each
   about 1 inch round, cut in half
   lengthwise
   Salt and freshly ground black
   pepper to taste
¼ cup freshly grated Parmesan cheese
4 male squash blossoms

In a medium skillet, heat olive oil over medium-high heat until it sizzles when a drop of water is added. Add chiles and garlic and sauté until garlic starts to turn brown, then remove both. Add squash and sauté until crisp. Season with salt and pepper.

Garnish with cheese and squash blossoms and serve with sautéed chiles on the side (only for passionate chile lovers).

Wine: Hinman Vineyard Riesling (Oregon)

Coll Walker

261 West Main Road

Little Compton, Rhode Island 02837

(401) 635-4719

*T*he country road runs from Fall River, Massachusetts, to Rhode Island Sound and the Atlantic Ocean. To the west is the undulating coast of the Sakonnet River. Sailboats and fishing boats are scattered out over the shining blue waters. Typical gray New England homes cloaked in weathered shingles or clapboard dot the landscape; usually they are surrounded by three-foot-high stone walls, the kind that divide the land throughout New England. It's beautiful country, little known to most of us, since tourists tend to go to the beaches of Newport or Cape Cod. Rhode Islanders try to keep this secret region for themselves. The rest of us only hear about it when a hurricane like Bob roars up the coast.

Johanne Killeen and George Germon of Al Forno and Lucky's in Providence took us to see this area, because their restaurants get the best produce, berries, and seafood out this way. From early spring to Thanksgiving, George's white truck makes its stops along Route 77, ensuring that the finest and freshest products available will be in their dining rooms each night.

Coll Walker's roadside stand is especially well represented in Johanne's and George's kitchens. When the tomatoes are prime, you'll find them all over their menus. When the corn is ready, it, too, appears in many guises.

On an early August day the stand is lined with baskets of fragrant berries, lettuces, basil, cucumbers, gorgeous leeks, tiny tomatoes, as well as the plump red and yellow varieties, and yellow, red, and green peppers. There are green and yellow zucchini, green beans, and yellow wax beans. A cart is filled with just-picked corn. And there are pails of dahlias and gladiolus. Soon there will be perfectly ripened Red Haven peaches and McIntosh apples, then turnips, Brussels sprouts, cabbages, chard, and broccoli. In fall, the tables and benches will be piled high with winter squash and pumpkins.

We feel there is a special flavor to vegetables grown by the ocean. Coll Walker farms 50 acres, land bordered along one side by the bay. "People say that things taste better because of the salt water spray," he said. "I really can't tell, but maybe it's because of all the seagull droppings."

If Coll's not riding the tractor or supervising field work, he's at the stand filling shelves or checking the tomato sorters. "I have to touch every tomato myself." He laughed as he tossed a tomato from the "perfect" basket to one for irregulars. "But it looks gorgeous," said Polly Gracia, the tomato sorter. "Ah," Coll responded, "but it's soft." Every tomato is sorted that way, and each is gently polished with a soft cloth.

There are 2 acres of tomatoes, a total of four plantings. The first begin in a plastic-covered greenhouse near the road. They are ready for the stand in June. By the time those run out, his field tomatoes begin ripening. He prefers the new hybrid varieties, believing that they are the most consistent for taste, appearance, firmness, and yield. While customers like the low-acid yellow tomatoes, Coll dismisses these from his own table. "There's no taste to them," he said. All of his tomatoes, though, are plump and tasty. "We have good, heavy soil here. The fog and dew from the ocean add something good, although if we get too much moisture, the tomatoes will crack." The main problem for tomatoes, however, is usually from Coll's own chickens, who enjoy pecking in the tomato fields. Since the chickens manage to deliver good eggs, especially one that actually deposits a blue egg daily at his bedroom door, Coll forgives them their penchant for tomatoes.

"See those gorgeous birds?" Coll said. "They are terrible, especially the red-wing blackbirds. So I use Mylar balloons, but I have to move them often." There are also problems from woodchucks and rabbits, and a family of raccoons that torment Coll out in the corn fields, but deer are not a problem in this area.

Coll prefers to grow for customers who will actually prepare and eat his vegetables and fruit; he is not growing for distributors. His operation is farmer-to-eater. The premium paid by the customer enables him to spend extra attention on each tomato, every ear of corn.

Coll is an independent New Englander who farms the way he thinks is right for his land and his customers. He wishes no part of anyone's doctrine, and is therefore unwilling to commit totally to organic farming. But he seldom needs to spray, and when he does, he uses as safe a chemical as possible, at night, spraying only those areas necessary. Of course he knows that food is best when it is as free of chemicals as possible, but there are times when one organic farmer, surrounded by heavy chemical users, will be set upon by something that threatens his entire crop, and a tough decision has to be made. Coll wants the option of using chemicals, although he rarely exercises it and never uses chemicals randomly. But because of his location along the bay, a wet summer can lead to crop-threatening fungus, so he will very carefully select a spray that can help. Sometimes it will be an agent that will not satisfy the criteria for organic certification. But Coll is still a very natural grower, responsible and dedicated.

Coll closes the market for Thanksgiving. After enjoying the holiday, he'll return to the stand and scrub it out. Then he relaxes. "I do nothing, absolutely nothing," he said. But the cycle begins again when it's time to order seeds. Soon it's the season for preparing the fields. Little by little his staff comes together again. "I hate to count how many it takes to run this place," he admitted. Somewhere between ten and fifteen was the final calculation.

What happens to the damaged tomatoes? The very bad ones go to a pig farmer, the slightly damaged ones are sold for sauce. And what does Coll take home? The damaged ones, of course. "I'm Scottish," he said. "I'm cheap, so I only cook the damaged vegetables for myself. Except for corn. I always pick my own corn, right before cooking it."

Nanni's Dill Pickles

Nanni was Dorothy R. Kight of Houston, Texas. This recipe comes to us from her daughter, Julie Arnim, our dear friend, who, with her husband, Buster, runs The House on the Hill in Ellsworth, Michigan—the best bed-and-breakfast establishment we've ever been to. Whenever we leave there they give us jars of these pickles and Buster's Jalapeño Peppers (page 43).

Makes about 40 quarts

    1 bushel small cucumbers
40–42 jalapeño peppers
80–84 cloves garlic
    3 or more large dill bunches with seed heads (40–42 seed heads)
     Approximately 6 cups kosher salt
    6 quarts cider vinegar

Distribute cucumbers, whole or sliced, among hot, sterile quart bottles. Take care not to force too many into the jars. Place 1 jalapeño pepper in each jar. Then add two garlic cloves, a dill seed head, and a long stalk of dill cut into several pieces. If you like them to be "dilly," add more dill. Set aside.

To make brine, put 6 quarts water in a large stock pot. Add one cup of salt and stir thoroughly, then let the water stand a minute. Try to float a whole egg in the water. If it doesn't float, gradually add more salt, stirring and letting it settle, until the egg will float. At that point, remove the egg, add 2 quarts of vinegar, and bring the mixture to a boil.

After brine has boiled for 2 minutes, remove from heat. Pour brine over prepared jars to fill. Seal jars and repeat brine-making process until all jars are filled.

Allow pickles to cure for at least 1 week before eating.

Puree of Winter Squash

This very simple dish is standard on our table for both Thanksgiving and Christmas. We find that baking the squash in a hot oven causes some of the natural sugars to caramelize, adding a superb flavor to the puree.

Serves 6–8

> 1 4–5-pound winter squash, such as butternut, Hubbard, or delicata
> ½ cup unsalted butter or margarine, or more if desired, softened
> 1–2 teaspoons freshly ground white pepper
> Salt to taste (optional)

Preheat oven to 425°. Place whole squash on a foil-lined baking pan and bake in preheated oven until very tender when tested with a long-tined fork, about 50 minutes. If your Hubbard squash was sold in pieces, place the chunks flesh side down in a baking pan. Add about ¼ inch of water and bake until tender. Remove from oven and let cool ½ hour.

Cut squash in half, discard seeds and strings, and scoop pulp into a food processor fitted with the metal blade. Cut butter into chunks and add to processor. Purée until smooth. Add white pepper and blend.

If you are making the dish ahead of time, spoon puree into a pretty ovenproof casserole, wrap tightly with plastic wrap, and store in refrigerator overnight, or as needed. Remove from refrigerator several hours

before serving and allow to come to room temperature.

Preheat oven to 350°. Cover casserole loosely with foil and bake in preheated oven until hot, about 30 minutes.

Bring casserole to the table and serve family-style.

Heavenly Pumpkin Cheesecake

It is interesting to make this cake with different kinds of cooking pumpkins. Even people who say that they don't like pumpkin pie will love this dessert. It's delicious on its own and even better served on a pool of caramel sauce.

Makes 1 10-inch cake

FILLING

> 1 4–5-pound pumpkin
> 1½ pounds cream cheese
> 1 cup superfine sugar
> ½ teaspoon ground ginger
> ½ teaspoon cinnamon
> ¼ teaspoon freshly grated nutmeg
> ½ teaspoon cardamom
> 1 tablespoon dark rum
> 5 jumbo eggs

SHORTBREAD CRUST

 2 cups unbleached flour
 ½ cup superfine sugar
 ¼ teaspoon cinnamon
 ½ cup unsalted butter, cut into 8
  pieces
 2 jumbo egg yolks
 1 tablespoon white rum
 1 egg white beaten with 1 teaspoon
  water

TOPPING

 3 cups sour cream
 ½ teaspoon superfine sugar
 2 teaspoons white rum
  Freshly grated nutmeg to taste

Preheat oven to 425°. Cut pumpkin in half and discard seeds. Place halves skin side down in a shallow baking pan. Add enough water to come ½ inch up the sides of the pan and bake in preheated oven until flesh is very tender, about 45 minutes. Remove from oven and scoop flesh into the bowl of a food processor fitted with the metal blade. Purée until smooth and set aside. Excess puréed flesh will freeze well.

Place one oven shelf in the top third of oven and the other shelf far enough below it to allow room for a large pan filled with hot water. Preheat oven to 375°.

To make the crust, sift flour, sugar, and cinnamon into the bowl of a food processor fitted with the metal blade. Add butter pieces and pulse about eight times, or until mixture is the texture of cornmeal. Add egg yolks and 1 tablespoon white rum and process about 12 seconds, or until mixture is evenly blended. It will not form a ball. Press about ⅓ of the dough over the bot-

tom of a 10-inch springform pan, covering it evenly. Bake for 13 minutes. Remove pan from oven and let cool on a cake rack. When cool, press remaining dough evenly around the sides of the pan. Carefully brush the prepared crust with the egg white mixture. This will help seal the dough. Set aside.

Now continue with the filling. Place cheese, sugar, spices, and 1 tablespoon dark rum in the bowl of an electric mixer. Beat until cheese is smooth. Scrape sides of bowl and add the 5 jumbo eggs. Beat on high speed for 5 minutes, scraping sides of mixer several times during this process. Then add 2 cups of the reserved pumpkin puree and beat until evenly blended. Pour filling into prepared pan.

Fill a large pan with hot water and place it on the lower oven rack. Place cheesecake on upper shelf and bake for 1 hour and 15 minutes. Remove cake from oven and place on a cooling rack while you make the topping. Remove water pan and increase heat to 450°.

Blend topping ingredients until smooth and spoon evenly over the cake. Smooth with a spatula. Return cake to oven and bake for 10 minutes. Turn oven off, leave oven door ajar, and cool cake for 1 hour. Then immediately place cake in refrigerator and chill overnight.

Run a sharp knife around edge of cake before removing the sides of the pan. If there are shortbread crumbs, you might wish to sprinkle them over the top.

Adele Straub

The Farmer Is Adele

36089 Neff Road

Grafton, Ohio 44044

(216) 926-3316

The Straub family lives in a rural community about 40 miles southwest of Cleveland. While Ron's job with Xerox has him on the road a lot, the family really cherishes their 6 acres of fields, woods, and pond. Adele was a full-time mother in the early 1980s, but as the children approached school age, she began to think about going back to work. Their little farm held the key.

The Farmer Is Adele was born in the summer of 1988, the summer of the Great Midwestern Drought. Her seedlings had been started in a greenhouse; they were transplanted before the drought began. Then the heat of June struck. "Luckily, we have this pond," Adele said. "We filled huge barrels with water from the pond and trucked them out to the fields. Then I hand-watered everything—an all-day project each time we had to do it." Her smile faded as she talked about that difficult time.

"It was horrible," she said, "but I had too much invested in the field to lose it." Somehow, everything survived. Then the first time she picked her "designer" lettuces to sell, the temperature went up to 100° and everything wilted before it got to market. It was on-the-job training at its toughest.

"To farm organically you have to have the three C's," Adele Straub told us. "You have to be crazy, courageous, and creative.

"It's crazy to spend all of your waking hours out in the sun," she said. And

when she's not weeding, or picking bugs off the plants, she's watering from her barrels. She now has a more efficient way of getting the water out to the field, but it still takes a full day to get everything watered. "I think you also have to be a bit crazy to squash bugs, but I've learned to do it and not even allow myself to think 'Yuk.'

"Being courageous is a part of all farmers' lives, but it's really essential for organic farming," she said. "If you think you have a problem, don't wait. You'd better attack it fast. If you hesitate and wait, it's often too late."

She is also creative in many ways. Purple martin houses, hummingbird feeders, and bluebird houses are all over the property. "We invite them for cocktails and hors d'oeuvres," she said about the hummingbirds. The more birds, the fewer insects that harm the vegetables. "We make sure we have lots of earthworms, praying mantises, and ladybugs. We also love the frogs. It's amazing what comes around when you don't use pesticides. We even get snakes in the greenhouse.

"You have to think out a problem rather than just buying a spray," she added. Once, she had a sudden infestation of cabbage moths. A pesticide would have killed them instantly. Without it, they had to be eliminated one at a time. So Adele bought butterfly nets for the kids and offered them a bounty of fifteen cents for each moth. The kids did well.

Then, to help solve her moisture problem, she decided to cover her rows with biodegradable plastic that has holes punched in it through which Adele can plant. Now she can water less frequently, since the plastic slows moisture evaporation. This approach also solved a problem with slugs, which don't do well under the ground cover.

Adele practices what she calls a knowledgeable amateur's version of IPM—integrated pest management. She has planted Queen Anne's lace to attract pollinating bees and insect-eating wasps. Traditionally, organic farmers have planted marigolds, which they believe repel harmful insects. Now there are some studies that document their effectiveness in controlling nematodes, a ground worm that can hurt the crops. So she plants them in profusion. "Even if they don't work at all," she said, "they are worth planting just for their beauty."

She has also become committed to the idea of companion planting, the pairing of different vegetables that research indicates do well together. So, for example, she plants corn, broccoli, and dill in companion rows and somehow there are fewer bad bugs. Her two varieties of watermelons are mixed with sunflowers to attract birds. Adele hopes those birds will eat some of the bugs that bother the melons. And she put electric fencing around the fields to protect against rabbits and woodchucks. Luckily, deer are not yet a problem.

During her first four years, Adele expanded considerably, seeking unusual varieties of seeds. Besides the usual tomatoes, for example, she now grows both green and purple tomatillos. By season's end she will have produced about five varieties of beans, numerous kinds of corn and squash, snow peas and snap peas, myriad salad greens, hosts of peppers, cool and hot, and all sorts and colors of broccoli, cabbages, and Brussels sprouts. And then there are the cantaloupes, watermelons, and pumpkins.

In addition to her on-the-job training in growing, Adele learned on the job that selling organic produce isn't easy. In this part of Ohio, consumers just don't celebrate the benefits of unsprayed, unchemicaled food. They do not see any reason to pay more for organic vegetables. And there are not the kinds of farmers' markets that one sees in so many other parts of the country, which allow the farmer to develop new customers.

So Adele became a Surrogate Farmer. For a mere $20 a year, a family can become a member of FarmEr Adele's Surrogate Team (F.E.A.S.T.). Besides receiving a discount on their treasures, members also get first crack at each day's harvest. They even get some input into what is planted in the first place. F.E.A.S.T. gave Adele a solid base on which to work. She now spends much less time using the telephone to drum up business. Lately, several markets in the region have also discovered Adele and now purchase her excess vegetables.

Is she tired? You bet. But is she happy? "Even when it hits 100°, I just love it. There's nothing better."

Our Caesar Salad

Fashions come, fashions go. Caesar Salad is one of those great dishes that have been on the menus of fine restaurants for decades, often as a great showpiece prepared tableside. It can also make a humble family supper into an event when garnished with some grilled chicken or salmon. Linda has been making this Caesar salad for thirty years; the only change is the introduction of young red and green romaine instead of the tough supermarket stuff.

Serves 4–6

>   1 cup ¾-inch dry bread cubes, made from good bread
>   3 tablespoons plus ⅓ cup extra-virgin olive oil
>   2 large cloves garlic, crushed
>   ¼ teaspoon dried basil
>   ¼ teaspoon dried thyme
>   1 teaspoon kosher salt
>   1 2-ounce tin anchovies, drained
>   1 teaspoon Worcestershire sauce
>   4 drops Tabasco
>   Juice of 1 lemon
>   1 pound young red and green romaine leaves, cleaned, dried, and torn into bite-sized pieces
>   1 jumbo egg, boiled 2½ minutes
>   ⅓ cup freshly grated Parmesan cheese
>   Freshly ground black pepper to taste

Let bread cubes stand uncovered a few hours ahead. Heat 3 tablespoons of the olive oil in a large skillet over medium heat. Add 1 clove garlic, the basil, and the thyme. Stir and cook for 1 minute. Add the bread cubes and sauté until golden. Remove bread cubes with a slotted spoon and drain on paper towels.

In a large wooden bowl, combine remaining garlic clove, salt, and 4 anchovy fillets. Mash thoroughly with a fork until mixture is a thick puree. Add Worcestershire, Tabasco, and lemon juice and mix thoroughly. Then slowly add ⅓ cup olive oil, blending vigorously until fully incorporated.

Place romaine in a large bowl. Add boiled egg and toss to coat all the leaves. Add to prepared dressing and toss again. Add cheese, black pepper, and croutons. Toss again. Garnish with remaining anchovy fillets and serve.

Wine: Floreal (Flora Springs) *Sauvignon Blanc* (Napa Valley)

Warm Duck and Red Cabbage Salad

Serves 4

  2 duck breasts, split
    Freshly ground black pepper to
    taste
  1 tablespoon dark soy sauce
  1 clove garlic, minced
  2 tablespoons red wine vinegar
  1 tablespoon Chinese black vinegar
    (available in Oriental markets)
  1 tablespoon dark sesame oil
  1 small red cabbage, thinly sliced
  1 small red onion, thinly sliced
  1 yellow bell pepper, cut into thin
    julienne strips
  4 thick slices smoked bacon
  2 tablespoons sesame seeds, toasted
  1 tablespoon minced fresh parsley
  1 tablespoon minced fresh chives

Carefully trim excess fat from each duck breast. Score skin and part of the fat by making two or three lengthwise parallel slashes along the top of each half. Rub each piece with some black pepper and soy sauce and let marinate for several hours.

Thoroughly clean the surface of a gas or charcoal grill with a metal brush; then coat the surface evenly with Pam. Heat the grill until very hot.

Combine garlic, vinegars, and sesame oil in a large bowl and whisk until mixture forms an emulsion. Add cabbage, onion, and bell pepper and toss. Set aside.

In a large skillet, sauté bacon until crisp. Remove, drain, crumble, and keep warm. Reserve skillet and drippings.

Place duck breasts skin side down on the grill and cook for 6 minutes (if very thick, allow 2 minutes more); turn and grill 2 more minutes. Allow to rest for 5 minutes.

While duck breasts are resting, heat bacon fat in skillet, add cabbage mixture, and toss. Cover skillet and cook over low heat, shaking pan several times, for 5 minutes. Add crumbled bacon.

Carve duck breasts across the grain in about 6 slices each. Divide cabbage mixture among each of four large serving plates. Fan half a breast next to the cabbage in overlapping slices. Sprinkle with sesame seeds, more freshly ground pepper, and the herbs.

Wine: Sokol-Blossor Riesling (Oregon)

Hartzler Family Garden Relish

Wilma and Arlo Hartzler live in Smithville, Ohio, not far from the dairy-farming Hartzlers, who may be distant relatives (page 114). This is rich farmland, yielding delicious fruits and vegetables when the vagaries of our weather systems permit.

Serves 6–8

  2 medium tomatoes, chopped
  1 cucumber, peeled and chopped
  1 onion, chopped
  1 green bell pepper, chopped
  1 hot chile pepper, seeded and
    chopped

DRESSING
  1 cup cider vinegar
  1 teaspoon kosher salt

¼ teaspoon freshly ground black
    pepper
½ teaspoon celery seed

Combine tomatoes, cucumber, onion, bell pepper, and hot pepper in a large mixing bowl. Place dressing ingredients in a medium-sized bowl with ½ cup water and whisk well. Pour dressing over vegetables and mix gently but thoroughly. Chill for several hours before serving.

Rose's Swiss Chard Fry

Rose Mustacchio, one of Adele Straub's F.E.A.S.T. members, has been making chard this way for eons. This is a wonderfully delicious recipe, simple and addictive, especially when you use olive oil.

Serves 4

½ pound Swiss chard leaves
1 jumbo egg
1 cup unbleached flour
¼ teaspoon baking soda
⅔ cup extra-virgin olive oil or
    vegetable oil
    Salt and freshly ground black
    pepper to taste

Remove ribs from chard leaves. Fill a large saucepan with water and bring to a boil. Add chard and simmer until tender, about 2–3 minutes. Drain and refresh chard in cold water to stop cooking process. Open leaves and pat dry.

Beat egg with ½ cup water in a shallow soup plate. Slowly add flour, mixing to keep smooth. Add enough additional water to make mixture the consistency of thin pancake batter. Mix in baking soda.

Heat oil in skillet over medium heat. Dip chard in batter and fry until golden brown on each side. Season and serve.

Patrick McCafferty

Ohio Maiden

27397 SR 751

Newcomerstown, Ohio 43832

(216) 897-1207

*Y*ou never know who you will find helping Patrick McCafferty on his little central Ohio farm. One season it was young people from the city, learning the meaning of back-breaking toil. Maybe an old college friend or someone he had worked with in his years on California farms will stop by to help. Or it might be a Sherpa guide with an impressive climbing résumé.

In actual fact, on a recent visit, that was precisely who was there, transplanting flats of frisée and purple mustard in Patrick's hydroponic salad-green and watercress operation. Nigma Gyalzen Sherpa is a twenty-seven-year-old trekking guide and expedition chef who gave up climbing when a cousin, a fellow high-altitude guide, was killed in a fall. After he retired, he decided he would visit the people around the world who had been his clients before he returned to his family's farm after a year. One of Patrick's friends who had climbed with Nigma told him of this organic hydroponic Ohio farm, so he came to set lettuces in Patrick's greenhouse and to learn something new to take back to Nepal.

"The guy is incredible," said Patrick. "I never saw anyone who is a better worker. The only thing is, he won't kill a Japanese beetle. His religion won't let him." In a way, Patrick's religion won't let him kill the beetles either, at least not with chemicals. He picks them off as he sees them and steps on them to be sure they don't procreate on his mizuna. He uses beneficial insects, like ladybugs and lacewings, to control pests. Only rarely will he spray and only in the face of a clear and present danger. He occasionally uses Rotenone, a compound made of chrysanthemum leaves and roots that is effective against aphids, or Dipel, which contains *Bacillus thuringiensis* and attacks the digestive systems of cabbage loopers and caterpillars. Both agents are neutralized in twenty-four hours by sunlight. And he uses diatomaceous earth, a harsh jagged soil that discourages nocturnal invasions by crawling bugs, around the perimeter of the greenhouse.

Patrick McCafferty is part of a well-known Cleveland family of doctors, dentists, accountants, judges, prosecutors, and lawyers. He set out to study medicine but switched to English and philosophy. On a pre–graduate-school travel hiatus, he took a job as a California farmhand. He found that he loved the work, and so he did it for a number of years. In 1988, he came back home to Ohio, bought a small farm near Coshocton, set up a small hydroponic greenhouse for watercress, and tilled a few acres for organically grown row crops. In 1989, under the name of Ohio Maiden, he went to market with his products and began to explore the possibility of raising other greens inside, in water. By 1990, he was selling a high-quality, varied mix of greens for salads, delivering it cleaned and ready to eat to the best restaurants in the region.

But it wasn't easy. He had heat problems, cold problems, water problems, flooding problems, delivery problems, labor problems. The first summer, he learned that the covered greenhouse was just too hot for the plants. Now he takes the plastic off after the last frost and doesn't reinstall it until mid-September. He found that the covers he pulled over young plants to shield them from the sun actually cooked them. Now he uses the covers to keep in moisture at night and, coincidentally, to keep out nocturnal insects.

There is a natural gas well on his farm, but he learned with some difficulty that its flow could not be trusted. He now uses a wood furnace with a fan to keep warmth in the greenhouse in winter. The gas is now relegated to an emergency backup.

Patrick's first greenhouse design left something to be desired. First, he had to create a patch of flat land to build it on. The floor had to slope down 1¼ inches per 10 feet for optimum results. But the low end of the greenhouse is near an embankment that forms a catch basin at the bottom. In the wet summer of 1990, so much rain came that everything was totally washed out; a lake formed at the bottom end of the greenhouse. He had to start from scratch, this time installing a high-capacity perimeter drainage system.

The floor of the greenhouse is covered with clear plastic sheeting. The plants are suspended on racks with their roots resting on the plastic. As the water flows by, the roots take what they need to grow. The water is rich enough in minerals that he is able to recycle it, pumping it back to the high end of the floor and letting it pass over the roots again. Seepage and evaporation cost him 300 gallons a day. But so far, his spring and well produce enough water to keep the operation, now expanded to three times its original size, going well. But there is not enough for the crops he raises in his organically certified fields. In the drought of 1991, he had to just watch as everything died. The up side of that was that he had time to build more hydroponic capacity.

McCafferty starts his lettuces in his basement from seeds. He uses small absorbent cubes of growing medium, 276 to a flat. Each cube gets two seeds. Once sprouted, the flats are placed in the greenhouse, where the new roots wick up the nutrients from the flowing water. The water is rarely more than a quarter of an inch deep as it goes by, but the plants are efficient at getting what they need. As they grow, he spreads them out until the 276 plants occupy as much as 12 square feet.

It usually takes five weeks from planting to the first picking. In ten days, the plants are in full leaf again, ready for a reharvest. And in another ten days, a third harvest. By this time, a successor plant has sprouted, ready for a place in the flowing water.

In the course of a year McCafferty will plant and harvest at least fifty different kinds of salad greens. And even in the middle of the winter there are never fewer than twenty varieties available. Watercress, which was to have been the key crop, is now only 10 percent of his hydroponic output.

Patrick McCafferty takes offense when people say that hydroponically grown produce is bland. Tell him that, and he is likely to pick off a leaf of Osaka purple mustard and have you taste it. If he does, hold on. It will pop your skull like fresh horseradish. "I'll admit that things get a little tame in the winter," said Patrick. "That's from the lack of sun and fresh air. But find me a leaf better than that. If you do this right, nothing is better."

Summer Salad with Fried Goat Cheese and Fresh Mint

Serves 4

DRESSING

 2 tablespoons red wine vinegar
 6 tablespoons extra-virgin olive oil
 1 tablespoon minced fresh mint
 1 teaspoon minced garlic
 1 tablespoon minced fresh chives

 6 cups baby hydroponic lettuces and mustard greens, washed and thoroughly dried
 ½ cup fine dry bread crumbs
 ¼ teaspoon freshly ground white pepper
 8 ½-inch-thick slices goat cheese
 1 jumbo egg, lightly beaten
 Approximately ½ cup vegetable oil

Salt and freshly ground black pepper to taste

Nasturtiums and mint leaves for garnish

Combine dressing ingredients and whisk briskly to form an emulsion. Set aside.

Place greens in a large bowl and set aside.

Combine bread crumbs and white pepper in a small bowl. Dredge slices of cheese in egg, then in crumbs. Into a large skillet, pour enough oil to coat the bottom; heat until hot. Fry cheese slices until golden, 2–3 minutes each side. Remove from skillet and keep warm.

Quickly toss greens with dressing and distribute among four serving plates. Place 2 slices of cheese on each salad. Add salt and pepper and garnish with flowers and mint.

Swordfish Steaks with Watercress and Tomatoes

Serves 4–6

MARINADE

    3 tablespoons red wine vinegar
    2 tablespoons fresh lemon juice
    ¼ cup olive oil
    1 clove garlic, finely minced
    1 teaspoon freshly ground black pepper
    Pinch of kosher salt
    ½ teaspoon dried basil
    ¼ teaspoon dried sage
    ¼ teaspoon dried thyme

    2 pounds swordfish fillets, each ¾ inch thick
    1 tablespoon olive oil
    ¼ cup finely chopped onion
    3 cloves garlic, minced
    6 peeled fresh tomatoes, chopped
    2 tablespoons capers
    1 tablespoon minced fresh parsley
    1 teaspoon fresh thyme
    1 teaspoon fresh rosemary
    3 bunches fresh hydroponically grown watercress, stems removed

    Fresh herbs for garnish

Several hours before serving, combine vinegar and lemon juice in a small bowl. Whisk in ¼ cup olive oil. Add garlic, pepper, salt, and herbs. Whisk well. Arrange fish in a single layer in an ovenproof glass baking dish and pour all but 2 tablespoons of marinade over fish. Marinate, turning fish several times, for 4–5 hours. Reserve remaining marinade.

Preheat broiler or grill. Heat 1 tablespoon olive oil in a nonstick skillet. Add onion and garlic and stir over low heat for a few minutes. Add tomatoes, cover, and cook over low heat for 20 minutes. Stir in remaining ingredients except watercress and cook, uncovered, for a few more minutes. Transfer mixture to a warm bowl and set aside. Add reserved marinade to skillet.

Remove fish from marinade and gently pat dry. Grill or broil fish about 4 minutes on one side and 3 on the other. While fish is cooling, bring marinade in skillet to a boil and simmer, covered, for 5 minutes. Toss watercress with hot marinade, then divide among serving plates.

Place fish on watercress bed and spoon tomato sauce over one side. Garnish with fresh herbs.

Wine: Matanzas Creek Winery Chardonnay (Sonoma County)

The Ultimate Cole Slaw

In summer, Patrick's hilltop fields are planted with organically grown cabbages, corn, squash, tomatoes, and specialty potatoes. He also works with neighboring Amish farmers who grow to his specifications.

Serves 8–10

DRESSING

    2 cloves garlic
    ⅓ cup cider vinegar
    3 tablespoons sugar
    1 teaspoon kosher salt

1 teaspoon freshly ground white
   pepper
1¼ cups Hellmann's mayonnaise
½ cup sour cream
½ cup buttermilk

2 carrots, trimmed, scraped, and
   finely grated
1 tablespoon minced fresh tarragon
1 large Savoy cabbage, cored and
   finely shredded
1 bunch scallions, trimmed (with 1
   inch of green) and finely shredded

Combine dressing ingredients with ½ cup water in the bowl of a food processor fitted with the metal blade. Pulse 8 times and set aside.

Mix remaining ingredients in a large bowl and add dressing. Mix thoroughly, preferably with your hands. Cover bowl with plastic wrap and chill for at least 6 hours. Adjust seasonings and serve.

Rosemary Mashed Potato Cakes

Johanne Killeen and George Germon of Al Forno in Providence, Rhode Island, make some of the best food we've ever had. Their mashed potatoes are extraordinary and are the inspiration for these potato cakes, which taste even better when prepared with Patrick McCafferty's organically grown potatoes. It is Johanne's brilliant suggestion to add corn when it is in season.

Serves 8

2 pounds uniformly small red or
   yellow potatoes, scrubbed
5 tablespoons unsalted butter or
   margarine, cut in pieces
¼ cup milk, or more if necessary
2 cups lowfat sour cream
½ cup fresh corn kernels
   Kosher salt and freshly ground
   black pepper to taste
½ cup fine dry bread crumbs
4 tablespoons unsalted margarine
6 tablespoons extra-virgin olive oil
1 sprig fresh rosemary

Fresh rosemary sprigs for garnish

Several hours before serving, place potatoes (do not peel) in a 3-quart pot covered with water. Boil potatoes until tender, about 20 minutes. Drain well, then return potatoes to the pot over very low heat. Mash coarsely with a potato masher, then stir in butter. Add milk, sour cream, corn, salt, and pepper. Stir until well mixed; add more milk if mixture is too dry. Remove from heat and allow to cool. When cold, form mixture into rounded patties that are about 3 inches in diameter and 1 inch thick. Lightly dredge in bread crumbs.

Place margarine, olive oil, and 1 sprig rosemary in a large cast-iron skillet. Heat until a water drop sizzles when dropped into the oil. Add a few potato cakes and reduce heat to medium. Fry cakes for 5 minutes on each side. If the first side did not get golden brown in 5 minutes, increase heat for other side. Keep the finished cakes warm while you cook the remainder. Garnish with rosemary sprigs and serve.

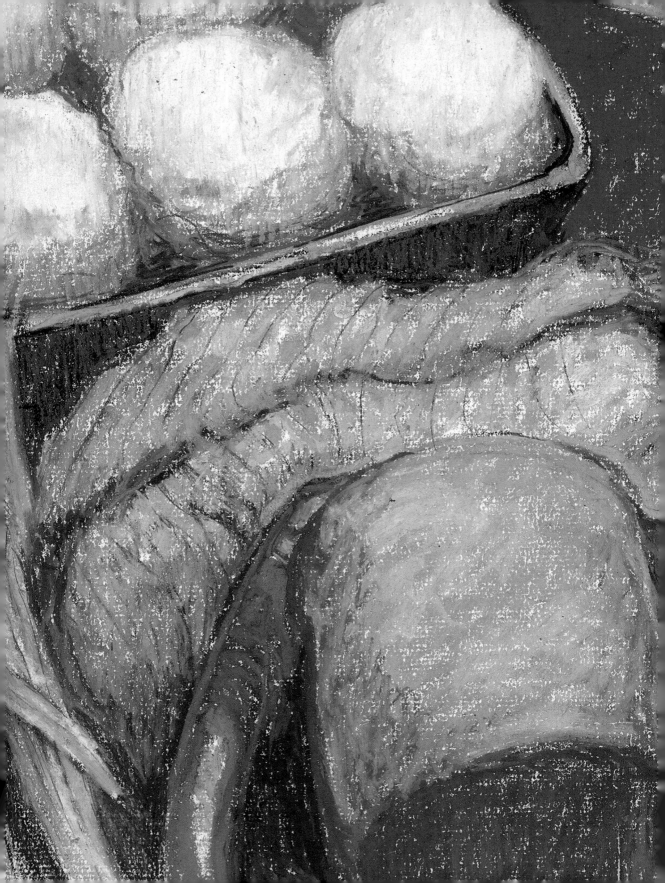

Grains and Millers

Frank Ford

Arrowhead Mills

Box 2059

Hereford, Texas 79045

(806) 364-0730

*T*he key to understanding Frank Ford is to go back to 1960. He had grown up farming the flatlands of Deaf Smith County in the northern Texas panhandle. He earned a degree in agronomy at Texas A&M and served as an artillery officer in the army. After his discharge, he became an organic grain farmer. Because he wanted his organically grown grain to be available to people who wanted "clean food," he got involved in setting up an alternative approach to processing the grain. But at the time, grain growers grew to a price, and every farmer's harvest went into the same big bin.

For Ford it just didn't seem a very satisfying arrangement. He did not want to grow grain for an agricultural monolith. The wheat of Deaf Smith County was already, he believed, the best in the world. It bothered him that chemicals were being used whether they were needed or not. And it bothered him that his premium grain brought only a commodity price that was set by forces over which he had no control; it was worth no more on the market than indifferently grown or inferior grain from other places. This led to the establishment of Arrowhead Mills in Hereford in 1960.

By the early 1990s, one of his two other founding partners had moved on to other things, but Ford continues as chairman of the board of what is arguably one of the most successful natural and organic milling operations in the world. Grain growers who can meet the high standards set by Arrowhead are able to draw a far better living from their land. Today, virtually all of Arrowhead's suppliers are determinedly organic.

Frank Ford continues to fight noble battles. The CBS television program *60 Minutes* brought one to the attention of a national audience in 1990. There are insects that eat grain. Sometimes the insects come with the grain from the field to the elevator and continue to feed. But Arrowhead does not use the chemical fumigants that other processors use to kill these insects. Many enlightened farmers used beneficial insects to kill the pests in the field, and the idea at Arrowhead Mills was to introduce these predator insects into the storage bins. They would kill the grain-eating bugs, and when the grain was processed, the dead insects, both the predator and the prey, would be removed. The USDA was aghast. In 1988 a suit was brought to block the practice. The Arrowhead Mills argument was simple. If you add chemical poisons you end up with dead insects and chemical poisons in the grain. If you add beneficial insects you end up with dead insects in the grain, which are easily cleaned out. Which was better? Arrowhead Mills won.

On another occasion, the adversary was the U.S. Department of Energy. In the early 1980s, word was out that the government intended to build an underground waste dump for nuclear waste. It would be packed in salt over 2,000 feet below the surface of the rich Deaf Smith County wheat fields. Those fields do so well in part because of the Ogallala aquifer, the underground water table that undergirds the entire region. To Frank Ford and his neighbors, the pollution of the aquifer seemed an enormous risk. They fought in over a dozen hearings, but the government refused to back down or reconsider and contested the case for eight years. But there is not now, nor will there ever be, a repository for nuclear waste below the panhandle wheat fields.

In addition, in the late 1970s, U.S. defense strategy dictated the building of mobile missiles that would be on the move constantly. The Texas panhandle was big and flat, so the Department of Defense decided to build a network of concrete tracks across great expanses of the region. The MX missiles would then stay in motion, to minimize their being preemptively struck by the enemy. That didn't sit too well with Ford and his neighbors either. This was a four-year court battle that cost the Department of Defense many millions of dollars as well, all to no avail.

In recent years Ford has focused on establishing consistent standards and regulations for organic farming. The criteria vary dramatically from place to place, and there is no single widely accepted definition. There have been dozens of organizations set up to examine and rule on a farmer's practices, deciding whether he can be called "organic." In an effort to bring some order out of the chaos, the 1990 Farm Bill mandated the Department of Agriculture to set up the National Organic Standards Board. Then Ford's concern became ensuring that farmers who actually grow organically were given a role on the new board. Again he and his allies have had some success.

Arrowhead employs a lot of people and enriches the Hereford and Deaf Smith County economies. Boyd Foster, president of Arrowhead now, is responsible for the company on a daily basis. It is he who has led the company as it has broadened its product base to include such products as pancake mixes, cold breakfast cereals, and even blue cornmeal muffin mix. Today there is also an agricultural

consultant, Gary Brownd; it is he who travels the country meeting with farmers who are either producing for Arrowhead or hoping to.

Frank Ford and his associates would like to see other organizations like Arrowhead Mills come into being. Ford feels that his progress since 1960 has demonstrated that they will work. He fears for the future of family agriculture and the small farmer. "It will be a disaster," he said, "if the small organic farmer is preempted by red tape and bureaucracy; if he is killed by bad regulations. The economics of the 1980s virtually destroyed the future of small business. And now all we can do to help the small farmer is to encourage the entrepreneurial spirit in him or her as best as we can."

How did his concern for this kind of farming, clean farming, come about? He thought for a while. "Once, as a kid," he said, "I found a ladybug in a pond where I was swimming. It appeared drowned. I squeezed it gently. I blew on it. In a few minutes it stirred, spread its wings, and flew away. I haven't thought about that for a long time. But I never forgot it."

Challah

Over the years, this bread has welcomed many a Rosh Hashanah, when it is served along with a bowl of really good honey. Linda also made this bread for her sons' bar mitzvahs.

Makes 1 large loaf

>   1 cake compressed fresh yeast (about 0.6 ounce)
>   2¼ cups warm water
>   ⅓ cup sugar
>   2 jumbo eggs
>   ¼ cup vegetable oil
>   6–8 cups unbleached flour
>   1 teaspoon salt
>   1 egg yolk beaten with 2 teaspoons water

In a small bowl, combine yeast, ¼ cup of the warm water, and 1 tablespoon sugar. Mix well and let rest in a warm place until mixture is bubbling, about 15 minutes.

In the bowl of an electric mixer fitted with a paddle, combine remaining warm water and sugar, turn motor on low, then add eggs and oil. Add yeast mixture; then, very gradually, add the flour, then the salt. Turn dough out onto a well-floured surface and knead until smooth and elastic, about 10 minutes, or knead in the mixer with a dough hook. Place dough in a well-oiled bowl, cover with plastic wrap, and let rise in a warm place until doubled. Punch down and let rise for 40 minutes longer. Divide dough into three or four parts and braid on ungreased baking sheet. Let rise in a warm place, loosely covered with plastic wrap, about 45 minutes.

Preheat oven to 400°.

Brush top of bread with egg wash and bake in preheated oven for 45 minutes, or until golden brown. Let cool on rack.

Brioche Loaf

Our friend Lydie Marshall, food writer and cooking teacher *par excellence,* is the one who first made us think about making brioche in a loaf pan. This way, it is perfect for toast, which can be served with hors d'oeuvres or turned into a splendid french toast.

Makes 1 9x5 loaf

- 1 tablespoon active dry yeast
- 1 tablespoon sugar
- 1 tablespoon warm water
- 2 tablespoons warm milk
- 1 cup unsalted butter, very soft
- 3 jumbo eggs
  Approximately 3 cups unbleached flour, or more if necessary

- 1 teaspoon kosher salt
- 1 jumbo egg yolk beaten with
  1 teaspoon warm water

Combine yeast and sugar in a small, warm bowl. Add 1 tablespoon warm water and the milk; mix well to dissolve yeast. Let rest in a warm place until mixture begins to bubble, about 5 minutes. If bubbling does not occur, discard mixture and get new yeast.

In the bowl of an electric mixer fitted with the paddle, beat the 1 cup butter until creamy. Add eggs, one at a time, beating thoroughly after each one. Blend in yeast mixture. Add 1 cup flour and the salt, beating thoroughly. Slowly add more flour and blend until mixture is no longer very sticky.

Change to a dough hook and knead for 5 minutes, or until dough is shiny and ever-so-slightly sticky. (Or knead the dough by hand on a floured surface.)

Thoroughly butter a large, warm mixing bowl. Place dough in the bowl, cover with plastic wrap, and let rise in a warm place until doubled, about 2–4 hours.

Liberally butter a 9x5 loaf pan. Punch dough down, knead for one minute, then shape into a loaf and press into pan. Cover pan with plastic wrap and let rise until doubled again, about 1–2 hours.

Preheat oven to 400°.

Using a pastry brush, coat surface of bread with egg-yolk mixture. Place bread in upper third of preheated oven and bake for about 30 minutes, or until surface is brown and bread sounds hollow when rapped on the bottom of the loaf.

Remove bread from pan and let cool on a rack.

Fried Polenta

This is wonderful with grilled sausage, or grilled anything for that matter. We also like to serve it garnished with a skillet of sautéed wild mushrooms.

Serves 8

>   6 cups rich chicken stock
> 1¾ cups medium-ground yellow cornmeal
>   1 teaspoon kosher salt
>   1 teaspoon freshly ground black pepper
>   Approximately ¾ cup grated dry Jack or pecorino cheese (see pages 139–141)
>   Approximately ⅓ cup olive oil
>
>   Fresh basil leaves for garnish

Bring stock to a boil in a heavy-bottomed, deep 3-quart pot. Very gradually add cornmeal (you can try letting it fall through a sieve or through your fingers as you hold it in a fist), stirring constantly to incorporate it evenly into the stock. Whisk vigorously to eliminate all lumps. Then lower heat to a slow simmer and stir with a wooden spoon, scraping bottom and sides of pot very thoroughly. Stir polenta in this fashion for 30–45 minutes. Polenta is done when it pulls away from the sides of the pot when you stir.

Remove pot from heat and stir in salt, pepper, and ½ cup cheese. (One could add some mixed fresh herbs to the polenta at this point.) Wipe a cold surface with some olive oil and dump polenta onto it. Smooth polenta into a 1¼-inch-thick square and cool.

Cut polenta into squares of the desired size and then into triangles. Brush with olive oil. Polenta can be chilled at this point, but bring to room temperature before proceeding to the next step.

Pour 3 tablespoons olive oil into a large skillet and sauté polenta until browned on both sides. Polenta triangles can be grilled over charcoal as well. To serve, sprinkle generously with more cheese and garnish with fresh basil leaves.

Wine: Roberta Pecota Gamay Beaujolais Nouveau (Napa Valley) (with grilled spicy sausage)

Chappellet Vineyard Chenin Blanc (Napa Valley) (with sautéed shiitake mushrooms)

Ma Griffith's Salt-Rising Bread

Leona Griffith, Fred's mother, brought this bread to our attention. Her stepmother, Inez Burdick, frequently made it in the summer on her little patch of farm in Ovapa, West Virginia. Like so many houses in that region, hers had a summer kitchen in an outbuilding a few steps away from the main house. That meant that when the fermenting starter got really pungent, the smell didn't permeate the house. Even though it's smelly to cook, the taste of this bread is divine. According to our research, this bread is called "salt-rising" because the early settlers who made it kept the bowl of developing starter warm by surrounding it with heated salt. Heat is very important to the process; make sure that your equipment and ingredients are nice and warm. We let the starter develop right on our stove, where the warmth from the pilot light is perfect.

Makes 3 loaves

Starter
- 1 large baking potato
- ½ teaspoon salt
- ½ teaspoon sugar
- 1 teaspoon baking soda
- ½ teaspoon ground ginger
- 2 cups boiling water
- ¼ cup cornmeal
- ¼ cup unbleached flour

- 2 cups warm milk
- 2 cups warm water
- 1 tablespoon salt
- Approximately 14 cups unbleached flour
- 3 tablespoons vegetable oil or lard
- 1 jumbo egg yolk beaten with 1 teaspoon water
- 2 tablespoons unsalted butter, melted

Slice the potato into a 1-quart mixing bowl. Add salt, sugar, soda, and ginger. Pour the boiling water over the mixture and stir. Sprinkle cornmeal and flour on top and stir. Place bowl in a warm place for 24 hours.

Stir mixture well and swish potatoes around to rinse them of as many solids as you can, then remove the potatoes and dis-card. Add ¾ cup of flour and whisk mixture to make a smooth, thin batter. Return bowl to a very warm place until surface is well covered with bubbles. This should take about 3–5 hours.

In a warmed 4-quart mixing bowl, combine starter with the milk, the 2 cups warm water, and the salt, and add enough flour to thicken. We find that it takes about 4 cups of flour. Mixture should be the texture of thick pancake batter. Cover the bowl with plastic wrap and return it to a warm place until a very thick sponge develops, about 3 hours.

Add vegetable oil and 4 cups of flour to sponge and stir very well. Add two cups more flour and blend. Dough should still be wet and shaggy. Sprinkle 1–2 cups of flour on a clean surface, turn out dough, flour your hands, and knead. Add more flour as needed. Dough should be smooth and silky, although still a tad tacky, after 10 minutes of kneading.

Lightly oil three warmed 9x5 loaf pans. Divide dough into thirds. Form into loaves on a lightly floured surface by patting each third into a flat oval. Then fold each oval in half and flatten down on the seam, tucking the ends under. Place into prepared pans, cover with plastic wrap, and let rise in a warm area until dough has at least doubled. This may take 3 hours.

Preheat oven to 375°. Brush tops of loaves with egg-yolk mixture and bake in preheated oven for 55 minutes, or until the bread sounds hollow when rapped on the bottom of the loaf. Brush with melted butter. Remove from pans after a few minutes and let cool on racks. This bread freezes very well.

Our Fabled Satin Pancakes

These pancakes have become a regular feature of our Sunday morning breakfasts. The sour cream gives them a beautiful satin-like texture. Don't forget—the batter has to rest for an hour.

Makes about 28 pancakes

> 1 tablespoon sugar
> 1 cup unbleached flour
> 1 cup whole-wheat flour
> 2 teaspoons baking soda
> 3 jumbo eggs
> ½ cup unsalted butter, melted
> 1½ cups sour cream
> 1½ cups buttermilk, or more if necessary
> 1–2 tablespoons vegetable oil
>
> Whipped butter at room temperature, warm maple syrup, fresh berries, and fresh mint leaves for garnish

In a large mixing bowl, combine the dry ingredients.

In another mixing bowl, whisk together the eggs, melted butter, sour cream, and 1 cup of the buttermilk until smooth. Add wet ingredients to the dry and whisk well to make a very smooth batter. Let batter rest at least 1 hour.

Add the remaining half cup buttermilk and whisk. Add more buttermilk if mixture is too thick to drop from the spoon into the skillet.

Into a large and well-seasoned cast-iron skillet, pour only enough oil to coat the bottom and heat until a drop of water dropped on the surface sizzles. Spoon enough batter onto the skillet to make 4-inch pancakes and reduce heat slightly. Fry pancakes until brown on each side. (Handle them with care. These pancakes will be very silky if you don't kill them with too much oil during the frying process.) As pancakes are done, remove them from the skillet, place on an ovenproof platter, and keep warm in the oven. When ready to serve, top with whipped butter and warm maple syrup, plus some berries and fresh mint leaves.

Ralph Diller

Route 1
Hereford, Texas 79045
(806) 258-7392

*T*he land is especially flat in this part of the Texas panhandle. In addition, the soil is exceptionally fertile. There is an underground water supply, the Ogallala aquifer. And with a higher altitude than most of the state, the region usually enjoys cold, snowy winters and breezy summers, making it ideal country for growing grain.

Deaf Smith County, of which Hereford is the county seat, is one million acres large. There are 300,000 acres planted in wheat, yielding 22 to 24 bushels per acre. There is also an enormous amount of corn. There are also more feedlots in Deaf Smith than in any other county in Texas. Before cattle are taken to market, they are "finished," or fattened, on a feedlot. They stand around and eat corn until they are ready to be sold. Paradoxically, the cattle do not feed on the Deaf Smith corn. That is food corn—corn for people. The cattle get feed corn brought in from outside the county; most of it comes from Wisconsin. But one good by-product of all of this feedlot activity is manure, a good, natural fertilizer prized by serious farmers.

Ralph Diller's place is about 12 miles out of Hereford, the last 2 miles traveled over dirt roads. Off in the distance, a large tractor stands in the field. Farmers here feel it makes more sense to leave their tractors where they'll start the next day's work rather than to drive it back to the barn every night. The next morning they'll drive out to the tractor in the pickup.

Like most young farmers in this area, Ralph Diller grew up in the business. He started this wheat, corn, and rye operation in 1975 on land that was already in the family. Of the 1,100 acres he farms, 640 are leased from his mom; the rest belong to Ralph and his wife, Michaele.

Water has become an enormous concern in Deaf Smith County. In 1900 there was water from the aquifer right at the surface. Now you have to drill to at least 200 feet—or, better, to 350 feet, where the water has a lower mineral content. And at those levels you have to pump hard, using a lot of fuel. By the early nineties the cost of water had reached $8 per acre-inch, the amount required to cover an acre of land to a depth of one inch. If your crop requires 20 inches of water and nature has only given you 10, then, if your crop is to survive, you have to get the rest from your wells. So if you need 10 inches of water on 1,000 acres you have spent $80,000. Some farmers say that with commodity prices so low, it hardly makes sense to farm.

Ralph fears that in twenty years the Ogallala aquifer will be gone. Right now he has only half of the water he had when he started in 1975, judging by how deep he has to go to get it. Although Ralph's fields are piped, and he works with a combination of irrigation ditches and circular sprinklers, he never forgets that water is finite.

"The oil crisis is nothing compared with the water crisis," said Ralph Diller.

He also said that farmers must keep water in mind when they decide what crops to grow. "Why plant cotton, which requires a huge amount of water, in an area that is especially arid? Try not to fight Mother Nature."

Ralph shakes his head at some aspects of our government's approach to farming. Since the New Deal days the federal government has subsidized the growing of several basic crops. The subsidies are meant to encourage the farmer to produce for a market where the prices are artificially low. He says that the subsidies are the only reasons many operators have survived. "If you are to make it, you must do everything the regulations require, take advantage of every loophole, every gap, every opportunity," he told us. "Because at commodity prices there is no way to make it by just raising stuff and taking it to market."

In addition, Ralph grows increasingly frustrated with bureaucratic regulations. In this part of Texas most farmers practice circular irrigation. Water is pumped through a pipe to the middle of a field, where it goes into a long radial wheeled sprinkler. It goes around the central axis like a hand on a watch, watering a large circle; so the main field is a circle. The corners of the field don't get water, so it makes sense to forget about them. But it is still acreage, and regulations require that it be planted or you lose out on subsidies. Yet nothing planted in the corners will really grow, so buying seed for these areas is money thrown away. But rules are rules and Ralph plants the corners anyway.

Wheat is planted in September. It grows until November, when it goes dormant and the cattle begin to graze on it. The grazing helps to reduce the insect population in general by eliminating the food supply for the bugs. Also, when the wheat is nibbled back to the ground, the stubble develops a deeper root system that helps it to tolerate the early summer heat. And fields that have been trampled by cattle are firmly packed and will retain moisture better.

When the price of wheat is reasonable, farmers pull the cattle off by March 15 and let the wheat grow until harvest at the end of June. When wheat is too cheap, the growers leave the cattle to graze out the fields. Diller runs about 400 cattle on his wheat. Sometimes he gambles on prices and buys the animals himself, selling them after they have eaten the fields. Other times the cattlemen will pay him for the use of his fields.

It's hard for the farmer to make much money on wheat; the mathematics are pretty simple. Fields have to be rotated; one year a crop, the next year fallow with a nourishing cover crop. So if you average 23 bushels per acre every other year, with wheat at $2.40 a bushel, you realize less than $28 per acre per year. And, of course, if you water, you have to factor that into the price, along with chemicals, farm equipment, and fuel. Even though you do realize a little income from the owners of the cattle that graze on the fields, at $2.40 a bushel you might as well not harvest it.

If your grains are top-quality, however, and your land has had no chemicals for three years and can be certified organic so that the grain meets Arrowhead Mills' standards, then you can get perhaps $3.25 a bushel for your wheat. That 85 cents more than commodity market price makes all the difference to the farmer.

Right now, Ralph has a circle and a half that are not organic. Everything else is, and he is working toward getting it all certified.

In addition to corn, rye, and wheat that are used for Arrowhead Mills' organic flours, he grows a lot of popping corn for Weaver, the world's largest popcorn company. Ralph likes to raise corn. "It's easy on the land, it takes less water than the wheat, and you can plant corn after corn, rather than having to let the field lie fallow," he told us.

Many farmers in this region do spray their fields with herbicides and pesticides from the air. Ralph told us of the precision with which aerial sprayers can hit a field. Using the same kind of navigation system that was used in the Gulf War and by people walking to the North and South Poles, pilots can know exactly where they are within a meter. Amazingly, though, most planes still use flaggers, people who stand in the fields and let the pilots know where to spray.

The spraying companies use computer models to predict when the bugs will be hitting, factoring in humidity, temperature, and rainfall, among other considerations. Then they start selling their spraying programs to the farmers on a contract basis. "Most farmers don't even look in their fields," Ralph told us. "They just buy the program."

· · ·

We asked Ralph Diller how he decided to go organic. He told us that early in the 1978 season a man called him at 5:30 in the morning. It was going to be another 100° day; Ralph was angry and worried. "Gonna spray?" the pilot asked. For some reason Ralph just said no. After he hung up the phone, he thought, "What did I do?" But as the day passed, he did not change his mind. And at the end of the season, the lack of spraying had made no difference to his production, although it took more of his time and anxiety to keep his fields free of weeds and pests. "The only thing that happened," he said, "is that I didn't get a spraying bill." And he has not had a spraying program since. Of course, he also has to work harder to compost the fields and to nourish them with legumes.

Ralph is also a champion of "beneficials"—that is, the good bugs, such as lacewings, wasps, and ladybugs—which kill the bad bugs. Ralph delivers the bugs to his fields in Quicksilver Ultralight, a 32-horsepower canvas frame plane that he and his young son, Nathan, learned to fly from a computer program. The first time Ralph ever flew it, he stayed up for an hour and a half, not really trusting himself to land it. But finally he did. He has also ordered a kit for a Streak Shadow from England, a very sophisticated ultralight; it should take him 500 hours to build this new one. He will then sell his services to other organic farmers for the distribution of beneficials. He puts the lacewings in sugar, and as he flies over the fields he sprinkles the fields with sugar—and, with it, the bugs.

This is a thoughtful man, one who worries about both his legacy and the future that he builds for his children. He wonders if it will be possible for the small family farm to survive. As for organic farming in this region, Ralph Diller told us, "The risk you'll take depends on how fast your heart beats." We gather he means in going organic, in dealing with the bureaucrats, and in flying an ultralight to 25,000 feet.

Cinnamon French-Toast Bread

Juilleret's is a small diner in Charlevoix, Michigan, that makes splendid french toast out of cinnamon bread. That's the inspiration for this bread. It's terrific toasted and served with good jam. But if you want great french toast, make thick slices and soak them in a mixture of good eggs, milk, vanilla extract, and nutmeg. Fry in butter or margarine, and serve with Maverick maple syrup (see page 345) and sautéed pecans.

Makes 1 9x5 loaf

     1 cake compressed fresh yeast (about
       0.6 ounce)
    ¼ cup warm water
     1 cup sugar
  1½ cups warm milk
    ¼ cup vegetable oil
4½–5 cups unbleached flour
     2 tablespoons cinnamon
    ½ cup raisins (optional)
    ½ cup chopped pecans (optional)
     1 tablespoon unsalted margarine,
       melted

In a small bowl, combine yeast, water, and 1 tablespoon of the sugar. Mix well, then let stand in warm place until bubbly, about 15 minutes. In the bowl of an electric mixer fitted with the paddle, mix milk, oil, 2 tablespoons sugar, and yeast mixture. Slowly add 4 cups of flour. Change to dough hook and knead until dough is smooth and elastic, adding more flour if too sticky. Place dough in a warm, well-oiled bowl, cover with plastic wrap, and let rise until doubled, about 1 hour.

Preheat oven to 375°. Punch dough down and turn out on a lightly floured board. Roll into a rectangle that is 9 inches wide and 18 inches long. Combine cinnamon with remaining sugar and mix well. Sprinkle evenly over surface of dough, then sprinkle with raisins and pecans. Roll rectangle from the short end, jelly-roll fashion, so it is 9 inches across. Place roll seam side down in a well-greased 9x5 bread pan. Loosely cover with plastic wrap and let rise until top is about 2 inches above pan, about 30 minutes.

Bake loaf in preheated oven for 35 minutes, or until bottom sounds hollow when bread is rapped on bottom of loaf. Immediately brush top of bread with margarine and place on a rack to cool.

Country Cornbread

This cornbread will be as good as the cornmeal you use. It works with yellow, white, and even blue cornmeal, and it is best with Arrowhead's cornmeal.

Makes 1 loaf

    1 cup unbleached flour
    1 cup stone-ground cornmeal
    1 tablespoon baking powder
   ½ teaspoon baking soda
    1 teaspoon kosher salt
    2 tablespoons sugar
    2 jumbo eggs, beaten
    3 tablespoons unsalted butter, melted
      or margarine
 1½ cups buttermilk

Preheat oven to 375°. Butter an 8x8 cake pan and set aside.

Combine dry ingredients in the bowl of an electric mixer. Combine remaining ingredients in another mixing bowl. With mixer running on low, add wet ingredients to the dry and mix well. Scrape sides of bowl once and mix briefly.

Pour batter into prepared pan and bake in preheated oven until browned on top and dry when a toothpick is inserted into the center, about 40 minutes. Remove pan from oven and cool on a rack.

Early-Morning Baking-Powder Biscuits

Biscuits like these were part of Fred's childhood. Linda's first attempts yielded results akin to hockey pucks, but she persevered. Now these are part of most Sunday breakfasts at our house. We use sweet butter and slather the biscuits with Rob Bialic's honey (page 353). What could be better?

Makes about 12 biscuits

> 3 cups unbleached flour
> 1 tablespoon plus 2 teaspoons baking powder
> ¾ teaspoon baking soda
> 1 rounded tablespoon sugar
> ½ teaspoon salt
> 3 tablespoons Crisco
> 1½ cups buttermilk, or more if necessary

Preheat oven to 475° and place the top shelf in the upper quarter of the oven.

Combine all ingredients except buttermilk in the bowl of a food processor fitted with the metal blade. Pulse twice. Add the buttermilk and process just until mixture leaves the sides of the bowl. It should be fairly moist; if not, add a bit more buttermilk and pulse again.

Turn dough out on a floured board and lightly knead for 30 seconds. Pat flat, to a thickness of about ½ inch. Fold in half, then pat into a rectangle, again about ½ inch thick. Cut dough into circles with a 2- or 2½-inch biscuit cutter. Place biscuit rounds close together on an ungreased heavy baking sheet.

Bake on top shelf in preheated oven until nicely browned, about 10–15 minutes.

The Best Chocolate Chip Cookies Ever

Mark Haynes has been of enormous help to Linda in her effort to become an exercise jock. Hard to believe, then, that he would present her with six of these luscious cookies at the conclusion of one of her heavy workouts. But he did. And to increase the temptation, he had his mother pass along a copy of her recipe. Hats off, Betsy Haynes—these are, indeed, the very best!

Makes about 30 cookies

> 2 cups unbleached flour
> 1 teaspoon baking soda
> ½ teaspoon salt
> ½ cup Mrs. Filbert's margarine, softened

½ cup butter-flavored Crisco
   shortening
½ cup granulated sugar
¾ cup dark brown sugar, firmly
   packed
1 large egg
1 teaspoon vanilla extract
12 ounces large chocolate chips
½ cup chopped pecans

Sift together flour, baking soda, and salt and set aside. In the bowl of an electric mixer, combine margarine, shortening, and sugars; cream well on medium speed. Then add egg and vanilla and blend well. Add flour mixture and mix on low speed just until blended. Add chips and nuts and mix again on low speed, just until blended. Cover bowl with plastic wrap and refrigerate for several hours or overnight. If dough is too hard to scoop, let stand at room temperature a few minutes to soften.

Preheat oven to 350°. Drop dough by rounded tablespoonfuls onto ungreased cookie sheets, about 9 to a sheet. (This dough also works well for very large cookies.) Be sure to allow room for batter to spread. Bake in preheated oven until golden brown, about 10 minutes. Let cookies cool on cookie sheets for a few minutes before transferring them to a rack. Store in an airtight container.

Our Thin-Crust Pizza Dough

This dough will keep in the refrigerator for several days before using. Just let it come to room temperature before stretching.

Makes enough for 4 small or 2 12-inch pizzas

¼ cup warm water
1 tablespoon wildflower or raspberry
   honey
2½ tablespoons active dry yeast
2 tablespoons olive oil
¼ cup whole-wheat flour
¼ cup rye flour
2½ cups unbleached flour, or more if
   necessary
1 teaspoon salt
¼ cup milk
2 tablespoons cornmeal

Blend warm water, honey, and yeast in a small bowl. Let rest in warm place until mixture bubbles, about 10 minutes.

Combine olive oil, flours, salt, and milk in a food processor fitted with the metal blade. With motor running, pour in yeast mixture, then almost ½ cup water. Process just until dough leaves sides of bowl and forms a ball. The dough should be smooth and elastic. If it is too dry, add a bit more water; if too moist, add a bit more unbleached flour.

Lightly flour a board and knead dough for a few minutes. Place dough in a lightly oiled bowl, cover with plastic wrap, and let rise in a warm place until doubled, about 1 hour.

Divide dough into two balls. Keep one covered while you work with the other. Sprinkle each of two 12-inch pizza pans with a tablespoon of cornmeal.

Flatten the first ball into a 6-inch circle. Then lift the circle onto the top of your fist. Make a fist with the other hand, then gently begin to stretch the dough over both fists, moving it in a circular motion, until it becomes a 12-inch circle. (With a little practice, this process becomes simple, but you can always resort to using a rolling pin.) Lower the dough onto the prepared pan and repeat the process with the other ball. Top as desired.

Andy's Schnecken

These go back to Linda's childhood and Aunt Jennie Bloomberg. But they are most often associated with Linda's son Andy, who receives a tin of them every time he visits Nana Gert LeVine. Because of the amount of butter in the dough, it is very sticky, so you will need patience in rolling.

Makes 36 rolls

> 2 tablespoons active dry yeast
> ¼ cup warm water
> 2 cups unsalted butter, cold
> 1 cup milk
> 3 jumbo eggs, beaten
> 5 cups unbleached flour, plus more for rolling
> 1¼ cups granulated sugar
> 2 tablespoons cinnamon
> 1¼ cups dark brown sugar, firmly packed
> 1 cup raisins

Combine yeast and water in a small bowl and mix. Set aside to bubble, about 5 minutes. Meanwhile, melt 1 cup of the butter in a small saucepan and add the milk. Remove from heat and set aside; mixture should be warm, not hot. In the warmed bowl of an electric mixer fitted with the paddle, combine yeast and butter mixture. Add eggs and mix. With motor running, add flour and ½ cup of the granulated sugar. Scrape sides of bowl and blend thoroughly. Cover bowl with plastic wrap and let mixture rise in a warm place until it doubles, about 1½ hours.

Mix dough with a wooden spoon; cover with plastic wrap again and let rise in a warm place for 1 hour.

Preheat oven to 375°.

Combine remaining sugar with the cinnamon and set aside. Slice remaining cup butter into very thin slices, about 20 slices to the stick. Spray 3 muffin tins with Pam. Place 1 slice of butter in bottom of each cup. Divide the brown sugar among the cups.

Dust a large surface with flour and divide dough into thirds. Roll first third into a 12x9 rectangle that is about ¼ inch thick. The dough will be sticky, so roll lightly, reflouring the rolling pin and surface as needed. Sprinkle surface generously with cinnamon mixture, then with raisins. Starting with the longer side, roll into a long tube. Slice into twelve 1-inch pieces and place one piece on top of butter and sugar mixture in each muffin cup. Repeat with remaining dough. Allow schnecken to rise 30 minutes, then bake in preheated oven until brown, about 15–20 minutes.

Remove pans from oven and allow to cool for 2 minutes on racks. Then invert pans on rack and allow to stand for about 1 minute to enable syrup to settle on the pastry. Remove pans. (You may need to help some of the schnecken come loose.) Store in a tightly sealed tin when cooled.

Randy Smith

9893 County Route 76

Hammondsport, New York 14840

(607) 868-3064

*T*he Smith family's agricultural odyssey is all too typical of what is happening in American farming today. Back in the early fifties, Randy's grandparents bought three tracts of farmland, a total of about 200 acres, on the escarpment above Keuka Lake. They did general farming well enough to raise a family. But when it came time for their son Fred to take over, prices had fallen so low that he could not make farming pay. So he took the some of the skills he had developed working the farm and put them to work in construction.

His family lived in the charming little resort town of Hammondsport. But for years, when he would get home from work, Fred Smith would drive the 5 miles to the farm and do chores there. He held on to the farm, working it when he could, not because he expected to make it pay, but because it was theirs and it was there. When he was forty-eight, he decided not to do it anymore. It had meant two decades of 18-hour workdays, and he was tired.

For a couple of years nothing much happened on the Smith family farm. But then Randy, who had spent most of the summer days of his youth working on it, felt the call and took up where his father had left off. Now it is he who works an eight-hour day as an inspector in a factory and then toils on the farm every evening until past dark.

Randy Smith grows oats and corn and raises a few bulls and steers. But he is intrigued with buckwheat. It is quixotic; you can never be sure what it is going to do. On the day we visited, a 15-acre field of it was in full bloom, looking like cotton. He had planned to grow 30 acres, but because of the heat and a lack of rain, he lost half of it. "If you like to gamble," he said, "plant buckwheat."

In some ways, buckwheat is an ideal crop. Randy gets his seed from Birkett Mills at Penn Yan and signs a contract to grow it for a set price. It can be planted as early as late May and as late as early July. It grows quickly, its leafy canopy shading out competing weeds. In a month and a half it is in bloom. It is also a good cover crop—green manure, as they say—adding quality to the soil. And insects don't eat it. So no sprays are necessary. It needs nothing but good luck.

Randy found half a dozen ladybugs on one of the plants. "This is a good sign," he said. "They are good for pollination, and if other bugs try to get started here, the ladybugs will take care of them."

Buckwheat looks nothing like wheat. It is a leafy plant, not a grass. Seeds from its tiny white flowers turn into the triangular grains that when dried and milled yield the wonderful dark flour. But if there is a succession of very hot days followed by very cool nights, the heads will split, or "blast," ruining the crop.

Deer and wild turkeys love buckwheat. "A doe and two fawns were at the edge of the woods watching me plant," said Randy. "I think they were taking notes about where to come to when this stuff was ready." It's easy to lose several acres of buckwheat and corn to the turkeys and the deer.

An early planting will be swath-cut while green and piled in wind rows— long, even piles—to dry. Later the combine will pick it up and sort the grain from the plants. The later plantings will be combined after the first frost has killed the leaves. Randy usually gets about 25 bushels of grain per acre. He rotates crops, usually planting oats after he has used the field for buckwheat. The oats that follow can usually get by with relatively little weed problem, because the buckwheat will have kept the weeds from growing and going to seed.

Working this farm is for Randy Smith a labor of love. "This land is paid for," he said. "Otherwise we couldn't do this at all." His father keeps the taxes paid,

about $3,000 a year. Fuel for the machinery will run over $500 for the summer, and he had to spend $700 for tires for the two old tractors.

Why does he do this? All of this labor for so little return.

"You can't grow more land," Randy answered. "We owe it to this land to take care of it. Besides, it's very peaceful. I love coming out here."

Randy's wife, Gaylynne Faith, works for the county. "Gaylynne has a good job," said Randy Smith. "Maybe within five to ten years I will finally be able to work the farm full-time, to see what we can do with it."

"And raise buckwheat," said Randy's mother, Barbara. "Most people can't raise buckwheat. It takes a special touch."

"Yeah," said Randy with a laugh. "Touch is right. Touched in the head!"

Buckwheat Pancakes

There is a wonderful Appalachian folk festival in Ripley, West Virginia, that we love to attend around July 4. That's where Linda first tasted buckwheat pancakes. In the early years of our marriage, we would buy enough freshly ground buckwheat flour to store for a year in the freezer. Now it is easy to acquire really marvelous organically grown flour all the year round from Arrowhead or Birkett Mills. While most recipes for buckwheat pancakes call for yeast and need to rise for several hours, this recipe is easy to make at the last minute (but the batter will stand nicely overnight in the refrigerator).

Makes 12–15 pancakes

⅔ cup buckwheat flour
⅓ cup stone-ground whole-wheat flour
⅓ cup unbleached flour
2 teaspoons baking powder
½ teaspoon baking soda
1 tablespoon sugar
1 jumbo egg
3 tablespoons unsalted butter, melted
1½ cups buttermilk, or more if necessary
1–2 tablespoons vegetable oil

Whipped butter, at room temperature, warmed maple syrup, fresh fruit, and fresh mint leaves for garnish

Combine dry ingredients in a large mixing bowl. Add egg, butter, and buttermilk. Whisk well to make a smooth batter. Let mixture rest for 15 minutes. Check to see if more buttermilk is needed—batter should be thick enough to hold some shape when dropped from a spoon onto a hot skillet.

Into a large and very well-seasoned cast-iron skillet, pour only enough oil to coat the bottom. Heat oil until a drop of water dropped on the surface sizzles. Spoon enough batter onto the skillet to make 4-inch pancakes and reduce heat slightly. Fry pancakes until brown on the bottom, then turn and fry other side until browned. Transfer to a heated platter and keep in a warm oven until all pancakes are prepared. Garnish with butter, syrup, fruit, and mint.

Buckwheat Black Bread

Buckwheat has no gluten, so its flour must be used in concert with flours that do; but it has a strong, nutty flavor and makes this delicious bread wonderfully dense and chewy. It is great for sandwiches, as well as for mopping up zesty sauces.

1 2-ounce cake compressed fresh yeast
1 teaspoon sugar
1 cup warm water
1½ cups buckwheat flour
1 cup rye flour (dark, if possible)
1½ cups unbleached flour, or more if necessary
3 cups stone-ground whole-wheat flour
1 tablespoon salt
1 tablespoon crushed fennel seed
½ cup black molasses
¾ cup strong brewed coffee
¼ cup cider vinegar
¼ cup vegetable oil
2 tablespoons caraway seeds
2 teaspoons ground ginger
1–2 tablespoons cornmeal
1–2 tablespoons unsalted butter

Combine the yeast and sugar with the warm water and blend thoroughly. Set aside in a warm place until bubbly, about 15 minutes.

In the bowl of an electric mixer fitted with the paddle, mix buckwheat flour, rye flour, unbleached flour, whole-wheat flour, salt, and fennel. Add yeast mixture, molasses, coffee, vinegar, oil, caraway, and ginger. Mix on low speed until blended. If mixture is too wet, add more unbleached flour, a bit at a time. Turn out on a lightly floured work surface and knead for 10–15 minutes, until dough is smooth and pliable. Dough still may be a bit tacky, however.

Lightly oil a large, warm mixing bowl. Place dough in bowl, turning once to slightly oil all surfaces. Cover with plastic wrap and let rise in a warm place until doubled, about 2½ hours. Punch dough down.

Sprinkle cornmeal on cookie sheet or stone. Shape dough into a fat, round loaf and let rise, lightly covered, on the cookie sheet in a warm place until nearly doubled, about 1–1½ hours. Meanwhile, preheat oven to 400°. Bake in preheated oven for 1 hour, or until bread sounds hollow when rapped on bottom of loaf. Remove from oven, quickly rub surface thoroughly with butter, and let cool on a rack.

½ teaspoon salt
1 teaspoon ground cardamom
½ teaspoon freshly grated nutmeg
½ teaspoon cinnamon
¼ cup granulated sugar
2 jumbo eggs, beaten
½ cup maple syrup
1 cup buttermilk
½ cup apple cider
¼ cup vegetable oil
1½ cups chopped tart unpeeled apples
½ cup dried currants

Icing
2 tablespoons apple cider
2 teaspoons lemon juice
1 cup confectioners' sugar

Preheat oven to 375°. Thoroughly grease muffin tins and set aside.

Combine dry ingredients in a large bowl and set aside. Combine eggs and maple syrup in a mixing bowl and whisk vigorously. Add buttermilk and whisk again. Then add cider and oil. Pour mixture over dry ingredients, add apples and currants, then quickly fold together without overmixing. Spoon into prepared muffin tins, filling almost full. Bake in preheated oven for 25 minutes, or until a toothpick inserted in the center comes out dry. Remove from heat and let muffins stand in tins for 5 minutes on cooling racks, then turn out.

Make the icing by combining cider and lemon juice in a small saucepan. Bring to a boil over high heat, remove pan from heat, and quickly whisk in confectioners' sugar until mixture is very smooth. Dip warm muffin tops into the cider icing, then let cool on a rack.

Buckwheat Apple Currant Muffins

Makes 1 dozen

1 cup buckwheat flour
1⅔ cups unbleached flour
2 teaspoons baking powder
1 teaspoon baking soda

Lowell G. Raun, Jr.

Lowell Farms

311 Avenue A

El Campo, Texas 77437

(409) 543-4950

While it is rarely thought of as a big American crop, rice has been grown in this country for three hundred years. According to the Rice Council of America, the annual worldwide per capita consumption exceeds 143 pounds per person. And the United States is one of the world's largest exporters of rice. Initially, it was believed that rice could only be grown in the flat, marshy tidal lands of the Carolinas. In 1884, however, an Iowa farmer visiting the prairie lands of the Gulf Coast had an idea that dramatically altered the course of rice growing in this country.

He believed that the hot, flat terrain of southwestern Louisiana and southeastern Texas had the rich soil required for rice. He knew that the region offered the high rainfall and abundant water rice needs. But most important, he saw that the land itself was firm—much more solid than that of the Carolina marshes. It was this firm soil that prompted the Iowa farmer to suggest that the mechanized methods he employed on his own farms would work on this Gulf Coast land, enabling rice farming to be done mechanically rather than by hand. People thought he made sense and he was right. The rest is history.

Three generations of Rauns have now farmed rice in Wharton County, Texas, not far from the Gulf. Today, Lowell Raun, Jr., and his wife, Linda, farm over 400 acres of rice land; and Lowell manages another 1,400 acres with his father and brother.

Most of this land is planted with rices developed by geneticists at the Texas Agricultural Experiment Station at Beaumont specifically for this part of Texas. Texmont, Lemont, and Gulfmont are semi-dwarf varieties that are less vulnerable than taller rices to the fierce hurricanes that annually sweep the region. Maybelle is an early-maturing variety that is usually ready for harvest before the storm season begins. But one 32-acre patch of Lowell Farms is special. On it, the Rauns grow jasmine rice organically.

Lowell and Linda had been looking for something new and interesting to do, something that might at the same time provide a new income stream. On a recent trip to the West Coast, they had been impressed by the space given to organic and natural foods not only by health-food and specialty-food stores but by ordinary supermarkets as well.

They chose to plant jasmine rice this way for a number of reasons: First of all, it has an outstanding fragrance and delicate, flowery taste. Also, jasmine rice is extremely popular in Oriental communities in the United States, so there was a waiting market. At the time, all of the jasmine rice sold in this country was being imported, mostly from Thailand. In addition, this long-grained rice has always commanded a premium price. And jasmine seed was newly available from the Beaumont agricultural station.

Besides, Lowell felt that jasmine appeared to be especially good for organic growing. It is a hardy plant that grows quickly. Since you cannot use herbicides, the strategy is to get the rice growing before the weeds have a chance. Lowell soaks the seeds to speed up germination. He plants late so that the weather is warmer. Within five days, he has visible shoots, and within a couple of weeks, he has enough leaf on the rice plants that the soil below is shaded and the weeds are stunted. Then, when the rice is about 6 inches high, he irrigates, flooding the whole field and drowning the undesirable growth. Jasmine rice is also high tillering, meaning that there are a lot of heads of rice per plant, making a better shade and thereby reducing grass and weed competition.

The jasmine rice is harvested in August, the fields are again flooded, the stubble grows, and the canopy develops again. There is a second harvest in October or November.

At first, Lowell worried about insects. A pest called the stinkbug was his main concern. Stinkbugs nibble the rice grains and even in sprayed fields will damage about 1 percent of the crop. He was surprised and pleased, then, that in his organic field there was no more damage than in the fields that had been sprayed with insecticides.

Lowell had hoped for 3,000 pounds per acre from the first two harvests of jasmine, but was astonished to realize that in the end his yield was 5,200 pounds. Nonetheless, this is substantially less than the 8,500 to 9,000 pounds that the Rauns traditionally get from their conventional fields.

The field Lowell chose for planting jasmine was ideal. It had been fallow, free from all chemicals for twenty-five years. It was very rich, with a deep layer of topsoil. And he had only to level it to the degree of the rest of the farm before he could plant.

Lowell and his uncle have designed a lot of equipment for the fields. One of their inventions is a laser system that they use with their grader. The goal is to make the field as level as a tabletop, with not more than a couple of inches of slope per several hundred feet. This makes water use more efficient, since it won't run off. As the grader moves over the surface, the undulations are read by the laser, which immediately signals for soil to be scraped up if it is too high and laid down if it is too low.

Perhaps the most frustrating problem for the rice farmers here are the wild geese. They are supposed to fly north about the time the fields are planted. "They don't want to leave because we've made it so wonderful for them," Lowell told us. "In one 113-acre field, the geese ruined 7 acres. Altogether we lost 15 acres to the geese in the whole farm. It costs $700 to $800 per acre to farm. So the geese cost us $12,000. Sometimes there will be ten thousand of them." The Rauns have propane cannons that explode from time to time to scare the geese off, but they don't have enough of them.

The average annual rainfall in this region is 35 inches, but rice farmers prefer drier years. It minimizes fungal damage, and they can control their own water supply, irrigating when they need to. The yields are higher in the drier years.

The rice is harvested when its moisture content is 20 percent. The farmer can tell when it is ready by just looking at it and feeling the heads. After it has dried to about 12 percent moisture, they take it to the mill. Usually the millers buy it when it is delivered and pay according to quality. Of course, Lowell usually gets a premium.

The jasmine (60,000 pounds of it yearly) undergoes what is called toll milling: It is processed for a fee, and the Rauns keep ownership while it is in storage at the mill. As orders come in, the mill will bag the rice and ship it. The Rauns hired an advertising firm to design their handsome package. Now Lowell and Linda find that their biggest challenge is, in fact, researching the market and finding ways to sell their certified organic rice.

The quality of the Rauns' jasmine is clearly evident to anyone who knows rice. The grains are all the same size, shape, and color. The flavor, fragrance, and texture are superb. It is understandably more expensive than regular rice. But aficionados think it's a bargain.

Most rice growers never even know where their rice is shipped, let alone who is eating the results of their labors. But Lowell and Linda Raun sell their jasmine rice themselves. They now have tasted the pride of ownership and found that they enjoy this closer, more personal connection with the consumer and the fact that anyone who eats their jasmine knows the name and address of the people who grew it. Cautiously optimistic, Lowell has identified a nearby field as a likely place for growing more jasmine.

Linda's Paella

This is the first dish that Linda ever prepared for Fred. While it's a long recipe, it is not difficult to make; much of the preparation can be done early in the day.

Serves 8–10

1–2 pounds chorizo
¾ cup olive oil
¼ cup vegetable oil
3 pounds chicken breasts and thighs, cut in half
Salt and freshly ground black pepper
2 ounces lean boneless pork, cut into small cubes
2 ounces smoked ham, cut into small cubes
½ cup finely chopped onion
¼ cup finely chopped shallots
1 tablespoon minced garlic
1 red bell pepper, cut into julienne strips
½ green bell pepper, cut into julienne strips
1½ cups peeled, seeded, and chopped fresh tomatoes
8 cups Fish Fûmet (page 204)
½ teaspoon powdered saffron
¼ teaspoon cayenne pepper
1 lobster, stomach and intestines discarded
12–14 raw shrimp, peeled and deveined
1 cup sea scallops
10–20 littleneck clams, scrubbed
10–20 mussels, scrubbed and debearded
4 cups uncooked jasmine rice
¾ cup fresh or frozen peas
8–10 lemon wedges
2 hard-boiled eggs, chopped

Prick sausages in several places, place them in a saucepan, cover with water, and bring to a boil. Simmer for about 5 minutes, drain, and pat dry with paper towels. Slice into ¼-inch slices.

While sausage is cooking, pour ½ cup of

the olive oil and all the vegetable oil into a large skillet. Heat on high until oil is hot, then carefully brown chicken pieces over medium heat until golden on both sides. Remove chicken and set aside. Sprinkle with salt and pepper to taste.

Add sausage slices to the skillet and brown on both sides. Remove sausage and set aside.

Drain oil from skillet, then add remaining olive oil and heat until hot. Add pork and ham cubes and sauté these for a few minutes. Add onion, shallots, garlic, and peppers. Continue to sauté for a minute. Then add the tomatoes. Stir and cook over medium heat until liquids in the pan have evaporated. This mixture is called *sofrito*. Remove from heat and set aside.

One hour before serving, remove racks from oven and preheat to 400°. Combine stock and saffron in a large saucepan and bring to a boil. Add ½ teaspoon salt, ½ teaspoon freshly ground pepper, and cayenne. Stir well.

Cut lobster tail into slices. Try to break claws into a few parts. Cut lobster body into six parts and set aside.

Combine the rice and *sofrito* in the bottom of a 14-inch paella pan or 14-inch casserole that is at least 1½ inches deep. Mix well. Pour the boiling stock over this and place pan on high heat. Stir constantly until mixture begins to boil.

Quickly scatter chicken, sausage, and shellfish evenly around the pan. Sprinkle evenly with peas. Set the pan on the floor of your oven (if pan is too large to do this, place on rack in lowest portion of oven) and bake for 25–30 minutes, or until liquids are absorbed and rice is *al dente*.

Remove paella from oven and wrap the pan with a large bath towel. Let rest for 8 minutes. Then scatter lemon wedges over the top and sprinkle with chopped egg.

Wine: Forman Vineyard Chardonnay (Napa Valley) or *Amity Vineyards Pinot Noir* (Oregon)

Red Beans and Rice

It took time for Linda the New Englander to comprehend that red beans and rice could be good together. But she quickly understood why this dish is like manna from heaven to folks in the South.

Serves 10–14

   1 pound dried red kidney beans
   5 tablespoons vegetable oil or lard
   1 cup chopped celery
   2 cups chopped onion
1½ cups chopped green bell pepper
4–5 cloves garlic, finely chopped
   1 dried red chile pepper, chopped
   2 smoked ham hocks
   4 cups chopped canned tomatoes, with juice
   3 bay leaves
   1 tablespoon fresh thyme
   1 teaspoon freshly ground white pepper
   1 teaspoon freshly ground black pepper
   2 pounds andouille sausage, cut in ½-inch slices
     Approximately 1 tablespoon Tabasco

Kosher salt to taste
½ cup chopped fresh parsley
5 cups cooked jasmine rice
(preferably cooked in chicken
stock), buttered

Fresh parsley sprigs for garnish

In a large bowl combine red beans and water to cover (at least 2½ quarts); soak overnight.

The next day, heat 3 tablespoons of the oil in a large cast-iron pot, then sauté celery, onion, green pepper, garlic, and chile over medium heat until nearly tender. Drain and rinse the beans. Add beans, ham hocks, tomatoes, bay leaves, 1½ quarts water, thyme, and white and black pepper. Bring to a boil, reduce heat, and simmer, partially covered, for 1½ hours, adding water as needed.

In a large skillet, combine 2 tablespoons oil and the sausage and lightly brown over medium heat. Add sausage to bean mixture along with Tabasco and salt; continue cooking until hocks and beans are tender, about 1 more hour. Add more pepper if desired.

Remove ham hocks and slice meat off the bone. Return meat to the pot and stir in chopped parsley.

Serve hot buttered rice and beans on the side. Garnish with parsley sprigs.

Wine: Charles Shaw Gamay (Napa Valley)

Simple Fried Rice

Serves 4–6

Approximately ½ cup vegetable oil
1 clove garlic, finely minced
¼ cup finely minced onion
1 dried red chile pepper, crumbled
2 teaspoons finely minced fresh ginger
½ pound ground pork or veal
2 jumbo eggs, lightly beaten
3 cups cooked jasmine rice
3 tablespoons dark soy sauce
3 tablespoons rich chicken stock
1 tablespoon dark sesame oil
¼ cup diced smoked Virginia ham (optional)
¼ cup cooked peas
1 tablespoon minced fresh cilantro
2 tablespoons minced fresh chives

Heat 1–2 tablespoons of the vegetable oil in a wok. When very hot, add garlic, onion, chile, and ginger, toss for 30 seconds, then add ground meat. Cook, tossing constantly, until meat is cooked. Remove from heat and place meat mixture in a small bowl.

Return wok to heat, add 1–2 tablespoons of oil, and heat until hot. Add eggs and cook, stirring constantly, until eggs are done. Transfer eggs to a small bowl and set aside.

Add 1–2 tablespoons of oil to wok and heat. Return meat mixture to wok, along with rice, soy sauce, stock, sesame oil, and ham. Toss over medium heat until mixture is hot. Stir in eggs and peas and toss for 1 minute over heat. Remove from heat and stir in cilantro and chives.

Wine: Ponzi Vineyards Dry White Riesling (Willamette Valley, Washington)

Dave Reinke

Manitok Organic Wild Rice
Box 87
Callaway, Minnesota 56521
(800) 726-1863

*I*ts history is almost as old as the lakes themselves. For as long as there have been the Anishinabeg, or Chippewa, Indians, wild rice from their lakes has been a major culinary and economic part of their lives. In fact, the weeks of harvesttime between August and September are referred to as *Manominekegisis,* the Rice-Making Moon.

Despite its importance, however, real lake wild rice came perilously close to disappearing. Fortunately, the White Earth Band of the Anishinabeg tribe has found a way of strengthening this great resource. They have done so with the help of Minnesotan Dave Reinke, now marketing manager of the Manitok Wild Rice Cooperative.

Over the last thirty years, wild rice has been plentiful and fairly cheap. That's because most of it is not hand-harvested lake rice; rather, it is combine-harvested paddy rice, a cultivated rice that was developed years ago by researchers at the University of Minnesota when the demand for wild rice exceeded the wild supply.

Paddy rice tends to be very black and hard, requiring at least an hour of cooking. That it has few of the fine qualities of the real thing matters little to the average consumer—it virtually ruined the market for the Anishinabeg's hand-harvested lake rice.

Wild rice, *Zizania aquatica* (water weed), is not a true rice but a grass, an annual plant that grows from seed in the shallow lakes of the Great Lakes watershed, an area often referred to as the "wild-rice bowl." Wild-rice lakes are most common in northern Minnesota, but there are also wild-rice lakes in the northern parts of Wisconsin and Michigan. Wild rice comes in a number of colors and sizes. It can be gray, green, brown, or reddish; it can be long-grain or short-grain. These characteristics are determined by the nature of the soil. For example, in the western part of Minnesota, where the soils are highly organic (containing a large amount of decayed plant matter), the rice has a shorter grain than in the eastern part, where the soil is richer in minerals.

Wild rice is a fragile plant that requires a perfectly balanced ecosystem for its survival. Seeds germinate in early March, as the ice is melting; germination begins, in fact, under the ice. A very delicate, very thin plant begins to take root in the soil under the water. By June it has reached the water's surface. Wild rice grows best in pristine water that is 12 to 18 inches deep, but it will survive in waters that are 6 inches to 30 inches deep. If the water is too deep, the plant uses too much energy for growth and dies. If the water is not clear enough for photosynthesis, the plant dies from lack of nutrition.

When the leaves break through the surface, they begin using oxygen; if the water gets too high, the plant drowns. So proper water management is essential. Aerial leaves begin to develop in July and the plant grows rapidly, from 2 to 8 feet above the water's surface. Soon the plants are so thick that they obscure all signs of water.

About one plant grows per square foot of area, and each plant has six or seven heads. There are 30 to 100 kernels, or seeds, per head. About 10 percent of the kernels ripen each day, so a strong wind can do a lot of damage if it comes before the harvest. In a good year, only about 20 percent of the rice actually gets harvested; the rest falls into the lake to reseed for the future.

A good harvest requires ideal conditions in the lakes. By the early 1980s, the Minnesota lakes were in bad shape. Pollution had damaged some, but most had been hurt by an uncontrolled beaver population. Beaver dams wreaked havoc on the rice fields by causing too much water in some lakes, too little in others. Dave Reinke was hired in 1984 to help the White Earth Band reestablish the wild rice beds in the northwestern part of the state. Many beavers were relocated so that old dams could be destroyed and new ones made. Lakes were reseeded where necessary. By the end of the decade, the yield had increased dramatically.

The harvest usually begins the last week in August. Lower Rice Lake has 1,500 acres of wild rice, so dense that you never see open water. Big Chippewa, Bonga, and Big Bear are among the more than 800 bodies of water that are over 10 acres in size on this reservation. While there are 10,000 people living on the 36-square-mile reservation, only 4,100 actually belong to the tribe. By law, all harvesting must be done by hand and must be done only by members of the tribe.

The only tools are a canoe and ricing sticks. Traditionally, there will be two people in the canoe, usually a couple. The man guides the canoe through the water with the help of a long, forked pole. Using two light and smooth wooden ricing sticks, or "knockers," the woman pulls a head of rice over her lap with one stick and raps the ripe seeds loose with the other. Since the whole head does not ripen simultaneously, only the ripe grains fall. Each lake will be harvested several times more.

It used to be that harvesting was only done in the morning; afternoons were spent drying, parching, and "jigging." The seeds were first spread out on birchbark "sheets" for a short while to dry, then placed in a cauldron over a wood fire and stirred with a paddle to be parched. This parching process is what gives the rice its special flavor. Finally, the parched rice would be placed in a shallow pit lined with bark and deerskin and youngsters wearing special soft moccasins and leather leggings would dance, or jig, on the seeds in order to loosen the chaff from the kernels. Then the rice was placed in a special birch-bark tray, or winnowing basket, and gently shaken; the chaff would be carried off by the wind and the grain would drop to the basket below. The rice was then ready to be stored.

Today, the cooperative works with two nearby finishers. "It is important to complete the process in twenty-four hours," said Dave Reinke. "That's how we maintain this outstanding quality. We don't want the green seeds left unprocessed too long. That dries them too much, making a very black, hard grain with less flavor. When the rice is properly finished it will cook in only twenty minutes. Otherwise it will take at least an hour."

Parching is still done over a fire, but in a large motorized drum with paddle wheels. The rice must be brought to 260° to dry it to about 8 percent moisture, which will loosen the outer hull. "When the smoke rolls out of the parcher, it's ready," Dave said. "Then it's run through a thresher and fanning mills to remove the chaff." It takes 95,000 pounds of green rice to make 41,000 pounds of finished rice. It is almost all hand labor from harvest to packing. And this simple system is totally organic. It yields a product that is not inexpensive, nor should it be.

In 1978, the hand harvester got $2 a pound for his wild rice. In 1989, it had dropped to 50 cents a pound. Fortunately, by 1990 the price was up to $1 a pound and things seem to be changing for the better. Harvesting can be an important source of extra income, since the best harvesters can collect about 2,800 pounds of rice over an eight- to ten-day period.

Manitok Cooperative has representatives at each lake. They pay a premium price to each harvester and each purchase is recorded and assigned a number so they know which lake it came from and when. In 1990, Manitok Cooperative bought from two hundred harvesters; now, they might buy from as many as seven hundred. Dave Reinke is determined to maintain the high quality of his finished product, so he buys only as much rice as can properly be finished.

When it became clear that the White Earth Band's efforts were succeeding and the rice harvest was increasing, they developed a marketing plan that was funded by the U.S. Health and Human Services Department (Aid to Native Americans—ANA). Dave's assistant took over as crop manager and Dave took on the marketing. "We decided to go for organic certification," Dave said, "so that we could distinguish ourselves from the commercial producers." These lakes are pristine; all water is tested and certified for quality. There are no synthetically derived fertilizers, herbicides, insecticides, or fungicides. One cup of wild rice, when cooked, will serve six people. "Besides being so satisfying to the taste, it is higher in nutritional value than oats, barley, wheat, and rye," Dave reminded us.

Dave's goal is to help the tribe develop its financial base. Since a harvest of half a million pounds is possible, the potential for the tribe is considerable. But this rice is sold for its social value as well as for its quality. While many of the tribe's old traditions have been relaxed, the rejuvenation of the rice beds has put new vigor into the White Earth Band. The youth of the band have new enthusiasm for the traditions of their ancestors, and they are finding that these traditions are as rich in texture as the rice itself. The Anishinabeg call the rice *manomin,* "gift from the Creator." It can be an especially important gift as the tribe prepares for the twenty-first century.

Tim Anderson's Smoked Breast of Chicken with Wild-Rice Cakes, Cucumber-Melon Relish, and Cracked-Pepper Pear Sauce

In *The Best of the Midwest,* Tim Anderson, of Goodfellow's Restaurant, in Minneapolis, presented a splendid wild-rice compote and a variation of this cracked-pepper sauce. Tim's recipes are always very approachable; preparing them is the next best thing to dining at Goodfellow's.

Serves 4

RELISH
    ½ mango, peeled and seeded
        Juice of 1 lime
    1½ tablespoons finely diced red bell
        pepper
    ½ cup finely diced cantaloupe
    ½ cup finely diced honeydew melon

2 tablespoons peeled, seeded, and
finely diced cucumber
2 tablespoons minced fresh chives
Salt and freshly ground black
pepper to taste

SAUCE

2 tablespoons vegetable oil
1 tablespoon chopped carrot
1 tablespoon chopped celery
1 tablespoon chopped onion
1 tablespoon chopped fresh parsley
1 clove garlic, minced
¼ cup dry sherry
1½ cups rich veal or beef stock
½ cup rich chicken stock
½ ripe pear, roasted, peeled, and
puréed
2 tablespoons unsalted butter
½ ripe pear, peeled and cut into ¼-
inch dice
Salt to taste
1 tablespoon coarsely ground black
pepper

WILD-RICE CAKES

⅓ medium onion, grated
1 medium carrot, grated
1 medium white potato, grated
2 tablespoons chopped fresh parsley
¼ cup bread crumbs
⅔ cup cooked wild rice
2 jumbo eggs
Salt to taste
Approximately ½ cup vegetable oil

4 smoked chicken breasts, skinned,
split, and sliced on the diagonal

To make relish: In a food processor or
blender, purée mango pulp with lime juice.

Then combine puree with remaining ingredients in a small bowl and set aside.

To make sauce: In a medium saucepan,
heat vegetable oil, then sauté carrot, celery,
onion, parsley, and garlic until soft. Add
sherry and stir over medium heat, scraping
pan thoroughly. Add stocks and cook over
medium-low heat until liquids are reduced
by half. Strain to remove vegetables. Then
combine strained stock and pear puree in the
saucepan. Whisk in butter. Add salt, pepper,
and diced pear. Set aside and keep warm.

To make rice cakes: Combine all ingredients except oil in a mixing bowl and fold
together thoroughly. Generously oil a grid-
dle or cast-iron skillet and heat until oil is
smoking. Spoon a ball of batter (about
¼ cup) onto the skillet and pat it into a pancake shape. Cook on both sides until golden,
transfer to a heated platter, and keep warm
while you prepare the rest of the cakes.

To serve, spoon some sauce onto each of
four serving plates. Place a rice cake on top
of sauce, spoon relish onto cake, then fan
chicken slices around edge of cake with
part of each slice in the sauce. Serve hot.

*Wine: Girard Winery Chardonnay
(Napa Valley)*

Wild Rice with Pecans

This recipe is for Manitok wild rice or any
other natural lake rice. If you use paddy-
grown wild rice, the cooking time will be
about triple.

Makes 3¼ cups

1 cup Manitok wild rice
3 cups rich chicken stock
½ teaspoon kosher salt

3 tablespoons unsalted butter or margarine
¼ cup finely diced carrots
⅓ cup chopped pecans
½ teaspoon freshly ground white pepper
2 pinches cayenne pepper
1 teaspoon minced fresh thyme
1 tablespoon minced fresh parsley
1 tablespoon minced fresh chives

1 teaspoon cinnamon
Generous pinch freshly grated nutmeg
1 cup dried cherries
3 cups cooked wild rice
2 tablespoons sugar mixed with 1 teaspoon cinnamon
Michigan Dried-Cherry Zinfandel Sauce (page 399)

Rinse wild rice in three changes of hot tap water. Drain. In a heavy saucepan, combine rice, stock, and salt; bring to a boil. Cover, reduce heat, and simmer until rice has absorbed all water, about 20 minutes.

Meanwhile, place butter in a small skillet and melt over medium heat. When foaming, add carrots, reduce heat, and cover with a piece of wax paper pressed directly on the carrots. Sweat over low heat for 5 minutes. Remove paper, increase heat, and add pecans, pepper, and cayenne. Stir as pecans brown, then add herbs.

Combine carrot mixture with rice and serve.

Minnesota Wild Rice Pudding with Dried Cherries

Serves 8

   Butter and sugar for soufflé dish
3 cups hot half-and-half
⅔ cup sugar
¼ cup maple syrup
4 jumbo eggs plus 1 jumbo egg yolk, well beaten
2 tablespoons bourbon
1 tablespoon vanilla extract

Butter and sugar a 2-quart soufflé dish and set aside.

Preheat oven to 350°. In a medium-sized mixing bowl, slowly combine the half-and-half with the ⅔ cup sugar and the syrup. Stir until sugar is dissolved.

Place eggs and yolk in a large bowl and slowly add hot mixture, stirring very well. Add remaining ingredients except cinnamon-sugar. Blend thoroughly. Pour into prepared soufflé dish and sprinkle with cinnamon-sugar. Bake in preheated oven for 50 minutes. If pudding jiggles too much in center, bake for another 5–10 minutes. Remove from oven and cool on a rack for 20 minutes. Serve with dried-cherry sauce.

Wine: Mayacamas Vineyards Zinfandel "Late Harvest" (Napa Valley)

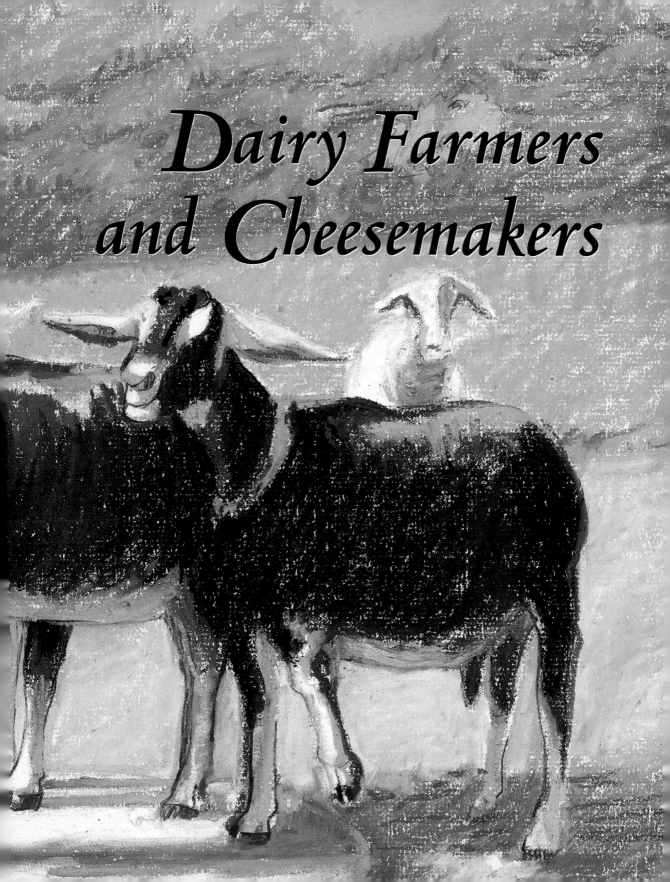

Dairy Farmers and Cheesemakers

Kip Rondy and Becky Ross

New Morning Farm

16232 Henry Road

Amesville, Ohio 44711

(614) 448-4021

Kip Rondy grew up middle-class. His father was a successful lawyer in Barberton, Ohio. And he himself traveled the usual middle-class route, to college to prepare for a profession, majoring in the social sciences and taking graduate work at Kent State.

But instead of searching out a comfortable niche in Barberton or Cleveland, he went to Lincoln County, West Virginia, one of the poorest regions in the nation. The poverty, Kip remembers, was extraordinary. He became involved as a paralegal in an advocacy office that helped people with Social Security problems and welfare-rights cases. He got caught up in the life and in the struggles of the people of the community. He bought a small farm, began raising chickens and producing eggs, started a family, and stayed there for twelve years.

In 1987, he came back to Ohio and, with the help of his father, bought a 123-acre farm in the beautiful hills near Athens. It had been a dairy farm, but Kip's interest was in eggs. He built a new barn and sold his silos, got in some Hy-Line Brown chicks, and soon started gathering eggs.

"It's a certified organic farm," said Kip. "Everything but the eggs is organic." He raises row crops—sweet corn, winter squash, kale and spinach—a lot of garlic, and spelts, 7 acres of it. Spelts is a wheatlike grain, common in Switzerland and France, which is often good for people who are allergic to ordinary wheat. It is his biggest cash crop; he can get 80 cents a pound for it in the health-food market.

"My eggs can't be organic," he said, "because I can't afford to use organic feed. The eggs would be just too costly." Still, he feeds a relatively expensive mix of corn and protein supplement. "The big producers have two rations. One for hens that lay fertile eggs for chicks, and another, lesser ration for the hens that produce eggs for the market. It stands to reason that the ration for the fertile eggs is best, so that's what I use."

Supplement can be made of any food that is high in protein. Soybeans, whey, brewer's yeast, and the by-products of various food-processing operations are commonly used. Supplement is usually 42 percent protein and contains added vitamins and minerals. It is much more costly than corn, so Kip mixes his corn and supplement to achieve a feed that is 19 to 20 percent protein. The big egg operations—Kip's competitors—which are always looking for ways to reduce costs, usually feed a mixture that is 16 percent protein.

The hens in the big egg factories are bred to lay. At an early sexual maturity their ovaries go into high gear. Four or five hens are put into each of thousands of small cages, where they stay for months, laying eggs. A really efficient hen might produce an egg a day. They are often debeaked so they can't hurt each other. Their food and water are presented mechanically, their eggs carried off by a conveyor belt and then moved, handled, sized, graded, packed, and shipped automatically. When the hens' rate of production goes down, they are dispatched to the soup company.

"I think our chickens are ten times healthier than those caged birds," Kip said. "They exercise. Just like people who are active, they have less cholesterol. And it logically follows that their eggs will be better. They are never debeaked, never given hormones." The chickens are kept in the barns at night, out of the way of predators that roam the hills. But after the morning feeding, the doors are opened and the chickens have all day to scratch in the meadows.

The profit margin in the egg business is very low. If a big operation can net a dollar per bird per year, it is considered a good economic performance. If the operator has a million birds, or even 60,000 to 70,000, he can earn a decent living. But a farmer like Kip cannot live on that small a margin; he has to get more for his eggs. So he must find customers who can tell the difference between his eggs and those of his big competitors, and who are willing to pay the higher price for higher quality.

Kip's hens provide more than sixty dozen eggs a day. They are collected, cleaned, and sized by hand. Kip sells them to health-food stores, specialty markets, good restaurants, and anyone else who craves eggs with some character. He is usually able to get 40 cents per dozen above the price of ordinary eggs. "You can tell the difference," said Kip. "Our eggs are great." He especially likes pullet eggs, those produced by the youngest hens. "They've got energy and youth and they make the tastiest eggs. If someone doesn't like these eggs, I can't help him."

Kip Rondy has gotten involved in organic farming organizations, and it was through one of them that he met Becky Ross, now his partner and wife. Her love of the out-of-doors led her to take a job as a landscaper in Cincinnati. She now owns Bekatha's Garden. She creates and tends English gardens and maintains golf courses and large yards. What she does brings in a steady income, so Kip and Becky divide their week. Late on Sunday evening, they drive the three hours to Cincinnati and work their landscaping accounts from sunrise to dark, through Wednesday. Then late Wednesday night, they drive back to Amesville and the chickens.

While they are gone, a friend gathers the eggs and feeds the chickens. When they return, they have four intense days during which they catch up on everything that has gotten behind, clean the hen houses, mix the feed, wipe the eggs, package the orders, do the deliveries, keep the books, and attend to the fields.

Kip had just returned from an organic farmers' conference in Columbus. He told us that a couple of farmers, both in their early sixties, had been talking about their money troubles, wondering how they could continue and what they would live on if they had to retire. "At that age," said Kip, "you shouldn't have to worry about money anymore. You've worried about it all your life."

But he thinks they can succeed with their little farm. They will produce crops that are good enough to command a better price and then he and Becky will take an active role in the marketing. "It will take most of my adult life to get it working. But that's what I want!"

Andy's Strawberry Meringue Cake

Since he was a small child, Linda's son Andy has requested this dessert as his annual birthday cake. It can also be filled with raspberries and cream or chocolate mousse.

Makes 1 10-inch cake

>   1–2 teaspoons vegetable oil
>   1 cup egg whites, at room
>   temperature
>   Pinch salt
>   1¾ cups superfine sugar
>   1½ teaspoons white vinegar
>   1 quart fresh strawberries
>   2 tablespoons kirsch
>   2 cups heavy cream
>   ½ cup sour cream
>   ¼ cup confectioners' sugar

Preheat oven to 325°.

Lightly coat bottom and sides of a 10-inch springform pan with the oil and set aside.

In the bowl of an electric mixer fitted with the beater, beat egg whites and salt until very soft peaks begin to form. With motor running on high, add the superfine sugar, a tablespoon at a time, until all is absorbed and the mixture is stiff and shining. Beat in vinegar. Spoon mixture into the prepared pan, rap on a hard surface to eliminate any air bubbles, and smooth top with a spatula. Bake in preheated oven for 1 hour. Remove pan from oven and let cool on a rack. (The middle will sink as cake cools.) Do not remove sides of pan.

No more than 4 hours before serving, prepare filling. Set aside 10 whole berries for garnish, then hull and thinly slice remaining berries. Toss with kirsch and set aside. Combine creams in the bowl of an electric mixer fitted with the beater. With motor on high, beat in confectioners' sugar and continue to whip until mixture forms soft peaks. Remove bowl from mixer and fold in berries. Spoon filling into meringue cake and smooth top with a spatula. Decorate with reserved berries and keep refrigerated until serving time.

Just before serving, carefully run a very sharp knife between the cake and the sides of the pan to loosen any part of the meringue that may have stuck there. Remove sides of pan and serve.

Wine: Joseph Phelps Vineyards "Delice"
(Napa Valley)

Herb and Chestnut Stuffing

In western Massachusetts, and perhaps other places, this is called stuffing—other parts of the country call it dressing. Whatever the name, it's simply delicious and a great light dressing. The legendary Paul Kovi, founder of the Four Seasons restaurant, taught us what most Hungarian cooks already know—sauté paprika with a little white wine to enhance its flavor. It is great for turkey, goose, and chicken.

Makes about 8 cups

>   3 cups corn flakes
>   1 jumbo Challah (see page 70), sliced
>   and torn into chunks
>   8 pullet eggs (or 4 jumbo eggs),
>   beaten
>   1 cup unsalted butter or margarine, or
>   more if necessary
>   1½ cups finely chopped onion
>   ¾ cups finely chopped celery
>   2 tablespoons minced garlic
>   ½ cup minced fresh parsley
>   ¼ cup minced fresh chives
>   1 tablespoon minced fresh oregano
>   1 tablespoon minced fresh thyme
>   1 tablespoon minced fresh sage
>   1 tablespoon mild paprika
>   ¼ cup dry white wine
>   Kosher salt and freshly ground
>   black pepper to taste
>   1½ cups fresh roasted and peeled
>   chestnuts, broken into pieces

Place corn flakes and bread in a large bowl and cover with water. Soak at least 1 hour. Drain well, pressing out as much water as possible. Blend eggs into bread mixture with your hands and set aside.

Melt 1 cup butter in a large skillet over medium heat. Add onion, celery, and garlic. Sauté for 5 minutes but do not brown. Add herbs, paprika, and white wine and stir over heat for a few more minutes. Reduce heat to very low.

Add bread mixture to skillet and blend very well. Add more butter if needed and salt and pepper to taste. Cook over low heat until most of the liquid is gone, just a few minutes. Remove from heat and let cool. Stir in chestnuts to blend evenly.

Gert's Brownies

Thanks to our friend Neil O'Donnell, a.k.a. Cornelius of Corning, we have lots of Pyrex around our house. So we've made these for years in a Pyrex baking dish; if you use metal, reduce the baking time about 10 minutes. These brownies may be frosted with your favorite icing.

>   1 cup unsalted butter
>   4 ounces unsweetened chocolate,
>   chopped
>   2 tablespoons Dutch cocoa powder
>   2 cups sugar
>   4 jumbo eggs
>   2 teaspoons vanilla extract
>   1 cup unbleached flour
>   1 cup coarsely chopped walnuts

Preheat oven to 300°.
Grease a 7x11 Pyrex baking pan.

Place butter and chopped chocolate in a heavy-bottomed saucepan and melt over low heat. Stir in cocoa.

Remove saucepan from heat and stir in sugar until well blended. Add eggs, one at a time, blending thoroughly after each one. Add remaining ingredients, one at a time, blending very well after each.

Pour into prepared pan, smooth surface, and bake for 65 minutes. Cool on a rack, cut into squares, and serve.

Cheese Soufflé with Shellfish Sauce

Years ago, our friend Craig Claiborne published a recipe for a soufflé that was baked over its sauce. The taste memory of that delicious dish inspired Linda to prepare endless variations over the years, including this one, which originated with our Parisian friend, Danièle Giusti, who lived with Linda one summer. Linda's notes from those days, however, refer to ingredients measured not in cups but in portions of a milk glass!

Serves 4–6

  ¼ cup extra-virgin olive oil
  ¼ cup finely minced shallots
  ¼ cup finely minced celery
  2 teaspoons finely minced garlic
  ¼ cup Sauvignon Blanc wine
  1 cup fresh Roasted Red Tomato Sauce (page 20)
    Salt and freshly ground white pepper to taste
  2 teaspoons finely minced fresh tarragon or ½ teaspoon dried
  1 tablespoon minced fresh parsley
  5 tablespoons unsalted butter
  2 tablespoons grated Parmesan cheese
  ¼ pound shucked mussels
  ½ pound small scallops or peeled shrimp
  1⅔ cups milk
  5 tablespoons flour
  1 teaspoon dry mustard
  6 large egg yolks, beaten
  4 ounces shredded aged sheep's-milk, Gouda, or dry Jack cheese (see pages 139–141)
  7 large egg whites

Heat olive oil in a medium-size skillet. Add shallots, celery, and garlic; sauté over low heat until shallots and celery become translucent. Add wine and continue to cook for 2–3 minutes; then add tomato sauce and stir until warmed through. Add salt, pepper, and herbs; blend and set aside.

Use 1 tablespoon of the butter to grease a 2-quart soufflé dish. Then dust it evenly with the grated cheese. Butter a foil "collar" and tie it around the soufflé dish so that the top extends 2 inches above the rim of the dish. Place an oven rack in the middle of the oven and preheat to 400°. Spoon raw shellfish into prepared dish, add tomato mixture, and set aside.

Scald milk and set aside. Melt remaining butter in a heavy saucepan over medium-low heat. Whisk in flour and mustard, blending well, then slowly whisk in scalded milk. Cook, whisking constantly, until a very thick béchamel sauce is made. Reduce heat and stir for a few minutes (this additional cooking reduces the floury taste). Remove sauce from heat and stir some of the hot béchamel into the beaten egg yolks. Whisking constantly, add enough béchamel to egg mixture to heat it thoroughly. Then stir the now-tempered egg yolks into the pan of remaining béchamel sauce. Season with salt and pepper to taste. Fold all but 1 tablespoon of the shredded cheese into the sauce and set aside.

Beat egg whites with a pinch of salt just until they hold a stiff peak. Stir about 2 spoonfuls of egg whites into the cheese mixture to lighten it, then fold remaining egg whites into the cheese mixture. Spoon over the tomato sauce in the prepared soufflé dish and sprinkle with remaining shredded cheese.

Place soufflé on middle rack of preheated oven, reduce temperature to 375°, and bake for 35 minutes. Soufflé should be nicely browned and firmly set. To serve, use two forks to pull portions of soufflé apart and spoon sauce from bottom.

Wine: Honig Cellars Sauvignon Blanc (Napa Valley)

Imperial Crème Caramel

Linda established her culinary reputation on this dessert when a dear friend, the late Sidney Sachs, touted its glories to all of Cleveland.

Serves 10–12

> 2¼ cups granulated sugar
> 8 jumbo eggs, plus 1 jumbo egg yolk
> 6 cups half-and-half
> ¾ cup milk
> 1 tablespoon kirsch
> 1 teaspoon vanilla extract
> 2 cups Crème Fraîche (see page 350)
> ½ cup confectioners' sugar

Fresh whole strawberries for garnish
Fresh mint leaves for garnish
Heavenly Strawberry Sauce (page 382)

Melt ¾ cup of the granulated sugar in a caramel pot or saucepan, stirring until sugar turns a rich, deep brown. Pour caramel into a 12-cup ring mold and carefully coat the sides. Be sure to use oven mitts to do this, because mold gets very hot. Set mold aside and let cool.

Put eggs and yolk in the bowl of electric mixer and beat well. Add remaining granulated sugar and beat thoroughly. Add half-and-half, milk, kirsch, and vanilla. Beat again. Let mixture rest for 1 hour at room temperature.

Preheat oven to 350°. Pour egg mixture through a fine strainer into the prepared mold. Fill a large baking pan with hot water, place the filled ring mold in the center, and carefully place pan in preheated oven. Bake for 1 hour, or until a knife inserted into the custard comes out clean. Remove mold from the hot water and let cool on a rack, then chill in refrigerator.

Just before serving, beat the crème fraîche with the confectioners' sugar until soft peaks are formed. Carefully loosen sides of custard by pressing a finger gently around the custard and the outer and inner rings of mold. Invert serving platter on top of mold, then turn whole thing over and shake gently. Remove mold, fill center with the whipped crème-fraîche mixture, and garnish with whole berries and fresh mint. Spoon strawberry sauce over each individual serving.

Joe Hartzler

Hartz Desire Farm

3287 Apple Creek Road

Smithville, Ohio 44677

(216) 669-3267

Hartz Desire Farm is a beautiful, clean, and tidy organic dairy farm. And it is only 5 miles from Wooster, Ohio, and the Ohio Agricultural Research and Development Center, Ohio State University's bastion of establishment agricultural practices.

Joe's father, Harold Hartzler, is, as he says, "sort of retired." His wife, Pat, works at the hospital. Two sons, John and Jeff, run the home place. Two of Joe's brothers, Gene and Greg, along with Joe, have their own farms. Daughter Janis and her husband, Dan Steiner, also farm. Of the clan, only one son and one daughter are not farming.

"I was one of the first around here to use herbicides," said Harold. "Back in the late fifties, I put them on my fields and I said, 'This is slick. No weeds.'" But there were problems. On one occasion, after Harold had applied a chemical, there was a big rain. The chemical washed over into a neighbor's field and killed his hay. Harold recalled that the neighbor came over to his house and told him not to "let any more of that come over here." Another nearby farmer thought that if a little was good, a lot would be better. So he put on so much that he ruined his land for four years.

There was something else that caught Harold Hartzler's notice. As a farmer, he had always celebrated the humble earthworm. Then one day he realized that he just didn't have earthworms on his land. Another neighbor told him that if he had no earthworms now, he should try to imagine what it was going to be like on this land in twenty years.

So in 1964, Harold Hartzler stopped using chemicals. He admits that he didn't know enough to do it right. "You just can't quit cold turkey," he said. "By the third year all we got was weeds. Other guys were getting two hundred bushels of corn per acre and I think we got about fifty. Everybody laughed."

"But they don't laugh at us anymore," said Jeff. "We get great yields."

John recalled that when he was twenty-two years old, in 1982, he became ill. A kind of malaise, a chronic fatigue. All he wanted to do was sleep. He was given antibiotics for what was presumed to be some kind of infection. Nothing helped, so his family brought him up to Cleveland to see a specialist. "The doctor told me I had DDT in my system and it had hurt my liver," said John.

He recalled that the DDT had to be mixed before it could be put in the sprayer. "It was fun," he said, "like playing in the sandbox, and I always asked Dad if I could help with it."

"That was when he was four years old," said Harold. "And eighteen years later he pays the price for it."

Once the problem was diagnosed, an appropriate treatment set him on the road to recovery. Harold shakes his head. "I wonder how many other young people were not as lucky as John."

We drank Hartz Desire milk with our sandwiches and had Harold's homemade ice cream with our cobbler. We could not recall when either had been better. Milk this good, we thought, ought not be pumped into the giant vat of the dairy industry.

It turns out that Harold has long had the dream of having a creamery. Now, with 200 cows on 700 organic acres and 1,000 gallons of milk a day, they feel the time is at hand.

"Our milk is worth more," said Harold. "We treat it better. We think it hurts milk to pump it the way most operations do. And homogenized milk is blasted through a pump under pressure. We won't do that. By handling our milk with respect and care, we're adding value."

We went out to Joe's barn to meet the cows. Thirty-seven of them were in their stalls. A huge fan moved air through the building. "It's best for them to be inside on such a hot day," said Joe. "But they get to stay out all night when it's cool."

He introduced us to Trixie. Her awesome udder produced 30,000 pounds of milk in one year. She is the champion of the whole operation. During one four-year period, after one of the farms had been certified organic, the average yield had gone from 16,000 pounds to over 20,000. Now, on the five farms in the Hartzler family, the average is 21,000 pounds per cow.

"Cow health suffers when the animals are on a conventional chemical farm," said Joe. "You get a lot of reproductive problems. Our animals now are so healthy that our vet bill for thirty-seven cows is under two hundred dollars a month."

He thinks it is what they eat that makes the difference. The Hartzlers raise almost all of their own feed—soybeans, hay, oats, and corn. And when there is a rare shortfall, they share among the farms. Their careful crop rotation schedule has, as Harold says, "healed the land." No longer do neighbors laugh at the Hartzlers. In their corn fields they now get 35 bushels per acre above the county average. And a visiting scientist recently counted 2,300 earthworms per square meter.

"Now when you write this up," said Harold, "don't make it look so hard that no one else will want to try it, because anyone can do it. After five years it's a snap. Under our system," he continued, "the soil takes care of itself."

"It's not so much changing your fields that's important," said Greg. "It's changing your mind."

At the edge of a field Joe rubbed a little chunk of the earth loose with his hand. Dry as it was in the drought of 1991, Joe said, "this soil is full of good stuff. It's loaded with life. That's the secret. Life."

Wonderful Cinnamon Ice Cream

Tim Anderson, the talented chef at Goodfellow's, in Minneapolis, taught us to use crème fraîche in our ice cream to make it especially rich and creamy. We also suggest adding ¾ cup of pureed peaches to the cooled custard right before freezing. Whatever you do, let the ice cream stand at room temperature for a few minutes before serving if you make it more than 12 hours ahead.

Serves 8

>   3 cups milk
>   1 6-inch vanilla bean, slit in half
>   lengthwise
>   2 cinnamon sticks
>   7 jumbo egg yolks
>   1 cup sugar
>   ½ teaspoon cinnamon
>   1 cup Crème Fraîche (see page 350)

In a small saucepan, bring the milk, vanilla, and cinnamon sticks to a boil. Remove from heat and cover. Let stand for 30 minutes.

Put yolks and sugar in the bowl of an electric mixer fitted with the beater; beat at high speed until the yolks are pale and form a ribbon when dropped from the beater. Beat in ground cinnamon.

Remove vanilla bean from the milk, scraping the seeds into pot. Remove cinnamon sticks. With motor running, gradually pour the milk into the egg mixture, then pour all into a heavy-bottomed saucepan.

Fill a large mixing bowl with ice and set aside.

Cook egg mixture over low heat, stirring constantly, until it forms a very thick custard (mixture should reach about 180° on a candy thermometer).

Remove from heat and place pan on the bed of ice. Stir in the crème fraîche. Keep stirring until mixture has cooled, then chill completely. Freeze in an ice-cream maker according to manufacturer's directions.

Grandma Weller's Chocolate Pudding

While Linda knows that her grandma's chocolate pudding probably came from a package, her memory of that pudding is that it was wonderfully smooth and chocolaty, and very special.

Serves 4–6

>   ⅓ cup Dutch cocoa powder
>   ½ cup superfine sugar
>   3 tablespoons cornstarch
>   1 teaspoon unflavored gelatin
>   2 jumbo eggs, beaten
>   1⅔ cups milk
>   1 cup half-and-half
>   2 teaspoons vanilla extract
>   2 tablespoons Kahlúa
>
>   Confectioners' sugar or whipped
>   cream and candied violets for
>   garnish

Sift cocoa, superfine sugar, cornstarch, and gelatin into a heavy-bottomed saucepan. Add eggs, milk, and half-and-half and whisk thoroughly. Cook over medium heat, stirring constantly, until mixture thickens and begins to bubble. Remove from heat, add vanilla and Kahlúa, and whisk vigorously until mixture is smooth.

Pour into custard cups and chill. Serve garnished with confectioners' sugar or whipped cream and a candied violet.

Crème Anglaise

Crème Anglaise, pooled under almost any dessert, makes it festive. Add a tablespoon or two of any liqueur or brandy to the sauce and the sauce totally changes character. Try it with some applejack over a simple baked apple.

   2½ cups milk
     1 6-inch vanilla bean, slit in half
       lengthwise
     ¾ cup superfine sugar
     8 jumbo egg yolks

Combine milk and vanilla bean in a heavy-bottomed saucepan and cook over medium heat until milk is scalded but not boiling. Remove from heat, cover, and let stand 30 minutes. Remove vanilla bean from milk, scraping seeds back into pot.

Combine sugar and egg yolks in a medium mixing bowl and whisk vigorously until mixture forms a ribbon when dropped from whisk into bowl.

Return saucepan to heat and scald milk again. Then temper the egg yolks by gradually adding half the hot milk to the yolks, beating constantly. Add yolk-and-milk mixture to saucepan containing remaining scalded milk and whisk to blend.

Place pan on medium-low heat and stir continuously until mixture forms a custard that coats the back of a wooden spoon. Plunge saucepan into a sink filled with cold water to stop the cooking. Leave for 10 minutes, stirring often. Store in a sealed container in the refrigerator until needed. Let come to room temperature before using.

Ali Barker's Milk Punch

Ali Barker drew national attention as the chef at New York's Union Square Café. He and his charming wife, Marcie, formerly with New York's Gotham Bar and Grill, recently moved back to Marcie's home town, bringing their considerable skills to downtown Cleveland. Since its April 1992 opening, their restaurant, Piperade, located in a landmark building in the heart of the city, has wowed Clevelanders. This milk punch really warms one after a chilly afternoon of cross-country skiing.

Serves 10

    2 quarts milk
    1 cup half-and-half
     Zest of 1 orange, finely minced
     Generous pinch ground allspice
     Generous pinch ground cloves
  2¼ cups Gentleman Jack or other
     unblended bourbon
   ½ cup Grand Marnier liqueur

Combine milk, half-and-half, orange zest, and spices in a large pot; bring just to the boiling point over medium heat. Add bourbon and liqueur and heat through. Taste, adding more bourbon if desired. Pour into punch bowl or pitcher for serving.

Sally and Roger Jackson

Star Route 1, Box 106

Oroville, Washington 98844

(509) 485-3722

Sally Jackson is one of the legends. She is talked about across the world, wherever serious cheesemakers toil. And yet, on her little farm in the Okanagan wilds of north-central Washington, she makes only 15 pounds of cheese a day.

She had only recently gotten a telephone, and somehow we got her number. We had heard that people just don't pop in on the Jacksons of Oroville. But on the day we arrived, Roger Jackson, Sally's husband, gave us a hearty greeting and explained that they were rigging up a cheese smoker. He had built a firebox about 1½ feet square. A 6-inch pipe ran from the firebox to a sheet-metal cabinet where he would put the cheese, a distance of about 5 feet. He said he would use apple wood and hickory wood and keep the fire going for 24 hours. With this arrangement, he said, the smoke will get to the cheeses, but not the heat. The cheeses will go into a special cradle that he designed in order to keep them round.

In due course, he took us to the cheese house to meet Sally. She was dipping into a big deep pan on a wood-burning stove and was transferring curds into small paper cups into which she had punched some holes. These small chèvres, she said, would continue to drain for a day or two, then be removed from the cups and put into herbed olive oil. She sells jars of these delicious cheeses to eager chefs in Seattle.

She continues her work as we talk, and most of the talk is about the business at hand. She told us everything about the cheese, but she seemed reluctant to speak of the circumstances that led this New England couple to this remote farm. We do learn that they met on Martha's Vineyard and that Roger's family had been farmers. They came to Washington originally to run an apple farm but have now been involved in cheesemaking for fifteen years. Before he became a farmer, Roger had been a teacher in New York and an indexer for Prentice Hall Press.

Sally decides what kind of cheese she is going to make according to her mood. Some stores have difficulty with that side of her, since they never know what to expect; it forces them to market her cheeses using only her name. She prefers to make large wheels of cheese, coating them with herbs, cocoa, ash, or whatever natural material appeals to her. The coatings add flavor to the wheels while protecting them from unwanted molds. In recent days, she has used paprika, oregano, basil, sundried tomatoes, sweet peppers, garlic, jalapeños, and chives to flavor her various cheeses. The day before our visit, she made a marbled mix of goat's-milk and cow's-milk cheeses. She uses milk from brown Swiss cows to make mozzarella; when she has chestnut leaves, she mixes some Jersey cow milk into sheep's milk to make a fatty, zesty cheese that is wrapped in the leaves and aged two months.

Sally milks about fifteen goats and eight sheep. She supplements that with Jersey, Guernsey, and brown Swiss cow milk that she buys from her neighbors. While milk from different kinds of cows tastes alike, the butterfat content is different. Sally utilizes those differences to add variety to her cheeses. Eventually, she would like to buy all her milk and get completely out of the milking business.

The cheese-aging room is below ground and is pleasantly cool. There is an air conditioner put there at the insistence of the state inspectors, but the Jacksons rarely run it. There is no electricity here, so Roger, perpetually inventive, has rigged up an old-fashioned slow-running generator. In fact, after reading Galileo on levers, he concocted the mechanism that helps form big cheese wheels by pressing them into a mold under 60 pounds of pressure. He has also figured out a way to save winter snow for warm-weather refrigeration. He piles it up in large mounds and covers it with straw. It lasts all summer, its melt water providing natural cooling for the milk house and natural refrigeration for the farmhouse.

There is also a large freestanding straw "house," an enormous mound that covers a small room that was their first aging room. Inspectors told them that the presence of straw and the lack of air conditioning constituted a violation, so they built a more modern aging room in addition to the old one. Never mind that European cheesemakers had used such structures for centuries.

At first, the state and federal inspectors didn't know what to make of this little operation; it was a paradox. It produced only 15 pounds of cheese a day and yet it was cheese that the best chefs wanted and that the top food writers extolled. Roger said that now they generally get along well with the inspectors who come to call. Today they have a creamery license, which is all they need to do what they do.

The setting is extraordinary. The farm sits at 4,400 feet above sea level only 3 miles from the Canadian border. It is always cool at night, and they have frost in every month of the year. The Cascades can be seen in the west, snow-capped peaks easily visible from 50 miles. The farmstead is in a little hollow, or draw. There is higher ground to the south rising up a couple of hundred feet to a ridge. It is forested with aspen, birch, and pine and is the watershed for the springs that never fail.

"I keep my animals out of that region," said Roger. "It is a small price to pay for such wonderful drinking water."

The Jacksons were preoccupied with a major chore that faced them that evening. Roger was going to rent a backhoe to cut a ditch in which to bury their new telephone cable. Now they pay the penalty for having brought their farm into the modern era—they get calls from people who want cheese.

"Sorry," is all they can say. "It's already all spoken for."

Maybe they will take the phone out.

Cheese Blintzes with Smoked Salmon and Caviar

Bruce Naftaly of Seattle's Le Gourmand restaurant was one of the first chefs on the national scene to work hand-in-glove with organic producers and to commit himself to working exclusively with regionally grown products. We first ate Sally Jackson's cheese in his superb blintzes, which inspired ours, below. The batter is our version of one that Linda's mother, Gert LeVine, has made for years.

Makes 18

Blintzes
  2 jumbo eggs
  ¼ teaspoon salt
  ½ teaspoon freshly ground white pepper
  3 tablespoons unsalted butter, melted
  1 cup unbleached flour
  2 tablespoons whole-wheat pastry flour (available in health-food stores or from Arrowhead Mills, page 67)

Filling
  8 ounces fresh soft sheep's-milk cheese or fresh goat cheese
  6 ounces ricotta cheese
  1 jumbo egg
  2 teaspoons minced fresh dill
  1 tablespoon minced shallot
  ½ teaspoon salt
  ½ teaspoon freshly ground white pepper
  3 tablespoons finely diced smoked salmon

  Approximately 4 tablespoons unsalted butter or margarine

  Softly whipped Crème Fraîche (page 350), fresh dill, thinly sliced smoked salmon, and natural salmon caviar for garnish

First, make blintzes: In the bowl of a food processor fitted with the metal blade, combine eggs, 1¼ cups water, salt, pepper, and 2 tablespoons of butter. Pulse to mix well. Add flours and pulse until well blended. Scrape sides of bowl and pulse about four more times. Refrigerate batter for 30 minutes. If mixture is too thick to pour easily into a skillet, thin with some more water. (The density depends upon the protein and gluten content of your flour.)

While batter is chilling, combine all filling ingredients except salmon in the bowl of the food processor and pulse until smooth. Scrape mixture into a mixing bowl and fold in salmon. Cover with plastic wrap and chill until needed.

Put 2 teaspoons remaining butter into a well-seasoned 6-inch crêpe pan and heat over high heat. When hot, add a scant 2 tablespoons of cold batter to the skillet. Quickly tilt to distribute batter evenly over pan. Reduce heat to medium and cook about 1 minute. Turn the blintz gently with your fingers or a spatula and cook about 30 seconds on the other side. Turn out on a clean kitchen towel; repeat until all of the batter is used. Add more butter to pan only if necessary.

Arrange blintzes browned side up on your work surface. Place a heaping tablespoon of filling in middle, just a bit closer to you than to the center. Fold short end over filling, fold sides over, and roll. Each package should be about 3½ inches long and 1½ inches wide. Arrange blintzes seam side down on a large plate and keep chilled until just before serving time.

When ready to serve, melt remaining 4 tablespoons butter in a cast-iron skillet over medium-high heat. Fry blintzes until browned on both sides.

Garnish with dollops of crème fraîche, dill, a slice or two of smoked salmon, and some salmon caviar.

Wine: Domaine Chandon Blanc de Noirs Sparkling Wine (Napa Valley)

Salad of Fennel, Walnuts, and Aged Sheep's-Milk Cheese

We love the French tradition of following dinner with salad and then cheese. In fact, while we may not always have a cheese course, we always have salad following our main course. And when there is really good cheese in the house, we try new ways of combining it with a salad course. This is one of our favorite combinations. We have also added thin batons of Sally Jackson's mozzarella when we have it.

Serves 6

> 2 large fennel bulbs, trimmed
> 3 ounces aged sheep's-milk cheese, shaved
> 12–18 walnut halves
> 4–6 ounces mixed baby lettuce leaves
> 3 tablespoons balsamic vinegar (extra-aged preferred)
> 6 tablespoons walnut oil
> Salt and freshly ground black pepper to taste
> 2 teaspoons minced fresh tarragon
> 2 teaspoons minced fresh fennel fronds
> 2 tablespoons minced fresh chives

Slice fennel horizontally as thinly as possible and place in a large salad bowl. Add shaved cheese, walnuts, and lettuce leaves.

Pour vinegar into a small bowl. Slowly whisk in walnut oil until mixture forms a thick emulsion. Whisk in salt, pepper, tarragon, and fennel fronds.

Pour dressing over salad and toss well. Taste, adjust seasonings, and sprinkle with chives.

Savory Cheesecake with Basil and Pine Nuts

The wonderful Pete Peterson of Tapawingo, in Ellsworth, Michigan, makes outstanding savory cheesecakes. When we received a large quantity of soft sheep's-milk cheese from Sally Jackson, we turned to Pete for inspiration. This cake is equally delicious with walnuts and fresh thyme instead of pine nuts and basil.

Serves 12

1 tablespoon unsalted butter, softened
¼ cup fine, dry bread crumbs
5 ounces grated Parmesan, extra-aged sheep's-milk, or dry Jack cheese (see pages 139–141)
¼ cup fresh basil
¼ cup coarsely chopped fresh parsley
2 tablespoons olive oil
1 clove garlic, peeled
Pinch salt
12 ounces soft sheep's-milk or goat cheese, at room temperature
8 ounces cream cheese, at room temperature
8 ounces ricotta cheese
½ cup sour cream
4 jumbo eggs
¼ teaspoon freshly ground white pepper
⅓ cup pine nuts, toasted

Fresh basil leaves and parsley sprigs for garnish

Preheat oven to 325°.

Thoroughly butter bottom and sides of an 8-inch springform pan. Combine bread crumbs and ⅛ cup of the Parmesan and spoon into pan. Toss pan so that it is well coated and shake out excess.

Combine basil, parsley, olive oil, garlic, and salt in the bowl of a food processor. Pulse until mixture turns into a smooth paste. Scrape sides several times during this process. Set aside.

Combine sheep's-milk cheese, cream cheese, ricotta, sour cream, and remaining Parmesan in the bowl of an electric mixer. Beat until mixture is completely smooth. With motor running on high, add eggs, one at a time, and beat until well blended after each egg. Beat in the white pepper.

Transfer about ⅓ of this mixture to a small bowl and set aside. Combine basil mixture with remaining cheese mixture and blend well. Spoon into prepared pan and smooth top. Spread remaining cheese mixture (without the basil) over the top. Sprinkle with the pine nuts. Bake in preheated oven for 1 hour and 20 minutes. Turn oven off, open door slightly, and cool for 1 more hour, then transfer to a rack to cool completely. Serve at room temperature or slightly warmed, garnished with basil and parsley.

Wine: Kennwood Vineyards Sauvignon Blanc (Sonoma County)

Bob and Letty Kilmoyer

Westfield Farm

28 Worcester Road

Hubbardston, Massachusetts 01452

(508) 928-5110

*B*ob Kilmoyer, a professor of mathematics and computer science at nearby Clark University, in Worcester, was certain that he and his wife, Letty, working together, could make a farm meet virtually all the nutritional needs of their growing family. So, in 1972, Letty gave up her career as a nursing instructor to be a full-time mother and they bought a 20-acre farm. Their plans looked great on paper; rarely did they have to buy more than the basics. But it sure was hard, endless work!

"We thought by raising our own food it would be cheaper. Ha! What a jolt it was," said Letty, "when we spent a sabbatical year in Oregon. We bought all our food that year and the cost was about the same as raising it."

Cheesemaking came along by accident. When a pair of goats was virtually thrust upon them by a friend, the Kilmoyers had more milk than they could consume and made some into cheese. It was very casual in the beginning. The pasteurizer was hooked up to the furnace; cheeses were ripened in a small pantry off the kitchen. Unexpectedly, they were the first makers of goat cheese in New England.

After three years, they built a separate building for the cheese and enlarged the barn. Although their cheeses were always in demand, it took them five years to turn a profit. Even then, the volume was so small that one car breakdown in Boston would eat up the entire profit for a year. It became an interesting dilemma. Their son and daughter were grown and gone. Their cheeses were being lauded by all who tasted them; they were selling all they could produce. They were constantly exhausted, and yet they saw no way to turn the farm into a dependable business, until the day when they calculated that if they dramatically increased their volume their profitability could also improve significantly. Otherwise, the best they could hope for was a continuation of their exhausting effort only to break even.

It was so obvious. The farmhouse was practically empty with the children gone. Why not hire labor from colleges that sought cooperative learning and working experience? Today, there are usually three students living with the family at Westfield Farm, and many others waiting for their chance to work there.

The herd of goats has also grown to seventy Saanens and Nubians. Letty likes the white-haired Saanens for volume and the floppy-eared Nubians for protein and butterfat. Three energetic and loutish bucks take care of the entire herd. Of the two Saanen bucks, one is a newcomer from New Zealand, representing an entirely new bloodline on the farm. He has already sired Spock, a charming kid whose white face is punctuated by black bushy eyebrows that are almost perpendicular to her eyes. Two Jersey cows keep the household—and young kids—in milk, the richest, most wonderful milk Linda has ever tasted. In addition, the Kilmoyers now buy goat's milk from four other farms in the area in order to meet their production goals.

Their herd is trained to stay within the bounds of movable electric fences; this enables them to rotate pastures easily. While the Kilmoyers use no chemicals and pesticides in their fields, they decided not to purchase certified organic feed; it is prohibitively costly. But they try to purchase feed that is as chemical-free as possible.

The milking parlor is pristine. Four goats can be milked at a time. With Bob's profession being what it is, things are well computerized. Goats are monitored daily for volume; their protein and butterfat levels are analyzed monthly. Each "family line" produces a different level of butterfat content and volume of milk. Sassafras, Alyssum, and Gentian are part of the "Flower" line. Francesca, Babette, and Nicolette are part of the "French" line. These genealogical records, in the computer, are also of great help when breeding time comes around.

Goats can be milked for ten months; they are dry for two before they give birth. Letty tries to rotate things a bit so that all the kids are not born at the same time. But still, between January and April it gets pretty hectic, with more than a hundred kids born on the average every year. Of these, the Kilmoyers keep about ten and sell the rest.

It takes about 6 pounds of milk to make 1 pound of cheese; the Kilmoyers make about 300 pounds of cheese a week. Federal law requires that unless cheese is aged at least sixty days, all milk used to make it must be pasteurized. The Kilmoyers pasteurize milk about five times a week in a large tank in the cheese building. Rennet and culture are added after the milk is cooled, and the mixture sits undisturbed for eighteen hours.

A number of styles of goat cheese are made at Westfield Farm. The creamiest is Capri, which is made in logs. The curds and whey are placed into log-shaped baskets lined with cheesecloth and left to drip for a day. Then the basket is removed and the cheesecloth is hung from a hook for another day, to extract still more whey. The cheese is then placed in a mixer with salt, or salt and herbs. It is then packaged and is ready to eat in four to five days.

Capri is also made in rounds; the process, however, is a bit different from that for the logs. After the eighteen-hour rest following the addition of rennet and culture, the Kilmoyers dip the curd and whey into round molds, which either have holes or are elevated on drain mats so that the curd separates from the whey. After twenty-four hours, the cheeses are removed from the molds, placed on racks, and salted. On the fourth day, the cheeses are turned several times and allowed to dry.

On day five, the cheeses are either packaged plain or are coated with pepper or herbs, labeled, double-wrapped, and refrigerated. Now the rounds are ready to eat.

While Capri represents a very large part of their production, Camembert, Hubbardston Blue, and the Blue Log are the cheeses that bring national acclaim to Westfield Farm. A goat's-milk Camembert is made by adding some *Penicillium candidum* to the milk before adding the rennet. Hubbardston Blue, which has won its share of blue ribbons from the American Cheese Society and other cheese competitions, is made from an addition of *Penicillium roqueforti*. These cheeses are aged in a cool place while mold grows on the outside; the ripening takes place from the outside toward the center.

Each style of cheese must be kept physically separate from the others to prevent cross-contamination of molds. Hubbardston Blue is aged from six to eight weeks; Camembert takes four to six weeks. The rich and wonderful Blue Log is made by using a combination of the above methods and may be eaten either fresh or aged. It, too, has won a number of first-place ribbons.

Although Letty and Bob still handle most of the sales themselves, they also have found some outstanding distributors. A number of good articles in some national publications were great for business; Westfield Farm goat cheeses are sold around the country today. While the Kilmoyers have yet to study cheesemaking in France, they no longer regret that they were unable to afford the trip when they most wanted it. "Now I'm glad we didn't go and get locked into standard cheesemaking methods," Letty told us. The cheese the Kilmoyers make is uniquely theirs—rich, flavorful, with wonderful texture.

Now whenever they go to the refrigerator to pour a chilled glass of that lush Jersey milk, Bob and Letty pass a sign on the kitchen wall that states quite clearly: "These are the good old days."

Four-Cheese Pasta Sauce with Smoked Salmon

Serves 4–6 as an appetizer, 2–4 as an entrée

- 2 cups heavy cream
- 4 tablespoons unsalted butter
- 4 ounces plain young goat cheese, crumbled
- 4 ounces aged goat cheese with mold, crumbled
- 4 ounces ripe Camembert or Brie, cut in chunks
- 2 ounces aged sheep's-milk or sharp cow's-milk cheese, grated
  Freshly ground white pepper to taste
- ½ cup cooked fresh peas
- 8 ounces smoked salmon, cut into strips
- 1 pound cooked pasta

  Fresh basil leaves, cut into julienne strips, for garnish

Pour cream into a deep, heavy saucepan. Simmer briskly until reduced by half. Add the butter and the four cheeses and stir over low heat until mixture is smooth. Add pepper to taste. Add peas and salmon and stir over low heat until peas are heated through.

Pour over pasta and toss. Sprinkle with fresh basil and a few more grindings of pepper.

Wine: Qupé Chardonnay
(Santa Barbara County)

Goat Cheese Pizza with Caramelized Onion and Sun-Dried Tomatoes

Have fun experimenting with different varieties of goat cheese. We've also made this with Westfield Farm's Blue Log and found it to be terrific.

Makes 1 12-inch pizza

- 3 tablespoons unsalted butter or margarine
- 1¼ pounds Spanish onions, very thinly sliced
- 1 tablespoon sugar
- ¼ cup olive oil
- 2 cloves garlic, minced
- 2 tablespoons cornmeal
  Dough for 1 12-inch pizza (page 82)
- 5 ounces Capri (young) goat cheese
- 6 oil-packed sun-dried tomatoes, drained and cut into strips
- 2 ounces shredded fontina cheese
- 1 tablespoon minced fresh basil
- 2 teaspoons minced fresh rosemary
- 1 tablespoon minced fresh chives
- ¼ cup grated dry Jack (see pages 139–141) or dry goat cheese

Melt butter in a large skillet over medium heat. Sauté onions until they begin to get tender, sprinkle with sugar, and increase the heat, tossing until onions caramelize. Set aside.

Heat olive oil and garlic in a small saucepan. Sprinkle pizza pan with cornmeal. Roll, pat, and stretch pizza dough into a thin 10-inch circle and place on cornmeal. Generously brush the surface with the warm garlic-oil mixture, reserving the remainder.

Distribute reserved caramelized onions evenly over the surface. Crumble the goat cheese and distribute it evenly over the onions. Arrange sun-dried tomato strips over the pizza, then sprinkle with shredded fontina. Combine herbs in a small bowl and sprinkle half over pizza. Dust with grated cheese and drizzle with remaining garlic–oil mixture.

Place oven shelf in upper third of oven and preheat to 500°. Bake pizza for 8–10 minutes. Remove and sprinkle with remaining herbs.

Wine: Trentadue Zinfandel (Sonoma County)

Chèvre Pound Cake with Lemon Glaze

Makes 1 10-inch cake

CAKE
- ½ pound plain Capri or other young goat cheese
- ½ cup unsalted butter, at room temperature
- 2½ cups granulated sugar
- 5 jumbo eggs
- 3½ cups whole-wheat pastry flour (available in health-food stores or from Arrowhead Mills, page 67) Pinch salt
- ½ teaspoon baking powder
- ½ teaspoon baking soda
- 1 tablespoon fresh lemon juice Zest of 1 lemon, grated
- 2 teaspoons vanilla extract
- ½ cup buttermilk

GLAZE
- 2 tablespoons fresh lemon juice
- 1 teaspoon vanilla extract
- 1 cup confectioners' sugar

Fresh berries and mint leaves for garnish

Preheat oven to 325°.

Thoroughly oil, then flour, the bottom and sides of a 10-inch Bundt pan and set aside.

Cream the cheese and butter in the bowl of an electric mixer fitted with the paddle. Gradually add granulated sugar, scraping sides thoroughly several times. With motor running on high speed, add eggs, one at a time, scraping sides of bowl after each addition. Reduce speed and add flour, mixing only until blended. Scrape sides, add remaining cake ingredients, and blend.

Pour batter evenly into prepared pan. Bake in upper third of preheated oven until a tester inserted into the middle of the cake comes out clean, about 1½ hours. Let cake cool in pan on a rack for 15 minutes, then remove from pan.

While cake is cooling, make the glaze: combine lemon juice and vanilla in a small saucepan and bring to a boil. Remove pan from heat and whisk in confectioners' sugar until mixture is very smooth. When cake is cool, slowly drizzle glaze over top of cake. Garnish with mint leaves and fresh berries.

Wine: Ferrari-Carano Vineyards "El Dorado Gold" Sauvignon Blanc Late Harvest (Alexander Valley)

Rick and Lora Lea Misterly

Quillisascut Cheese Company
2409 Pleasant Valley Road
Rice, Washington 99167
(509) 738-2011

Thirty-five milk goats—including Shangalang, Khizzi, Tinkerbell, Blanchette, Shara, Nectarine, Omni, Flo, Sinn Bein, and Phenomena, so named because she was found practically frozen in a snowdrift and tenderly nursed back to life ("A phenomenon," said Rick Misterly, "with a feminine ending")—Bossie, the Jersey cow, and her progeny, Happy Jack and Baby Honey (now also a mother); Major Tom, the turkey, many years beyond the Thanksgiving table he ought to have graced; Toddy and Poddy, the Muscovy ducks; chickens galore; some Karakul sheep; assorted kittens; and a dog named Jelly are fed and loved by Lora Lea and Rick Misterly and their daughter, Willow. They live in the rocky, fertile hills of northeastern Washington, not far from beautiful Lake Roosevelt and the upper Columbia River Valley, a six-hour drive to Seattle and their customers. In that city's restaurants today, when the cheese in a dish is Quillisascut, it is so identified on the menu.

All the animals and their masters eat food grown without chemicals. What the Misterlys cannot produce themselves they try to obtain by the barter system. Their cheese house, adjacent to the main house, is built into the hillside, allowing them to have a naturally cool cellar room for aging. The cheesemaking room is white and pristine; the house is chaotic, cozy, and casual, filled with books and pictures, toys and dolls. It is the home of people who enjoy life but who sometimes have more of it than they can manage.

The Misterlys began producing cheese in the summer of 1987. Rick does most of the physical work on the farm, while Lora Lea is in charge of cheesemaking. "In fact," she confided, "I almost hate to teach him how, because I so enjoy having this for myself." But she has, although she tries to confine him to making feta when she must leave the farm. Lora Lea, alone, makes the pressed-curd or mold-ripened Quillisascut cheese.

They do, however always share milking chores every morning and every evening. It's a sight to see. Rick and Lora Lea each have a private milking space. "We have automatic equipment here, but we do it by hand because it gives us some absolute private time, alone with our own thoughts, and alone with each animal." The goats, a cross between Alpine and Saanen, line up in the paddock, each trying to get in front of the others. Two at a time are selected; one turns right, the other left. A short jump up on the specially designed milking stand and then the goat begins to chomp on the grains offered in a bucket. A halter secures the hungry goat and milking begins. Each beast has her own pattern. Some are not tethered at all; others like to kick at the bucket and have to be tethered. But the milking moves quickly, and a few minutes for each goat is all it takes. Meanwhile, each little cutie gets a few hugs along the way. (Lora Lea "cannot bear to have any farm animal killed, since they trust us so much.")

When finished with the goats, Rick then milks Bossie, who was a thank-you gift after Rick took care of a neighbor's farm during a prolonged illness. Sometimes Bossie's milk goes into mozzarella; sometimes Lora Lea makes a creamy, rich yellow cow's-milk cheese with black pepper and garlic or rosemary and savory. These are firm cheeses with mellow flavors; as they age, they become drier and sharper. Other times Lora Lea makes Robiola, a soft cheese similar to fresh chèvre.

They use eleven pounds of goat's milk to make one pound of cheese. Currently, the Misterlys make about seven different kinds of cheeses, totaling 6,000 pounds a year. They use an old Spanish Manchego-cheese recipe to make their firm and full-flavored aged pressed-curd goat cheeses, which get their flavor from

bacterial action rather than from mold formation. Curado, aged between two and four months, is soft and flexible, with a sweet nutty flavor when young. Viejo, the aged Curado, is firm and zesty, superb for grating. Some Curados are delicately flavored with lavender and fennel or pink peppercorns and dill. These, by the way, are wonderfully fragrant as well as tasty.

Lora Lea also makes mold-ripened *crottins* that are satisfyingly reminiscent of fine French chèvres in flavor, fragrance, and texture. The curd is slowly coagulated, formed more from the natural lactic acid in the milk than from the rennet. The curd is then placed in small molds with holes for draining. When the whey is completely drained, the shaped cheeses are either placed in the aging room for mold formation or wrapped in grape leaves and aged in virgin olive oil.

Their feta is rapidly coagulated cheese; it is brine-aged, tender but firm and very full-flavored. *Macères* is a French-style potted chèvre that Lora Lea sometimes mixes with sun-dried tomatoes or garlic, chives, and rosemary. It's a big favorite at Ray's Boathouse, in Seattle. The Misterlys grow all the herbs, tomatoes, and grape leaves on their farm.

Lora Lea feels that a part of her is in every cheese they make. "I feel it is important for farmers and customers to know each other, to understand our responsibility to each other. How lucky I am to live on a farm and do the things I love to do, like talk to our livestock, grow food for myself and my family, and make cheese."

"I have been a good girl, putting up food for winter," she wrote to us in a recent letter. "Thirty-five quarts of Red Haven peaches, 35 quarts of Hale peaches, 30 quarts of paste tomatoes. I'm also still drying fruit, all of the above peaches, Roma and Heinz paste tomatoes, Bartlett pears. Yum. And I froze 25 pounds of corn and still need to do some more. It's a Golden Jubilee corn, which is a favorite for home gardens. Sweet corn flavor, long ears, perfectly straight rows of kernels, a nice yellow, buttery color. I am very happy to have all this food to feed my family. There is such joy in growing it, all this magic. You plant this little seed and end up with all this food. How did all that life get put into a little seed?"

Potted Cheese with Herbs

This is so very simple to make. Be sure to experiment and try different combinations of cheeses and herbs. You can also add dried tomatoes. Spread on hearty black-pepper crackers and use the leftovers to spread on pizza or mix with pasta.

Makes about 1 ½ cups

>   4 ounces fresh goat cheese
>   3 ounces blue-rind goat cheese
>   3 ounces fresh goat's-milk ricotta
>   6 tablespoons sour cream
>   1 tablespoon minced fresh chives
>   1 tablespoon Cognac or Calvados
>   1 teaspoon fresh thyme, or lemon
>   thyme, if possible
>   1 teaspoon minced fresh mint, or
>   pineapple mint if possible (optional)
>   1 teaspoon freshly ground white
>   pepper
>
>   Scented geranium or dandelion
>   petals for garnish

Combine all ingredients in the bowl of a food processor and pulse until smooth. Spoon mixture into an attractive serving bowl, sprinkle with flower petals, and chill until ready to serve.

Shirred Eggs with Chèvre, Sun-Dried Tomatoes, and Prosciutto

For this dish, it is unimportant whether the cheese is very young or somewhat aged—these eggs are delicious either way as part of a Sunday brunch. We especially enjoy having them instead of the poached eggs as a garnish for the Corned Beef Hash (page 245).

Serves 10

>   3½ tablespoons unsalted butter, melted
>   2 tablespoons olive oil
>   10 scallions, trimmed and minced
>   10 jumbo eggs
>   3–4 ounces prosciutto, coarsely
>   chopped
>   4–5 ounces peppered chèvre, cut into 10
>   pieces
>   5 sun-dried tomatoes, chopped
>   1¼ cups heavy cream
>   2 tablespoons minced fresh chives

Preheat oven to 375°.

Coat 10 half-cup ramekins with the melted butter and set aside.

Heat olive oil in a small skillet and sauté scallions for about 1 minute, then divide them among the ramekins.

Break one egg into each ramekin, distribute the prosciutto evenly over them, crumble the chèvre over the prosciutto, and top

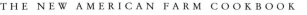

it off with the tomatoes. Pour 2 tablespoons of cream over each ramekin.

Arrange ramekins on a cookie sheet and bake for 13 minutes in the preheated oven. Sprinkle with chives and serve.

Baked Penne with Tomatoes, Sausage, Basil, and Goat Cheese

Serves 6

- 1 pound penne
- 6 cups Roasted Red Tomato Sauce (page 20)
- ¼ cup tomato paste
- 1 teaspoon minced fresh oregano
- ¼ cup chopped fresh basil
- ¼ cup chopped fresh parsley
- 1 teaspoon salt
- 1 teaspoon freshly ground black pepper
- 1 teaspoon crushed red-pepper flakes
- 3–4 ounces soft goat cheese (plain or with pepper), diced
- ½ cup ricotta cheese
- 1 pound fresh hot Italian sausage, grilled and cut into slices
- ½ cup grated aged sheep's-milk cheese, or more if desired

Preheat oven to 500°.

Bring 6 quarts of salted water to a boil and cook penne until almost *al dente*. Drain and return to pot.

Meanwhile, combine tomato sauce and paste in a saucepan and simmer over medium heat until blended. Remove from heat.

Add tomato mixture, herbs, salt, pepper, pepper flakes, diced cheese, and ricotta to pot with penne. Mix until blended, then mix in sausage.

Spoon pasta into a 3-quart baking dish, sprinkle with grated cheese, and bake in preheated oven for 10–12 minutes.

Wine: Santino Wines Barbera (Amador County)

Minted Peas

Serves 8–10

- 4 cups shelled fresh or frozen peas
- 4 tablespoons minced fresh mint
- 1 red bell pepper, cut into julienne strips
- 1 yellow or orange bell pepper, cut into julienne strips
- ½ cup finely diced celery
- ½ cup diced scallions (white part and 1 inch of green part)
- 1 teaspoon kosher salt
- 2 teaspoons coarsely ground black pepper
- 4 ounces 2–4-month-old goat cheese or goat's-milk feta, crumbled
- 2 tablespoons Dijon mustard
- 6 tablespoons red wine vinegar
- ⅓ cup extra-virgin olive oil

Fresh mint leaves for garnish

No more than 4 hours prior to serving, combine peas, mint, bell peppers, celery, scallions, salt, black pepper, and cheese in a large bowl.

In a small bowl, blend mustard and vinegar. Gradually whisk in the olive oil until mixture emulsifies, then gently blend into vegetables. Carefully spoon vegetables into an attractive serving bowl (we use a large glass cylinder). Garnish with mint leaves before serving.

Ignazio Vella

Vella Cheese Company

315 Second Street

P.O. Box 191

Sonoma, California 95476

Tom Vella, father of Ignazio, came to Sonoma County from Italy in the early 1920s. He worked in a creamery, then became a contract milk hauler. In 1931, a group of dairymen asked Tom to set up a cheese factory that would use some of their milk on a regular basis. With a partner, Celso Viviani, Tom set up a business that has remained healthy and quality-conscious to this day. In 1981, he left the business to Ig and his three sisters, and has continued to make award-winning cheeses in Oregon.

Today, Ig Vella and his associates make mostly variations on a cheese first made by a gold-rush-era Scottish cheesemaker named David Jacks, who settled in California and is credited with inventing Monterey Jack cheese (somewhere along the way Jacks lost the S). He found the culture and perfected the technique for this dense and fragrant cheese, edible either young or aged.

Fresh Jacks are often seasoned with garlic, onion, caraway seeds, or hot peppers. Some are made with partly skimmed milk, but there are also double-cream versions. Ig also makes a fontina and a number of cheddars. But the stock in trade of the company, the cheese for which it is famous, is dry Jack. This cheese is more dense than the fresh Jack, richer in flavor, sharper, more intense. It develops a nutty flavor that lingers long on the tongue, becoming almost sweet before it disappears.

Vella's Guernsey milk is purchased through the California Cooperative

Creamery. For the dry Jack, they use the evening milk from one specific farmer and the daytime milk from three others. They also use a starter culture that gives a higher acidity to the dry Jack. Charles Malkassian and Roger Ranniker work closely with Ig in this process, which varies in frequency depending on business, using 1,300 gallons of milk at a time to make 108 wheels of cheese. The rennet they use is a vegetable microbial enzyme, not the more commonly used calf rennet; so Vella dry Jack can be enjoyed by dedicated vegetarians. Despite the quantity, this cheese is still handmade: curds are cut, cooked, and stirred by hand, then scooped into cheesecloth, tied into balls, pressed by hand against the side of the milk tank, and formed into wheels by a wooden press. When the cheese is ultimately shipped, it still bears the imprint of the original knot from the cheesecloth.

After the wheel is firm, it is cured in brine for three days. Then the cured wheels are rubbed with cocoa, pepper, and vegetable oil and stored on curing racks in one of a number of temperature- and humidity-controlled storerooms for a minimum of seven months. As they age, the wheels shrink and lose moisture. The cheesemaker tests his product for ripeness by tapping it and sometimes by cutting into it with a special cylindrical tool and taking a little taste. Some dry Jacks age longer, getting better and more expensive the longer they sit. There are 18,000 to 20,000 cheeses aging at one time at Vella, so there is always considerable money tied up in inventory.

The ultimate dry Jack, bearing Ig Vella's Bear Flag brand label, is called California Gold. Those dry Jacks that seem to have exactly the qualities Ig wants for special aging are carefully selected and signed into the storage house, where they rest on shelves for two to three years, until it's time to be wrapped for market. It is a grating cheese of wonderful texture and taste.

There are seven full-time cheesemakers and a total of thirteen employees at Vella. Ig never sets quotas, and he does whatever he can to keep his staff interested. And Ig takes his turn with the others in the storage room, coating, turning, and oiling the richly flavored wheels that are being aged.

Most of the market that the company was founded to serve has long since been taken away by big-time cost-cutting producers and by inexpensive imports.

Ig Vella has held the course, however, taking no shortcuts, handling and rehandling every wheel, coating it, rubbing it, and selling and packing it with loving care. It is a labor-intensive process that produces a gem among cheeses, and there are buyers out there for every ounce that he and his friends can produce.

Above Ig Vella's desk is a sign. It reads "No amount of planning, hard work, intelligence, cunning, or shrewdness will ever replace blind, stupid luck. Ig Vella, June 20, 1976."

Don't you believe it!

Winter Cheese Soup with Beer

Serves 8

- 4 tablespoons unsalted butter
- ⅓ cup sliced shallots
- 10 cloves garlic
- 1 tablespoon sugar
- 2 teaspoons dry mustard
- 3 cups heavy cream
- 5 cups rich chicken stock
- 1 12-ounce bottle dark beer
- ½ pound aged cheddar cheese, grated
- ¾ pound Vella dry Jack cheese or well-aged Gruyère, grated or shredded
- Salt and freshly ground white pepper to taste
- Minced fresh dill for garnish

In a small skillet, melt butter over medium heat. Add shallots and garlic, sprinkle with sugar, and cook over medium-high heat until garlic cloves are caramelized and tender. Blend in mustard.

Combine garlic mixture with cream in a large, heavy saucepan. Cook over medium-low heat until mixture begins to thicken. Carefully pour into food processor and purée. Return mixture to saucepan and add stock and beer. Cook over medium heat until hot. Slowly add the grated cheeses and stir until soup is smooth. If soup needs more thickening, just cook a bit longer over medium-low heat, stirring often. Add salt and white pepper to taste. Ladle into heated soup plates and sprinkle with fresh dill.

Macaroni and Cheese with Tomato

If you prepare this ahead, don't combine sauce with macaroni until just before baking.

Serves 8

- 1 cup fine, dry bread crumbs
- 1 cup finely grated extra-aged Vella dry Jack cheese or Romano
- 3 tablespoons minced flat-leaf parsley
- 6 tablespoons unsalted butter

¼ cup flour

4 cups warm milk

6 ounces Vella dry Jack cheese or well-aged Gruyère, grated

8 ounces sharp yellow cheddar cheese, grated

1 teaspoon freshly ground white pepper

1 medium onion, minced

1 large clove garlic, minced

1 fresh hot red chile pepper, seeded and minced

1 tablespoon minced fresh chives

2 teaspoons minced fresh thyme Kosher salt to taste

1 pound cooked elbow macaroni

2 large fresh tomatoes, peeled, seeded, and diced

¼ cup fine, dry bread crumbs

Combine bread crumbs, extra-aged Jack, and 2 tablespoons of the parsley in a small bowl and set aside.

In a large, heavy saucepan, melt 4 tablespoons of the butter over medium heat. Whisk in flour, then gradually whisk in warm milk and bring to a boil. Reduce heat to a simmer, stirring for a few minutes, until thickened. Stir in dry Jack, cheddar, and white pepper and set aside.

In a nonstick skillet, melt remaining butter over medium heat. Add onion, garlic, and red pepper. Cover with a piece of wax paper pressed directly on the vegetables and sweat over low heat for 5 minutes. Stir vegetables into cheese sauce with the remaining parsley, the chives, and the thyme. Add salt and macaroni and blend well. Fold in tomatoes.

Preheat oven to 375°.

Butter a 4-quart ceramic casserole, then lightly dust with bread crumbs and shake out excess. Pour macaroni into casserole and cover with cheese-and-crumb mixture. Bake in preheated oven until hot and bubbly, about 30 minutes.

Wine: Charles Krug Chenin Blanc (Napa Valley)

Boneless Chicken à la B.J.

The inspiration for this recipe goes back to Linda's early years in Cleveland and the delicious meals prepared for her by her friend B. J. Adelson.

Serves 4

1½ cups grated Vella dry Jack cheese or Parmesan

½ cup fine, dry bread crumbs Salt and freshly ground white pepper to taste

2 jumbo eggs

2 chicken breasts, boned, split, and slightly flattened

½ cup unsalted butter or margarine, or more if necessary

12 fresh asparagus spears, cooked crisp

Freshly minced parsley, chives, and basil for garnish

Whole leaves of fresh basil and spears and flowers of fresh chives for garnish

Combine 1 cup cheese, bread crumbs, salt, and pepper in a shallow soup plate. Break eggs into another soup plate and beat thoroughly. Dip chicken breasts first into the egg, then into cheese mixture. Coat each piece thoroughly, then place on a rack.

Melt butter in a large skillet over medium heat. When very hot, add prepared chicken breasts and sauté 6 minutes per side, or until brown. Preheat broiler during the last 6 minutes.

Remove breasts from skillet and place in a single layer in a flameproof pan or baking dish. Place 3 asparagus spears on top of each breast and sprinkle evenly with remaining cheese. Pour butter from skillet over the prepared breasts; if butter is too brown, melt additional butter for this process.

Place pan beneath a hot broiler until cheese has browned. Garnish with minced and whole herbs and sprinkle with the petals of chive flowers.

Wine: Chalk Hill Winery Chardonnay "Chalk Hill" (Sonoma County)

Potatoes and Onions au Gratin

Serves 6–8

    Olive oil for greasing baking dish
3 pounds russet (baking) potatoes, peeled and thinly sliced
1 clove garlic, finely minced
3 cups milk
    Salt and freshly ground black pepper to taste
1 large sweet onion, about ¾ pound, thinly sliced
1 cup grated Vella dry Jack cheese or well-aged Gruyère
2 jumbo eggs, beaten
1 cup heavy cream
¼ cup fine, dry bread crumbs
4 tablespoons unsalted butter, cut into small pieces
    Freshly grated nutmeg to taste

Preheat oven to 350°.

Rub a shallow 3-quart ceramic baking dish with olive oil and set aside.

Combine sliced potatoes, garlic, and milk in a heavy-bottomed saucepan and bring to a boil. Cover and simmer for 15 minutes. Remove from heat and stir in salt, pepper, and sliced onions.

Using a slotted spoon, arrange potatoes and onions evenly in the prepared casserole, sprinkling layers with half the cheese as you go. Temper the eggs by slowly whisking in a small amount of the hot milk; then combine the eggs with the hot milk remaining in the saucepan. Add cream to the mixture and whisk well. Pour this mixture evenly over the potatoes.

Sprinkle top with bread crumbs and remaining cheese. Dot with butter and grate some fresh nutmeg over the top.

Bake for 1 hour and 15 minutes, or until potatoes are tender when pierced with a skewer.

Fish and Shellfish

Jon Rowley

Fish Works!

Fishermen's Terminal, C-10 Building

Seattle, Washington 98119

(206) 283-7566; fax (206) 283-1714

You usually don't expect to learn about strawberries when you go to the fishmonger's. Nor did we expect to eat perhaps the sweetest strawberries we had ever had sitting with Jon Rowley, the fish guru.

Early on a Friday morning we had gone to the office of Jon's company, Fish Works!, which provides services to the seafood industry and to restaurants and markets that deal in seafood.

Within minutes we found ourselves awash in information about the Northwest seafood scene. We were hearing about the region's restaurants and their chefs. We were learning about the fishermen—who they are, where they came from, how they work, what makes some better than others. And we heard for the first time one of Jon's favorite terms, "creative sourcing."

That's where the strawberries come in. A tall slender man with a beard and long hair, wearing coveralls, came into the office.

"Jon," he said excitedly, "I have Hoods."

"My God," Rowley answered. "I thought it was too wet."

The man put a quart of the berries onto Jon's big conference table. Jon asked his assistant to wash off the mud in cold water. In moments they were back. He dumped them onto some paper towels and told everyone to dig in.

"Eat fast," he said. "They have a very short shelf life."

We suspended our talk of shellfish farmers and fishermen and plunged in.

"These last one day," he told us. "If they don't get eaten the first day, it's too late." He encourages his restaurant and supermarket clients to use this perishable strain that has to be consumed the same day it's picked. They might cost a little more, and they might be a little more difficult to work with, but the extra effort is made up for in flavor.

"That's what I do in the seafood industry," he said. "I try to convince users that there is no substitute for quality. And I want them to understand that flavor depends on proper handling and timely distribution."

When he left Portland's prestigious Reed College, instead of going on to graduate school, which most Reed graduates do, Jon became a salmon fisherman in Alaska. But almost at once he became aware of the inherent conflict between the fisherman and his market. Jon saw seafood that had been carefully handled by the fisherman abused the instant it got to the dock, and abused still more in the distribution, and abused yet again in the restaurant kitchen. Also, fish carefully handled by one fisherman got mixed with fish that hadn't been, and both fishermen got the same price. The consumer paid the same price regardless of the quality, and the fisherman received a standard price regardless of the care he might have taken.

What caused these problems? Greed or ignorance or both. Fish Works! came into existence when Jon Rowley decided to be the industry advocate for a quality product. He has now become enormously successful doing that, and thousands of restaurant and supermarket customers eat a lot better as a result of what he does.

A case in point is the example of halibut. Halibut can only be fished for a short period of time—by law, the season is 24 hours long. That means that 5,500 fishing boats gather over the Alaskan fishing grounds with hooks baited. Then, at exactly the opening minute, miles of longlines are dropped overboard. Sometimes, to beat the clock, the fishing is so furious that there is simply no time to ice the fish, let alone gut them. And they lie for hours "round," or uncleaned, on the deck until the fishermen can find time to put them below. Often, they are just left topside.

When the 24-hour season is over, there is transportation gridlock. The halibut are brought to shore, and several million pounds or more are dumped into the market at one time—much of it, by the time it is processed, not very good. Ninety-five percent of the halibut arrives at the market frozen. In fact, Jon told us about F.I.S.H. (Find Intelligent Solutions for Halibut), a national coalition of retailers, restaurants, fishermen, and distributors who want to change the way halibut is managed. In 1989, for example, projected waste from bycatch mortality, cut-gear loss—dead halibut or nonhalibut that are tossed back into the water—and spoilage was estimated by the International Pacific Halibut Commission to be nearly 20 million pounds, 30 percent of the allowable catch. Jon's photographs from the 1990 season were not pretty. And the 1991 season turned out to be just as bad. Fortunately, as the public becomes better informed, pressure is being put on the North Pacific Management Council to improve the management of the fisheries.

Jon's view is that a public or private bureaucracy that imposes all these kinds of conditions on a fishery is doing the fishermen, the fish, and perhaps most important, the consumer a disservice. He feels that the way fishermen are forced to operate compromises quality and encourages waste. He advocates an individual transferable quota system that would give each vessel entitlement to a fixed amount of fish. The fisherman could land fish anytime during the year. This would provide year-round fresh fish.

That night we had dinner at the first of several restaurants that take Jon Rowley's advice. We had Bruce Gore's extraordinary salmon and his exceptional black cod (see page 153). At another restaurant, we had Dungeness crab. ("Have it cold with nothing but mayonnaise," Jon had told us. "And just get one. One is big enough for two.") And after a wonderful dinner at Elliott's Oyster House, one of Seattle's great pierside restaurants, the waiter persisted when we told him we were too full for dessert.

"You have to have our strawberry shortcake," he told us. "It's the best. Hood strawberries, just picked." We did and it was wonderful.

"It's Jon Rowley's recipe," he said.

Jon Rowley's Strawberry Shortcake for Elliott's Oyster House

Serves 8

    2 quarts ripe strawberries, unrefrigerated, picked the same day
½ cup sugar, or more to taste

DROP BISCUITS
    4 cups unbleached flour
    2 tablespoons sugar
    2 tablespoons baking powder
    1 teaspoon salt
½ cup unsalted butter, cold
    1 cup plus 1 tablespoon heavy cream
    1 cup milk

    1 pint heavy cream, cold
    1 teaspoon vanilla extract
    2–3 tablespoons sugar

Quickly rinse and hull 1 quart strawberries. Slice a third of them, cut another third of them in quarters, and cut the remainder in half (or crush all berries slightly by hand to desired texture). Sprinkle with sugar, stir gently, and macerate at room temperature for 3–4 hours, or until berries are sufficiently juicy.

To make the biscuits, preheat oven to 375°. Mix dry ingredients together in a large bowl. Cut in butter until mixture resembles coarse meal. Add 1 cup cream and milk and mix just until mixture begins to pull away from bowl. Divide dough into 8 parts and drop onto cookie sheet. Brush with remaining cream and bake in preheated oven until golden brown, about 20 minutes. Place biscuits on rack.

Rinse, hull, and cut remaining 1 quart strawberries as you did the first quart and mix gently with macerated berries.

Place heavy cream in bowl and beat with vanilla and sugar until mixture holds soft peaks.

Cut warm biscuits in half and place each bottom half in its own wide, shallow serving bowl. Spoon on about half the prepared berries, making sure to include ample juice. Add about ¾ of the whipped cream. Top with biscuit tops, remaining berries, most of the juice, and a dollop of whipped cream on each biscuit top. Drizzle with remaining juice.

Shaw's Crab House Garlic-Basil Dungeness Crab

It's not the neatest eating, but it sure is wonderful! We thank Chef Yves Roubaud for sharing this recipe with us.

Serves 6

- 6 Dungeness crabs, cooked and cracked
- 2 cups extra-virgin olive oil
- 12 cloves garlic, finely chopped
- 1 heaping tablespoon finely chopped fresh basil
  Juice of 4 lemons
  Dash Worcestershire sauce
- 2 sliced lemons and 2 loaves crusty Italian bread, sliced, for garnish

Separate each leg of the crabs with a section of body meat. Crack legs thoroughly with mallet. Place all crab pieces in a large serving bowl.

Combine olive oil, garlic, basil, lemon juice, and Worcestershire in a small bowl. Whisk thoroughly, then pour over crabs. Chill, stirring frequently, for several hours.

Garnish with lemon slices and accompany with crusty bread for dipping.

Wine: Chateau Potelle Chardonnay "Reserve" (Napa Valley)

Jon Rowley's Guide to Eating Crayfish, also Known as Crawfish

In the course of his consulting business, Jon Rowley plans some unusual dining events for his clients. The following instructions were provided to diners who enjoyed the Crayfish Festival at Shaw's Crab House in Chicago.

1. Dress for roll-up-your-sleeves conviviality.
2. Abandon your timidity. At this step, many will quaff a shot of chilled aquavit.
3. Hold the crayfish's head in one hand.
4. With the other hand, twist and pull the tail.
5. With thumb and forefinger, pinch the edges of the tail toward its underside until the shell cracks.
6. Turn the tail over and place your thumbs on its inside edges. Press until the shell gives way.
7. Pull out the tail meat in one solid piece. Victory! Pop it in your mouth.
8. Lift the carapace (shell) from the part of the body that has the legs and claws.
9. Scoop out the buttery-flavored juices and fat from the carapace with your thumbnail. Delicious!
10. Chew and suck the juices out of the abdominal section and legs.

11. Crack open the claws with your teeth. Suck out any meat and juices.

12. Use a finger bowl and napkin for cleaning your hands.

13. Chase with beer and/or aquavit.

14. Well done! Repeat steps 3 through 13.

Shaw's Crab House Sautéed Salmon with Spicy Cucumber Relish

While one can use Norwegian or Scottish (Atlantic) salmon, this dish is definitely better with the Pacific salmon for which it was intended. Chef Yves Roubaud, born and trained in France, has become a master at preparing these wonderful fish dishes for his Chicago restaurant, Shaw's Crab House.

Serves 4

Cucumber Relish
- 2 English cucumbers, peeled and thinly sliced
- ½ red bell pepper, cut into thin julienne strips
- ½ yellow bell pepper, cut into thin julienne strips
- 1 tablespoon dark sesame oil
- 1 teaspoon balsamic vinegar
  Pinch crushed red pepper flakes
  Pinch salt

- 4 8-ounce salmon fillets
- 1 cup unbleached flour
- 2 tablespoons vegetable oil
- 4 lemon wedges for garnish

Combine relish ingredients in a bowl and mix thoroughly. Set aside.

Dip salmon fillets into flour and shake off excess, then heat oil in large skillet until hot.

Sauté salmon over medium-high heat for 4 minutes; turn and sauté another 4 minutes.

Place salmon on serving plates and garnish each plate with cucumber relish and a lemon wedge.

Wine: Adelsheim Pinot Noir (Willamette Valley, Oregon)

Shaw's Crab House Braised Alaskan King Salmon

Serves 2

- 2 tablespoons olive oil
- 2 8-ounce fillets Alaskan king salmon, pin bones removed
- ½ cup dry white wine
- ¾ cup medium-diced fresh tomato
- ⅓ cup finely diced celery
- ⅓ cup finely diced onions
- 2 finely diced carrots
- 1 teaspoon minced garlic
- 1 cup bottled clam juice
  Freshly ground white pepper to taste

Preheat oven to 400°.

Heat olive oil in an ovenproof skillet until hot. Add salmon fillets, skin side down, and sauté over medium-high heat for 5 minutes on one side only. Add wine, vegetables, and garlic, then place skillet in preheated oven for 3 minutes. Add clam juice and cook for an additional 3 minutes. Season with white pepper.

Wine: Williams & Selyem Pinot Noir "Olivet Lane" (Sonoma County) or Alexander Valley Vineyards Chardonnay (Alexander Valley)

Bruce Gore

Triad Fisheries

P.O. Box 11702

Winslow, Washington 98110

(206) 842-1620

Bruce Gore, the salmon guru, is an expert in both the biology of death and the politics of fishing. His understanding of these two dissimilar fields enables him to bring to the market perhaps the finest, freshest ocean fish the American consumer can buy. Like a wine connoisseur who can taste a wine and name the vineyard and the year, Bruce Gore can taste a piece of fish and tell you the fishery and the condition of the catch. At lunch one day, we gave him a sample of salmon.

"Farmed. British Columbia almost certainly," he said. "Murky. Muddy. No muscle tone. Red color from something U.S. farmers aren't allowed to use. And it was frozen after rigor."

Most of the salmon farmed on the West Coast are kept in large offshore enclosures created by netting. What they are fed bears little resemblance to what they would eat if they were "free-range" fish. Bruce will grant that sometimes salmon farming is done well, but it was his concern over the lack of quality in so much American salmon, both farmed and caught at sea, that led him to his personal revolution.

He and his wife, Kathy, had always been meticulous in the handling of their catch. They line-caught, killed and eviscerated quickly, and chilled at once. But when they got back to the shore and to the market, their carefully handled salmon were tossed in with what everyone else had caught.

They had gone through all the business of getting licensed to do what they do.

They spent much of their lives fishing. And it just didn't seem right that there was no reward for the higher quality they delivered to market. So they took a big gamble. Bruce remembered from a college geology class that ice crystals are smaller when formed quickly. If the salmon were frozen in extreme cold, there would be less cellular breakdown in the fish. Bruce and Kathy equipped their boat, the *Triad,* with a state-of-the-art freezer of Bruce's own design, which would blast-freeze their catch at minus 35° Fahrenheit. Most seagoing freezers work at 0 to −10.

They line-catch, pulling the fish on board one at a time. The fish are instantly stunned to unconsciousness, before they get hurt from thrashing about or from the production of adrenaline. Then the main artery is cut so that the heart will pump out most of the blood. Immediately after that, Bruce and Kathy eviscerate them, making sure that they massage the fish to get every drop of blood possible out of the flesh. Then comes the process that leaves the animal solidly frozen within two hours after it was caught.

"Rigor mortis is deferred," Bruce said. "Most fish will be allowed to go completely through rigor before freezing. But this way we stop the process of biochemical change at the instant it begins. And when the fish thaws on the chef's counter, it is a fish that is as fresh as it was the moment it was pulled from the water."

Bruce had prejudices to overcome within the fish business. Few fish lovers would believe that frozen could be better. So Bruce had to show the best restaurants and the best markets that a frozen Triad salmon with Bruce Gore's name on the tag was the best salmon money could buy and worth the premium price that the new process required.

It was a hard sell, but he had help. Jon Rowley, Seattle's fabled seafood consultant, became an advocate. Now there are a dozen more boats that work with Bruce, using his approach and marketing their pink, king, chum, coho, and sockeye salmon, albacore tuna, halibut, ling cod, and black cod under the Triad label. They sell all they can catch. And the product carries a money-back guarantee of freshness.

From its numbered tag, Bruce can trace a fish back to the day it was caught and to the fisherman who caught it. So if there is a problem—if someone let a fish thaw out prematurely, for example—he will find out exactly what happened. He is also very careful about the distributors and retailers that sell his fish. If they don't have the right equipment or if they don't handle his fish carefully, they can't be his customers.

Like all conscientious fishermen, Bruce and Kathy Gore worry about the health of the fisheries, the condition of the seas, the possible extinction of a species, archaic licensing procedures, and the shabby and careless handling of a catch that makes so much of what we buy so much less than it ought to be.

But these concerns fade when they climb on board the *Triad* with their two children and head for their rendezvous with the salmon. It is 1,000 miles from their home to the place where they begin fishing. And they will work the coast for over three months, until the *Triad* is groaning low in the water with its catch. Then they will come home with perhaps 15,000 pounds of fish after having sailed as many as 5,000 miles in pursuit.

It is a wonderful life, they say, with long hours of hard work. The sun at their fishing latitude keeps them company almost twenty-four hours a day.

"We live our summers looking at the curvature of the earth," Bruce said. "It is about as free and independent a life as one can live."

Salmon Fillets
Steamed in Lettuce Leaves

This is a lovely and light dish that we especially enjoy with Our Home Fries (page 278) and a very simple, very fresh vegetable.

Serves 6

- ¼ cup dry white wine
- 1 slice fresh ginger, lightly crushed
- ¼ teaspoon freshly ground white pepper
- 6 salmon-fillet pieces, 3–4 ounces each, skinned and with pin bones removed
- 6 tablespoons unsalted butter, softened
  Zest of 1 lemon, finely minced
- 2 teaspoons finely minced fresh ginger
- 2 teaspoons finely minced fresh chives
- 12 large leaf-lettuce leaves, stems removed
  Salt and freshly ground white pepper to taste
- 24 long spears fresh chives

Combine wine, slice of ginger, and ¼ teaspoon white pepper in a shallow dish. Add salmon fillets and marinate, turning several times, for at least 30 minutes.

Combine butter, lemon zest, minced ginger, and minced chives. Blend well and form into a log; wrap in wax paper and chill until ready to use.

Fill a skillet with water and bring to a boil. Quickly dip lettuce leaves in the water just long enough to soften them. Remove and pat dry. Arrange 6 leaves on a work surface. Remove salmon from marinade and set each piece on one of the lettuce leaves. Slice the butter log into 6 pieces and place one piece on each fillet. Sprinkle with salt and white pepper. Form each piece into a packet and wrap with another lettuce leaf. Tie each packet together with a chive spear.

Place a plate in the bottom of a flat steamer basket. Put the lettuce packages in a single layer on the plate. Place the steamer in your wok and add enough water to enable you to create steam WITHOUT the water bubbling onto the plate. Bring to a boil and steam for 10 minutes. Remove steamer from wok and let packages rest about 1 minute. Place each package on a serving plate and garnish with remaining long chives.

Wine: Kistler Vineyards "Dutton Ranch" Chardonnay (Sonoma County)

Gravlax with
Cilantro Mustard Sauce

Serves 10–15

- 2 2-pound salmon fillets, cut from thick end
- ¼ cup kosher salt
- ¼ cup superfine sugar
- 1 tablespoon coarsely ground white pepper

20 dried juniper berries, crushed
1 large bunch fresh dill
1 large bunch cilantro
   Cilantro Mustard Sauce (recipe
   follows)
   Capers, finely diced sweet onion,
   thinly sliced Buckwheat Black
   Bread (page 88), and softened
   unsalted butter for garnish

Check fillets for bones by slowly running your fingers along the fillets against the grain; carefully remove any bones remaining with a pair of tweezers. Combine salt, sugar, pepper, and juniper in a small bowl and set aside.

In a large, shallow glass bowl, put ⅓ each of the dill and the cilantro. Sprinkle with ¼ of the combined seasonings. Place one of the salmon fillets, skin side down, on top. Sprinkle surface of salmon with another ¼ of the seasonings and gently rub with your fingers. Then distribute another third of the cilantro and dill. Rub another ¼ of the seasonings on the flesh of the remaining fillet and carefully lay it skin side up over the other piece. Sprinkle skin side with remaining seasonings; evenly distribute remaining cilantro and dill.

Cover the glass dish with plastic wrap and place at least 3 pounds of weight on the fish. Make certain that the edges of the dish are well sealed. Store salmon in refrigerator.

Carefully turn fish at least three times during the first 48 hours; be certain to replace weight and to seal the mixture tightly with plastic wrap. After three days, remove salmon from the dish, scrape off herbs, and wrap tightly. It will keep nicely for at least five days.

To serve, rinse fillets and pat dry. Using a very sharp knife, slice salmon very thin on the diagonal. Serve with mustard sauce, capers, finely diced sweet onion, and buttered black bread.

Wine: Jepson Vineyard Brut Sparkling Wine (Mendocino County)

Cilantro Mustard Sauce

This is superb with fish, but we also like to serve it with smoked or roasted fowl. When your butcher is able to obtain turkey tenderloins (page 303), just grill them and serve them with some of this sauce. This will keep nicely for a week in a tightly sealed container in the refrigerator. It would be equally delicious with most varieties of fresh basil instead of cilantro—just use champagne vinegar in place of the cider vinegar.

Makes 1 generous cup

   ¼ cup Dijon mustard
   1 teaspoon dry mustard
   1 jumbo egg yolk
   1 tablespoon cider vinegar
   1 tablespoon fresh lemon juice
   2 tablespoons sugar
   ½ cup extra-virgin olive oil
   ¼ cup vegetable oil
   3 tablespoons finely minced fresh
      parsley
   1 tablespoon finely minced fresh
      chives
   3 tablespoons finely minced cilantro
      Salt and freshly ground white
      pepper to taste

Combine mustards, egg yolk, vinegar, lemon juice, and sugar in a bowl. Whisk well to combine. Slowly whisk in oils until a very thick emulsion is formed. Add herbs and blend, then add seasonings to taste. Allow to stand in refrigerator for at least 24 hours before serving. Will keep for several weeks in refrigerator if tightly covered.

Salmon en Papillote with Fennel, Tarragon, and Lime

Serves 8

    ½ cup extra-virgin olive oil
    1 pound fennel bulb, trimmed
    4 tablespoons unsalted butter
    8 scallions, trimmed and cut into julienne strips (white part and 1 inch of green part)
    2 medium carrots, scrubbed and cut into thin julienne strips
    4 oyster mushrooms, thinly sliced
    1½ pounds salmon fillet, skinned and cut into 8 pieces
      Salt and freshly ground white pepper to taste
      Zest of 1 lime
    1 tablespoon minced fresh tarragon
    1 tablespoon minced fennel fronds
    4 tablespoons Fish Fûmet (page 204)
    7 tablespoons Sauvignon Blanc wine
    1 tablespoon fresh lime juice
    1–2 tablespoons unsalted butter, melted

Cut 8 10-inch circles of parchment paper. Fold them in half, then open and brush lightly with olive oil. Set aside.

Thinly slice fennel bulb, then cut slices crosswise into ⅛-inch matchsticks. Melt butter in a large skillet over medium heat. Add fennel, scallions, and carrots. Cover with wax paper pressed directly on the vegetables. Reduce heat and cook for 10 minutes. Add mushrooms and sauté for 5 minutes more.

Distribute vegetables among the parchment circles, placing them to one side of the fold.

Check salmon for bones by running your fingers along the fillets against the grain; carefully remove any bones remaining with a pair of tweezers. Place a fillet on each vegetable bed and season with salt and pepper.

Preheat oven to 475°.

Combine zest, tarragon, and fennel fronds. Combine stock, wine, and lime juice. Drizzle about 2 teaspoons of olive oil over each fillet and sprinkle with the herb mixture. Then, working with one packet at a time, drizzle 1½ tablespoons of the stock mixture over the fish, fold over the top half of the packet, and quickly crimp the sides together to seal the packet before the liquids run out. Brush exterior of packet with a bit of melted butter for better browning. Place packets on a large cookie sheet.

Bake for 8 minutes in preheated oven. Let each guest slit his own packet open; the fragrance is wonderful.

Wine: Carmenet Sauvignon Blanc (Sonoma County)

Donald M. Bell, Donald R. Bell, and Roy Cole

Bell's Fishery

P.O. Box 902

Mackinaw City, Michigan 49701

(616) 436-7821

*I*n Clifford Ross Gearhart's wonderful history of commercial fishing in the upper Great Lakes, *Pity the Poor Fish Then Man*, Donald M. Bell, affectionately nicknamed Ding Dong, is one of the central figures. He grew up packing whitefish in his father's fishery and icehouse at Cheboygan, Michigan, about 20 miles south of Mackinaw City. When his father died suddenly in 1947, Donald felt that he did not have the necessary business skills to carry on, so he found other employment. Ultimately his brother sold the facility and the land for other purposes.

But an opportunity came in 1949 that Donald could not resist. Another fish operation in Mackinaw City became available. For two years he had worked in the office of a grocery chain, an experience that had taken some of the mystery out of the art of business. He had missed the society of fishermen, and this was a fishery very like his dad's. The price was right and no down payment was asked, so he bought it.

It was no accident that in those days people in the fish business were usually also in the ice business. No one knows better than a fish packer that you can't ship one without the other. It was on Donald Bell's total dedication to the connection between ice and freshness that he built his reputation as one of the most responsible fish men on the Great Lakes. When he was a kid, Donald's father's crews cut up the winter lake ice and stored it under straw or sawdust for the summer. Now the fishery has efficient ice-making equipment that turns out 8 tons of shaved ice a day.

How well a fisherman handles his catch determines whether Bell's Fishery will buy it. There are about thirty commercial fishermen from whom the company buys most of its product. They catch chub, perch, whitefish, trout, walleye, and salmon. They work the waters of Lake Huron, Lake Michigan, and Lake Superior. If they don't have their own ice-making equipment, and most do not, they come by the fishery to load up before they set out with their nets for three or four days of work.

"I don't care how much ice they take with them," said Ding Dong, "as long as they have plenty on the fish when they get back."

We Will is the determined name of one of the fishing boats that brings in whitefish to the fishery. On the day of our visit, a little radio had just let us know that she was coming in. We watched as the two fishermen on board maneuvered the stubby little boat up to the dock. This day *We Will* didn't do so well. "How was it?" we asked. "I'm almost embarrassed to say," said one of the fishermen. "We sure had our nets in the wrong place today. We got half a tub." Hardly enough to pay for the fuel they burned, Ding Dong figured. Usually, they come in with five or six tubs of whitefish. But as every fisherman knows, tomorrow is another day, and *We Will* will certainly have a better day tomorrow.

Not all of the fish is brought to the dock out back of the office. The company has refrigerated trucks that make the rounds to other fishing communities to pick up the product and hurry it back to the plant, where it is packaged and shipped. Similar trucks then carry the boxed fish to the company's customers in New York, Chicago, Detroit, and other cities. Bell sells to eight to ten wholesalers, and in addition the company deals directly with fifty to sixty quality restaurants, an arrangement that chefs like.

The fishery has seen some bad times. Widely publicized talk of industrial pollution in the lower Great Lakes a couple of decades ago nearly killed commercial fishing in the upper Great Lakes. And in 1963 an outbreak of botulism traced to some smoked lake fish put several companies out of business and nearly got Bell's. Their plant was found blameless, but it took a long time to rebuild consumer confidence.

Smoking is still an important part of the operation; the wonderful fragrance hangs over everything. The fish are soaked in a simple brine, then put in a wooden smoker for 5 to 8 hours, until the inside temperature of the fish is 180°. "It's just an old Boy Scout bonfire," said Ding Dong. "No gas, no electricity. Just hard maple." The smoker can handle 1,200 to 1,400 pounds. By law, since the botulism tragedy, the process has to be monitored continually and all data recorded to verify that the temperature is high enough for long enough to kill any bacteria in the fish.

When one talks about quality fish with the good chefs of the Midwest or New York, Bell's is a name that inevitably comes up. Now that Donald has handed the business over to his son, Donald R., and his son-in-law, Roy Cole, he no longer works full-time. But the new generation, now comfortably at the helm, follows the tradition that put quality above all else. Roy's children are too young, but Donald's two college-age sons work in the plant whenever they can, perhaps considering whether to become a fourth generation of Bells in the lake-fish business.

Ding Dong's desk is like the console of a pipe organ. The keys and the stops are rubber stamps, hanging in parallel rows above the desktop. There are dozens of them, each representing one of the company's customers. Need to make a shipping label? Call out the name and his hand goes unerringly to the rubber stamp bearing the appropriate name and address.

The prospects are good for the continued success of Bell's. The upper Great Lakes are still healthy. There has been some environmental degradation, of course, but development has not been as destructive as it has been in other parts of the country. Fishery management has, for the most part, been enlightened about proper resource management. And there is growing demand: the public's hunger for "a good fish" has increased as health concerns have changed eating habits. (A sign on the front window reads: "Make a cow happy; eat a fish today.")

Donald R. recalls that a few years ago one of the New York customers called, screaming at a new employee. "Where's Ding Dong?" he demanded. "The chubs are too small. Get him on the phone." The shaken clerk explained that he couldn't, that Ding Dong was at the barbershop. "Well, I hope the barber cuts his goddam throat," he roared. A while later Bell was back, shaved and shorn. He called his angry customer, calmed him down, told him there was nothing wrong with the chubs, that he should go back and take another look. "And by the way," he added, "my throat is still intact."

That angry customer still calls Bell's Fishery. But he is sad that it isn't Ding Dong who answers the phone these days. For scores of buyers, telephone encounters with Ding Dong were a highlight of the work week, a time for a good laugh, a chance to talk about serious concerns, a celebration of business friendship at its best.

"He enriched people's lives," wrote Cliff Gearhart in his book. "He had a warmth that drew people to him." If you go by Bell's someday to buy fish, maybe you'll be lucky. Maybe it will be one of those busy end-of-the-month days and Ding Dong Bell will be there behind the counter, helping out.

Jimmy Schmidt's Lake Perch with Red Tartar Sauce

Jimmy Schmidt is one of the great talents among American chefs. Author of *Cooking for All Seasons* and owner/chef of the Rattlesnake Club and Tres Vite, both in Detroit, he can always be counted upon for simple and delicious recipes.

Serves 6

2 cups unbleached flour
2 tablespoons mild paprika
1 teaspoon salt
¾ teaspoon freshly ground white pepper
2 large eggs, lightly beaten
1 cup milk

2 pounds lake perch fillets, skinned
½ cup clarified unsalted butter
1 cup Jimmy Schmidt's Red Tartar Sauce (recipe follows)
2 lemons, cut into wedges or crowns, and 4 sprigs fresh parsley for garnish

Combine flour, paprika, salt, and pepper in a sifter and sift mixture into a medium-sized bowl. Combine eggs and milk in another bowl. Dip perch fillets into the egg mixture, shake off excess liquid, then dredge in flour mixture to coat evenly. Shake off excess flour and place fillets on a rack.

In a large skillet, heat the butter over high heat. Cook fillets until golden, about 2 minutes on one side. Turn fillets and cook about 1 minute on other side. Remove to a rack or paper towels to drain.

Mound fillets on serving plates and serve with Red Tartar Sauce. Garnish with lemons and parsley.

Wine: R. H. Phillips Chardonnay (California)

Jimmy Schmidt's Red Tartar Sauce

Makes 2 cups

2 large egg yolks
1 tablespoon Dijon mustard
¼ cup fresh lemon juice
1 cup corn oil
2 red bell peppers, roasted, peeled, seeded, and diced
1 poblano pepper, roasted, peeled, seeded, and diced (or use green bell pepper for a milder flavor)
2 tablespoons diced red onion
¼ cup capers, minced

2 anchovy fillets, minced (optional)
1 tablespoon minced scallion (green part only)
1 tablespoon minced fresh parsley
½ teaspoon salt
Tabasco to taste

In the bowl of a food processor fitted with the metal blade, combine yolks, mustard, and lemon juice. With motor running, gradually add corn oil in a steady stream until mixture is thickened. Add half the red pepper and purée until smooth. Stop motor, add remaining ingredients, and pulse to combine. Adjust seasonings. Refrigerate in a tightly sealed container for up to four days. Serve leftovers with grilled chicken or smoked turkey.

Jimmy Schmidt's Whitefish with Citrus "Aïoli"

Serves 4

½ cup fresh lemon juice
1 cup fresh orange juice
1 large egg yolk
1 tablespoon Dijon mustard
1 cup virgin olive oil
Salt and freshly ground white pepper to taste
Tabasco to taste (optional)
¾ cup chopped fresh parsley
¼ cup chopped fresh chives (optional)
4 8-ounce whitefish fillets, trimmed, with pin bones removed
Mild paprika

Fresh parsley sprigs and long chive spears for garnish

In a small saucepan, combine the lemon and orange juices and bring to a simmer over high heat. Cook until reduced to ¼ cup, about 7 minutes. Cool. In the bowl of an electric mixer fitted with the whisk, combine reduced juices, egg yolk, and mustard. With motor running on high speed, add the olive oil in a steady stream. Season with salt. Add pepper or Tabasco, if using. Fold in herbs and refrigerate.

Preheat the broiler. Season fish with salt, pepper, and a generous dusting of paprika. Place fillets skin side down on ovenproof broiling pan. Broil under preheated broiler until done, about 8 minutes, depending on thickness of fillets. Remove from oven.

Remove skin by carefully inserting a thin spatula between fish and skin. Invert fillet and remove the dark fatty tissue. Place whitefish on each of 4 serving plates. Spoon some "aïoli" over the fish, garnish with herbs, and serve.

Wine: Girard Winery Chardonnay (Napa Valley)

Shaw's Crab House Planked Lake Superior Whitefish with Duchess Potatoes

The first time we ate planked whitefish was at the wonderful Shaw's Crab House in Chicago in the company of Steve Lahaie, managing partner. Steve grew up in St. Ignace, just across from Mackinaw City; it is he who suggested we pay a visit to the Bell family and he who introduced us to this superb dish.

Serves 4

6 tablespoons unsalted butter, softened
1 tablespoon chopped fresh parsley
½ teaspoon fresh lemon juice
½ teaspoon Worcestershire sauce
Dash Tabasco
Salt and freshly ground black pepper to taste
4 hickory-wood planks (9- or 10-inch ovals) (see Note)
2–3 tablespoons vegetable oil
6 medium Idaho potatoes, peeled and quartered
2 large egg yolks
⅔ cup heavy cream
1 pinch freshly grated nutmeg
4 8-ounce fillets Lake Superior whitefish, trimmed and with pin bones removed

Combine 4 tablespoons of the butter, parsley, lemon juice, Worcestershire, and Tabasco in the bowl of a food processor fitted with the metal blade. Add salt and pepper to taste; then blend until smooth. Place mixture on a sheet of wax paper and roll into a plump log. Refrigerate until time to use.

Preheat oven to 275°. Brush planks with oil, lightly covering both sides. Place on cookie sheets and heat in oven for 1 hour.

While planks are being seasoned, place potatoes in a 3-quart saucepan and cover with water. Boil over high heat until tender when pricked with a fork, about 15 minutes. Remove from heat and drain. Place potatoes in the bowl of an electric mixer. Add remaining butter, egg yolks, cream, salt, pepper, and nutmeg. Combine ingredients by cutting them into the potatoes with two knives. Then attach paddle to mixer and beat until mixture is well blended and potatoes are stiff. Set aside in a warm place.

Increase oven temperature to 350°. Lightly brush more vegetable oil on seasoned hickory planks. Place whitefish, skin side down, on planks. Bake in preheated oven for 10 minutes.

Remove fish from oven and heat broiler. Fill a pastry bag fitted with a decorative tip with the potato mixture and pipe potatoes around rim of plank. Put 1 tablespoon of reserved seasoned butter on each fish fillet. Place under broiler for 2–3 minutes, until potatoes are browned and butter has melted. Put planks on a charger or larger plate and serve immediately.

Note: Hickory planks are available at restaurant-supply stores, gourmet shops, and some hardware stores.

Wine: Chateau Woltner "Estate Bottled" Chardonnay "Howell Mountain" (Napa Valley)

Jean Joho's Braised Lake Superior Whitefish with Brioche Crust and Tomato Butter

Lucky the Everest Room patrons who can enjoy this dish and the spectacular view of Chicago all at the same time. Chef Jean Joho is one of the very best.

Serves 4

- 2 slices Brioche Loaf (page 71)
- 6 tablespoons unsalted butter, softened
- 1 teaspoon minced fresh chervil
- 1 teaspoon minced fresh tarragon
- 2 tablespoons minced fresh chives

Salt and freshly ground black pepper to taste
- 4 7-ounce fillets Lake Superior whitefish, pin bones removed
- 4 shallots, minced
- ½ pound fresh tomatoes
 Pinch sugar
- 3 ounces Alsatian Riesling wine

The day before serving, dry slices of brioche by leaving them exposed to the air.

The next day, grate dried brioche into crumbs. Mix with 2 tablespoons of the butter, chervil, tarragon, 1 tablespoon of the chives, salt, and pepper. Lightly season fish with salt and pepper, then coat with crumb mixture.

Lightly butter a large shallow baking pan. Sprinkle with the shallots, salt, and pepper. Arrange fish fillets over shallots and set aside.

Preheat oven to 425°.

Blanch tomatoes in boiling water for 10 seconds, then cool in ice water. Peel skin from tomato and remove seeds. Purée through a Foley food mill into a saucepan; add sugar.

Simmer tomatoes over low heat until liquid is slightly reduced. Meanwhile, pour wine over fish and place pan in preheated oven for 10 minutes, or until crust is golden.

To finish sauce, slowly add remaining butter, a bit at a time, to the simmering tomato mixture. Whisk vigorously between additions. Season with salt and pepper, then add remaining chives. Spoon sauce over fillets and serve.

Wine: MacRostie Winery Chardonnay (Sonoma County)

Josh Goldman and Scott Lindell

AquaFuture

P.O. Box 783

Turner's Falls, Massachusetts 01376

(413) 863-8905

The landscape of Israel is dotted with fish farms, where tons of tilapia are raised every year. There, tilapia, which require a very warm environment, are out in the open, nurtured by the hot sun—truly a sun-kissed fish. The sun stream golden tilapia of AquaFuture are grown indoors, along with sunshine bass and an assortment of herbs and baby lettuces. Instead of being grown in the naturally warmed open-air fish ponds of the Promised Land, however, these fish are grown in 150,000-gallon tanks, in a controlled indoor environment located in a west-central Massachusetts industrial park. It is an operation that has created a host of synergistic relationships that address myriad nutritional and social issues.

Josh Goldman was a Philadelphian who moved to the area as a student at Hampshire College. There he first began to investigate bio-engineering and aquaculture systems. And he began to think about alternative ways of providing inexpensive, high-quality food sources for the future.

Scott Lindell went to Berkeley in the mid-1970s. His interests there ranged from aquaculture to the counterculture to the gourmet counter, and he followed with great interest the development of Alice Waters' restaurant, Chez Panisse. "That's really where my vision comes from," he said with a smile.

AquaFuture was conceived in 1987. The two men spent eighteen months researching and designing the technology for farming fish and plants in a greenhouse environment. The first year of cultivation began in a space of 4,000 square feet early in 1989. By mid-1991, the company had grown to 40,000 square feet. They produced 60,000 pounds of fish their first year and project 1 million pounds for the 1991–92 year. This is a biologically integrated operation, and the same warm environment and water in which the fish grow are used to organically fertilize hydroponically grown produce. AquaFuture produces about 10,000 pounds of herbs, baby lettuces, and edible flowers per year.

The principal fish that AquaFuture grows is sunshine bass, a relative of the striped bass, which has the same delicate flavor and firm white flesh of its seagoing cousin. The brood stock for both bass and tilapia have been selected for hardiness, high yield, and consistent availability of fingerlings. The sunshine bass fingerlings are grown in ponds in the southern United States until they are about 3–4 inches long. Then they are trucked to the Northeast and AquaFuture's round 150,000-gallon tanks, where they are fed a carefully formulated grain diet that is rich in natural vitamins and minerals. It takes ten months for the fish to reach 1¾ pounds; some fish will have to spend a few more months in the tank, since many chefs want to purchase fish that weigh over 2 pounds. With careful planning, AquaFuture is able to supply fish to their customers most of the year.

AquaFuture's water filtration process is quite ingenious. Water is constantly recirculated through the round tanks, which are easier to keep clean than rectangular tanks because there are no corners to scrub. About thirty times a day the water is filtered through clarifying and cleansing devices, and out of about 30 million gallons of filtered water there is less than a 1 percent loss. Most of this waste water, discharged into a nearby river, meets drinking-water standards, and some is converted to plant fertilizer as it passes through a tank that converts its ammonia into nutrients. Food production is free of all pesticides.

The water for the fish is supersaturated with oxygen by means of a device for mixing oxygen and water. In this oxygen-rich environment, fish gills are very efficient, so the fish puts its energy into growth and not into extracting oxygen from the water.

As a further conservation measure, AquaFuture has entered into a cooperative arrangement with Mohawk Plastics, a neighbor, which uses a large volume of

water to cool its equipment. AquaFuture now takes that warmed water and extracts heat from it through a heat exchanger and sends it back to the plastics plant again. This recycling of water and heat enables both companies to save money, not only on the water bill but on the electric bill as well.

The general environment in the greenhouse-like AquaFuture building is kept at a temperature above 80°. When the natural warmth from the sun is not enough, they supplement it with propane-powered heaters, and the humidity level is kept at 80 percent. This is a setting that is especially nurturing for herbs, such as basil, and for the nasturtiums and marigolds, as well as for the baby lettuces. In the old building, these were grown in trays above the fish tanks. The staff found it too awkward working above the fish, however; sometimes a worker would slip and take an unscheduled swim. In the new facility, the plants are grown off to the side.

Sunshine bass and tilapia were selected for the project for a variety of reasons. First, they are warm-water fish. Warm-water fish grow faster, so they can be at market sooner. And they move in schools—they stay together and do not require large uncrowded growing spaces. So the building can be small enough to be economically feasible and not require lots of expensive land. Since the building is small and efficiently designed, it is possible to create and maintain a warm environment, even in the cold New England winters, without breaking the bank, and a warm environment is good for growing greens. Also, Tilapia and sunshine bass are well received by chefs because they hold up well in cooking and are compatible with a variety of sauces. And perhaps most important of all, they are delicately flavored fish that people like. Whereas many farmed fish seem to taste muddy and have a mushy texture, AquaFuture's tilapia and bass are sweet-tasting and firm, thanks to their constantly filtered water and carefully planned diet.

As the fish grow, they are placed into tanks according to size. When it is time to go to market, they are moved to a cleansing tank, full of clean water, without food, for a day. During that time, the fish purge themselves of all waste. They then go straight into ice water, where their systems slow down and stop. It is a humane death and the fish are not traumatized, so no hormones are released that could damage flavor and texture. They are processed instantly, packed in special containers, and in customers' hands within twenty-four hours of leaving the water.

Both Josh and Scott strongly believe that this kind of fish farming is essential for the future. While tilapia is hardly a well-recognized product in this country, the popularity of striped bass is universal. One of the most loved of wild fish, and historically one of the most available, it has suffered enormously from overfishing and pollution during the last two decades. In 1970, 15 million pounds of striped bass were taken from ocean waters. For many years there was no fishing for this species; in 1989, the year that the striped-bass fishing season was reopened, only a half million pounds of bass were taken—most from contaminated waters, so the quality of the fish is highly suspect. It is commonly accepted that fish farming is the only way to guarantee a stable and healthy food source for the future.

Currently, AquaFuture only distributes their products within Massachusetts. But their plan is to expand as the production facility begins to operate at full capacity. Ultimately, they hope to build other facilities in other states and to grow other species. And as word spreads, there have even been inquiries from other continents. The company is doing well, and the men are enjoying watching their dreams materialize.

Grilled Tilapia with Cilantro Mustard Sauce

Serves 4

> 8 tilapia fillets
> 4 tablespoons olive oil
> Salt and freshly ground black pepper to taste
> 1 tablespoon green peppercorns
> Cilantro Mustard Sauce (page 157)
>
> Cilantro for garnish

Rub tilapia fillets with olive oil. Thoroughly clean the surface of a gas or charcoal grill with a metal brush; then coat the surface evenly with Pam. Heat the grill until very hot. Grill fillets for 4½ minutes per side (shift slightly during grilling to achieve the "X" pattern from grill). Season with salt and pepper.

Mix green peppercorns with cilantro mustard sauce. Garnish each fillet with a generous dollop of sauce and fresh cilantro.

Wine: Babcock Vineyards "Eleven Oaks" Sauvignon Blanc (Santa Barbara County)

Tilapia with Capers and Sage

Serves 4

> 1 jumbo egg
> 1 cup fine, dry bread crumbs
> 2½ pounds tilapia fillets
> Salt and freshly ground black pepper to taste
> 4 tablespoons unsalted butter or margarine
> ¼ cup extra-virgin olive oil
> ⅓ cup Sauvignon Blanc wine
> 2 tablespoons fresh lemon juice
> ½ teaspoon cayenne pepper
> 1 tablespoon minced fresh sage
> ¼ cup minced fresh parsley
> 2 tablespoons capers
>
> Fresh chive spears and lemon slices for garnish

Break egg into a flat soup plate and beat thoroughly with one teaspoon of water. Put bread crumbs into another soup plate. Dip fish fillets into egg, then coat well with crumbs. Place prepared fillets on a rack and sprinkle with salt and pepper.

Melt butter in a large cast-iron skillet over medium heat. Add oil and increase heat. Sauté fish fillets for 2 minutes on each side, or until golden. Transfer fish to a warm platter while you prepare the sauce.

Return skillet to medium heat, add wine and lemon juice, and stir to loosen any browned bits of fish adhering to the bottom of the pan. Add remaining ingredients and stir for one minute. Nap the fish with this sauce and garnish with fresh chives and lemon slices.

Wine: Ferrari-Carano Vineyards Chardonnay (Sonoma County)

Grilled Sunshine Bass with Green Salsa

If you are unable to find sunshine bass, substitute striped bass or small snapper.

Serves 4

> ¼ cup extra-virgin olive oil
> 1 large clove garlic, finely minced
> 1 tablespoon minced fresh chives
> Juice of ½ lemon
> 4 1½-pound sunshine bass, gutted, gilled, and scaled

Salt and freshly ground pepper to taste

SALSA

1 bunch flat-leaf parsley, stems removed
¼ fresh jalapeño pepper, seeded
1 small shallot
1 bunch watercress, stems removed
5 sprigs cilantro, stems removed
10 arugula leaves
2 teaspoons fresh thyme
3 fresh basil leaves
¼ cup extra-virgin olive oil
2 tablespoons fresh lemon juice
1 teaspoon salt
1 teaspoon freshly ground black pepper

Combine oil, garlic, chives, and lemon juice in a Pyrex dish. Mix well. Rinse fish and pat dry. Rub lemon mixture on fish and marinate in Pyrex dish for 1 hour.

To make the salsa, combine parsley, jalapeño, and shallot in the bowl of a food processor fitted with the metal blade. Process until finely minced. Add remaining greens and herbs; pulse to mince thoroughly. Spoon into a small bowl and add olive oil, lemon juice, salt, and pepper. Stir well and chill.

Thoroughly clean the surface of a gas or charcoal grill with a metal brush; then coat the surface evenly with Pam. Heat the grill until very hot. Remove fish from marinade and sprinkle with salt and pepper to taste. Make several vertical slashes on each side of fish. Grill for 5 minutes on each side and serve with the green salsa.

Wine: Honig Cellars Sauvignon Blanc (Napa Valley)

Pan-Fried Tilapia

Serves 4

½ cup finely ground cornmeal (see Note)
½ cup unbleached flour
1 teaspoon salt
1 teaspoon freshly ground white pepper
1 teaspoon dried thyme
1 teaspoon hot paprika
1 jumbo egg, beaten
¼ cup buttermilk
4 tilapia (about 12 ounces each), cleaned, gutted, and rinsed
½ cup unsalted margarine
Juice of 1 lemon
4 tablespoons unsalted butter

In a large, shallow bowl, combine cornmeal with flour, salt, pepper, thyme, and paprika. Blend well. Place beaten egg and buttermilk in another bowl and blend.

Pat tilapia dry, dip in egg mixture, then dredge thoroughly in cornmeal mixture. Place on a rack.

Melt margarine in a cast-iron skillet. Heat over medium heat until smoking. Carefully place fish in skillet and fry about 5 minutes per side. Fish should be golden brown on outside and moist on inside. Remove fish and drain on paper towels. Add lemon juice and butter to skillet and whisk for 1 minute. Serve fish with lemon butter.

Note: If cornmeal is not very fine, put it into the bowl of a food processor fitted with the metal blade and pulse 20 times.

Wine: Kenwood Vineyards Sauvignon Blanc (Sonoma County)

William D. Johnson

Rushing Waters Trout Farm

P.O. Box 386

Palmyra, Wisconsin 53156-0386

(414) 495-8327

Rhapsodic passages have been set down repeatedly over the centuries celebrating the joys of trout fishing. Many great fishing writers hold that the reward is the act of fishing itself; whether a trout was actually caught, killed, and eaten is, for some, irrelevant. And yet, for anyone with a palate and a taste memory, dining on a fresh rainbow trout, 3 or 4 pounds, just out of a pristine stream, can stand as one of the highlights of a lifetime of eating.

That trout, in order for it to have been truly memorable, had to have been a wild thing. It must have been taken from a clean stream after a hard struggle. It must have been nourished by the rich insect life of the stream, and it must have been fierce and powerful, its musculature solid from a lifetime of movement.

On a beautiful farm in the hills of south-central Wisconsin, William D. Johnson is addressing this problem. Until 1987, he had managed a foundry, pouring bronze. His brother-in-law, an investor, was looking for a business project. Somewhere, he had seen an article on aquaculture. Properly done, he thought, it could have good potential. He asked Bill Johnson to quit the foundry and look into the possibilities.

Bill had never so much as owned a pet goldfish, but he started reading, traveling, asking questions. He knew that to succeed he would have to have a special product of very high quality. It could not be the mushy, muddy fish often characteristic of pond farming. It would have to be a trout that would look and taste like the ever-scarcer wild trout. The water would have to be fresh and in motion. There could not be overcrowding. The fish would need freedom to move. They also decided early on that it would be a natural product, as close to organic as possible. No chemicals or antibiotics would be used. And no beta carotene or other artificial colorings would be fed to the fish. The pink of the flesh would come naturally, from the rations. And the food, high in fat and protein, would have to come close in content to what the fish would eat in the wild.

"Never forget," said Bill, "that feed equals flavor."

The site Bill chose had been a trout farm before. The water was from artesian wells fed by a rich aquifer; 3,000 gallons a minute bubbled up, more than enough. Previous owners had failed to make a go of it and the farm had stood idle for several years. Bill and his brother-in-law were able to buy it at a good price. They then invested over $1.2 million to rebuild the raceways, install aeration equipment, build a hatchery, overhaul the processing and packing facility, and add smoking equipment. In March 1987, the farm was ready. In June 1988, they sold their first trout. In 1989, they broke even. In 1990, they sold nearly 200,000 pounds of rainbow trout and were expecting to reach 300,000 pounds by 1991. The emphasis on quality worked. They harvest to order, and they will not ship unless there is certainty that the fish will be delivered absolutely fresh.

The process begins in a climate-controlled building where the brood stock is taken twice a year, in March and September. These are the best fish, the fastest-growing fish, selected for energy and color. Each female will be stripped of as many as 2,000 eggs. Milt will be expressed from the males and mixed with the eggs. At least 75 percent of the eggs will be fertilized, and 50 percent of those will eventually go to market. In thirty-one days, the fish hatch. They spend the first few weeks inside in large vats, being hand-fed several times a day. At about 3 inches, they go outside to the first of a series of long connected ponds that make up the raceway. Thousands of the tiny trout clump together, forming a black mass in the pond. "Protection from predators," Bill said.

The fish double in weight every three weeks until they are about 8 ounces. As they grow, they are moved several times from one raceway to another so that they are never crowded. They reach market weight, about 1 pound, in nine to fourteen months. At this weight they dress out at 8 to 10 ounces, an ideal size for the restaurant trade.

While scores of Wisconsin and Illinois restaurants use Bill's rainbow trout, the one closest to the farm is Heaven City in Mukwonago, Wisconsin. It is in an old building that, they say, had once been a house of ill repute. When the strumpets took their leave, mattresses on their backs, the restaurateur Scott McGlinchey turned it into a restaurant. It is the one Bill and his wife can visit easily whenever they have a taste for one of their own rainbows and don't want to cook.

So far, things have gone well. But there is plenty to worry about. "There is a heron rookery nearby," he said. "Seventy great blue herons at last count, and during migration this place is like McDonald's to them." Sometimes it is necessary to stand guard over the ponds to scare away the herons. Bill figures he loses 50 pounds of baby trout every day to the herons. "A guy raising crops can get insurance against acts of God," said Bill, "but there is no insurance against herons." Also, algal bloom in the ponds can make the fish taste muddy, so it is vital to keep fresh water flowing through the raceway. And he worries about the water. "If agricultural runoff gets into the aquifer," he said, "we will be in big trouble."

He is also concerned that his farm not create a problem for others, since it is at the source of a stream, the waters of which are captured midway, held, and used. At the end of the raceways, beyond the last pond, the water is allowed to go its natural way. But since it is an organic operation, the waters are healthy. As long as it stays that way, and the mature trout in the last pond are strong, then Bill knows that the operation is no threat to anything downstream.

Like so many other creative farmers, Bill Johnson tests the patience and understanding of the regulatory bureaucracies. The state fish and game people see trout hatcheries as their sole province. Yet here is a man doing what they do and making a profit at it. "The state should not raise fish, even for restocking fishing streams," Bill said. "Their legitimate concern is maintaining what is in the wild. They should just fund research." He feels the laws need to be rewritten to eliminate red tape and thereby encourage others to do what he has done.

The fact is, Bill Johnson could probably teach the fish and game people something about trout. He has become an expert; if there were a test for ichthyologists, he would surely pass. His house is full of extraordinary aquariums, both freshwater and saltwater. On his shelf is *Exotic Aquarium Fishes,* by William T. Innes, for half a century the classic aquarist's bible. The specimens in his tanks rival anything on its pages.

As we toured the farm, watching the workers feed, test, and harvest, we were accompanied by two handsome dogs. By the office door, uneaten, were their bowls of dry dog food. They had other things on their minds. They do not have the huge paws or the sharp claws of a bear, so they cannot fish with a swipe, but they have developed great skill. After moments of intense concentration followed by mere seconds of splashy activity, off they went with the ultimate snack in their mouths, a 1-pound trout as fresh as a fish could ever be. Having certainly enjoyed the sport of the catch, they would soon equally enjoy the pleasures of eating it.

Heaven City's Smoked-Trout Turnovers on Coarse Mustard Sauce

We thank chef Scott McGlinchey for this delicious recipe.

Serves 4

- 2 11x14-inch sheets frozen puff pastry, defrosted
- 2 large eggs, beaten
- 8 slices fresh mozzarella
- 1 pound Rushing Waters smoked trout, boned and flaked
- 1 tablespoon unsalted butter
- 1 tablespoon finely chopped shallots
- 1 ounce dry white wine
- 6 ounces coarse-grained mustard
- 3 ounces heavy cream

  Fresh watercress sprigs for garnish

Preheat oven to 425°.

Cut sheets into 8x8-inch squares. Cut each square evenly into 4 (4x4-inch) squares. Thoroughly brush pastry squares with beaten egg. Cut each mozzarella slice in half diagonally. Place a cheese triangle in one corner of each pastry square. Place 2 ounces of smoked trout on cheese, then cover with other cheese triangle and fold pastry over. Seal edges with tines of a fork and brush surface with beaten egg. Repeat until 8 turnovers are made. Place turnovers on nonstick cookie sheets and bake until golden, about 10–12 minutes.

Meanwhile, in a small saucepan, melt butter and sauté shallots until golden. Add wine, mustard, and cream. Bring to a boil, stirring constantly.

Place a pool of mustard sauce on each serving plate, top with turnovers, garnish with watercress, and serve.

Wine: Havens Cellars Sauvignon Blanc (Napa Valley)

Heavenly Smoked-Trout and Shellfish Pasta Sauce

This is one of the first dishes Linda taught in her classes; it has also been one of the most popular.

Serves 4

- 2 cups heavy cream
- 4 tablespoons extra-virgin olive oil
- 2 cloves garlic, minced
- 4 scallions, minced (white part only)
- 4 sun-dried tomatoes
- 3 tablespoons pine nuts
- 12–16 medium raw shrimp, peeled and deveined
- 1 pint bay scallops
- 6 ounces smoked trout, boned, skinned, and broken into small pieces
- 6 tablespoons unsalted butter, cut into pieces
- Salt and freshly ground black pepper to taste
- 3 tablespoons mixed minced fresh basil, thyme, and chives
- 4 tablespoons freshly grated Parmesan cheese
- 1 pound cooked pasta

Minced fresh chives and salmon caviar for garnish

Pour cream into a deep, heavy saucepan and simmer briskly over medium heat until reduced by half. Set aside.

Pour 2 tablespoons of olive oil into a skillet and heat; add garlic, scallions, tomatoes, and pine nuts and cook over low heat for 3 minutes. Stir often; do not burn. Remove mixture from pan, then add remaining olive oil and sauté shrimp for two minutes. Add scallops and cook just until they turn opaque. Do not overcook. Remove from heat and add smoked trout and garlic mixture.

Heat cream; do not boil. Carefully blend in fish mixture. Whisk in butter, a bit at a time, then add remaining ingredients. Spoon into heated flat soup plates and garnish with chives and a dollop of caviar.

Wine: Girard Winery Chardonnay "Reserve" (Napa Valley)

Trout Fillets with Pecan-Butter Sauce

Serves 8 as appetizer, 4 as an entrée

- 1 teaspoon kosher salt
- 1 teaspoon freshly ground white pepper
- 2 tablespoons finely ground pecans
- 2 tablespoons fine, dry bread crumbs
- 4 trout, filleted and butterflied
- 2 tablespoons olive oil
- ½ cup unsalted butter
- ½ cup ground pecans
- 1 tablespoon fresh lemon juice
- 1 tablespoon minced fresh chives
- 2 tablespoons minced fresh parsley
- ¼ teaspoon cayenne pepper

  Lemon slices for garnish

Combine salt, pepper, 2 tablespoons pecans, and bread crumbs in a shallow soup plate. Brush both sides of the fish with olive oil, then dredge fish in the seasoning mixture. Place fish on rack until ready to cook.

Melt butter in a small skillet, add ½ cup pecans, and sauté for a few minutes. Add the lemon juice, herbs, and cayenne; sauté a minute more, then remove from heat. Set aside.

Thoroughly clean the surface of a gas or charcoal grill with a metal brush; then coat the surface evenly with Pam. Heat the grill until very hot.

Arrange fish fillets skin side down on the grill. Cook for 4 minutes. Turn and cook 1 minute on other side. Transfer to a platter and keep warm. Reheat lemon-pecan mixture, arrange fish on serving plates, and garnish with the sauce and some lemon slices.

Wine: Eberle Winery Chardonnay (Paso Robles)

Carolyn Collins

Carolyn Collins Caviar

925 West Jackson Boulevard, Third Floor

Chicago, Illinois 60607

(312) 226-0342

*I*f you saw Carolyn Collins on Chicago's Michigan Avenue, you'd say she was the fashion coordinator at one of the fine avant-garde boutiques in town. She is not one to blend into a crowd. She'd never strike you as a sport fisherman, let alone a caviar processor. But she is both.

In her office and processing facility, just off Chicago's Loop, Carolyn speaks of "making" caviar. She and her daughter Rachel were avid fishermen who spent every spare minute they could on licensed Great Lakes chartered fishing boats. There would usually be five fishermen on board, and if each caught the limit it would mean not only a lot of fish but, if the season was right, a lot of caviar too. Carolyn, who loved caviar, was often given the roe from her companions' fish. Sometimes there was a lot of it—a fourth of the weight of a female can be roe.

She worked for years until she finally mastered the technique of handling the delicate eggs. In 1983, she started her business and soon found that chefs loved her product. Now the company is producing close to 15,000 pounds of caviar annually.

All species of game fish have roe at a certain periods of their lives. Carolyn Collins handles roe from whitefish, several varieties of trout, bowfin, and at least three varieties of American sturgeon. All roe needs to be processed (separated from the tissue and other matter that hold it together and cured for a while with salt) and then packaged. Unlike virtually all other commercial caviar, Carolyn Collins's caviar is processed completely by hand.

Traditionally, caviar is processed at the time of harvest—between October and March, depending upon the species. Many skeins of roe (kidney-shaped bundles held together by a fine membrane) are put into a machine that shakes the eggs loose. It is easy to understand that the eggs—or berries, as they are called—are often bruised. The berries are salted and cured in large tubs, then bottled and generally pasteurized for long shelf life. Pasteurization requires the use of heat, so the berries are often slightly cooked, making them somewhat crisp when they should be tender and creamy.

Carolyn, however, freezes the skeins at the time of harvest and processes them to order throughout the year. Some skeins are handled by shaking the berries loose through a large screen; with others, the berries are detached from the skein "piecemeal," by hand. Each skein is processed separately and cured in individual jars so that the berries are always uniform in size and color when in their final containers. It is a completely natural product; there is no coloring added and only enough salt to cure and stabilize the product. There is no pasteurization, so the caviar must be refrigerated until it is consumed.

Carolyn's business has become too large for her and her associates to catch all the fish themselves. There are thirty-one whitefish fisheries on the Great Lakes; she buys roe from only one. And this roe comes to the company already processed because she so trusts the company. Roe from all other fish comes in skeins; often Carolyn goes to the fishery at the time of harvest and selects each skein she wants. She is frequently amused to learn that her rejects are bought by nationally recognized companies and are sold at steep prices.

Her salmon roe comes from chinook in Lake Michigan—fish that were introduced decades ago to feed on the alewives that had gotten out of control. Chinook, which are able to live in either salt water or fresh water, have thrived in the lake and yield superb caviar. Carolyn says, however, that only 30 percent of the salmon or other roe she examines meets her standards; the quality depends on the manner of death and the cleaning of the fish.

Carolyn also processes several varieties of trout roe. Trout caviar is very delicate—a soft, juice-filled berry, either yellow or gold. Occasionally, Carolyn handles caviar from Apostle Island red-fin trout; it ranges in color from buttercup yellow to orange. Curiously, the same fish from Lake Michigan do not yield a good roe; it is too smelly and oily. The quality of the water, what the fish eats, and how it is handled when caught are all important variables in determining the texture and flavor of the roe.

There are nine species of sturgeon in the United States, inhabiting coastal waters, the Great Lakes, and the Mississippi and its tributaries. In the old days sturgeon were ubiquitous. But pollution, dams, and carelessness have hurt the population dramatically. You cannot harvest sturgeon roe without killing the fish, and if you kill a fish that is too young to reproduce you lower the population growth rate.

"The United States produced more than 150,000 pounds a year of sturgeon caviar during the last century, with almost half coming from the Great Lakes," Carolyn told us. "Unfortunately," she said, "such intensive harvesting almost destroyed the fish population, since people did not realize that sturgeon don't reach sexual maturity until twenty to thirty years of age and they only spawn once every six to eight years. They can live a hundred and fifty years. Today it is illegal to sell flesh or roe from Great Lakes sturgeon."

Sturgeon fishing is tightly regulated almost everywhere. "In fact, in Wisconsin," Carolyn said, "you can only catch one a year, and that can only be done with a spear through the ice." She showed us a photo of a friend's 104-pound catch.

Most of Carolyn Collins Caviar's sturgeon roe comes from the Mississippi River valley. Currently, the company is producing caviar from three varieties, each with a distinctive roe. One characteristic common to all three is a very long, sweet finish, or aftertaste.

The hackleback, or shovelnose, sturgeon produces small, naturally black caviar. The berries appear to be firm, although they are soft and almost buttery, nicely separate, with an intense, sweet flavor. Carolyn likes this caviar for garnishes and pasta dishes.

The paddlefish (spoonbill) is a scaleless fish belonging to the same class as sturgeon. It yields a larger berry than the hackleback. The berries are steel-gray in color, well separated, and slightly oily. This caviar is very mild, smooth, and not salty.

Finally, the ultimate—the "Chattanooga Beluga," the finest freshwater sturgeon caviar in the country. The berries are large and golden gray, with a sweet, nutlike flavor and a delicate, creamy texture. It is simply superb. Occasionally, there is an albino sturgeon that yields golden eggs, which seem to be a bit more intensely flavored. Unfortunately for most of us, Chicago chef Jean Joho, of the Everest Room, has a contract for all the albino sturgeon caviar Carolyn can get.

The company has distributors from one coast to the other, now supervised by Rachel Collins, a taller version of her striking mother. In addition to the various caviars, the company has a number of specialty products, ranging from caviar with Absolut pepper vodka and jalapeño peppers to applewood-smoked sturgeon. They also make a wonderful smoked caviar using gold-colored whitefish eggs. These products, too, adhere to the same standards of quality that Carolyn sets for the Chattanooga Beluga. Carolyn refers to these products as "expanded concepts."

Ludwig Bemelmans, a legendary caviar devotee, once said, "Caviar is to dining what a sable coat is to a girl in an evening dress." We know he would have waxed rhapsodic about Carolyn Collins caviar. What a pity he didn't get to taste any.

Smoked Sablefish Pâté with Caviar

One of the most extraordinary fish we've ever tasted, sablefish, or black cod, never seems to make its way to the Midwest, let alone the East Coast, except in the smoked form. While this dish works well with smoked whitefish or trout, sablefish has the best flavor and texture. We also like to combine different kinds of caviar to make a colorful and tasty garnish.

Makes about 1 ½ cups

12–14 ounces smoked sablefish
  ½ cup unsalted butter, at room temperature
  1 tablespoon heavy cream
  ¼ teaspoon freshly ground white pepper
3–4 ounces caviar from salmon, paddlefish, or trout
20 slices Melba toast

Separate the fish flesh from bones and skin. Put flesh into the bowl of a food processor fitted with the metal blade. Put butter into processor along with cream and white pepper. Pulse until mixture is very smooth.

Pack pâté into an attractive serving dish and smooth the top. Cover tightly with plastic wrap and chill until firm.

Let pâté stand at room temperature for 30 minutes before serving. Decorate the top with caviar and serve with Melba toast.

Wine: Domaine Carneros Sparkling Wine, Brut "Carneros" (Napa Valley)

Rachel's Smoked Caviar Butter

Rachel Collins, Carolyn Collins's daughter, recommended that we spread this onto hot crusty bread, use it as topping for baked potatoes, toss it onto hot pasta for an instant caviar sauce, or pipe it onto canapés of smoked fish.

Makes about 2 cups

  2 cups butter, softened almost to room temperature
  1 ounce lobster roe
  4 ounces Collins's smoked Chicago golden caviar

Put butter in the bowl of an electric mixer fitted with a paddle (do not use a food processor). With motor at medium speed, beat until butter is thoroughly creamed. Place mixer bowl in refrigerator until butter is thoroughly chilled, about 10–20 minutes. Then return bowl to mixer and whip butter until very light and fluffy, up to 20 minutes. Turn mixer to lowest speed and add lobster roe. Mix until roe is evenly distributed, then remove bowl from mixer and gently fold caviar into butter by hand. Divide mixture among small containers and store in refrigerator. Let butter come to room temperature, about 30 minutes, before using.

Wine: Au Bon Climat Pinot Blanc "Bien Nacido Vineyard" (Santa Barbara County)

David Schy's Tuna Sashimi with Bowfin Caviar and Wasabi Vinaigrette

Chef David Schy gives Chicago's Hat Dance Restaurant its distinctive spirit. Part of the fabled Lettuce Entertain You Enterprise group, Hat Dance is one of those places you always want to revisit because the food is terrific and the place is fun.

Serves 6

VINAIGRETTE
    ½ tablespoon Dijon mustard
    1 tablespoon grated fresh ginger
    ¼ teaspoon minced garlic
    1 jumbo egg yolk
    1 teaspoon fresh lemon juice
    1 tablespoon rice wine vinegar
    ¼ teaspoon salt
    Pinch freshly ground white pepper
    1 ounce wasabi powder
    1 tablespoon soy sauce
    ¾ cup extra-virgin olive oil
    ½ teaspoon dark sesame oil
    1 tablespoon chopped cilantro

    6 ounces cucumber, cut into julienne strips
  12 ounces thinly sliced high-quality yellowfin tuna
    3 ounces bowfin caviar
    1 ripe avocado, sliced into 18 equal pieces

    Fresh cilantro for garnish

Combine mustard, ginger, garlic, egg yolk, lemon juice, vinegar, salt, pepper, wasabi, and soy sauce in a bowl and blend. Slowly add olive oil, whisking vigorously. Then whisk in sesame oil. Add cilantro and blend; set aside.

Just before serving, divide cucumber among the centers of six chilled serving plates. Fan tuna slices over the cucumber. Spoon 2 tablespoons of vinaigrette over each serving. Add caviar and avocado to the plates and garnish with fresh cilantro.

Wine: Iron Horse Vineyards Sparkling Wine Brut "Green Valley" (Sonoma County)

Justin Taylor, William J. Taylor, and Paul Taylor

Taylor United
SE 130 Lynch Road
Shelton, Washington 98584
(206) 426-6178

Justin Taylor and his sons, Bill and Paul, are a world away in time and place from the old-time Chesapeake Bay oystermen with their skiffs and rakes, trusting nature for their livelihood. They are contemporary oystermen, high-tech specialists, students of the biological sciences.

In fact, the days of the uncultivated oyster are virtually over. Oyster lovers today must rely on people like the Taylors, who have studied science, developed cultivation techniques, lobbied for stringent antipollution laws, leased the tidal flats, invested money, built farming facilities, and added their back-breaking toil.

Bill and Paul are the fourth generation of their family to work the waters of Puget Sound. Their great-grandfather harvested Puget Sound Olympias until his death in 1930, when the coastal railroad was still taking barrels of fresh oysters down to the gourmets of San Francisco. But the industrialization of the Puget Sound region, and especially the pollution from paper mills that were built all around it, virtually destroyed the oyster beds. The native Olympia oyster, which was once so plentiful that it was used as ballast on ships, was nearly driven to extinction by the 1950s.

Olympias are tough to propagate: the male broadcasts his sperm, but the female keeps her eggs within, taking in the spermy water. Fertilization takes place and larvae develop to swimming size before she expels them and sends them in search of culch, a

piece of shell to which they will attach themselves to grow. But they take three years to get to market size, and that isn't very big at all. So the Taylors and other operators, armed with increased environmental awareness, began to introduce hardier strains, mainly Pacifics, in the cleaned-up tidal flats, and the industry began to come back.

By the late 1970s, hatcheries in the region had become a dependable source of seed, as the larvae are called. Justin buys the seed and transports it, along with the groceries, in the back of his pickup truck. On the day of our visit, he opened an ice chest and carefully took a resealable plastic bag from the chipped ice. In it was a cloth-covered ball, secured with rubber bands. He unwrapped it to reveal what looked like a mass of black, wet sand.

"Twenty million larvae," said Justin Taylor. "Twenty million oysters. And two thousand dollars."

Taylor United will propagate some larvae as is, culchless, for the half-shell market. The larvae will be released directly on the prepared oyster bed, where they will grow until maturity, about eighteen months. Others will be placed in special plastic-mesh growing bags, about 150 larvae to a bag. The bag is then placed on the bed. These protected oysters will have a better yield—only about ten animals will fail to reach maturity, since they are much less vulnerable to predators.

Justin will place still other larvae in a big tank with pulverized shell fragments—culch—on which the larvae will attach themselves. Pacific oysters, for example, which make up the largest segment of the West Coast market, tend to cluster together in a clump on one old shell, making them unsuitable for the half-shell market. Most, but not all, culched larvae will grow in clumps. Clumped oysters are shucked and sold in containers for stewing, frying, or stuffing; they don't bring as good a price as the fine singles. (Interestingly, shucked oysters represent the greater volume of sales on the West Coast; on the East Coast, half-shell oysters win out.) Culched larvae spend about forty-eight hours in the tank, then they are taken to the oyster beds—the soil of the tidal flats, rich with glacial gravel. Of course, the quality of the water and the sea bottom, the topography of the area, and the movements of the tides all have an impact on the oyster. Because of varying currents and water temperatures, some culched oysters mature in two years, others require three.

Taylor United's oyster beds are located in a variety of locations. The company holds 1,500 acres of tidal land, of which 400 acres are farmed. In the rest of the spread either it is too muddy or there is too much wind. But the Taylors work all the time to improve their tidelands, adding gravel and shell to the muck.

In some regions along the coast, if the oysters are kept too close to the bottom, they could have a muddy taste; here, the glacial gravel prevents this. Then, too, if they are too close to the surface, where there is not enough salt in the water, the oyster's life could be at risk. But if you distribute the seed on the tidal flats and leave them to grow there, they will be in and out of the water regularly. When they are exposed at low tide, the oysters close tightly and develop very strong adductor muscles. If they are in a region where there are drills, an oyster predator, the oysters sense their presence and devote more energy to the growing of shell. And the tidal currents roll the oysters around in the sand, causing their shells to take on the characteristic gnarled shape.

Where the waters are deeper, some farmers grow the oysters in lantern nets, a series of shelves strung together inside a protective web, so that they are never out of the water. Since they are not abraded by the sand, their shells are more elegant. And since they don't have to be tightly closed periodically, most of their energy goes into the production of the meat. These are the oysters coveted by the half-shell market, especially on the East Coast.

The Taylor United plant is large and airy. The big Pacifics are brought in in huge baskets. Those for the half-shell market are sorted and bagged in one area. The clumped oysters go to another, where men and women with knives and chain-mail gloves slice into them with blinding speed (top shuckers earn $1,800 to $2,000 per month). A sign at the doorway of the Taylor processing plant reads: "All clams and oysters must be tagged with the name, date, and area harvested." If there is something wrong, this information enables the oyster detectives to trace the problem. Now, as in the early days of Puget Sound oystering, most—more than 80 percent—of the harvest goes to California. A Saturday oyster is Monday dinner in Los Angeles, traveling there by refrigerated truck.

Research to undergird the oyster trade goes on all the time. For example, there is the business of the months without an "r." The reason you don't eat oysters in May, June, July, or August is that those are the months when the creatures get sexy. They devote their energy to the production of egg or sperm, and an oyster in the throes of sexual activity just doesn't taste good. There is a controversial procedure called the triploid process, which in essence consists of bathing newly fertilized eggs with an antibiotic that interferes with ordinary development. In effect, it neuters the baby oyster, which then grows up with a chromosomal aberration that keeps it from getting sexual in the summer. That, in turn, means you can go to market in months without an "r," when other, sexier oysters, diploids, are unfit to eat because of the presence of egg and sperm. Some argue that the triploid is overall not as tasty an oyster and that it would be best to leave things as they are and simply abstain from dining on oysters in the breeding season. But for many the goal is to create sexless oysters—except, of course, for those needed by the hatchery.

So how do they like them? Justin said, "Give me Olympias fried in lots of butter." His son, Bill, is the purist of the family: "Don't wash them. Don't put anything on them. Just open them and eat them."

Oyster Stew

Devoted as he is to oysters in any form, Fred counts this as one of his favorites for the Christmas table.

Serves 8

- 1½ cups Crème Fraîche (page 350)
- 2 jumbo egg yolks
- 1 teaspoon kosher salt
- 1 teaspoon freshly ground white pepper
- 2 teaspoons dry vermouth
- ½ teaspoon Tabasco
- ½ teaspoon Worcestershire sauce
- ½ cup unsalted butter
- ¼ cup finely minced shallots
- 1 bay leaf
- 1 large sprig fresh thyme (lemon thyme, if possible)
- 1 quart shucked oysters with their liquor
- 4 cups half-and-half
- 1 tablespoon minced fresh chives
- 1 tablespoon minced fresh parsley

Softened unsalted butter for garnish

Combine crème fraîche, egg yolks, salt, pepper, vermouth, Tabasco, and Worcestershire in a mixing bowl. Whisk vigorously until very well blended, then set aside.

Using a deep skillet large enough to hold all the ingredients, melt butter over low heat. Add shallots, bay leaf, and thyme sprig, cover with wax paper pressed directly on the vegetables, and sweat until shallots become translucent, about 5 minutes. Discard bay leaf and thyme sprig. Add oysters and half-and-half. Increase heat slightly and simmer briskly until oysters begin to curl.

Working quickly, temper the egg yolk mixture by gradually adding small amounts of hot half-and-half mixture to it, whisking well. Quickly add the tempered yolks to the oyster skillet, stirring constantly until hot. Do not let stew come to a boil or it will curdle. Taste and adjust seasonings.

Ladle stew into heated shallow soup plates and sprinkle with chives and parsley. Garnish with a dollop of butter if you wish.

Wine: Jepson Vineyard Sauvignon Blanc (Mendocino County)

Simply Fried Oysters

Serves 12 as an appetizer, 4 as an entrée

- 24 shucked oysters, with their liquor
- 6 tablespoons milk, or more if necessary
- ⅔ cup unbleached flour, sifted
  Salt and freshly ground white pepper to taste
- 2–3 cups vegetable oil
- 1 jumbo egg

  Lemon slices and finely minced fresh chives and parsley for garnish
- 1¼ cups Rémoulade Sauce (page 203)

Drain oysters and measure liquor. If necessary, add enough milk to make a full ¼ cup and pour into a medium-size mixing bowl. Add 6 tablespoons milk and mix thoroughly. Gradually beat flour into liquid, then add salt and pepper. This should be a fairly thick batter. Add more milk only if batter is too thick to coat the oysters.

Heat oil in a wok, then beat egg in a small bowl. When oil is hot enough to quickly brown a cube of bread, quickly dip each oyster first into the beaten egg and

then into the batter, and then place in the hot wok. Do not crowd. Fry until brown on both sides, about 4 minutes per side. Drain on paper towels, garnish with lemon and herbs, and serve with sauce on the side.

Wine: Flora Springs Wine Company "Soliloquy" (Napa Valley)

Hot and Spicy Sautéed Oysters

Serves 8 as an appetizer

- 6 tablespoons unsalted butter
- 6 tablespoons olive oil
- 2 tablespoons minced shallots
- 2 cloves garlic, minced
- ½ teaspoon kosher salt
- 1 teaspoon freshly ground white pepper
- ½ teaspoon cayenne pepper
- ¼ teaspoon Tabasco
- 4 dozen shucked oysters, with their liquor
- 1 tablespoon dry white wine
  Juice of one lemon, or more to taste
- 2 teaspoons fresh lime juice
- 2 teaspoons Worcestershire sauce
- ⅓ cup minced fresh parsley
- 2 tablespoons minced fresh chives

- 8 toasted slices French bread, rubbed with some olive oil

Fresh parsley sprigs and lemon
slices for garnish

Combine butter and oil in a large skillet
and melt butter over medium heat. Add
shallots and garlic and cook over low heat
for a few minutes, but do not brown. Add
the salt, pepper, cayenne, and Tabasco.
Quickly add the oysters and sauté until the
edges begin to curl. Add remaining ingredients. Turn up the heat and toss the oysters
for 30 seconds. Taste and add more lemon
juice if desired.

Put one round of toast on each of 8
warmed serving plates. Divide the oysters
among the plates, letting some spill off the
toast. Garnish with parsley and lemon.

Wine: Girard Winery Dry Chenin Blanc
(Napa Valley)

Oyster Loaf

Serves 2

      1 loaf crusty Italian bread
      5 tablespoons unsalted butter
      2 teaspoons Tabasco, or more to taste
16–20 shucked oysters, with their liquor
      ½ cup buttermilk
      1 jumbo egg
      1 cup finely ground cornmeal
      1 teaspoon kosher salt
      ¼ teaspoon cayenne pepper
      ¼ teaspoon freshly ground black
        pepper
      5 tablespoons corn flour (available in
        health-food stores)
        Pinch freshly grated nutmeg
   2–3 cups vegetable oil

        Juice of 1 lemon
      1 tablespoon minced fresh chives
      1 tablespoon minced fresh parsley

        Mayonnaise mixed with cayenne
        pepper for garnish

Preheat oven to 425°.

Cut a large oval out of the top of the bread
and scoop out the soft center. Combine butter and 1 teaspoon of the Tabasco in a small
saucepan; melt over low heat. Lightly brush
the inside of the bread shell with some of the
butter mixture and keep remaining butter
warm. Place bread shell on cookie sheet and
bake in preheated oven until lightly
browned, about 5 minutes. Set aside.

Drain oyster liquor into a bowl and combine with buttermilk, remaining Tabasco,
and egg; mix well. In another bowl, combine cornmeal with salt, cayenne pepper,
black pepper, corn flour, and nutmeg and
blend.

Heat oil in a wok. When oil is hot
enough to quickly brown a cube of bread,
quickly dip each oyster first into beaten
milk mixture and then into the cornmeal
mixture, then place in the hot oil. Repeat
with remaining oysters, but do not crowd
them in the wok. Fry until nicely brown on
both sides, about 3 minutes. Drain on paper
towels and keep warm while you fry remaining oysters.

Place cooked oysters in prepared bread
shell. Quickly add lemon juice, chives, and
parsley to remaining butter mixture and
pour over oysters. Slice bread in half and
serve with cayenne mayonnaise on the side.

Wine: William Wheeler Chardonnay
(Sonoma County)

Ian W. Jefferds

Penn Cove Mussels

P.O. Box 148

Coupeville, Washington 98239

(206) 678-4803

Whidbey Island is in upper Puget Sound, an hour and a half northwest of Seattle; it is the longest island in the continental United States. In a region known for lush forests, Whidbey is a farming island of meadows, pastures, and bare, undulating hills.

In the early 1970s, Peter Jefferds, an army officer who had a particular fondness for mussels, decided to retire there. He and his wife, Beryl, were devoted students of the iridescent beauties; they decided that the icy waters of Whidbey's Penn Cove would be a perfect place to start a mussel farm. After study in Spain, Peter and Beryl planted their first mussel seed in 1975, making Penn Cove America's oldest operating commercial mussel farm. Ian and Rawle Jefferds soon joined their parents in the project, and, with Ian's wife, Karen, bought the business from them in 1986.

While a very popular shellfish in Europe, mussels were nearly impossible to find in American fish stores and restaurants in 1975. Wild mussels grew on both coasts, but they were ignored by all but a few true aficionados. Quality was uneven and it was almost impossible to purge them of the sand. If you ate mussels, you ate grit. Peter learned early on, however, that quality control and excessive sand are not problems with farmed mussels.

Three species of common blue mussels are found wild on both coasts—on the East Coast, *Mytilus edulis;* on the West Coast between California and Oregon, *Mytilus galloprovencialis;* and between Washington and Alaska, *Mytilus trossu-*

lus—the variety cultivated at Penn Cove. In farmed form, *M. trossulus* is character-ized by a fairly thin shell and pale ivory meat and is usually about 2½ inches long.

Penn Cove utilizes the spawn from wild native mussels right at its location. All mussels spawn in late spring; there is a lesser spawn in the fall as well. The spawn hatches at once. Within a few weeks, the wild larvae metamorphose into mussel shape and naturally attach themselves to one of thousands of collection lines hung from Penn Cove's 40x80-foot rafts. Once planted, the larvae extrude byssel threads (the beard), which strengthen their attachment to the rope's surface. As the mussels grow, the rafts have to be surrounded by long nets to protect the mussels from thousands of diving ducks that would prefer to pick cultivated mus-sels off the suspended ropes than to forage for wild ones on the ocean floor.

When the young mussels reach ¾ inch in length, they are stripped from the col-lection ropes, or seed lines, and transplanted into 20-foot net "socks" that are then hung from the rafts. These socks are made of a very flexible material. Gradually, as the mussels grow, they grow through the net socks completely and the sock becomes nothing but a rope in the middle of a big mass of mussels. Once the mussels reach ap-proximately 2 inches in length, they need no further protection from hungry ducks.

This method of culture keeps the mussels in the top part of the water, nearest their food source. Farmed mussels feed efficiently, sifting algae and other plankton from the constantly moving water and taking only a year to reach maturity. Be-cause they grow so fast in this environment (wild mussels can take two to three years to grow 2 inches), they develop a thinner shell and more energy goes into growth of meat, ultimately yielding more meat per pound. Since they are never near the bottom, they never pick up sand and grit; in fact, Penn Cove mussels never need to be purged of sand. This saves a step in preparation and makes them very popular with chefs.

Mussels are stripped from the lines, brought up on a conveyor belt, cleaned, and graded; those that are too small get socked up and returned to the water for more development. Every shell that is opened is tapped; if it doesn't close instant-ly, it is presumed dead and discarded.

The process is so efficient that mussels are delivered to the customer less than twenty-four hours after they left the water. Each custom-packed 10- or 25-pound bag of mussels is dated and given a certification number, then sold to a wholesaler, broker, or restaurant in Washington or elsewhere around the country. When properly stored, buried in ice, mussels have a shelf life of about a week, but Ian Jefferds prefers to deliver more often to his customers.

Penn Cove also farms oysters, although not in this bay, since the seed spillover from the mussels would result in oysters covered with wild mussels and barnacles. They are growing two varieties of Pacific oysters: Lasqueti golden, with a fluted and light-colored shell and very briny meat, and Penn Cove select, a thicker and coarser oyster that is beach-raised. They have recently added a European oyster called Lasqueti flat, kin to the French belon. The oysters are kept in a lantern net, a series of shelves strung together inside a protective webbing, which is suspended from a raft on the surface of the water so they, too, have a nonstop flow of food. This way, they stay out of the mud and develop a beautiful shell, making them prized by restaurants.

In 1990, Penn Cove processed nearly 500,000 pounds of mussels. They expect to handle 1 million pounds by the mid-1990s. Their oyster production is still considerably smaller, but the potential for growth is substantial as people realize just how delicious these Pacific oysters can be.

Since no visit to Penn Cove would be complete without a plate of their wonderful products, we headed for nearby Coupeville and Toby's Tavern, a smoky hundred-year-old building all paneled in dark wood, with a big bar at one end and a pool table in the middle. There, seated by windows overlooking the bay, we feasted on huge bowls of steaming Penn Cove mussels, while Ian showed us how to use one-half of a mussel shell as a spoon to scoop out all the others. The meat was sweet, moist, and tender.

"The bottom line," Ian told us, "is sitting down to lunch with someone, giving him a bowl of mussels, and seeing him enjoy them. That's what all this comes down to."

Ian's Favorite Marinated Mussels

Ian Jefferds of Penn Cove Mussels tells us that there are, on average, 35 farmed mussels to the pound and 20 wild mussels to the pound. To serve this as an appetizer, presume an average of 5 farmed mussels per person. This dish goes well with cold beer—it's too acidic for wine.

Serves 20–28 as an appetizer

- ½ cup dry white wine
- ¼ cup chopped shallots or scallions (white part only)
- 2 cloves garlic, minced, or more to taste
- 1 tablespoon minced fresh parsley
- 1 tablespoon minced fresh basil or thyme
- 4 tablespoons unsalted butter
- 4 pounds Penn Cove mussels, rinsed and debearded

MARINADE
- ½ gallon cider vinegar
- 2½ cups sugar
- ½ large red onion, thinly sliced
- ½ cup chopped scallions (white part only)
- 2 tablespoons chopped pimientos
- 2 tablespoons chopped garlic
  Freshly ground black pepper to taste

Place wine, scallions, garlic, parsley, basil, and butter in a large, heavy saucepan and bring to a boil over high heat. Add mussels and cover pan. Steam for 5–6 minutes, or until shells are open and meats are opaque. Remove from heat.

Remove steamed mussels from the broth and set in a large bowl in the refrigerator to chill. Discard any mussels that did not open.

To make the marinade, combine vinegar and sugar in a mixing bowl and stir until sugar is dissolved. Add remaining ingredients. Pour marinade over the thoroughly chilled mussels. Drain marinade, then pour it over mussels again. Repeat this process several times to make certain that all mussels are soaked. Pour mussels and marinade back into bowl, cover, and keep refrigerated until mussels are ready to be served, at least an hour but not more than a week. Be sure to pour marinade over mussels right before serving.

Sinful Mussel Stew

Like Peter and Beryl Jefferds, Linda has been devoted to mussels for years. She still remembers a wonderful week in Brussels when she ate them at least twice a day. This recipe is based on the French *mouclades*— or mussels on the half shell. It is wonderfully rich and satisfying. Do not debeard the mussels ahead or they will die and spoil. Serve this with some good French bread and a big salad for a satisfying supper.

Serves 6

- 1 cup Crème Fraîche (page 350)
- 3 jumbo egg yolks
- 4 tablespoons unsalted butter
- ½ teaspoon curry powder
  Pinch powdered saffron
  Pinch cayenne pepper
- ⅓ cup finely minced shallots
- 3 tablespoons fresh lemon juice
- 4 pounds mussels, scrubbed and debearded
- 1 clove garlic
- 2 cups Sauvignon Blanc or Sancerre wine
  Salt and freshly ground white pepper to taste

  Minced fresh parsley and chives for garnish

Preheat oven to 250°.

Combine crème fraîche and egg yolks in a small bowl and whisk thoroughly. Set aside.

In a medium-size saucepan, melt the butter over medium heat, then add the curry powder, saffron, and cayenne; stir for 1 minute. Add shallots and cook just until they become translucent. Add lemon juice and set aside.

While shallots are cooking, combine mussels, garlic, and wine in a heavy six-quart pot. Cover and cook over high heat, shaking from time to time, until the mussels open, about 3–5 minutes. Remove mussels from the broth with a slotted spoon; discard any that haven't opened, along with garlic clove. Remove and discard top shell from good mussels and place these mussels in a large ovenproof dish. Cover dish with foil and place in a larger dish or pan filled with hot water. Place both dishes in the oven to keep warm.

Strain wine mixture through cheesecloth to eliminate any grit, then add to saucepan with shallots and return to medium heat. When mixture is very hot, temper the reserved egg-yolk mixture by adding some hot wine mixture to it, a bit at a time, whisking well. When yolk mixture is warmed, add all of it to shallot saucepan, reduce heat to low, and stir constantly for 4 minutes. Do not allow soup to get too hot or it will curdle. Mixture should be creamy but not thick. Add salt and pepper.

Arrange mussels in large, shallow soup plates (concentric circles are beautiful if you have the patience). Ladle soup over the mussels, sprinkle with parsley and chives, and serve.

Wine: Long Vineyards Sauvignon Blanc (Napa Valley)

Warm Ragout
of Mussels and Scallops

Serves 8 as an appetizer

- ½ cup unsalted butter
- 1 pound scallions, chopped (including ½ inch of green)
- 2 leeks, washed, trimmed, and chopped
- ⅔ cup chopped sweet onion
- ¼ cup minced shallots
- 1 small dried red chile pepper, crumbled
- ½ cup Fish Fûmet (page 204)
- ¼ cup Chardonnay wine
- ¼ cup minced fresh parsley
- ¼ cup minced cilantro
- 1½ teaspoons curry powder
  Salt and freshly ground white pepper to taste
- 1 cup heavy cream
- 1 pint bay scallops
- 1 pint shucked mussels

  Golden caviar for garnish
  Cilantro and fresh parsley for garnish

In a heavy sauté pan, melt 4 tablespoons of the butter over low heat. Add scallions, leeks, onion, shallots, and chile; toss to coat well. Cook mixture for 2 minutes, stirring often. Cover with a sheet of wax paper pressed directly on the vegetables and sweat over low heat until onions are tender, about 15 minutes.

Discard wax paper and add stock, wine, parsley, cilantro, and curry powder. Stir over medium heat for a few minutes. Then remove sauté pan from heat and purée contents in the bowl of a food processor fitted with the metal blade.

Return puree to the sauté pan and add salt, pepper, and cream. Heat slowly, stirring often. Adjust seasonings.

Melt remaining butter in a large skillet. When hot, add scallops and mussels. Toss often over medium-high heat until scallops are opaque, about 2 minutes.

Combine shellfish and sauce. Divide among 8 warm small gratin dishes and garnish with a dollop of caviar and fresh herbs.

Wine: Acacia Winery Chardonnay (Carneros)

Curtis Hutcherson

1733 Acadian Drive

Houma, Louisiana 70363

(504) 876-4564

Curtis Hutcherson is a handsome middle-aged man who has been shrimping all his life. He goes out regularly in his 45-foot diesel-powered boat with his helper, 6 tons of ice, and 600 gallons of diesel fuel, plying the close-in waters for brown shrimp in May and white shrimp from August to December. He tests the waters first, deploying a small "try-net" to see if there is enough to make it worth putting out the big ones. It costs a lot to outfit the boat to go out; Curtis says he needs to catch about 500 pounds of shrimp a day to make it.

The shrimp boat drawing up its nets makes you think of an angel's arms outstretched in benediction. The vessel's two long booms pull up the nets, which trail into the water like the folds of long flowing sleeves. The nets are roughly cone-shaped. The open leading edge is wide, maybe 40 feet, and held open by a set of trawl boards. There are floats on the top of it and weights on the bottom. For hours the boat moves slowly through the coastal and estuarial waters. The nets, immersed just below the surface on each side, at right angles to the boat, gather up thousands of the shrimp that flourish in these rich Louisiana waters.

The nets, heavily laden if it has been a lucky day, are drawn up and their contents spilled out onto a huge sorting tray. Lucky fish, squid, and other noncommercial creatures of the deep are culled out and tossed back, returned to the food chain. The shrimp are destined for an icy hold, for safekeeping until the boat gets back to shore. The boat may be out for several days before concern for the cargo, or a shortage of ice or fuel, requires a return.

Curtis likes to catch and deliver quickly, so he does not make the longer journeys into the gulf, where the season has no limits and where, with a larger boat, you can stay out for two weeks or longer. He also prefers to chill the shrimp with their heads on. Browns can hold for seven days with their heads, whites ten days. But if they are to be on ice in the boat for longer than that, they must have the heads removed before they are stowed.

His father, Rudolph, is an old-time Cajun netman. In his late seventies, he still mends, rigs, and fits the tools of his son's trade. Rudolph was widowed a few years ago, but he is always attended by members of his family and nearby friends. The talk seems always to be about food and the catching of it, and about the problems that make the shrimper's life ever more uncertain.

Among the people whose lives are connected so directly to the waters around them, there is an undercurrent of pessimism, a sense that it is a bad time for shrimpers of Terrebonne Parish.

Nowadays, shrimp nets must be fitted with a TED, an acronym for turtle excluder device, which supposedly senses the presence of any large sea turtle that may unwittingly wander into the net and triggers the opening of the cone end of the net, releasing everything that is in it, including whatever shrimp have been caught—and very occasionally a turtle. The shrimp fishermen chafe against the rule, made, they say, by people who haven't the vaguest notion of how their craft works. Since most shrimpers never caught a single turtle, and the rare one caught was seldom endangered, they resent the TED, which slows the boat, burning extra fuel.

But environmentalists insist the TED is here to stay. Eventually, the shrimpers will have to adjust, or perhaps a better device will be developed.

Furthermore, the oil companies have left their mark. Wherever there is drilling, there is always detritus. And as hard as the companies might try, there will always be spills. In addition, much of the drilling is shallow. As oil has been pumped out, the earth beneath the shallow waters has settled, deepening the swamps and fundamentally changing wildlife habitats. Effluent from sewage systems, agricultural runoff, and industrial pollution has also had an impact. The Army Corps of Engineers is no friend of the shrimpers, either. It has created an inland waterway southwest from New Orleans to the gulf to facilitate shipping. But this waterway acts as a funnel in bad weather, allowing storm-driven seawater to flood areas deep inland. There is also the erosion of the coastal islands that in the past had acted as a protective storm barrier. So hurricanes, which can be so devastating to the estuarial waters on which these people depend, now upset the ecosystem over enormous stretches of the bayou country.

And there is the constant threat that one day the Mississippi, which wants desperately to change its course, may overrule the Army Corps of Engineers, leave its present banks, and flow west into the Atchafalaya, thereby eliminating many shrimp beds.

This is legendary Cajun country. Nearby are towns with names like Montequt, Presque Isle, Petit Caillou, Chauvin, and Bourg. Many of the houses stand on 9-foot stilts, in case there is another hurricane. The shrimp boats are tied up along the narrow bayou. And strangers who venture into this country are treated as though they are members of the family, long-lost friends.

On Rudolph Hutcherson's patio a dozen or more people are enjoying his hospitality and the fruit of his conviction that one does not cook just for oneself.

"How long will all of this last?" we asked Rudolph about his famous home-made jambalaya. "Depends on how many people know about it," he answered. He had made several jars of fig preserves and he saw that everyone had some to take home. He likes the preserves as an accent with the jambalaya. "Don't worry about the calories," he told everybody. "Fish don't have 'em anyway. You can eat fish like candy. And the preserves—you just cook 'em hard and fast and you kill the calories."

Bayou-Style Boiled Shrimp

If you've never been, you have to go to Sportsman's Paradise in Chauvin, Louisiana; the food there, prepared under Connie Scheer's watchful eye, is simply wonderful. Allow enough time to go fishing for the region's delicious speckled trout and to tour the beautiful bayous and swamps. You can buy the crab boil called for in this recipe by writing directly to Zatarain's Inc., New Orleans, Louisiana 70114.

Serves 2–4, depending on appetites

> 3 tablespoons kosher salt
> 1 3-ounce bag Zatarain's Crab Boil (see above)
> 2 lemons, sliced
> 2 tablespoons cayenne pepper
> 4 pounds large raw shrimp, unpeeled, preferably with heads still attached

In a large stockpot, combine 3 quarts water, salt, crab boil, lemons, and cayenne. Bring mixture to a rolling boil and add shrimp. Boil for 6–10 minutes, depending upon size. Shrimp are done when you can see a bit of space between the shrimp and their shells. Remove from heat and quickly add lots of ice to pot. Let stand for 5 minutes. (This helps the shrimp to absorb some of the flavors of the seasonings.) Drain and serve in large bowls. Break the heads from the body, peel off the shells, and enjoy. If you are a real aficionado, suck the juices from the heads.

Wine: DeLoach Vineyards White Zinfandel (Sonoma County)

Shrimp with Legendary Rémoulade Sauce

When Linda was a bride of just six months, she found herself preparing a New Year's Day party for a hundred guests. Since that day in 1961, shrimp with rémoulade sauce has been a house specialty.

Serves 8 as an entrée, 16 as an appetizer (Makes 1 quart sauce)

RÉMOULADE SAUCE

- 3 teaspoons dry mustard
- 3 cups homemade mayonnaise
- 2 jumbo hard-boiled eggs, coarsely chopped
- 3 tablespoons capers
- 2 ounces flat anchovies, rinsed, dried, and coarsely chopped
- ⅓ cup minced fresh parsley
- ⅓ cup minced fresh chives
- 1 tablespoon Worcestershire sauce
- ¼ cup chili sauce
- ¼ cup grated fresh horseradish
- 1 teaspoon Tabasco
  Zest of 1 lemon, finely minced
- 1 quart Fish Fûmet (page 204)
- 750 ml. Sauvignon Blanc wine
- 2 shallots, finely minced
- 3 bay leaves
- 2 lemons, thinly sliced
- 1 tablespoon salt
- 1 tablespoon black peppercorns, bruised
- 1 tablespoon mustard seed
- 4 pounds raw shrimp, unpeeled

At least 5 days before serving, blend mustard with mayonnaise in a large bowl. Gently fold in the remaining sauce ingredients and blend evenly. Pour into a container that has a tight lid and refrigerate until needed. (Sauce will keep well for several weeks if stored properly.)

The day of serving, combine 1 quart water, stock, and wine in a large stockpot. Bring to a boil, then add remaining ingredients. Bring to a boil again, and boil an additional 5–10 minutes, depending on the size of the shrimp. Turn off the heat, add a big bowl of ice, and let stand for 5 minutes. Drain shrimp and chill.

If shrimp are to be served as an entrée, let people peel their own shrimp at the table. Otherwise, peel ahead, after chilling. Serve with rémoulade sauce on the side.

Wine: Domaine Carneros Sparkling Wine Brut (Carneros)
or *Schramsberg Vineyards Blanc de Noirs, Late Disgorged* (Napa Valley)

Chauvin Shrimp, Smoked Sausage, and Okra Gumbo

When we talked with Connie Scheer at Sportsman's Paradise in Chauvin, Louisiana, she said that the women who make her wonderful gumbo begin with lots of okra and onions and cook them long and slow; they do not make a roux. Having this dish at home is almost as wonderful as eating it at Connie's!

Serves 4–6

- 3 tablespoons vegetable oil
- 1½ pounds okra, trimmed and sliced
- 1½ pounds onions, chopped
- 3 cloves garlic, chopped
- 2 fresh cayenne peppers, chopped
- 1 cup chopped red, green, or yellow bell peppers
- 1 pound andouille sausage, sliced and browned
- 2 teaspoons kosher salt
- 1½ teaspoons freshly ground black pepper
- 1½ teaspoons freshly ground white pepper
- ½ teaspoon cayenne pepper

2 teaspoons fresh thyme
¼ cup chopped fresh parsley
2 bay leaves
2 pounds very ripe tomatoes, peeled and chopped
3 cups Fish Fûmet (recipe follows)
Tabasco to taste
1 pound raw shrimp, peeled and deveined
3 cups cooked rice, preferably jasmine

Chopped chives for garnish

Heat oil in a 5-quart pot. Add okra and onions and cook over low heat, stirring often, until mixture is thoroughly softened, about 1 hour. Toward the end of the hour, the okra will turn quite golden and the pot will need frequent scraping. Add garlic, fresh peppers, sausage, salt, and ground peppers. Cook over medium heat for 10 minutes, stirring frequently. Add herbs, tomatoes, and fish fûmet. Reduce heat, cover, and simmer for 1½ hours. Taste, add Tabasco, and adjust seasonings. Shortly before serving, bring mixture to a fast simmer. Add shrimp and cook for 6–10 minutes, depending on size of shrimp. Serve over rice and sprinkle with chopped chives.

Wine: Elk Cove Vineyards Pinot Gris (Willamette Valley, Oregon)

Fish Fûmet

Let your fish merchant know a few days ahead of time that you want to make a fish fûmet so that he has time to gather some good bones for you. Do not use bones from strongly flavored fish, like tuna, or oily fish, like mackerel. Please note that when we sweat the vegetables we do not use butter, because fat will make the stock rather cloudy.

Makes 7 cups

2 cups chopped onion
1 cup chopped carrots
1 cup chopped celery
3 pounds fish heads, bones, and trimmings
1 bunch celery
1 bay leaf
2 sprigs fresh thyme
10 white peppercorns, bruised
1 teaspoon fennel seed
1 strip orange peel
2 cups Sauvignon Blanc wine

In a large stockpot, place onions, carrots, chopped celery, and 1 quart water. Cover with wax paper placed directly on the vegetables and bring to a boil. Reduce heat immediately and simmer for 15 minutes. Discard wax paper, then add 1½ quarts more water and the remaining ingredients. Bring to a boil, reduce heat to a very brisk simmer, and cook for 1 hour. Remove scum as it accumulates on the surface of the liquid.

After 1 hour, remove from heat. Use a large, flat Chinese strainer to remove as much of the fish and vegetables as you easily can. Then pour stock through a colander that has been lined with two layers of cheesecloth. Return stock to a clean pot and simmer until fûmet is reduced to 7 cups. Chill until ready to use.

Harold and Cheryl Bowers

Route 1, Box 534
Palacios, Texas 77465
(512) 972-2737

Harold Bowers has lived in the Palacios (pronounced like pa-*la*-shus) area all his life. He started growing rice as soon as he graduated from high school, in 1958. In the mid-seventies, Harold added some row crops to his rice operation—corn, soybeans, and milo. He and Cheryl initially thought about shrimp farming back in 1985, when it was first discussed in their region. It made economic sense to diversify. But they quickly learned that while the folks at the Texas Department of Agriculture encouraged this new activity, the Texas Parks and Wildlife Department discouraged it. To one group it made sense in terms of providing farming opportunities for the community, but the other group feared that it could cause biological contamination of the Gulf of Mexico if some farmed species of shrimp were washed into the gulf.

There are all kinds of regulations the Bowerses must follow. For example, because the shrimp are an exotic, or introduced, species, one rule states that in the event of a hurricane the farmer must kill his shrimp to prevent their being washed live into the gulf. The chemicals required for this have to be kept on hand at all times. So consider this scenario. It is near harvesttime. The shrimp have been fed $100,000 worth of fish meal. A big storm is coming; the authorities order the kill, then the storm veers off in another direction or dies down. The Bowerses will have lost everything, and there is no insurance to protect against this.

The
Bowerses have 50 acres of
ponds. Harold dug them in an old worn-
out field, 100 yards or so from the gulf. They built a pier
into the water to support the intake pipes through which water from the
gulf is pumped to the ponds. Another rule required filtering this intake water, even
though it didn't seem especially necessary. A specific size mesh for the filter was
prescribed. But it was so fine that the water just wouldn't go through it. They were
stymied until Harold appealed the rule and convinced the officials that their fine
filter wouldn't work.

Each spring the Bowerses begin by preparing the pond water for the arrival
of seed stock, or PLs (post larvae). They add nitrogen and cottonseed meal to the
water to create an algal bloom on which the PLs will feed to get started. Then, in
May or June, the PLs arrive in plastic bags, which are kept cool in Styrofoam
boxes. The bags are put into a large vat of pond water for half a day so they will get

acclimated to the local temperature. Then the PLs go into the pond. There are 19,000 PLs per box, and on one day the Bowerses may unload 76 boxes. They got their first seed stock from Panama. Now the larvae come from Laguna Madre, a few miles down the Texas coast, which makes things simpler and less costly.

The larvae grow quickly and will be ready for a fall harvest. There should be a 60 percent survival rate, and the Bowerses are pleased they often do better than that.

As the shrimp grow, it is necessary to aerate the ponds. Electric paddle wheels mounted on rafts turn all the time, churning the water. If the electricity fails, or even if it weakens, the process stops and the shrimp die. There are also dangerous viruses that can destroy a crop. And aquatic birds eat more than their share. In fact, Harold and Cheryl use the same kind of propane guns at the ponds as they do in their rice fields to scare away birds.

The shrimp, as well as the water, are tested twice a day for contamination, temperature variation, and other problems. Two employees paddle across the ponds four times a day, feeding the shrimp with fish meal manufactured in Idaho. The rations contain 45 percent protein, which is reduced to 35 percent protein later in the season. Shrimp are fairly efficient; 3 pounds of food convert to 1 pound of shrimp.

Harold and Cheryl used to grow the big *Penaeus stylirostrus* shrimp, which run 6 to 8 per pound. But they found the species too fragile and suffered a considerable loss from it. Now they raise *Penaeus vannamei,* a much hardier species, which run 18 to the pound.

When the shrimp are mature, all hands gather for the harvest. The ponds are drained, one by one, into huge catch basins. At first, the Bowerses tied big net bags onto the drainpipe. When the bag was full of shrimp, they would close the valve and put on another bag. It was exhausting work. Now the shrimp are mechanically scooped out of the escaping water and put onto a conveyor belt that carries them to vats of ice water. They are killed instantly by hypothermia. As the water in the pond gets lower, high-powered jets of seawater from hand-held hoses are used to wash any reluctant shrimp into the catch basin. After the pond is empty, some shrimp still remain. Harold and Cheryl, their family, their employees, and extra hired help harvest the remainder by hand off the bottom of the drained pond.

If all goes well, they will ultimately harvest 3,000 pounds per acre. With 43 acres under cultivation, they could have 129,000 pounds of shrimp that sells for $3 per pound—more than a third of a million dollars from one crop. Needless to say, that would be ideal circumstances. And that is before the Bowerses' considerable expenses have been deducted, although they do get a better price for their shrimp because of its freshness and high quality.

Their next goal, however, is to develop a successful marketing strategy. Shrimp boats are often out for a week or two before their harvest is brought ashore and sold. All these shrimp are sold frozen. The Bowerses' farmed shrimp are chilled at the instant of harvest and ready for sale all in one day. The advantage is obvious. Harold and Cheryl want to sell directly to markets where such freshness is worth a little something extra.

Instead of being tempted to pull the plug on a complicated, challenging, and sometimes frustrating operation, Harold Bowers is doing what all creative, pioneering people do, whatever their calling. He is persevering.

Shrimp and Corn Chowder

Serves 6–8

- 1 pound raw shrimp, peeled, deveined, and coarsely chopped
- 1 teaspoon minced fresh ginger
- ¼ cup Sauvignon Blanc wine
- 5 ears fresh corn
- 4 cups rich chicken stock
- 2 cups milk
- 1 teaspoon kosher salt
- ½ teaspoon freshly ground white pepper
- 1 cup Crème Fraîche (page 350)
- 2 tablespoons minced cilantro
- 2 tablespoons minced fresh chives

Combine shrimp, ginger, and wine in a small bowl and mix well. Set aside.

Using a very sharp knife, carefully slice corn kernels off the cobs. Place corn and cobs in a large saucepan with stock, milk, salt, and pepper. Bring mixture to a brisk simmer over medium heat; reduce heat to low, cover, and cook until kernels are tender, about 25 minutes. Remove from heat and discard cobs.

Using a slotted spoon, transfer half of the cooked kernels into the bowl of a food processor fitted with the metal blade. Pulse until corn becomes a smooth puree. Add puree to saucepan and whisk until well blended. Return saucepan to heat and add shrimp mixture and crème fraîche. Simmer until shrimp is opaque and soup is hot, about 5 minutes. Taste and adjust seasonings.

Ladle into heated soup plates and garnish with cilantro and chives.

Wine: Calera Wine Company Chardonnay (Santa Barbara County)

Texas Spicy Shrimp with Hot Sauce

Serves 6

SAUCE
- 2–3 tablespoons olive oil
- ½ cup finely chopped green bell pepper
- ½ cup finely chopped red bell pepper
- ½ cup minced red onion
- ½ cup minced scallion (white part only)
- 1 cup chopped celery
- 1 tablespoon finely minced garlic
- 6 cups peeled, seeded, and diced fresh tomatoes
- 1 tablespoon Worcestershire sauce
- 1 tablespoon minced fresh thyme
- 1 tablespoon minced cilantro
- 1 tablespoon lemon zest
- 1 teaspoon freshly ground white pepper
- 2 teaspoons Tabasco
- 1 tablespoon fresh lemon juice

- 2 cups unbleached flour
- ½ teaspoon salt
- 1 teaspoon freshly ground black pepper
- 2 jumbo eggs
- 1 cup beer
- 1 tablespoon Tabasco
- 2 cups vegetable oil
- 24 large raw shrimp, peeled and deveined
- 3 cups cooked rice, preferably jasmine, buttered

Fresh herbs and sliced lemons for garnish

To make the sauce, heat the olive oil in a large, heavy skillet; add peppers, onion, scallion, celery, and garlic and sauté until vegetables are wilted. Add remaining sauce ingredients and cook over medium-low heat for 20 minutes, or until tomatoes are very tender.

While sauce is cooking, prepare shrimp batter. Put flour, salt, and 1 teaspoon black pepper in a shallow bowl and blend well. Mix eggs, beer, and 1 tablespoon Tabasco in another bowl and beat thoroughly. Combine the two mixtures and blend.

Heat vegetable oil in a large skillet until very hot. Coat shrimp with batter and fry, a few at a time, until golden brown, about 5 minutes. Drain on paper towels and keep warm while you fry remaining shrimp.

Serve fried shrimp on a bed of rice with a dollop of sauce. Garnish with herbs and lemon slices. Pass more sauce on the side.

Wine: Domaine Montreaux Sparkling Wine "Brut" (Napa Valley)

Skewered Shrimp

These make a wonderful appetizer. Or serve them with Algesa's Spinach and Feta Pie (page 7) and salad for a delicious and simple supper.

Serves 4 as an entrée, 6–8 as an appetizer

MARINADE
    Juice of 3 limes
    ½ cup vegetable oil
    1 tablespoon minced garlic
    1 tablespoon minced shallots
    1 tablespoon minced cilantro
    1 teaspoon freshly ground white pepper
    1 teaspoon cayenne pepper
    1 teaspoon ground cumin
    Salt and freshly ground black pepper to taste
    2 pounds large raw shrimp, peeled and deveined
    ½ cup unsalted butter or margarine, melted
    1 teaspoon medium-hot chile powder
    1 red bell pepper, cut into 8 1-inch squares

    Lime quarters and minced cilantro for garnish

Combine marinade ingredients in a glass dish and whisk vigorously. Add shrimp and toss thoroughly, so that shrimp are completely coated. Cover dish with plastic wrap, place in refrigerator, and marinate for several hours, turning at least once.

Soak 8 bamboo skewers in water for 30 minutes. Meanwhile, thoroughly clean the surface of a gas or charcoal grill with a metal brush; then coat the surface evenly with Pam. Heat the grill until very hot.

Combine melted butter with chile powder and blend well. Remove shrimp from marinade and thread about 4 shrimp on each prepared skewer. Add a square of red pepper to the end of each skewer. Place skewers across grill and baste with melted butter mixture. Grill for 2–3 minutes on each side. Garnish with lime quarters and minced cilantro.

Wine: Preston Vineyards Chenin Blanc (Dry Creek Valley)

Seth Garfield

Cuttyhunk Shellfish Farms

Box 51

Cuttyhunk, Massachusetts 02713

(808) 636-2072

"On a clear day you can see the Vineyard," said Patrick Flynn from one of the high hills of Cuttyhunk Island. A high school student and one of the "summer folk," young Patrick has become an expert with oyster lines and cages through his years of work with science teacher and oyster farmer Seth Garfield.

Cuttyhunk is one of the Elizabeth Islands, between Buzzards Bay to the northeast and Vineyard Sound to the southwest. Cuttyhunk Island is small, about 2 miles long. People walk or use golf carts and bicycles. There is a wealth of wildlife; deer meander everywhere. Thousands of water birds come by for the summer. There is glorious sailing and outstanding fishing. The beaches are pristine; the quiet is deafening.

Seth Garfield, a great-great-grandson of President James Garfield's, was a zoology major at the University of Rhode Island. After graduating in 1978, he realized that oyster and clam farming just might be the wave of the future. He had access to one of the finest possible farm sites in the Northeast. So with the encouragement of his wife, Dorothy, he began to do his homework.

The greatest obstacle to aquaculture is often people who complain that farm sites hamper recreational activities or interfere with commercial fisheries. Seth, however, believed the people of Cuttyhunk would understand and approve of his plan. And he was right; he had no trouble getting support for aquaculture in these waters.

Seth began by growing both oysters and clams. But he abandoned the clam farming because there was such a plentiful supply of wild clams nearby. Today, he farms oysters and harvests wild clams.

Seth grows two species of oysters, the American (*Crassostria virginica*), known in his parts as the Cuttyhunk, and the European flat (*Ostrea edulus*), the belon. He begins by buying oyster seed, usually when it is about ⅛ inch long. It will take the seed between one to three years to grow. Seth raises culchless oysters, which means that they grow separately, or singly—not in clumps on old shells. These will be premium oysters, not for shucking and canning but for the half-shell trade. In fact, there is little demand for shucked oysters along the East Coast.

The oysters are grown in long nets enclosed in protective cages, which in turn are suspended from the surface of the water. There are about 350 oysters in each net. This kind of "off-bottom" aquaculture allows the farmer to manage the

animal density, giving him better quality control, something especially important for culchless oysters. Seth and his helpers monitor the nets frequently, moving the oysters as they grow, and sorting the nets to prevent overcrowding and to allow room for uniform development. With 1,200 nets to deal with, this is a labor-intensive operation.

Seth farms in two locations. The West End Pond, a salt-water bay virtually surrounded by land, is his primary site from November to April. There he uses only 10 of the 50 acres available to him. Sheltered from the rough seas, yet rich in phytoplankton, the food of oysters, it is a perfect place for the oysters in winter. In summer, the West End Pond becomes a water-bird center. So Seth moves all the nets and cages he needs for his summer harvest to another farm site, a 2-acre area of water off tiny Penikese Island, a short boat ride across Cuttyhunk Harbor. The fairly calm, cold waters yield a medium-sized oyster that is extremely sweet and crisp. These are raw-bar oysters at their absolute best.

Cuttyhunk Harbor is usually filled with boats of all sizes. It's a perfect place to drop anchor for the night, well sheltered from rough seas, yet with beautiful beaches nearby. To take advantage of this ready-made market for fresh seafood, Seth started the Raw Bar, a food stand, in a small shed right on the dock, selling oysters, shrimp Seth bought from local fishermen, and clams he dredged himself. People would buy a plate or two, complete with cocktail sauce and crackers. The Raw Bar took off. And from it grew a Floating Raw Bar; every night Seth's employees take the *Half Shell* and float among the sailboats in the harbor, selling plates of briny-fresh oysters, littleneck and cherrystone clams, and boiled shrimp. And now the *Down Island Raw Bar*, another boat—this one going "down-island" toward the Cape to Naushon Island, the largest of the Elizabeths—is in operation, as well as a catering business that is active on the mainland.

In summer he sells all the oysters he can harvest, all the littlenecks and cherrystones he can dredge, right from his boats. In winter he has a waiting list of mainland wholesale customers. One of his favorites is New York's Grand Central Oyster Bar. "Our oysters can be on their tables less than twenty-four hours from harvest. That makes them really fresh," Seth said.

In season there are fifteen to twenty employees, mostly summering kids with their families on the island or students from South Dartmouth Friends Academy, where Seth has been teaching general science and environmental issues for a number of years. His two careers complement and support each other. In winter, Seth operates the oyster farm with four or five students who weekend on the island with him, harvesting oysters in the West End Pond. There is generally a hurried midweek trip as well.

"Whatever the weather, we'd go out," said Patrick Flynn. These are the tough ones who enjoy the adventure of the frigid thirty-minute trip from Padanaram Harbor across the rough waters of Buzzards Bay no matter how fierce the elements. "We wear protective clothing, and stay within the small shelter at the front of the boat, a twenty-four-foot Privateer," said Seth. "It's all part of living with Mother Nature."

The summer of 1991 was a good reminder of lessons to be learned. The poor economy kept tourism down. Seth anticipated that and didn't even start his Down Island Raw Bar. Also, the starfish, crabs, and drills—natural predators of the oyster—were especially abundant. But the clam operation was doing well. "We'd bring up between two thousand and nine thousand pounds of quahogs each day of dredging," said Seth. He was planning to expand his clam operation, then Hurricane Bob hit. "We lost about fifty thousand oysters, about a third of our seed," he continued. "While the loss at Penikese was bad, the pond was worse. There, the hurricane drew water right up out of the pond, the pond became deoxygenated, and the oysters just died." It meant new seed, new lines, new cages, and more money.

Meanwhile, Seth has a waiting list of wholesale oyster and clam customers. Those who buy his large quahogs ("They use them for stuffies, tasty stuffed baked clams," he said) take all he can get. "People know I'm responsible. My clams don't come from contaminated waters, and they are kept fresh and chilled." And so life goes on at Seth's usual frenetic pace. He and his students continue to learn the lessons of living with Mother Nature.

Scalloped Oysters

Serves 12 to 14

- 1 cup fine, dry bread crumbs
- 2 cups crushed oyster crackers
- 1 cup crushed Ritz crackers
- 1 cup unsalted butter, melted
- ⅓ cup fresh lemon juice
- ¼ cup chopped fresh parsley
  Freshly ground white pepper to taste
- ¼ cup minced fresh chives
- 2 teaspoons fresh thyme
- 2 quarts medium oysters, with their liquor
- 2 cups heavy cream, or more if necessary
- 3 tablespoons amontillado sherry
- 1 tablespoon Worcestershire sauce
- 15 drops Tabasco

  Fresh herbs for garnish

Combine bread crumbs, crushed crackers, butter, lemon juice, parsley, pepper, chives, and thyme. Mix well and set aside.

Drain oysters, combine liquor with remaining ingredients, and set aside.

Preheat the oven to 350°.

Butter a large baking dish and scatter ⅓ of the crumb mixture over the bottom of the dish. Add half the drained oysters. Distribute another ⅓ of the crumbs, then the remaining oysters, then the remaining crumbs. Pour liquor mixture over casserole. Add more cream if liquid is not visible near the top of the dish. Bake in preheated oven for 50 minutes, or until bubbling and browned on top.

Wine: Ponzi Vineyards Pinot Gris (Oregon)

Our Stuffies

In Rhode Island and Massachusetts they call them quahogs. But the rest of the country calls them littlenecks, cherrystones, and chowder clams.

Serves 4 as an appetizer

- 4 very large chowder clams, well scrubbed
- 3 slices smoked bacon, minced
- ¼ cup minced shallots
- 3 cloves garlic, minced
- 1 stalk celery, finely minced
- ½ teaspoon kosher salt
- 1 teaspoon freshly ground black pepper
- ½ teaspoon Tabasco
- 1 teaspoon Worcestershire sauce
- ¼ teaspoon dried sage
- 4 tablespoons unsalted butter or margarine
- ⅔ cup fine, dry bread crumbs
- 2 tablespoons minced fresh parsley
- 2 teaspoons minced fresh tarragon
- 1 tablespoon minced fresh chives
- ⅓ cup grated dry Jack (see pages 139–141), aged sheep's-milk, or Parmesan cheese
- 4 tablespoons unsalted butter or margarine, melted

Open clams, reserving liquor and shells. Remove meat and chop. Place chopped clams in a large bowl and add reserved liquor.

Preheat oven to 425°.

Cook bacon in a heavy skillet until almost crisp; remove bacon, chop, and add to clams. Add shallots, garlic, and celery to skillet and sauté until vegetables are translucent. Add salt, pepper, Tabasco, Worcestershire, sage, and the 4 tablespoons butter and stir until butter has melted. Add crumbs and herbs and stir for 1 minute. Combine crumb mixture with clams and bacon and mix thoroughly.

Lightly butter the inside of each reserved clamshell, then fill with crumb mixture. Sprinkle with cheese and drizzle with melted butter. Place stuffed shells on a cookie sheet and bake in preheated oven for 15 minutes.

Wine: Kistler Chardonnay "Estate" (Sonoma County)

Red Pepper Vinaigrette and Lime Vinaigrette for Cuttyhunks on the Half Shell

In a flash, Linda devoured a plate of Cuttyhunks and littlenecks just standing on the dock of Cuttyhunk Harbor—all with just a squeeze of lemon. Then she came home and asked Zack Bruell of Z Contemporary Cuisine, in Cleveland, to create some garnishes for these delicacies. The results appear below. Serve the fresh oysters with small bowls of these sauces on the side. A little bit goes a long way.

Makes about ½ cup

RED PEPPER VINAIGRETTE
  1 red bell pepper
  2 small shallots, finely minced
  2 tablespoons balsamic vinegar
  2 tablespoons extra-virgin olive oil
    Salt and freshly ground black
    pepper to taste
  ½ teaspoon finely minced jalapeño
    pepper (optional)

Heat broiler or grill until hot. Grill pepper until blackened on all sides, about 15 minutes. Place in a paper bag, close top, and let cool. Peel, seed, and devein pepper. Dice finely, then combine with remaining ingredients in a small bowl and mix well. Let stand 1 hour before serving.

Makes about ⅔ cup

LIME VINAIGRETTE
  2 limes
  ½ cup Crème Fraîche (page 350)
  2 teaspoons minced shallots
  1 scallion, minced (white part only)
  2 teaspoons minced chives (garlic
    chives preferred)
    Salt and freshly ground black
    pepper to taste

Remove zest from limes and mince finely. Squeeze juice from limes into a small bowl and combine with zest. Add remaining ingredients and serve.

Wine: Sanford Winery Sauvignon Blanc (Santa Barbara County)

James A. Wesson

Freeport Enterprises

Route 2, Box 356

Gloucester, Virginia 23061

(804) 693-6575

On the wall of Jim Wesson's office is a cartoon from the *New Yorker* magazine. A man with some lawn equipment has just knocked on the door of a house. "Like to have your lawn fertilized by a Ph.D.?" he asks. Jim Wesson can relate to that. He, too, is a Ph.D. (in animal physiology). He spends all his time not in scholarly or academic pursuits but in making his living catching and marketing soft-shell crabs, wondering how many people might like to have a crab dinner that was sent to them by a doctor of philosophy.

Jim Wesson grew up on the beautiful Piankatank river, a tributary of the Chesapeake Bay. Since property records for this area were burned during the Civil War, when the Gloucester courthouse was torched, his family can only trace its history in the region to the mid-nineteenth century. But he is certain that his barn dates from 1740. His ancestors were farmers, but they were also watermen, taking much of their livelihood from the rich waters of the bay and its tributaries.

Jim is only forty, but in his lifetime he has seen the quality of these waters erode to such an extent that only the tough, omnivorous, scavenging blue crab continues to thrive. There are fewer full-time watermen these days. Most of them do other work and catch a few crabs just to supplement their income. Those who still try to make a living as full-time watermen are near poverty level. "And yet," said Jim, "they still believe God's going to bring everything back. They said the same thing about the buffalo."

Blue crabs leave the bay and go into the ocean to spawn. Their eggs are brought back into the brackish waters up the bay by the ocean currents and winds. If the winds and currents are not favorable, it will ultimately be a bad season for crabs. It takes a blue two years to grow to its maximum size of 6 inches from point to point; during this period the crab will molt forty to fifty times. Although all blue crabs molt around May, the rest of their shedding is unpredictable and occurs throughout the year according to each individual's schedule.

A soft-shell crab is a crab that has just shed its shell. After blue crabs have come out of their winter torpor, when they have eaten a bit and grown a little, it's time to come to shore to shed. They gather in the marsh grasses, where they pray that nothing will eat them while they molt and are vulnerable to predators. A crabber like Jim Wesson will ignore their prayers. He will have set up traps fashioned of vinyl-coated chicken wire. The crabs, moving along the shore, come up against a wire barrier fence and follow it into a trap from which they cannot escape.

Jim keeps forty "pounds," or crab traps, around these waters. Regularly, several times a day, they are checked and emptied. He takes the crabs by skiff to the crab sheds, right by the shore, where there are twenty-eight large shedding floats, as they are called. These are actually wood and/or fiberglass tubs, 4x8 feet and 8 inches deep, filled with continuous flowing brackish water right from the river.

Ten to thirty dozen crabs are placed in each float. Jim can tell from looking at a crab just where it is in the molting process. He and his two helpers keep a constant watch over them to follow the shedding status of each. Once they notice that the hard shell of one of the crabs has opened across the back, they will watch for the couple of minutes it takes for the crab to literally back out of the outgrown shell. The now-soft crab is quickly placed in a smaller holding tank for the short time it takes it to harden just a little. This slight firming makes the crab better able to withstand the subsequent travel to market. When the time is determined to be right, the crab is immediately refrigerated to stop the hardening process. Since it only takes four hours for the soft shell to harden to inedibility, the waterman has to be on his toes all the time.

Cold but alive, crabs are packed in trays, covered with fresh hay, and dispatched to restaurants and fish markets across the country. At some point in the next five or six days, the live crabs will be dispatched by a deft chef, who will do a thirty-second cleaning before breading and frying them.

Jim is sad over the deterioration of the river and the bay system of which it is a part. Agricultural runoff, sedimentation, and industrial pollution have killed the grasses that are essential food for the crabs as well as for other species. These days, Jim has to run forty traps to catch what his grandfather did with just seven. Too much untreated sewage has found its way into the bay. Uncontrolled development along the shoreline has further degraded the environment. And there has been too much fishing—unscientific, careless fishing.

"Virginians deserve clean water," he said. He believes that if the Chesapeake Bay and its tributaries are ever to come back, there will have to be massive reform in agricultural practices, stern measures to control population growth in the region, and stringent rules on pollution. To help achieve reform, he has become an outspoken activist and president of the Working Watermen's Association.

Jim will tell you that the best soft-shell crabs are the smallest allowable, about 3 inches across. They have been chilled immediately after they shed, while they are still "super-soft." He likes them best just lightly breaded and fried. Unfortunately, Jim said there is no incentive for the waterman to ship the fragile super-softs when he can get the same $5 a dozen for the tougher paper-shelled crabs. A soft crab in the 5½-to-6-inch range is called a "whale," the largest marketable size. This is what most buyers prefer; the consumers get less taste but more crab for their money.

If you were lucky, however, perhaps the very soft-shell crab you had for dinner tonight was caught in a galvanized wire mesh trap, assisted out of its outgrown shell, chilled, packed in straw, and shipped by a man who is an authority on wildlife physiology.

If the soft-shell crab business loses its economic viability, Jim promises he'll use his skills to help manage and restore the fisheries on the bay. Jim is too committed to this beautiful region and its way of life to turn his back and walk away.

Shaw's Crab House Soft-Shell Crabs with Lemon Butter and Almonds

The world is very small. Just as we were about to leave Jim Wesson's place, he casually mentioned that he was flying to Chicago in a few weeks along with a tank of almost-ready-to-shed crabs. He was going to participate in a crab festival at . . . Shaw's Crab House. We quickly called our friend Steve Lahaie, Shaw's managing partner. The result is this delicious recipe from Chef Yves Roubaud.

Serves 4

　12 soft-shell crabs
　 2 cups unbleached flour
　¾ cup unsalted butter
　½ cup dry white wine
　Juice of 1 lemon
　 1 teaspoon minced shallots
　¼ cup heavy cream
　 3 ounces blanched slivered almonds, toasted

　Watercress and lemon slices for garnish

Clean crabs by removing lungs, eyes, and intestines (or ask your fish merchant to do this for you when you buy the crabs). First, lift up sides of upper shell and remove gills. Place crab on a wooden board and, using a sharp knife, cut off head immediately behind eyes. Use a butter knife to scrape out the lungs and intestines through this opening. Rinse well under running water. Then turn crab over and pull open the "apron," or turned-under tail, and cut it off with a sharp knife or scissors.

Dry crabs with paper towels and dredge in flour. Heat a 12-inch skillet over medium heat until hot, then add 2 tablespoons of the butter. Place 4 crabs in skillet, shell side down, and sauté until brown, about 3 minutes. Turn with spatula and cook until other side is brown. Transfer crabs to a warm platter and keep warm in oven while you fry remaining crabs, adding up to 2 tablespoons more butter as necessary. Cut remaining 8 tablespoons butter into pieces and reserve.

Drain skillet of excess butter. Add wine, lemon juice, and shallots. Cook over medium heat until liquid is reduced to 2 tablespoons. Slowly whisk in heavy cream and cook over medium-low heat until mixture is reduced and thickened. Lower heat, add butter pieces, and whisk until smoothly blended. Remove from heat.

Place 3 crabs shell side up on each of 4 heated serving plates and drizzle with lemon butter. Garnish each plate with 2 tablespoons of toasted almonds, a sprig or two of watercress, and a lemon slice.

Wine: Kent Rasmussen Chardonnay (Carneros)

Fresh Herbed Crab Cakes

Blue crabs with hard shells are often steamed for delicious crab boils. But they also can be picked for their sweet meat, which makes spectacular crab cakes.

Serves 8 as an appetizer

 2 tablespoons unsalted butter
 2 tablespoons minced shallots
 1 large clove garlic, minced
 1 small dried red chile pepper, crumbled
 1 tablespoon minced fresh parsley
 1 tablespoon unbleached flour
 ½ cup heavy cream
 2 teaspoons dry mustard
 1 tablespoon fresh lemon juice
 1 pound fresh blue-crab meat
 1 jumbo egg yolk
 1¼ cups fine, dry bread crumbs
 3 tablespoons white cornmeal
 1 tablespoon minced fresh chives
 1 teaspoon minced fresh tarragon
   Salt and freshly ground white pepper to taste
 1 jumbo egg, beaten
 ½ cup milk
 2 tablespoons unsalted margarine
 2 tablespoons vegetable oil
   Summer Salsa (page 43) or Rémoulade Sauce (page 203)

   Bunches of watercress and fresh tarragon for garnish

Melt butter in a small skillet. Add shallots, garlic, and chile pepper and sauté until softened. Stir in parsley, then sprinkle with flour and stir over low heat for 1 minute. Add cream and cook until mixture has thickened, stirring constantly. Remove pan from heat and transfer contents to large bowl. Add mustard, lemon juice, and crab meat. Blend. Then add egg yolk, ¼ cup bread crumbs, cornmeal, herbs, and seasonings. Blend thoroughly and chill for 1 hour.

Divide mixture into 8 portions and form each into an oval cake. Combine egg and milk in a shallow soup plate and put remaining bread crumbs in another soup plate. Dip cakes first into egg mixture, then into crumbs. Let cakes rest on a rack for a few minutes.

Combine margarine and vegetable oil in a cast-iron skillet and heat until hot. Sauté crab cakes until golden brown on both sides, about 5 minutes per side. Serve with salsa or sauce and a garnish of herbs.

Wine: Hacienda Wine Cellars Chenin Blanc (California)

Fried Soft-Shell Crabs with Cayenne Mayonnaise

When we ate at Sportsman's Paradise in Chauvin, Louisiana, we had a huge platter of shellfish that had been battered this way and deep-fried. They were fabulous. Delaune's Cajun Bronze Seafood Seasoning may be purchased directly from Delaune's Foods, 3425 West Main Street, Houma, Louisiana 70360.

Serves 4

 1½ cups cornmeal
 ⅔ cup corn flour, available at health-food stores
 1½ teaspoons salt

 2 teaspoons freshly ground white pepper
 2 tablespoons Delaune's Cajun Bronze Seafood Seasoning, or more to taste
 8 soft-shell crabs, cleaned and dried as on page 220
 Approximately 6 cups vegetable oil

 Lemon wedges and mayonnaise mixed with cayenne pepper for garnish

If cornmeal is not very fine, put it into the bowl of a food processor fitted with the metal blade and pulse 20 times. Then, in a large, shallow bowl, combine cornmeal, corn flour, salt, pepper, and Delaune's Seasoning. Blend well.

Dredge crabs thoroughly in this mixture. Let rest on a rack for a few minutes.

Pour oil into an electric deep-fat fryer and heat to 370°. Fry crabs, about 3 at a time, until golden brown, about 6 minutes. Keep warm while remainder are fried. Serve with lemon wedges and cayenne mayonnaise.

Wine: Joseph Phelps Vineyards Johannisberg Riesling (Napa Valley)

Charlie Coppola and Mike Gorman

Manchester Seafoods

2139 Main Road

Tiverton, Rhode Island 02878

(401) 624-8000

Sakonnet Bay runs from Fall River, Massachusetts, in the north down to Rhode Island Sound and the Atlantic. The main industry of the region is fishing, although summer tourists who come to enjoy the water might eventually present a challenge to the industry. In fact, most of the development around the bay is residential.

Mike Gorman is a Tiverton native and is now in his thirties. He has spent his life around these waters. As one of the partners in Manchester Seafoods, he is continuing a long local tradition of handling shellfish in the best possible manner, treating it as the fragile, perishable treasure it is.

The company has a long history in Tiverton, going back nearly sixty years. In 1984, the company closed; the owners retired and there was no one interested in continuing it. Fortunately, Marshall's Smoked Fish from Brooklyn, New York, one of the largest purveyors of smoked fish in the country, bought the company two years later. They were looking for an opportunity to diversify, and they hired Mike Gorman to run the plant. In time, Charlie Coppola, a young, energetic New Yorker, was hired as manager. Charlie had been working at Dean & DeLuca, one of the country's premier specialty-food stores. By emphasizing high standards of quality and special handling of lobsters and clams, Charlie was able to create the market Manchester needed.

The company grew quickly, only to be almost wiped out when Hurricane Bob virtually destroyed the plant in 1991. The holding tanks were literally upended, and it was weeks before the place could function. Then, too, the clam beds were a wreck; lobstermen's traps were destroyed. Things came to a grinding halt for several months, since there were no products to ship. Finally, Marshall's lost heart and was ready to close. So Charlie and Mike joined forces and in November of 1991 they bought the company from Marshall's. Once again, ownership of Manchester Seafoods is back in the community, which depends upon its continued growth for employment of area clamdiggers and lobstermen.

Clams have become a huge part of the business. Charlie likes clams and saw their potential for the company, which has gone from selling 20 to 30 bags of clams a day to their present level of about 150, or about 8,000 pounds of clams. It is up to Mike to make certain that Manchester sells only top-quality clams.

Quahogs, as hard-shell clams are known in the east, can be found year-round in great quantities along the New England coastline. The very large ones with very chewy meat are known as chowder clams. The next size down is cherrystone, probably the most versatile clam, since it tastes great cooked or raw. The most popular for half-shell eating are littlenecks, the smallest of the quahogs, which are usually so clean that they do not need to be purged of grit before serving. Littlenecks are the favorites of clamdiggers, since they are the easiest to harvest. Quahogs are found farther offshore, usually in waters about 15 feet deep. Manchester also sells a soft-shell clam, which is especially good for steaming. These clams are dug out of the sand at the shore.

"It is essential to buy from good diggers," said Mike Gorman. "There are guys out there who dig where they shouldn't. Some areas are closed because the water is polluted; others are protected areas, where the beds have to regenerate." Many diggers try to fool Gorman, but he will only buy from certain suppliers, the ones he knows abide by the rules.

The diggers, who call themselves "shellfisherman," come in daily and are paid by the piece. Some like to go out early in the dawn, others like the afternoon breeze. Usually they work from boats with outboard motors and find the clams with a long aluminum pole and rake. There are even some people who are doing this with diving tanks. Legally, the clam harvested must be a minimum of 1 inch in diameter. A good digger might bring in 1,000 pieces at a time.

Manchester's clams are not sold for bulk or for canning but only for the half-shell market. So if the shells are chipped or cracked, their customers will reject them. Also, each clam must be tightly closed. Customers will pay a premium for perfectly uniform, high-quality pieces.

Every clam is carefully graded with the help of very special equipment. Clams are placed on a conveyor belt, which leads to rollers that gently sort them by size into chutes. Once in the chute, each clam is further measured with the help of fiberoptics and then sorted again. All this work is done carefully in order not to damage the clamshell, and there are up to three experienced graders who supervise the operation. Size in this part of the operation, by the way, is determined by the number of rings on the shell.

Locally, the clams are delivered in large baskets. Those shipped have traditionally been bagged in burlap sacks, but Manchester is switching to waxed boxes, which will give more protection during shipping. Clams are kept in coolers off the floor to protect them from bacteria, and the floors are also scrubbed frequently.

While he likes clams, Mike Gorman just loves lobsters. He can tell at a glance what shape each is in as he supervises the unloading. Some arrive by truck from the pier in New Bedford; others arrive right at Manchester's dock, where the lobsterman can sell his load, buy more bait, and take off again. As with the clamdiggers, Manchester is very specific about the lobstermen with whom they will do business.

Within minutes of arrival, the lobsters are sorted by size and placed in huge tanks of refrigerated, recirculating seawater. "We like to keep them around 42 to 44 degrees so that they will be less active," said Mike. Lobsters are rather aggressive creatures, and the strong will eliminate the weak in a hurry. And while lobsters arrive with their claws already banded (done by the lobsterman while emptying his pots), they can still wreak havoc if not slowed down.

Mike is very skilled at spotting the weak lobsters and separating them out from the rest. "Our profits go down if the weak get eaten up by the others," he said—a phenomenon that often occurs in supermarket lobster tanks. At Manchester, lobsters that are weak or damaged get cooked for the retail shop and sold for salad. All the others are packed in huge crates, then floated in holding tanks until they are ready to be packed into trucks and shipped, generally within twenty-four hours or less. While many go to Providence, the bulk go to New York and New Jersey. Now Manchester is also shipping to France and Japan.

Manchester Seafoods, currently handling about 100,000 pounds of lobster a year, depends on high quality to hold its position in a very competitive market. Seasonal fluctuations often take the price of shellfish so low that it is hardly worth bothering to harvest them. Lobsters, for example, get soft when they molt, making them less desirable and harder to sell, even though the quality of the meat is not affected. With careful planning, however, Manchester can get Maine lobsters when local lobsters are soft, and sell local lobsters when Maine crustaceans are less desirable.

"They are the best, just the very best," said Johanne Killeen, owner/chef of Lucky's and Al Forno, in Providence. For a company on its second life, such praise is true music.

Tea-Smoked Bluefish

Linda's favorite fish from the New England waters around Manchester Seafoods is bluefish, and this is a simple and delicious preparation for it. Just accompany it with thin slices of buttered bread and slices of lemon.

Serves 4–6

>3 tablespoons dark soy sauce
>2 tablespoons minced fresh ginger
>4 scallions, trimmed and minced (white part only)
>2 tablespoons Sauvignon Blanc wine
>1 teaspoon granulated sugar
>2 tablespoons dark sesame oil
>2 pounds bluefish fillets
>½ cup dark brown sugar, firmly packed
>4 tablespoons crushed star anise
>½ cup loose black tea leaves
>Coarsely ground black pepper to taste

Combine soy sauce, ginger, scallions, wine, granulated sugar, and 1 tablespoon sesame oil in a large Pyrex dish. Whisk well. Add bluefish and marinate for several hours in the refrigerator, turning frequently.

Place one oven rack in the middle of the oven and one on the lowest level possible without touching the bottom. Preheat oven to 475°. Line a pie plate with several layers of foil. Combine brown sugar, anise, and tea on the prepared plate and mix well. Place pan on lower shelf and close door. Wait until oven begins to smoke, about 5 minutes.

Turn fillets skin side down in Pyrex dish. Grind lots of pepper over the surface of the fillets and press gently into the flesh. Place fish in oven and cook for 13 minutes. Turn oven off and let fish remain in closed oven for 5 minutes.

Carefully remove fish from the plate and brush surface with remaining sesame oil. Chill and serve cold.

Wine: Roederer Estate Sparkling Wine (Mendocino County)

Rob's Lobs

It must be coded in the genes! As a child, Linda considered stuffed baked lobster the greatest treat she could have. Much to her amazement, her son Rob has requested the very same thing as his birthday dinner ever since he was old enough to say "lobster."

Serves 6

>6 lobsters, 1½–2 pounds each
>2 shallots, finely minced
>2 cloves garlic, finely minced
>1 small bunch of chives, minced

4 sprigs tarragon, minced
¼ pound minced clams
¼ pound bay scallops, cut in half
¼ pound crab meat
⅓ cup grated aged sheep's-milk cheese
½ cup grated Gruyère cheese
1 tablespoon fresh lemon juice
10 drops Tabasco
½ cup unsalted butter, melted
1 teaspoon freshly ground white pepper
2 cups soft, fresh bread crumbs
½ cup heavy cream
6 tablespoons unsalted margarine, melted

Melted butter with lemon and minced fresh parsley for dipping

Ask your fish merchant to prepare the lobsters for you by splitting each on the underside lengthwise and discarding the stomach. Arrange lobsters split side up and scoop roe and tomalley, if there are any, into a large mixing bowl.

Preheat oven to 375°.

Add all the other ingredients to the mixing bowl, except the margarine, and mix very well. Divide the stuffing among the lobsters and mound it attractively into the cavity. Arrange lobsters on cookie sheets and pour the melted margarine over the stuffing.

Bake lobsters in the preheated oven for 20–25 minutes, or until lobsters are red and the stuffing is lightly browned.

Serve with bowls of parsley-lemon butter on the side.

Wine: Patz & Hall Chardonnay (Napa Valley)

Hatfield Steamed Lobster

Lisa and Lou Ekus, who live in Hatfield, Massachusetts, have one of the finest kitchens we have ever seen. They also turn out some of the best meals we've ever eaten. This is how Lou prepared lobster for Linda, and she has raved about it ever since.

Serves 6

3 pounds very good-quality kielbasa
6 live lobsters, 1½ pounds each, claw bands removed
12 ears fresh corn
½ cup prepared honey mustard
Salt and freshly ground black pepper to taste
1 cup unsalted butter, melted
3 lemons, cut in half

Fill a very large lobster kettle or stockpot with 2 inches of water. Add sausage and bring to a boil, then add lobsters, tails tucked under body. Cover and steam for 15 minutes. Remove and check each lobster for doneness this way: Pull curled tail back and let go. If it instantly snaps back, like a rubber band, the lobster is cooked. If it is a bit sluggish, return lobster to the pot for a few minutes more.

When lobsters are done, place them on a large serving platter. Return water to a fast boil and add corn. Cook until done, about 4 minutes. Remove corn and place on heated serving platter. Remove sausage and slice into large chunks.

Slice and serve sausage with mustard on the side. Sprinkle corn with salt and pepper. Pour melted butter into individual shallow bowls for dipping. Garnish lobster platter with lemons and serve.

Wine: Girard Winery "Reserve" Chardonnay (Napa Valley)

Linguine with Red Clam Sauce

While you can always substitute canned tomatoes for fresh, this dish is best when prepared in late summer, when the rich Roma and San Marzano plum tomatoes are at their peak. Try serving this with Lemon Fettuccine (page 393).

Serves 4–6

- ½ cup extra-virgin olive oil
- 1 clove garlic, crushed
- ½ cup white wine
- 3 dozen cherrystone clams, well scrubbed
- 2 large cloves garlic, finely minced
- ¼ cup onion, finely chopped
- 2 small dried red chile peppers, crushed
- 3 pounds fresh Roma or San Marzano tomatoes, peeled, seeded, and coarsely chopped
- 1 teaspoon minced fresh oregano
- 2 tablespoons minced flat-leaf parsley
  Salt and freshly ground black pepper to taste
- 1 pound cooked linguine or Lemon Fettuccine

  Chopped fresh flat-leaf parsley for garnish

Heat ¼ cup of the olive oil and the crushed garlic clove in a large saucepan over medium heat. Add wine and clams. Cover and cook over medium-low heat until shells open, about 8–10 minutes. Remove pan from heat and scoop clam meat from shells, being certain to spill clam juices into pot. Strain pot liquid through a coffee filter or cheesecloth to eliminate any sand and reserve. Coarsely chop clam meat and set aside.

In a large sauté pan, heat remaining olive oil over medium heat. Add minced garlic, onion, and chiles; reduce temperature and cook, stirring constantly, for 3 minutes. Add tomatoes, reserved clam juices, and oregano; increase heat until mixture begins to boil. Reduce heat and simmer for about 30 minutes, or until sauce is thick. Stir in parsley and seasonings. Add clams and heat through.

Toss sauce with linguine and divide among heated shallow soup plates. Garnish with more parsley.

Wine: Preston Vineyards Cuvée de Fumé (Dry Creek Valley)

Beef, Lamb,
and Pork

Mary Lou Bradley

B3R All Natural Beef
2100 West Highway 287
Childress, Texas 79201
(817) 937-3668

Childress is about a six-hour drive northwest of Dallas on the road to the panhandle, past small towns that seem to have had the heart knocked out of them—derelict storefronts, rusting cars and trucks, abandoned paraphernalia from oil drilling, and empty farmhouses that were once rich with the life of growing families.

But in the sunshine of mid-March, there is also a great deal going on. Tens of thousands of acres of green fields signal the growth of healthy winter wheat. There are freshly plowed fields as well. Most of the land is flat, with an occasional hill or gully. There are also miles of dry grasses and mesquite brush.

The B3R All Natural Beef office and packing facility is right on the highway in the town of Childress. There is a retail store in front that sells their beef and other Texas products.

The ranch itself is about 25 miles out of town. It's tough land, marked by an occasional flock of wild turkeys feeding among the mesquite. Billy Jack Bradley began ranching here in the 1950s, when he came home from the Korean War to be married. His fiancée, Minnie Lou, and his family had the ranch waiting for him. They built a successful and happy life, active in ranching circles; Minnie Lou, in fact, became the first woman to be a beef judge in national competition.

Their daughter, Mary Lou, was out of college at nineteen. For a while she was on the rodeo circuit, although she admits she wasn't very good as a barrel racer. What brought her home was the untimely death of her brother in 1982. Their parents, she told us, had been "using some energy to gather some country for him," and they planned for him and his young family to continue the ranch when they retired. With him gone, the family looked to Mary Lou, who made the decision that the ranch would become her future, too.

The Bradleys always raised beef naturally. They always practiced sustainable agriculture,* managing their farm in such a way that it could thrive without depending on resources from outside the farm itself. Their cattle always received all natural feed. They never used hormones, steroids, growth stimulants, or preservatives. Since none of the cattle went off to the feed lots to be fattened for market, there was no need for antibiotics to protect them from feed-lot diseases.

Mary Lou said, "People growing up in a good beef family have no idea how much more tasty and tender their beef is than the beef found in most supermarkets.

"We ate great beef all our lives. I didn't know the difference until I went to college." She went on: "Better-raised beef tastes better. Even ranchers who sent their cattle off to the feed lots were careful about how they fed the ones they kept for themselves." She finally convinced her folks that their beef was really better, and she got them to thinking that their beef just might be worth more than what they could get for it on the commodity market.

*Gordon K. Douglass of Pomona College in California, in an article entitled "When Is Agriculture Sustainable?" in G. K. Douglass, *The Meaning of Agricultural Sustainability* (Boulder, Colo.: Westview Press, 1984), gives this definition of sustainable agriculture:

" 'Agricultural Sustainability' means different things to different groups of people. One group thinks of sustainability as supplying enough food to meet everyone's demand. I call this the 'food sufficiency' or 'productivity' school. Agriculture, in its view, is primarily an instrument for feeding the world—or at least for feeding those who can afford to buy food on world markets—and preserving the resource base or the culture of rural life is usually of secondary importance.

"A second group regards agricultural sustainability as an ecological phenomenon. I call it the 'stewardship' school. Its proponents measure sustainable production not by total output, or output per unit of scarce input during a limited period of time, but by the average level of output over an indefinitely long period which can be sustained without depleting the renewable resources on which it depends."

Most chicken is known by the company name. But nobody has their name on beef. So that's what the Bradleys decided to do. B3R got started on Halloween in 1986.

At first, they began a home delivery program, slaughtering five head at a time and selling out before they slaughtered more. Finally, they prospered enough to start a wholesale operation. In 1990, they sold 5,000 head; in 1991, they sold 5,500 head.

Public interest in clean food has helped B3R expand. There are now other ranchers in their program, raising cattle according to the B3R standards and selling under their name; still more are interested in participating. Mary Lou says they collectively represent a thousand years of ranching experience. Given the low beef prices in the regular market, a rancher can survive only if his land is paid for, or if he can somehow get more for his product. In the B3R system, he does get more for his beef when the quality is there.

The Bradley family has 10,000 acres, and in this part of Texas, where the land is rough and dry, they calculate a full 36 acres of land per mother cow and calf to provide plenty of grazing. In addition, the Bradleys wean carefully, when a calf is at 500 to 600 pounds—half the mom's weight—and about seven months old.

The calf is moved just a short distance from its mother, rather than trucked what could be hundreds of miles to a feed lot. And for those last 120 days of feeding, the cattle are in spacious B3R paddocks, where they are fed a strict ration of corn. Other companies stop corn when the price goes up and feed the cattle cheaper grains.

The Bradleys use ultrasound to look at the eye of an animal's rib to see if it is big enough to slaughter; other companies slaughter after an animal has spent a certain number of days on feed, regardless of size.

B3R monitors each calf: is it efficient? After slaughter, each carcass is evaluated. A computer printout tells the Bradleys about a calf's weight, how much it ate, how efficient it was in turning the food into weight. This information is also used for breeding strategies.

There are 172 existing breeds of cattle, plus myriad crosses. Brahmas are popular in Texas because they do well in the hot, dry climate and they are impervious to most insects. But they are not good for the B3R program; the meat is too fibrous. B3R use Angus as the seed stock on their ranch. Mary Lou likes them because they have a good temperament and tend to cross well with other breeds. They marble nicely and have a good length (length is important in beef cattle, not height). They are also consistent in size, a factor that is especially important to the consumer, who does not expect a 1-inch rib steak to weigh 2 pounds, for example.

She said, "Old-time ranchers don't realize they are in the food business. They are startled when they see the steaks that come from one of their cattle, which they can do at B3R. But we are, after all, raising food and we must always remember that."

Mary Lou uses the word "learn" a lot. There are only about ten ranchers like her in the country, small outfits working on lower-cholesterol, tastier beef that is natural and organic. Still, it is difficult to get all aspects of the ranch certified as "organic" when you are managing thousands of acres and purchasing tons of corn. There is still much learning to do in order to make that happen economically.

But Mary Lou told us that she always says, "Yes we can" or "I don't know that I can't, therefore I can." It's because of this philosophy that she has never bowed down before her limitations.

"I drive cars fast and ride horses fast," she told us. She has also built a company fast. And done it well.

Roasted Smoked Brisket of Beef

We even make this in the winter, pulling our old Brinkman smoker onto the side porch, right by the door. That way it's easy to tend the fire or add water to the pan. This is great with Potato Pancakes (page 26) and the Minted Peas (page 138). Remember, if you use B3R beef it will require less cooking time.

1 whole beef brisket (about 10–12 pounds), point and flat attached
¾ cup Dry Barbecue Rub (page 238)
½ cup cider vinegar
750 ml. red Zinfandel wine
Several bunches mixed fresh herbs, such as marjoram, sage, oregano, parsley, rosemary, and thyme
4 cups mesquite, cherry, or apple-wood chips, soaked in water

2½ cups Wet Barbecue Mop (page 239)
3 cups Our Barbecue Sauce (page 239)

Two days before serving, place brisket in a large pan and sprinkle generously with Barbecue Rub. Massage thoroughly into the meat on both sides. Place meat in a ceramic or glass baking dish and drizzle with vinegar. Cover tightly with plastic and marinate in the refrigerator overnight. Remove from refrigerator first thing in the morning and allow to come to room temperature.

Prepare a large fire in a hot-water smoker. Fill smoker pan with boiling water, leaving room for the wine. Add the wine and the herbs. Then add half the soaked wood chips to the coals.

Place brisket fat side up on rack and baste with Wet Mop. Cover and cook for about 8 hours, basting twice an hour during the first three hours and once an hour after that. (Be sure to replenish water pan when the level gets low.) Brisket should be somewhat tender when pierced with a long fork.

Preheat oven to 325°. Remove brisket from smoker and place in a roasting pan. Add Barbecue Sauce, cover pan tightly, and roast until very tender, about 1½ hours. Transfer brisket to a platter, reserving sauce. Let meat cool, then chill meat and sauce overnight.

The next day, preheat oven to 325°. Skim any congealed fat from the surface of sauce. Place meat on carving board fat side up. Trim off excess fat from top, or point, section. Then carefully separate the point from the main, or flat, bottom piece using a carving knife. Remove as much fat as possible from surface of the flat as well. Carefully slice the point against the grain as thinly as possible. Neatly arrange slices in the bottom of a large ovenproof casserole. Repeat slicing process with the flat portion and arrange these slices over those from the point. Pour skimmed sauce over the meat. Cover tightly and bake until meat is hot, about 40 minutes.

Wine: Fetzer Vineyards Zinfandel (Mendocino County)

Oriental Flank Steak

This recipe makes enough marinade for at least four flank steaks. Save the unused marinade in the refrigerator; it is also good on tuna, pork, and chicken.

Serves 8

MARINADE
2 tablespoons grated fresh ginger
3 cloves garlic, finely minced
2 tablespoons minced scallions
2 tablespoons minced fresh chives
1 teaspoon Chinese chile paste (available in Oriental markets)
⅓ cup hoisin sauce
½ cup dark soy sauce (available in Oriental markets)
½ cup rice wine vinegar
⅓ cup dry sherry
¼ cup dark sesame oil
¼ cup vegetable oil
2 tablespoons sesame seeds

4 flank steaks, about 1 pound each
Salt and freshly ground black pepper to taste

Minced fresh chives and chive blossoms for garnish

At least two days before serving, combine ginger, garlic, scallions, chives, chile paste, hoisin sauce, soy sauce, vinegar, and sherry in a mixing bowl and mix well. Slowly whisk in the oils to form a thick emulsion, then add sesame seeds and blend. Pour into a container that has a tight cover, seal, and refrigerate.

Twenty-four hours before serving, arrange each flank steak in its own shallow glass or ceramic dish. Pour an equal portion of the marinade into each dish, cover, and refrigerate, turning steaks several times.

Several hours before serving, bring meat and marinade to room temperature. Carefully clean the surface of a gas or charcoal grill with a metal brush, spray with Pam, and heat grill until very hot. Remove steaks from marinade and place on hot grill. Turn after 3–4 minutes and grill on the other side an additional 3 minutes. Transfer steaks to a large cutting board and season with salt and pepper. Allow meat to rest for at least 5 min-

utes. Then slice steaks on the diagonal across the grain. Garnish with chives and serve.

Wine: Calera Wine Company Viognier (San Benito County) or *Saintsbury Pinot Noir* (Carneros)

Dry Barbecue Rub

This recipe will probably be enough for several different meals of ribs or brisket. Store the extra in an airtight container.

Makes almost 2 cups

- 1 cup brown sugar, firmly packed
- 2 tablespoons cayenne pepper
- 2 tablespoons freshly ground white pepper
- 2 tablespoons freshly ground black pepper
- 1 tablespoon fennel seeds, slightly bruised

1 tablespoon kosher salt
2 tablespoons garlic powder
¼ cup hot paprika
1 teaspoon powdered oregano

Combine all ingredients and blend well. Mixture should be sprinkled on the meat, then thoroughly rubbed in. Let rubbed meat stand overnight in the refrigerator.

Wet Barbecue Mop

Makes about 2½ cups

1 cup ketchup
¼ cup Worcestershire sauce
2 tablespoons medium-hot chile powder
¼ cup cider vinegar
¼ cup bourbon
1 cup very strong brewed coffee

Combine all ingredients in a small saucepan and heat over low heat until mixture is very hot. Mix well and use as basting liquid for beef or pork.

Our Barbecue Sauce

We first tasted the great barbecued delicacies of Kansas City with Larry "Fats" Goldberg, who, along with his good friend Calvin Trillin, is a maven on the subject. For weeks after our return, Linda played in the kitchen until she came up with a sauce that came close to the wonderful flavors we remembered from the smoky dining rooms of Kansas City. This sauce freezes very nicely.

Makes about 6 cups

2 tablespoons vegetable oil
1 large onion, finely minced
4 large cloves garlic, finely minced
4 cups ketchup
¾ cup cider vinegar
¾ cup dark brown sugar, firmly packed, or more if desired
¼ cup dark molasses
2 tablespoons dry mustard
2 teaspoons cayenne pepper, or more if desired
2 teaspoons freshly ground white pepper
2 teaspoons medium-hot chile powder
¼ cup Worcestershire sauce
2 teaspoons ground cumin
1 bay leaf

Pour oil into a heavy 3-quart saucepan and heat until just hot. Add the onion and the garlic; cook over medium heat, stirring often, for 5 minutes. Do not let onions brown.

Add the remaining ingredients and stir very well. Let mixture heat through slowly, then simmer over low heat for 30 minutes. Remove the bay leaf. Taste and sweeten if you wish. You may also wish to add more cayenne.

Grilled Skirt Steaks with Chile Pepper Relish

Cooks have to be creative and flexible with the peppers in this dish, since not all of the varieties are available everywhere. The idea is to combine peppers of varying degrees of piquancy so that the relish is flavorful and enjoyable. Those who like heat can use more hot peppers. Borage flowers have a delightful flavor akin to cucumber, which is why we suggest them as a garnish.

Serves 6

MARINADE
      Juice of 1 lime
    3 tablespoons red wine vinegar
    1 clove garlic, finely minced
    1 shallot, finely minced
    ¼ teaspoon medium-hot chile powder
    ½ cup extra-virgin olive oil
    1 tablespoon finely minced cilantro
      Freshly ground black pepper to taste
2–3 pounds skirt steak

RELISH
    2 red bell peppers
    1 yellow or orange bell pepper
    3 fresh mild green chiles, such as Anaheim or Cubanelle
    1 fresh poblano chile
1–2 fresh New Mexico red chiles
    1 red onion, thinly sliced
    2 tablespoons fresh lime juice
    ⅓ cup extra-virgin olive oil
    1 tablespoon capers
    ¼ cup minced cilantro
    1 tablespoon minced fresh chives
      Salt and freshly ground white pepper to taste

      Borage flowers for garnish

Combine lime juice, vinegar, garlic, shallot, and chile powder in a small bowl and blend. Slowly whisk in olive oil until a thick emulsion is formed. Add cilantro and black pepper; blend thoroughly.

Arrange skirt steaks in a large glass or ceramic dish and coat thoroughly with marinade. Allow to marinate at room temperature for at least 3 hours, turning several times.

Meanwhile, thoroughly clean the surface of a gas or charcoal grill with a metal brush, then coat the surface evenly with Pam. Heat the grill until very hot. Place bell peppers and chiles over the heat and grill until peppers are evenly blistered on all sides. Immediately place them in paper bags, seal tightly, and allow to cool.

Wearing rubber gloves to protect your hands, carefully remove the skin from all peppers, discard seeds, and devein. Rinse peppers, dry thoroughly, cut into julienne strips, and place in a medium-size dish with the onion slices. Place lime juice in a small bowl and slowly add olive oil, whisking briskly. Add capers, cilantro, chives, salt, and pepper. Taste and adjust seasonings as needed, then toss with peppers. Set aside to marinate.

Shortly before serving, thoroughly clean the surface of your grill as before; then coat the surface again with Pam. Bring back to high heat. Remove skirt steaks from marinade and place on hot grill. Turn after 2 minutes and grill on the other side for an additional 2–3 minutes. Transfer to a cutting board and let rest for several minutes, then slice in 1–2-inch strips. Divide strips among serving plates and top with relish. Garnish with borage flowers.

Wine: Quivira Vineyards Zinfandel (Dry Creek Valley)

Rex and Glenn Spray

Spray Brothers Farm

5690 Spray Lane

Mount Vernon, Ohio 43050

(614) 397-4207

*I*f you were making a movie about Midwestern farmers and called central casting for a couple of feature players, Glenn and Rex Spray would be what they would send.

When these men take you around their 700 acres in their big new 4x4 pickups, and when they stop to look at the corn or to assess the soil or examine the clover that is going to seed, you get the impression that you are participating in a film or documentary about an American archetype, a scenario that is too typical to be real.

The Sprays' father left Doddridge County, West Virginia, and came to Central Ohio with his family back in 1940. The farm he established here was 162 acres. Now, the farm has now grown to 650 acres, and the brothers lease another 50. These men operate an organic grain-and-beef operation that is more than four times larger than the farm they knew as boys.

The original farm was organic too. But in the 1950s, when the chemical revolution was beginning, the Spray brothers got caught up in it, along with millions of other American farmers. "We used a lot of herbicides," said Glenn. "We thought atrazine was wonderful. It killed everything but the corn. Then some new grass or weed showed up and we needed a tougher killer." The first time it was used on the farm, only a half pound was needed per acre of land. But as the resistant strains of weeds took hold, farmers found themselves using much more of it. "Some guys are now using five or six pounds of herbicide an acre," said Rex. "At those levels, it leaches into our water table. And at those levels you can't follow corn with beans."

"But even back then we used very few insecticides," continued Glenn. "We knew enough about insects to know that we didn't want to mess up the balance. Insects are part of nature's sanitation crew. We think farmers get bugs because their plants are under stress, vulnerable. A good example is that in the '88 drought, spider mites hit the conventional farmers much harder than they hit us. And they used insecticides and we didn't. It really wasn't any big catastrophic thing that made us change," he added. "It was just seeing what was happening to the soil." They stopped using chemicals in 1971.

In the grain part of their operation, the brothers fertilize naturally by means of crop rotation. Corn will usually be followed by soy beans, which then will be followed by clover, rye, or alfalfa. Whatever nutrients the corn takes out of the soil, the cover crops return.

When the brothers plant clover, it has other—economic—benefits besides rebuilding the soil. They harvest the flowers and winnow out three bushels of the tiny seeds per acre, valuable enough in a year of severe drought that the crop will bring in enough cash to cover the cost of buying supplemental organic feed for the cattle.

For the Spray brothers, being organic adds value to their crops. "The cost of growing organic produce is less, but we can't farm as many acres," said Rex. "So we need to get 20 to 25 percent over the conventional market price for any given product. Actually, we get 100 percent over for our organic soybeans, which are used for tofu."

They are raising organic Strawberry Popcorn for the first time. It's a contract crop and a new experience. And they have grown a lot of azuki beans, which they sell to a processor in North Dakota.

"Organic is what more and more folks want," he said. "And we've got to get this market before Heinz decides to switch over."

On the livestock side of the operation, they are still trying to figure out a way to market their organic beef better. "Beef is tough," Rex admitted. "We don't raise enough to keep the flow steady." There are 80 beef cattle on the place now. They finish the steers and keep some of the heifers as future breeders. They sell about 60 head of their Hereford-Angus mix a year, plus the cows that are no longer good breeders. Rex would like to have a contract to supply a specialty food store in a good-sized city. He says he would have to sell two or three head every week so the store would have a regular supply, which would mean they would have to more than double production. So in the meantime, although their cattle are certified organic—fed on organic hay, corn, oats, and pasture—Rex sends them to the conventional livestock market, where they bring the standard commodity price for beef on the hoof.

They recoil in horror at the idea of veal. "No way could you do organic white veal," said Glenn. "The way you produce white veal is to keep the calves anemic and give them medicines to keep them from dying."

We asked the Sprays about the high-tech cobalt-blue silos we had frequently seen when driving through farm country. There were four of them on a big farm nearby.

"They're called farmer's monuments," said Glenn. "You're told by the experts that you really need them to manage your silage better. They cost a lot. But you buy them and they become a permanent monument to your debt."

"But we do things our way because it's a way of life," said Rex. "It's the way we were brought up."

"No money in it," added Glenn, "and you work your tail off. But we know we are going to keep doing it. So why not do it the way we want? Organic is something that won't work, they tell us. And we're proving every day that it will."

New England Boiled Dinner

Serves 8

1 whole 8–10-pound cured (corned) beef brisket, with point and flat attached

3 bay leaves
2 tablespoons black peppercorns, bruised
2 large cloves garlic, crushed
6 whole cloves
¼ cup dark brown sugar, firmly packed

1 cup apple cider
2 tablespoons maple syrup
2 tablespoons Dijon mustard
24 small red potatoes, scrubbed
10–12 carrots, scrubbed and trimmed
2 Savoy cabbages, cored and quartered
4 tablespoons margarine, melted
Freshly ground black pepper to taste

Prepared horseradish and Dijon mustard for garnish

In a large saucepan, combine beef, bay leaves, peppercorns, and garlic. Cover with water and bring to a boil. Cover pot, reduce heat, and simmer for 3½ hours, or until meat is fork-tender. Carefully remove meat from pot, reserving liquids, and place in a shallow pan fat side up. Score fat in a diamond pattern and stud randomly with cloves. Meanwhile, keep pot liquid hot.

Preheat oven to 350°. Combine brown sugar, cider, maple syrup, mustard, and ¼ cup of the pot liquid in a small saucepan; whisk well to blend. Bring to a boil and simmer over medium heat for 4 minutes, then pour over beef. Place meat in oven and cook, basting several times, for 30 minutes. Let meat rest, then slice.

At the same time, return remaining pot liquid to a boil. Add potatoes and carrots. Cover and boil for 25 minutes. Add cabbage and continue to boil for 10 minutes more.

On a very large serving platter, arrange slices of meat at one end and mound boiled vegetables attractively at other end. Dress vegetables with melted margarine and black pepper. Serve with horseradish and mustard on the side.

Wine: Qupe "Los Olivos Cuvee" Syrah (Santa Barbara) or Kendall-Jackson "Durell Vineyard" Syrah (Sonoma County)

Three-Generation Stuffed Cabbage

This recipe has been passed from Grandma Weller to Gert LeVine, Linda's mother, and then on to Linda. It's a great dish, especially when served with jasmine rice (see page 91) and Buckwheat Black Bread (page 88), and is best when refrigerated overnight and reheated before serving.

Serves 6–8

FILLING
2 pounds lean ground beef
1 tablespoon kosher salt
2 teaspoons freshly ground black pepper
2 large cloves garlic, finely minced
1 tablespoon hot paprika
2 tablespoons minced fresh parsley
2 teaspoons minced fresh thyme
½ cup minced onion
⅔ cup fine, dry bread crumbs
1 jumbo egg

1 large Savoy cabbage (about 3¼ pounds), cored and steamed until softened
1 large onion, chopped
1 tablespoon minced fresh ginger
4 cups Roasted Red Tomato Sauce (page 20)
1 lemon, thinly sliced
½ 6-ounce can tomato paste
⅔ cup dark brown sugar, firmly packed
⅔ cup ginger-snap crumbs
1–2 tablespoons hot paprika

Combine filling ingredients with ½ cup water in the bowl of an electric mixer fitted with a paddle. Beat for 2 minutes.

Peel off 24–28 steamed leaves from the cabbage head and drain well. Slice remaining cabbage in julienne strips and place them on the bottom of a 6–7-quart oven-proof Dutch oven or casserole.

Form filling into small balls, about 2 ounces each, and wrap them in cabbage leaves. Place these rolls seam side down in the prepared pot. There will be several layers of meat rolls.

Combine remaining ingredients except paprika in a mixing bowl; blend thoroughly and pour over prepared rolls. Sprinkle generously with paprika, cover, and roast in preheated oven for 1 hour. Remove cover and roast for 30 minutes more.

*Wine: Eberle Winery Zinfandel
(Paso Robles)*

Corned Beef Hash

Serves 8–10

    4 pounds cooked corned beef, or leftovers from New England Boiled Dinner (page 243)
    4 large baked potatoes, cooled and peeled
    1 large onion
    ½ cup melted butter
      Salt and freshly ground black pepper to taste
    3 tablespoons Worcestershire sauce
    1 teaspoon Tabasco
    1 tablespoon minced fresh parsley
    1 tablespoon minced fresh chives
    1 teaspoon minced fresh marjoram
    1 teaspoon minced fresh thyme
 8–12 poached eggs
      Roasted Red Tomato Sauce
      (page 20)

      Sprigs of fresh parsley, chives, and thyme for garnish

Preheat oven to 425°.

Cut beef into chunks and mince the chunks a few at a time in a food processor fitted with the metal blade. Pulse only until chopped, not puréed. Put minced beef into a large mixing bowl. Mince potatoes and onions in a similar fashion in the processor and then combine with beef. Add melted butter, salt, pepper, Worcestershire, Tabasco, and herbs. Mix very well.

Rub a 9-inch cast-iron skillet with vegetable oil until well coated. Press hash into the skillet and pat down evenly. Place skillet in preheated oven and bake for 30 minutes, or until a crust develops.

Mound a spoonful of hash on each serving plate. Place a poached egg atop each mound of hash and pour some sauce over the eggs. Garnish with fresh herbs.

Wine: Joseph Phelps Vineyards Vin du Mistral Grenache Rosé (California)

Beef Stew with Prunes

This dish has its roots in southwest France and the town of Agen, the reputed prune capital of the world.

Serves 10

- 1 cup unbleached flour
- 1 teaspoon salt
- 1 teaspoon freshly ground black pepper
- 3 pounds beef top sirloin, cut into 2-inch pieces
- 4 tablespoons unsalted margarine
- 3 tablespoons olive oil
- 2 large onions, sliced
- 4 carrots, scrubbed, cut into 1-inch slices
- 3 large cloves garlic, thinly sliced
- 3 tablespoons sugar
- 750 ml. Syrah or Côtes du Rhône wine
- 4 strips smoked bacon, diced and blanched
- 2 cups rich beef stock, or more if necessary
- 2 bay leaves
- 2 teaspoons dried thyme
- 1 teaspoon dried rosemary
- 1 teaspoon dried marjoram
- ¼ cup chopped fresh parsley
- 10 ounces pitted prunes
  Peel of 1 orange, cut into julienne strips
- 3 tablespoons unbleached flour (optional)
- 3 tablespoons margarine, softened (optional)

Chopped fresh parsley for garnish

Preheat oven to 325°.

Mix flour, salt, and pepper in a shallow soup plate and blend. Dredge meat in flour mixture. Combine margarine and olive oil in a cast-iron Dutch oven and heat over medium heat. Add meat and brown well. Add onions, carrots, and garlic; stir over medium heat 2 minutes. Sprinkle with sugar, increase heat, and stir until sugar begins to caramelize. Add wine and thoroughly scrape bottom of pot. Then add bacon, stock, herbs, prunes, and orange peel. Add more stock if liquids do not cover solids in pot. Adjust seasonings, cover tightly, and place in oven for 2 hours. Taste for tenderness and cook an additional 20 minutes if necessary.

When meat is tender, remove pot from oven. If sauce needs thickening, make a *beurre manié* by combining the flour and margarine and slowly stirring this paste into the stew while it simmers on the stove. Ladle stew into flat soup plates and garnish with parsley.

Wine: Sean Thackary "Orion" Syrah (Napa Valley)

John and Sukey Jamison

Jamison Farm
171 Jamison Lane
Latrobe, Pennsylvania 15650
(800) 237-5262

*T*he voice on the phone puzzled John Jamison. It had a heavy rural French accent. "I want to see your lambs," said the caller. "Bring me some."

John and Sukey Jamison's farm and their lamb operation had been featured on a WCBS-TV news report. They had just advised Sukey's dad, retired and living in the south of France, that they were about to be on the air.

It's Sukey's dad, Bud, thought John. He's kidding us.

But something stopped him from treating the call as an intercontinental telephone joke.

The man, it turned out, had a French accent for good reason. It was the fabled Jean-Louis Palladin, the chef-owner of Jean-Louis, the restaurant at the Watergate Hotel in Washington, D.C. And it was no joke. Jean-Louis had not been happy with the American lamb he had been buying for his menu. Too big, too red, too fat. So when he heard about the Jamisons and their farming methods, he reached for the phone.

A couple of days later John Jamison drove the four hours from his hillside farm to the Watergate. He heard the echoes of history as he walked through the basement labyrinth where the famous Watergate burglars had toiled. On his shoulder he carried not the tools of the second-story man but two lambs, tightly wrapped in a shroud of paper and cheesecloth.

He found the entrance to the kitchen, where men in checked pants and white coats were scurrying around. From across the room came Palladin. There was not even a greeting. He grabbed one of the lambs from Jamison's arms and threw it onto a stainless-steel table. In seconds he had ripped off the paper and cloth and was bending over the carcass, looking into the cavity, feeling the fat, the ribs, the legs, and flipping it over as though it were as light as a chicken, feeling the backbone and the loin. He called all of his staff to the table and told them: at long last, lamb, real lamb.

French chefs are very serious about lamb. In the south, they tend to favor Sisteron lamb, with its taste of lavender and rosemary. In the north, many like the "salt lamb" of Brittany, animals that feed on the coastal salt marshes. (Southerners will sometimes say that salt lamb is okay if you like lamb that tastes like fish.) But for the chefs of southwest France, the region where Jean-Louis Palladin learned the craft and art of food, there is nothing like the little Pauillac lambs, milk-fed animals that are weaned and marketed as young as four months. In what Jamison took to him that evening from his Pennsylvania farm, Palladin had the lamb he had long hoped for but never expected to find.

John Jamison's family was in the coal business in western Pennsylvania. John's work in the family business involved management of a mine and the supervision of forty-five employees. He and Sukey, however, wanted to raise their children in a rural environment, and decided to try raising animals for a living. They bought a large farm (168 acres) with an old house (1875), and John left the coal business for good. They now own 800 ewes and have only four "employees"—a Great Pyrenees dog who guards the sheep (there are coyotes in this part of Pennsylvania) and three border collies who move them from paddock to paddock.

The traditional way of raising lambs in the United States is to wean spring-born lambs and send them to the feed lots, where they eat enough to come up to a particular weight. They are then sold, not according to quality but according to the market price for that weight. The Jamisons, however, decided to ignore weight. For the Jamison lambs, there would be no feed lot, no corn. Only milk and fresh grass, and a winter supplement of hay and oats.

The Jamisons make their marketing decision on what they call "age and finish." When the musculature of the lamb feels just right to the touch, the animal is ready for market. There should be a fat layer about the thickness of a dime covering the animal's backbone. If the bone feels too sharp, the lamb isn't ready. The animals could be from four to six months old and could vary in weight from 60 to 80 pounds, dressing out at 30 to 45 pounds. Jamison lambs have less fat and marbling than lamb we find in the supermarkets. Also, the meat is lighter in color when it is cooked.

The operation, while not certifiably organic, is natural. No hormones, no antibiotics, and no food additives are used. The Jamisons have divided their farm into paddocks of several acres each. When the grass is ready, the sheep are taken to one of the paddocks. In two days, after they have eaten that grass down, the dogs drive them to the next one. They dine there for a couple of days, and move on again. And so it goes, until the first patch has grown back, usually in about twenty days. This approach protects the land and maximizes its productivity.

And yes, when it comes time to freshen the ewes, it is done the old-fashioned way, by real rams, twice a year. Sukey feels that the ewes, a Dorset-Finn cross, are especially good mothers—they take care of their lambs from the moment of birth, reducing the need for Sukey's attention. The rams are Dorsets or Southdowns. The Jamisons' breeding program has enabled them to spread out the production and ensure that there will be product whenever it is wanted. Indeed, the Jamisons could produce as many as 2,000 lambs per year on the property. But how big they get will depend on how much lamb stew they can sell, said John. And he's not kidding.

Most of the customers want the loins, the chops, the legs. A few of the restaurants are starting to feature lamb shanks. But there is a lot left after the choice cuts are taken and shipped. Most of it—the shoulder, the brisket, the breast—goes into a splendid frozen stew prepared by the Jamisons according to a recipe developed by the devoted Jean-Louis Palladin. Other trimmings go into a delicious frozen pasta sauce. Both products are totally natural, free of preservatives, and selling beautifully.

Jamisons' Ground Lamb Stroganoff

This is very simple and delicious. If you want to get fancy, add sautéed mushrooms and a tablespoon of Madeira wine to the lamb just before it is done.

Serves 4

- 1–2 tablespoons vegetable oil
- 1 pound ground lamb
- 2 cloves garlic, chopped
- ½ teaspoon dried oregano
- ½ teaspoon salt
- ¼ teaspoon coarsely ground black pepper
- 1 cup sour cream
- 1 pound flat egg noodles, cooked and drained

Heat oil in a large skillet and add lamb and garlic. Brown meat lightly, drain juices from pan, then add seasonings and sour cream. Stir until heated through. Mix with noodles and serve.

Wine: Wild Horse Winery Pinot Noir (Central Coast)

Marinated Lamb Chops

Serves 4

MARINADE
- ¼ cup dry red wine
- ¾ cup vegetable oil
- ¼ cup minced cilantro
- ¼ teaspoon cumin
- 1 clove garlic, minced
- 1 shallot, finely minced
- ½ teaspoon minced fresh thyme
- ¼ teaspoon medium-hot chile powder
- 8 double-rib lamb chops
  Salt and freshly ground black pepper to taste

In a medium-size glass baking dish, whisk together wine and oil. Add the rest of the marinade ingredients and blend well. Rub mixture into lamb chops, then place chops in a glass or ceramic dish and cover with plastic wrap. Marinate in the refrigerator for 8 hours, turning several times.

Thoroughly clean the surface of a gas or charcoal grill with a metal brush; then coat the surface evenly with Pam. Heat the grill until very hot.

Remove chops from dish, reserving marinade, and season with salt and pepper. Place chops on grill and cook for 8 minutes, basting several times with marinade. Turn and grill on the other side for an additional 8 minutes. (Two-inch-thick chops should be medium-rare after 8 minutes per side, but check for an internal temperature of 140° for medium-rare.)

Wine: Laurel Glen Vineyard "Counterpoint" Cabernet Sauvignon (Sonoma County)

Jean Joho's Roast Leg of Lamb with Garlic Flan

The charming and talented Alsatian Jean Joho of Chicago's Everest Room restaurant was the chef who first told us about Jamison Lamb, which he has shipped weekly to Chicago from Latrobe, Pennsylvania.

Serves 6

> 1 leg of lamb, about 6 pounds, pelvic bone removed
> 3 tablespoons olive oil
> Kosher salt and freshly ground black pepper to taste
> 1 teaspoon fresh thyme
> 1 teaspoon minced fresh basil
> 12 small onions, peeled
> 12 cloves garlic
> ¼ cup dry red wine
> ¼ cup lamb or beef stock

GARLIC FLAN
> 10 cloves garlic
> 1¼ cups milk
> 1 cup heavy cream
> 3 jumbo eggs
> 2 teaspoons chopped fresh basil
> Salt and freshly ground black pepper to taste
>
> Bunches of fresh herbs for garnish

Have butcher bone, trim, and tie lamb with butchers' twine. Preheat oven to 450°. Rub lamb with about 1 tablespoon olive oil, salt, a lot of pepper, and the herbs. Place in a roasting pan and cook in preheated oven for 10 minutes.

Toss onions and garlic with remaining oil and add to roasting pan. Turn leg and reduce heat to 350°. For medium-rare lamb, roast for 1 hour and 15 minutes, or until internal temperature reaches 140° on an instant-read thermometer. Turn lamb and onions several times during cooking to be sure they brown evenly. Remove lamb from the pan and let rest on a carving board in a warm place for 20–30 minutes. The temperature should rise to 145° and the meat will retain most of its juices.

Transfer onions and garlic to a heated platter and keep warm. Add wine and stock to roasting pan and place over medium-high heat, scraping with a whisk to loosen any meat particles that may have adhered to it. Pour mixture into a small saucepan and keep warm.

To make flan, butter six 4-ounce ramekins and set aside. Preheat oven to 350°.

Place garlic in small saucepan, cover with water, and boil for 1 minute. Drain. Repeat this process two more times. Then purée garlic with the milk in a blender. Add cream, eggs, basil, salt, and pepper. Mix well, then pour into prepared ramekins.

Place ramekins in a shallow pan filled with hot water; water should come halfway up the sides of the ramekins. Bake in pre-heated oven for about 45 minutes, or until custard is set. Allow ramekins to rest in water bath before serving, about 10 minutes.

Meanwhile, slice the lamb and pour juices into the saucepan with the wine mixture. Arrange slices on heated serving plates, add onions and garlic, and pour sauce overall. Serve with warm flan.

Wine: Girard Winery Cabernet Sauvignon "Reserve" (Napa Valley)

Linda's Butterflied Leg of Lamb

If you use Jamison's natural lamb, which comes from animals that are smaller and leaner than those one buys at most supermarkets, you'll have to reduce your cooking time by about 10 minutes. This is great with Farfel (page 326). Because of the variations in thickness of this cut, you will have cooked meat in varying degrees of doneness—from medium-rare to well-done.

Serves 12

> 1 butterflied leg of lamb, about 6 pounds
> Freshly ground black pepper to taste

MARINADE
> ½ cup corn oil
> ½ cup extra-virgin olive oil
> Juice of 3 limes
> Juice of 1 lemon
> 3 tablespoons raspberry vinegar
> 2 cloves garlic, sliced
> 2 large shallots, chopped
> 2 thin slices peeled fresh ginger
> 1 teaspoon cayenne pepper
> 2 teaspoons ground coriander
> 2 teaspoons turmeric
> 1 teaspoon curry powder
> 1 teaspoon kosher salt
> 1 teaspoon ground cardamom
> 1 teaspoon freshly ground white pepper
> 6 sprigs cilantro

> Citrus Beurre Blanc (page 253)

The day before serving, butterfly the lamb by cutting the seam along the smallest edge of the leg, where the bone has been removed, with a sharp knife. Spread the meat out flat and rub with some freshly ground pepper. Arrange opened lamb in a large glass baking dish. Combine Marinade ingredients in the bowl of a food processor fitted with the metal blade. Pulse ten times, then process until ingredients are virtually puréed. Pour marinade over lamb and rub it well into the meat. Cover tightly and refrigerate overnight. Several hours before serving, remove bowl and bring ingredients to room temperature.

Thoroughly clean the surface of a gas or charcoal grill with a metal brush, then coat the surface evenly with Pam. Grill butterflied lamb over hot coals for 15 minutes per side. Insert an instant-read thermometer at the thickest point; the temperature should read 140°. If not, grill a few minutes longer. Let meat rest for 5 minutes before carving. Serve with Citrus Beurre Blanc on the side.

Wine: Heitz Wine Cellars "Martha Vineyards" (Napa Valley) or *Cabernet Sauvignon* (Napa Valley)

Citrus Beurre Blanc

Makes about 2 cups

- 2 shallots, finely minced
- 1 clove garlic, finely minced
  Juice and minced zest of 1 lime
  Juice and minced zest of 1 lemon
- 1 cup dry white wine
- 1 cup unsalted butter, cut into tablespoon-sized pieces
- 2 tablespoons heavy cream
- 1 tablespoon minced cilantro
  Salt and freshly ground white pepper to taste

Combine shallots, garlic, juices, and wine in a medium-size saucepan and bring to a boil. Lower heat and simmer briskly until liquid is reduced to 2 tablespoons. Over very low heat, add butter, a tablespoon at a time, whisking briskly. Whisk in cream, cilantro, citrus zests, and salt and pepper. Keep warm by placing saucepan in a larger bowl of hot water while you prepare the main part of the meal.

Grilled Lamb Burgers with Chile-Pepper Relish

Serves 4

RELISH
- ¼ cup minced cilantro
- 2 tablespoons minced fresh parsley
- 1 large mild red chile pepper, seeded and finely minced
- ½ small hot red chile pepper, seeded and finely minced
- 2 tablespoons minced onion
- ½ cup diced very ripe tomato
- 2 tablespoons olive oil
- 1 teaspoon red wine vinegar
  Salt and freshly ground black pepper to taste

- 1½ pounds lean ground lamb
- ¼ cup cilantro
- ½ cup minced onion
- ½ cup fine, dry bread crumbs
- 1 jumbo egg
- 1 teaspoon salt
- 1 teaspoon freshly ground black pepper
- 1 tablespoon Worcestershire sauce
- ½ teaspoon Tabasco

In a small bowl, combine ¼ cup cilantro, parsley, chiles, 2 tablespoons onion, tomato, olive oil, and vinegar. Mix well and season with salt and pepper. Chill until ready to serve.

Combine lamb with ¼ cup cilantro, ½ cup onion, bread crumbs, egg, salt, pepper, Worcestershire, ¼ cup water, and Tabasco. Mix thoroughly and form into plump patties about 1½ inches thick.

Thoroughly clean the surface of a gas or charcoal grill with a metal brush; then coat the surface evenly with Pam. Heat the grill until very hot. Grill the burgers to desired doneness (4 minutes per side if you like them rare). Garnish with the relish.

Wine: Rabbit Ridge Vineyards Cabernet Sauvignon (Sonoma County)

Maria Varela and Patricia Quintana

Ganados del Valle

P.O. Box 118

Los Ojos, New Mexico 87551

(505) 588-7896

During the late fall and early winter, remarkable lamb comes to Santa Fe and Taos from Los Ojos, in the north, near the Colorado border. Not much of it, but very special, milk- and grass-fed, and free of any of the chemical legerdemain that makes animals fat and big for the market.

The chefs of the good restaurants buy it for their holiday menus. And a few lucky families have been able to buy lamb legs or loins for their Thanksgiving or Christmas tables. What's more, it is not only good food but part of a vibrant experiment in the economic revival of a depressed rural community.

For generations, raising sheep has been the most significant agricultural enterprise of the Chama Valley. Some landholders can trace their families back not just generations but centuries. Traditionally, farmers took their sheep to high pastures in the summer and used their land for growing gardens and hay to sustain their sheep in the winter. But the average farmland holding today is about ten acres, barely enough for subsistence. Upland grazing has been foreclosed. There is no room to grow, and the economic health of the region has deteriorated.

The history and the culture of the region are rich, and the people who live here fervently want to protect their lifestyle.

So in 1983, with the help of Maria Varela, who has spent most of her adult helping rural communities organize for self-reliance, the community leaders formed a cooperative—Ganados del Valle (livestock growers of the valley). They decided that instead of selling the wool from their sheep they would work with it themselves. They would spin and dye the yarn, weave rugs and garments in traditional Hispanic patterns, and market the products through their own store and mail-order business. This business, Tierra Wools in Los Ojos, has created jobs and brought many professional opportunities to its members.

The cooperative also launched an effort to reestablish Churro sheep, the humble breed that came to the region with the Spanish four hundred years ago. The Churro wool, straight and clean, is ideal for traditional weaving, but over the years the breed had become virtually extinct. With help from experts at Utah State University, Ganados set up a breeding program that has snatched the Churro from the jaws of oblivion.

In addition, the community has pioneered several other enterprises, including a livestock-sharing program. It lends livestock to a fellow co-op grower who may want to expand or improve his flock. He or she repays the loan by returning animals of equal value after five or six years. Rio Arriba Wool Washing Service, a commercial facility for the washing of the fleece, was established in 1989. And in 1990, Ganados opened a feed store/general store that will keep more local money at home and feature arts and crafts from the region.

In the fifth year of Ganados's existence, a decision was made to go to market with both the Churro and the range lambs (nonspecific breeds). Patricia Quintana, who holds a master's degree in animal science from New Mexico State University, joined the co-op as a marketing specialist. Under the trade name Pastores Lamb, she sells meat to upscale restaurants and specialty stores in the region during the fall and winter. She wants to get an off-season breeding program going so she can deliver this organic lamb to her customers in the spring as well.

But wool and lamb production cannot increase without increasing the size of the flocks, and the flocks cannot grow without summer grazing in the highlands. And that is where Ganados del Valle has locked horns with environmentalists and the New Mexico Department of Game and Fish.

High above the floor of the Chama Valley are the upland meadows that traditionally were used by farmers for summer grazing. Forty-four thousand acres of these lands are controlled by the Department of Game and Fish. While it is not a designated wilderness area, it is land that environmental groups want kept pristine. It is, under the law, reserved for the use of elk and other wild animals. Recognizing this, Ganados has asked annually, since 1982, for a five-year test, monitored by experts, to determine if their sheep, carefully managed, would harm the highland meadows or in any way interfere with the life of the game—or if, as many experts believe, their presence would enrich the ecosystem and improve the health of the range. But despite broad public and editorial support for the test in New Mexico, the bureaucracy holds fast.

In 1989, when grazing land was unavailable, the sheep of the community were driven out onto the protected lands for grazing in an act of civil disobedience. Charges were brought but dropped. More recently, the co-op has leased grazing land from a private ranch.

Just before our visit to Ganados, the news came that Maria Varela had been awarded a five-year, $305,000 MacArthur Foundation grant. This "genius award," given unconditionally to people whose work is creative and uniquely valuable to society, usually goes to artists, novelists, scientists, and poets—rarely to a social activist. Suddenly, everyone wanted to find out about this woman whose vision was improving the fortunes and transforming the lives of scores of poverty-stricken farm families in New Mexico.

Maria is accustomed to tough battles. She has been in one after another all her life, and she does not intend to quit. And Pat Quintana, intense and energetic, is determined that the community will be saved, and that it will be based on the traditional values of the Hispanic people who have farmed here for more than two centuries. She believes that their efforts will make for a better tomorrow, even if development comes.

In the meantime, negotiations over summer grazing for the Ganados sheep continue. The parties to the dispute are talking and there is still hope.

"It's such a struggle," said Patricia Quintana. "But we'll keep at it."

Zesty Lamb on Skewers

This would be a great dish to serve with Grits Soufflé (page 37) and the Orange and Jícama Salad with Red Onion and Lime (page 394).

Serves 8

MARINADE

    1 cup Cabernet Sauvignon or Côtes du Rhône wine
    ⅓ cup vegetable oil
    2 tablespoons walnut oil
    1 tablespoon medium-hot chile powder
    1 tablespoon ground cumin
    3 large cloves garlic, minced
    1 tablespoon minced fresh ginger
    1 tablespoon minced onion
    1 tablespoon minced cilantro
    Juice of 2 limes

    2½ pounds boneless leg of lamb, cut into 1-inch cubes
    Kosher salt and freshly ground black pepper to taste

    8 slices of lime and fresh herbs for garnish

Pour wine into a large glass baking dish. Slowly whisk in oils to make a thick emulsion, then whisk in remaining marinade ingredients. Toss lamb cubes in the marinade and let stand, refrigerated or at room temperature, for several hours. Remove meat from dish, reserving marinade, then spear an equal amount of meat on each of 8 long skewers.

Thoroughly clean the surface of a gas or charcoal grill with a metal brush, then coat the surface evenly with Pam. Heat the grill until very hot. Place skewers on the grill and cook for 4 minutes per side.

Sprinkle with salt and pepper and garnish with lime and fresh herbs.

Wine: Girard Winery Cabernet Sauvignon (Napa Valley)

Hearty Lamb Stew

Serves 6

    3 tablespoons unsalted butter or margarine
    2½ pounds lamb shoulder, cut into 2-inch cubes
    1 teaspoon sugar
    ¼ cup flour
    ½ teaspoon kosher salt
    1 teaspoon freshly ground black pepper
    1 large clove garlic, finely minced
    2 cups rich lamb or beef stock
    1 cup dry red wine
    2 cups peeled, seeded, and diced tomatoes
    2 teaspoons fresh thyme
    1 bay leaf
    2 tablespoons minced fresh parsley
    1 sprig fresh rosemary
    18 small red or yellow potatoes, scrubbed

12 small white onions

12 small turnips, scrubbed, or 3 large turnips, quartered

12 small carrots, scrubbed

4 ounces green beans, trimmed and cut into 2-inch lengths

½ cup fresh peas

Minced fresh parsley for garnish

Preheat oven to 350°.

Melt butter in a cast-iron Dutch oven over medium-high heat. Add lamb and quickly brown on all sides. Add sugar and toss over high heat until sugar is caramelized. Then add flour, stirring until nicely browned. Add salt, pepper, garlic, stock, wine, tomatoes, thyme, bay leaf, parsley, and rosemary, then bring to a boil, stirring constantly until ingredients are well incorporated. Cover tightly and cook in preheated oven for 1 hour.

Remove pot from oven and skim as much fat as possible from surface. Add potatoes, onions, turnips, and carrots. Bring mixture to a boil, cover, and return to oven. After 40 minutes, add green beans and peas. Cook in oven for another 30 minutes, or until vegetables are tender. Skim, adjust seasonings, and serve garnished with a generous sprinkling of fresh parsley.

Wine: Cafaro Cellars Merlot (Napa Valley)

Paul Minnillo's Lamb Shanks with Flageolets and Pancetta

Paul Minnillo is owner and chef of Cleveland's Barricelli Inn. He elevates the humble lamb shank to ethereal heights. Be sure to have crusty bread for dipping.

Serves 4

3 cups dried flageolets

4 1-pound lamb shanks
Kosher salt and freshly ground black pepper to taste

6 tablespoons unsalted butter

Mirepoix

1 tablespoon dried juniper berries

1 tablespoon dried rosemary

1 tablespoon dried tarragon

1 cup diced pancetta

1 cup coarsely diced carrots

1 cup coarsely diced onions

2½ cups Sauvignon Blanc wine

2½ cups rich lamb or chicken stock

2 cloves garlic, finely minced

2 tablespoons extra-virgin olive oil

Soak flageolets in cold water overnight. Then drain, rinse, and place in a saucepan. Cover beans with cold water and bring to a boil. Lower heat and simmer until soft, about 30–45 minutes. Drain, rinse, cool, and set aside.

To begin the mirepoix, put the juniper berries in a coffee grinder and grind briefly. Add rosemary and tarragon and grind again. Set aside.

Season lamb shanks with salt and pepper. Melt butter in a skillet and add the lamb; sauté until brown. Meanwhile, in a large, deep skillet, finish making the mirepoix: Sauté the pancetta until golden. Then add carrots and onions; continue to cook over medium heat until carrots and onions are also golden. Add wine and stir over medium heat to loosen any particles that have adhered to the skillet. Add stock, garlic, and reserved herbs.

Add lamb shanks to skillet, cover, and simmer for 2½ hours. The meat should be tender and the liquids reduced by ⅔.

Heat the olive oil in a skillet. Add the reserved flageolets and cook over low heat until beans are heated through. Divide the sautéed beans among each of four serving plates and spread them to cover the plates. Then place a lamb shank in the center of each plate. Adjust seasonings in the sauce, then spoon some over each shank and serve.

Wine: Cain Cellars Cain Five (Napa Valley)

Grilled Marinated Rack of Lamb

This is a wonderful way to enjoy lamb, but it is costly. Cleveland's premier butcher, our wonderful Mr. Brisket, taught us that by totally removing the cap—or line of fat underneath the meaty part of the chops—you eliminate all of the unpleasant gristle. But that means you do discard a slim bit of meat that is in the middle of the cap. If you want a sauce, make one with wild mushrooms (page 324).

Serves 4

MARINADE

½ cup Cabernet Sauvignon wine
1 cup olive oil
2 large cloves garlic, sliced
1 tablespoon chopped fresh rosemary
1 teaspoon fresh thyme
1 teaspoon lavender flowers (optional)

1 rack of lamb, 6–7 chops per side, cap completely removed
Salt and freshly ground black pepper to taste

Sprigs of rosemary, thyme, and lavender for garnish

Early on the day of serving, pour wine into a large glass or ceramic baking dish. Slowly whisk in olive oil until an emulsion is formed. Add garlic and herbs and blend. Coat the two parts of the lamb rack with the marinade and arrange them in the dish. Let stand about 3 hours, turning several times. There is no need to refrigerate.

Thoroughly clean the surface of a gas or charcoal grill with a metal brush, then coat the surface evenly with Pam. Heat the grill until very hot. Remove lamb from marinade and season with salt and lots of pepper. Grill to desired doneness (6 minutes per side if you like it rare). Let rest on a cutting board for 10 minutes, then carve into chops.

Arrange 3 chops on each serving plate. Garnish with fresh rosemary, thyme, and lavender flowers.

Wine: Matanzas Creek Winery Merlot (Sonoma County)

Esther and Bill Welsh

Welsh Family Farm
Box 32
Churchtown, Iowa 52151
(319) 535-7318

*I*n many ways, the Welsh Family Farm is a typical Iowa farm. There are gently rolling hills against a huge blue sky and a handsome farmhouse with sturdy barns and sheds out back. The corn is about as high as it should be in late June, and there's lots of it. A big sign at the entrance proudly proclaims the name, and the place looks exactly the way one would expect a family farm to appear—comfortable, solid, nurturing, and prosperous. And it is totally organic.

"I'm just an Iowa farm boy," Bill Welsh told us. But in the 1950s, he was also in the United States Air Force. He was an instructor in atomic and biological warfare, teaching men the awesome power of these weapons, how to use them, and how to protect themselves against them. Ultimately, he left the military and began farming in Churchtown, not far from the Mississippi River. He and his wife, Esther, raised eight children.

Then in 1981, the evening before the Welshes' son Greg graduated from college, Bill found thirteen dead cows, a calamity for any farmer. After some remarkable detective work, the Welsh family learned a frightening lesson about farm chemicals.

At corn-planting time the previous spring, the Welshes were applying Dyfonate, a product containing organo-phosphate (something that becomes more toxic as it gets older), to the fields. Just before a storm came up, they pulled the wagon car-

rying the remaining bags of seed and Dyfonate into a shed to protect them from the elements. Apparently, one of the empty Dyfonate bags was left on the floor and no one noticed. Later, some bales of hay were stacked on the same spot. Early the following spring, when that hay was fed to the cows, those that ate it died.

"When I learned what went into that stuff I was horrified," Bill said. "Why, the same chemicals are used in poison gas. My father always warned me that I could kill us all with chemicals, but I always ignored him."

The picture of those dead animals is indelibly printed on Bill's mind. "When we really thought about what went into the products we used all the time, I vowed that I'd either quit farming or learn to farm another way," he added. And that was it for the Welsh family; from then on they did it differently.

In 1979, the Welshes had 480 acres. Bill felt that it would be best to be small, so he sold some of the land to neighbors. Now he realizes that organic farming is possible on a larger scale, but even with son Gary as a partner in the business, the days are almost too full.

The Welshes raise about 800 pigs a year, working with a breed developed for leanness and meatiness by a company in Kentucky. Bill has been very pleased with the results. Most are sold as certified organic pork through a distributor in Chicago.

The boars are right there at the farm; no artificial insemination for the Welsh sows! The 500-pound sows are put in farrowing pens, not crates; this way they have room to move around and turn. A sow averages 9 or 10 piglets per litter, 2.2 litters per year. Piglets nurse for four weeks, then just before weaning time, Bill starts them on a bit of feed. They get a well-balanced—and expensive—ration of organic corn, soy, proteins, and minerals. Whereas regular corn sells at $2.50 a bushel, organic corn is $3.50. A pig eats 10 to 12 bushels of corn before it reaches market size. The Welshes grow their own corn, but they do buy the soybeans. Since Bill does not use antibiotics, he gives the animals top-quality probiotics, bacteria that maintain the natural level of good bacteria in the intestinal tract.

Within five months or so, the animals reach about 250 pounds. At that weight, the animal has the optimum ratio of fat to meat. Bigger than that, the animal becomes more fat and less meaty. So slaughter is determined by weight, not age. The Welshes breed a sow for three years; then she goes off to market for sausage. Bill and Gary select the best of the piglets for replacement breeding on an ongoing basis.

The Welshes also raise about 2,500 certified organic turkeys a year, all bought as one-day-old chicks.

In addition, Bill and Gary are raising about 28,000 chickens a year. They work with HYPECOs, named for the company that developed the breed for the kosher trade.

Bill sells his pork fresh, but the poultry is flash-frozen immediately. He commented, "Even though we are very careful about contamination at our end, if a bird sits around too long when it leaves us, there could be a problem." This approach also enables him to ship to faraway places, so the fabled Bread and Circus markets of Massachusetts get large shipments of Welsh poultry every few months. Other trucks take frozen Welsh birds to Walnut Acres in Pennsylvania. And the fine restaurants in Madison, Wisconsin, arrange special pickups so they can get the chickens fresh.

The biggest challenge that Bill sees is trying to be both a producer and marketer at the same time. While the quality of his pork is outstanding, there are only a few distributors who will pay the premium for organically raised pork.

Fortunately, the state of Iowa is becoming supportive of the organic movement. Son Greg is now working for the Iowa agricultural extension office, developing markets for organic farm products. When Bill first began his organic effort, lending institutions would not give money to organic farmers, so risky was this type of farming thought to be. Now the state has real concerns about the effects of chemicals on the soil.

"The livestock health is much better, farming this way," Bill emphasized. "We really see a difference. And we're raising the best-quality product we can. But remember," he said, "just because it's organic doesn't mean it's automatically good. A farmer has to really work at being good."

Barbecued Smoked Spareribs

This recipe grew out of our taste memories of the great ribs we sampled in Kansas City. Then our friend George Germon, of Al Forno, in Providence, suggested that we add water to our Dry Barbecue Rub to make a brine. While he doesn't add water to the smoker, we feel more comfortable

doing so. If you use a dry smoker, be sure to check the ribs often, because they become tender faster.

Serves 8

    8 slabs top-quality spareribs, about 1
        pound each
    1 cup Dry Barbecue Rub (page 238)
        Approximately 3 gallons boiling
        water

At least 1 pound hickory-, cherry-, or apple-wood chips, soaked in water

3 bay leaves

8 sprigs fresh thyme or 2 teaspoons dried thyme

Approximately 1 cup cider vinegar

2 cups Wet Barbecue Mop (page 239)

3–4 cups Our Barbecue Sauce (page 239)

Rub meat with about 1 tablespoon of Dry Rub per side. Place slabs in a large roasting pan, add 1 cup water, cover, and marinate 24 hours in the refrigerator, turning several times. Bring to room temperature and cut slabs in half.

Make a large charcoal fire in the smoker. When the coals are white, quickly add the soaked wood chips. Then fill the water pan with 2 gallons boiling water, 2 bay leaves, 5 sprigs thyme, and ⅔ cup vinegar.

Slather ribs with Wet Mop. Arrange the slabs on the racks, overlapping a bit if necessary. Cover and smoke for 2 hours, basting several times and turning at least once. Add more water, herbs, and vinegar if liquids evaporate. The ribs should be quite tender. If not, smoke for another half hour.

Remove ribs from smoker, paint with a dab of Our Sauce, and set aside. (Too much sauce will cause the ribs to burn on the grill.) Thoroughly clean the surface of a gas or charcoal grill with a metal brush; then coat the surface evenly with Pam. Heat the grill until very hot. Meanwhile, heat the remaining Our Sauce in a saucepan and keep warm. Arrange ribs on the grill, reduce heat to medium, and cook about 6 minutes per side, turning several times. Then paint gen-erously with the heated sauce and serve with more sauce on the side.

Wine: Sausal Winery Zinfandel (Sonoma County)

Hot and Spicy Meat Loaf

This is the most often requested dish in our home; leftovers are especially splendid. The inspiration came from the brilliant Paul Prudhomme, who suggested that by blend-ing different peppers one could achieve a rounder heat. It is also he who taught us that evaporated milk in meat loaf adds a fla-vor that neither milk nor water can achieve.

Serves 10

2 teaspoons kosher salt

1 teaspoon freshly ground black pepper

1 teaspoon freshly ground white pepper

1 teaspoon cayenne pepper

1 teaspoon cumin

1 teaspoon powdered oregano or 1 tablespoon fresh oregano

1 teaspoon dried thyme or 1 tablespoon fresh thyme

1 bay leaf

1 cup finely chopped onion

½ cup minced scallion (white part only)

1 tablespoon finely minced garlic

⅔ cup minced celery

½ cup minced red bell pepper

½ cup minced Anaheim or Cubanelle chiles

½ cup unsalted margarine

½ cup evaporated milk
2½ pounds ground pork
1½ pounds ground veal
1 pound ground beef
3 jumbo eggs, beaten
2 cups fine, dry bread crumbs
1 tablespoon Tabasco
2 tablespoons Worcestershire sauce
½ cup chili sauce

Hot and Spicy Sauce (page 36)

Combine the salt, three ground peppers, cumin, and herbs and set aside. Combine the onion, scallion, garlic, celery, bell pepper, and chiles and reserve.

Melt margarine in a large, nonstick skillet and sauté seasonings for 3 minutes over medium heat, stirring often. Add vegetables and cook, stirring frequently, until tender. Add milk and heat through. Remove pan from heat, let cool, and discard bay leaf.

In the bowl of an electric mixer fitted with a paddle, combine the meats. Add eggs and beat until mixture is light. Remove bowl from mixer and blend in crumbs, Tabasco, Worcestershire, and chile sauce. Then add the cooled contents of the skillet and blend.

Turn the mixture into a 9x13 baking pan and shape into a long loaf, patting it firmly into shape. Chill for several hours.

Preheat oven to 400° and bake meat loaf for 1 hour and 15 minutes, or until nicely browned. Let rest in a warm place for at least 10 minutes before slicing. Serve with Hot and Spicy Sauce on the side.

Wine: Girard Winery Ol' Blue Jay (California)

Barbecued Pork Loin

Try this with Simple Fried Rice (page 96) and stir-fried vegetables. Boneless pork loin is usually about 2 inches thick and about 4½ inches wide, so it will cook fairly rapidly.

Serves 6–8

MARINADE
1 cup fresh orange juice
¼ cup dry red wine
¼ cup dark soy sauce
3 tablespoons Chinese chile paste (available in Oriental markets)
¼ cup hoisin sauce
3 cloves garlic, minced
2 shallots, finely minced
2 tablespoons minced fresh ginger
2 tablespoons dark sesame oil
3 tablespoons cilantro
2 tablespoons chili sauce

1 boneless pork loin, about 4½ pounds, silverskin removed

Combine all ingredients except the pork in a Pyrex baking dish and blend well. Immerse pork loin in the dish, coating it evenly with marinade. Cover and refrigerate for at least 8 hours, turning frequently.

Thoroughly clean the surface of a gas or charcoal grill with a metal brush; then coat the surface evenly with Pam. Heat the grill until very hot. Remove pork from marinade and place on grill. Lower hood, reduce heat to medium, and grill for 12 minutes. Baste, turn, and grill on the other side for an additional 12 minutes. Check with an instant thermometer; if the temperature registers 150°, the meat will be medium. Let roast rest for 10 minutes, slice, and serve with the natural juices that have collected on the carving board.

Wine: Saintsbury Garnet Pinot Noir (Carneros)

Braised Stuffed Pork Chops

We love to serve this with Grits Soufflé (page 37) and sautéed cabbage or Puree of Winter Squash (page 49).

Serves 4

> 3 tablespoons butter or margarine
> 2 thick strips smoked bacon, diced
> 1 clove garlic, minced
> 1 shallot, minced
> ½ cup fine, dry bread crumbs
> 2 tablespoons minced fresh herbs, such as sage, rosemary, thyme, or chives
> Salt and freshly ground black pepper to taste
> 4 loin or rib pork chops, each about 1½ inches thick and with a deep pocket
> Approximately ½ cup flour
> 2 tablespoons vegetable oil
> 750 ml. Cabernet Sauvignon or Rhône-style red wine
>
> Minced fresh chives and parsley for garnish

Melt butter in a large cast-iron skillet that has a tight cover and set aside. Transfer 1 tablespoon of the butter to a small skillet and sauté the bacon in it until meat is soft and brown but not crisp. Then add the garlic and shallot and stir over medium heat until softened. Stir in crumbs, herbs, salt, and pepper.

Divide this mixture into 4 portions and stuff each portion into one of the pork pockets, packing firmly. Holding the open sides together, dredge stuffed chops in the flour and carefully set aside on a cake rack.

Preheat oven to 325°. Add the oil to the remaining butter in the larger skillet, heat, then quickly brown the chops on both sides. Remove pan from heat and pour about 2 cups of wine over the chops, stirring up any particles that have stuck to the bottom of the pan.

Cover the skillet and place it in preheated oven. Braise for 1½ hours, basting several times. Add more wine as liquids evaporate or are absorbed.

Wine: Ponzi Vineyard Pinot Noir (Oregon)

Jodi and Ron Snyder

Great Bend Organic Farm

P.O. Box 158

Port Clinton, Pennsylvania 19549

(215) 562-5502

Great Bend Farm, 170 acres near Port Clinton, about 20 miles north of Reading, is certified organic. In 1988, Jodi and Ron Snyder were raising field corn and hogs on another Pennsylvania farm when they encountered a want ad in the *Lancaster Farmer*. Great Bend Farm was looking for a manager, someone who was dedicated to organic methods. Owners John Spang and Tanya Russ were returning to Belize, in Central America, where both had worked in the past, and where they owned another organic farm. They met, and the chemistry—so to speak—was right. The Snyders' assignment: raise superior hogs organically and develop a market for them.

The pigs on this farm are "free-range"; they live in the pastures. When he was studying agriculture at Ohio State University, Ron worked for a farmer who raised his pigs in the fields. "I saw it could happen," he said, "and I never forgot it." Initially, Ron brought the sows into a shed to farrow, but in recent times he has let them have their babies in the fields, and it has worked. There are 40 acres of pastureland, divided into a number of smaller fields by an electric fence. There is usually enough water, there is plenty of both sunshine and shade, and the pigs love the clover and timothy in the meadows. They are never confined.

On the day of our visit, as we had walked the farm, all of us drenched from the stifling heat, Ron looked at his pigs and mother sows as they searched for whatever comfort they could find in the dryness of the meadows. Their water in this long, hot, dry period has had to come from the bass pond, the level of which is low enough to cause Ron some concern. There was plenty of water for them to drink, from pressure-sensitive nozzles on large drums, but there was little water to be spared for a wallow, something swine not only want but need, especially during the year's hottest days. Ron shook his head sadly. "Well, at least they are outside," he said, "and under the trees. That's better than how most pigs live."

But in one meadow, a dozen coal-black sows and a couple of boars were taking their ease under the hemlock trees. "A different breed?" we wondered. No; a small spring in this meadow was still yielding a little water. It had mixed with the coal silt that is part of most bottomland in this eastern Pennsylvania farm country, and the swine had wallowed in it. Pink noses, white teeth, and sparkling brown eyes stood out on their ebony faces as they watched us walk by.

The downside of this free-range approach is that pigs sometimes get under the electric fence and don't come back for a while. On one occasion, forty piglets wandered off. But they all knew where the good food was and eventually they came home.

In addition to raising hogs, the Snyders farm about 50 acres. They raise a lot of corn and rye, but not enough for the several hundred hungry animals. So Ron is always looking for organic feed. "The pigs get what I can find at a reasonable price," he said.

As the pigs grow, a few females are chosen to be bred. The older breeding sows go to market when they are about three and have passed their peak efficiency. The rest of the animals, about 400 in number as of 1991, go to market at about six months, or 225 pounds.

"These are high-maintenance animals," said Ron. "You work hard for what you get." And good help is hard to find. "Most high school kids just can't cut it," Ron tells us. "We have a nineteen-year-old college student now and he is terrific. But in a few weeks he'll be gone."

Another concern is the deer. "It's a deer epidemic," Ron said. "They eat everything—the clover, the corn, the pear trees and apple trees, the grain we leave out for the pigs. Some evenings we will count more deer in the pastures than pigs." He has installed more and higher fencing to keep them out, but it doesn't always work. He doesn't hunt, and doesn't much like it when hunters come through, so the deer will continue to be a problem.

And then there are the vagaries of the market. "I just don't listen to the farm reports on the radio," said Ron. "Hear those prices and it makes you sick."

In actual fact, the Snyders hope that they will never have to listen to the commodity prices. Their approach is based on creating a superior product and getting a better price as a result. "Our pork is better," says Jodi. "Anyone can tell. Our kids can tell." Jodi is working to develop an organic smoked ham—no chemicals, nitrites, or nitrates—and to grow certified organic spices and herbs. Also in the works is apple sausage made with organically grown apples.

The Snyders' children, Jamie and Josh, are growing up on one of the most beautiful farms we have ever seen. It is neat, clean, and orderly, the payback for their daily toil. There is a pond for swimming and fishing, for bass and sunfish, and for the thirsty animals. There is the old canal bed, the towpath, and the locks that helped the boats laden with coal or pork or grain get to market. And the stone walls of the lock master's house still stand after a hundred and fifty years, long enough for a great tree to grow up within them, live its life, and die, its bare branches still spread out over the ruins and the towpath.

"I wish we were where we are now when we came three years ago," Ron said. "It's been slow going. But we are making progress. This is important to do. Maybe three years from now we'll be where we want to be."

Fred's Fried Pork Chops

This dish goes back to Fred's West Virginia roots. We love to serve it on a cold winter's night with some hearty soup and great potatoes. Best of all is to make it in the late summer, when it can be served with Fred's Fried Green Tomatoes (page 7).

Serves 4

      2 jumbo eggs
     12 drops Tabasco
      1 cup finely ground cornmeal
      3 fresh sage leaves, minced
      2 teaspoons salt
      2 teaspoons freshly ground white
          pepper
      1 teaspoon garlic powder
      8 pork chops, each ½ inch thick
     ½ cup vegetable oil

Combine eggs and Tabasco in a shallow soup plate and beat thoroughly. Combine cornmeal, sage, salt, pepper, and garlic powder in another shallow soup plate and blend. Dip chops in egg mixture, then dredge in meal mixture, coating well. Place coated chops on a cake rack.

Heat the oil in a large cast-iron skillet. Add chops, reduce heat, and fry for 5 minutes. Turn and fry on other side for an additional 5 minutes, or until golden.

Wine: Dehlinger Winery Pinot Noir "Estate" (Sonoma County)

Braised Pork and Smoked Sausage with Sauerkraut and Beer

Serve with some great potatoes and crusty bread. Beer could also be substituted for the wine recommendations at the end of the recipe.

Serves 6–8

     ⅓ pound smoked bacon, diced
    5–6 cups drained canned sauerkraut
      1 cup chopped peeled apple
     ⅔ cup chopped onion
      2 teaspoons caraway seeds
      1 teaspoon dried thyme
      2 teaspoons freshly ground black
          pepper

12 ounces dark beer, or more if
   necessary
¾ cup rich chicken stock
1 tablespoon dried juniper berries
1 bay leaf
2–3 tablespoons unsalted margarine
1 large clove garlic, minced
1 boneless pork loin, about 4 pounds,
   silverskin removed
   Salt and freshly ground black
   pepper to taste
2 pounds smoked sausage

Preheat oven to 350°. In a cast-iron Dutch oven, cook bacon over low heat until fat is partially rendered. Add sauerkraut, apple, onion, caraway, thyme, and pepper. Stir well and cook over low heat for 15 minutes. Add beer, stock, juniper berries, and bay leaf. Cover and braise in preheated oven for 2 hours. Add more beer if mixture becomes dry during cooking.

About 20 minutes before sauerkraut is done, melt margarine in a cast-iron skillet over high heat. Add garlic and pork loin. Quickly sear pork on all sides. Remove from pan and season with salt and pepper. Sear smoked sausage in same fashion. Place pork and sausage on braised sauerkraut, baste with garlic/margarine mixture, and spoon some braised sauerkraut over the meats. Baste with the drippings in the sauerkraut pot. Cover and return to oven for 1¼ hours. Slice meats and serve with sauerkraut on the side.

Wine: Steven Thomas Livingstone Dry Riesling (Columbia Valley)
or *Chateau Ste. Michelle Gewürztraminer* (Columbia Valley)

Grilled Pork Chops in Cracked-Pepper Marinade

Serves 2–4

MARINADE
¼ cup vegetable oil
¼ cup coarsely ground red, white,
   green, and black peppercorns
2 tablespoons Dijon mustard
1 teaspoon cayenne pepper
1 teaspoon salt
1 tablespoon minced fresh parsley
1 tablespoon minced shallots
1 tablespoon Worcestershire sauce
1 tablespoon Cognac or brandy

4 loin pork chops, each about 1 inch
   thick
2 cups apple- or cherry-wood chips,
   soaked in water

Combine all ingredients except chops (and wood chips!) in a small bowl and blend thoroughly. Coat chops with this mixture, pressing the peppercorns in firmly. Transfer meat and marinade to a glass baking dish, cover, and let chops marinate in refrigerator for at least several hours.

Thoroughly clean the surface of a gas or charcoal grill with a metal brush; then coat the surface evenly with Pam. Heat the grill until very hot, then add the wood chips to the fire. Place chops on grill, and carefully sear on each side for 1 minute. Then lower heat, cover with hood, and grill for 8 minutes. Turn chops and grill on the other side for an additional 7 minutes.

Wine: Rex Hill–Maresh Vineyard Pinot Noir (Willamette Valley, Oregon)

Sam Edwards

S. Wallace Edwards & Sons
P.O. Box 25
Surry, Virginia 23883
(800) 222-4267

We'll never know for sure how it all started, but we do know that long before the white man established the first permanent English settlement on Jamestown Island, in 1607, local Indian tribes cured and smoked their own meat right in their wigwams.

The premier contemporary practitioners of this art, S. Wallace Edwards & Sons, do not quite go back to those early days. And the pork these days is as likely to come from Ohio as from Virginia. But the techniques followed in curing the hams still have their roots in the Indian practices that go back centuries.

Samuel Wallace Edwards, Sr., the company's founder, grew up in Isle of Wight County, Virginia. His father-in-law operated the Jamestown-Surry ferry in the early 1920s, and the enterprising young man saw a great opportunity: he would serve ham sandwiches to the ferry customers. From that small but very successful operation grew this outstanding business. The president today is the founder's son, Samuel Wallace, Jr. (Wallace), and the vice president, Samuel Wallace Edwards III, is the founder's grandson.

It used to be that Virginia hogs would be finished on peanuts left in the fields after the harvest. Rarely will you find peanut-fattened hogs today. Automation now makes certain that all the peanuts are harvested. Peanuts are dear, so hogs are fed a standard grain ration. In fact, today's hogs are usually killed at around 250 pounds, much leaner than the slaughter weight of twenty years ago. Until the 1960s, the Edwards company slaughtered its own pigs. Now they demand absolutely fresh cuts from their suppliers. And they never use meat that is frozen.

"We're really picky about the meat we use," Sam said. "We want it here within twenty-four hours of the slaughter." Also, the temperature of the fresh meat is critical; it must be cooled properly—to between 38° and 43°—immediately after slaughter and cutting. Edwards has three principal suppliers; and because every delivery is recorded, and each ham lot labeled, they can track quality problems instantly.

Tradition says that the ham first needs to be put in cure, then aged six months to a year. The longer the aging, the more intense the flavor. Sam said, "We take the best of Mother Nature—temperature, humidity, and time—and duplicate it." If a ham is to be aged for a long time, it will be cut long on the hock and high toward the loin. The hock cut will be through the ankle joint to minimize the meat that is exposed to the air, preserving its natural moisture. Other hams, those set for shorter curing and a quicker turnover, will be cut short on the hock, with short butt ends and skinned backs.

The curing process consists of several stages. First, the meat is hand rubbed with a curing mixture of flaked salt and sodium nitrate. While salting is essential for preservation, the Edwards hams are noted for their superior flavor and lack of excessive saltiness. "We use as little sodium nitrate as possible, but we must use some; the special salt is used because it holds to the ham better than any other," Sam explained. Extra attention is given to areas that are not covered with skin. The hams are stacked in refrigerated rooms to simulate winter. After five days, the meat is hand-rubbed with the curing mixture again; this is known as "overhauling." The hams stay in this first room about a month, depending on their size and trim.

Each piece is individually inspected to determine when it is ready for the next step, which is washing and (usually) pepper coating. "Pepper really doesn't do much for the flavor," Sam said, "but it used to be needed to protect the meat from flies. Now we still do it for the hams that will be left uncooked, since people like the look, but we don't pepper the hams that will ultimately be cooked, since the pepper gets washed off in that process anyway." After peppering (or not), the ham is put into a stockinette. Then it goes into the next room—springtime—where it is hung on wooden racks at a moderate temperature for two weeks. During this time, the humidity level will be closely monitored so that the meat does not become too dry on the surface.

Then slowly, over a three-day period, the meat is brought up to a temperature of 85°, simulating summertime. Then the hams are rolled in their racks into one of the smokehouses, where they will be kept at that 85° for a week in a pure hickory-chip smoke.

The traditional Virginia ham consists of a whole long leg bone, which can weigh well over twelve pounds. These hams are the only ones smoked in the original smokehouse, a high wooden structure in which the hams hang at various levels above a basement smoke pit. Getting to them requires a long ladder. "Someone has to do the ladder duty," Sam admitted, "but no one really enjoys it." The smaller hams, the bacon, and the sausages are done in newer smokehouse facilities.

After smoking comes "summer" aging. The long hams, called Wigwam Brand, are aged for one year. Hams for grocery stores are aged only three months; those for restaurants, specialty-food stores, and the majority of what's offered in the Edwards catalogue are aged six months. The longer the aging, the drier and saltier the ham becomes and the more intense the flavor. It's the higher amount of natural juices still left in the ham that cuts the saltiness. From the day the meat arrives to the completion of this aging process, each piece of meat loses an average of 25 percent of its weight.

The Edwards family watches these hams as closely as a winemaker watches his wine barrels. Large ceiling fans circulate the air to assure an even temperature. Sam can insert a special long pick into each piece of meat and tell from smelling it exactly how the aging process is proceeding. When sold at the time of peak flavor, a ham will maintain its best quality for at least two months, if properly handled.

When fully aged, most hams are taken from their stockinette, put into a huge kettle of water, and simmered at 185–190° for six or seven hours, until they reach an internal temperature of 158–162°. Other hams are sold uncooked, and all varieties are available either bone in or boneless. The uncooked Wigwam Brand ham tastes like fine prosciutto. Any uncooked ham will not spoil when kept at room temperature but will continue to age and ultimately become too dry to enjoy.

The bacon cure is a mixture of salt, sugar, and sodium nitrite. Because the belly meat is so thin, curing lasts only one week, after which the meat is hickory-smoked for 18 hours at a high temperature. Then it is hung at 30–40° for a few days to stabilize and firm up. It is finally ready to sell. No chemicals or water are injected into this bacon; it's a natural product.

Edwards also makes a Surry Brand sausage with pork butt, ham trimmings, and a secret mixture of seasonings that includes a very robust sage. The sausage is put into natural hog casings and tied at 3-inch intervals. Then it, too, is hickory-smoked.

In the peak period, October through December, Edwards has forty employees; the rest of the year there are about fifteen. Besides their ever-expanding mail-order catalogue, they have a small retail shop near the plant and another in Williamsburg. In recent times, they have added such products as barbecued spareribs and smoked turkey to their line.

When asked about his favorite way to eat ham, Sam Edwards said, "In a sandwich, made with my grandmother's bread and some real butter." And then he commented, "But no one will bake bread for me, they're too busy."

Today his father concentrates on the scheduling and the wholesale end of things and Sam does the public relations, plus the wholesale specialty-food and retail sales. "Because I've always been here, we're used to working together, so if we disagree, we just have very up-front, intensive discussions." Sam's mother, Yvonne Edwards, his wife, Donna, and Paul Harte, his brother-in-law, are also very active in company operations.

Consistency and careful attention to every detail are what has made this company so successful since the early part of this century. That's why there will be yet another generation of Samuel Wallace Edwardses in the Surry, Virginia, smokehouse in the next century.

Sam Edwards's license plate reads HAM NO 1.
Wallace Edwards's—ED HAM
Yvonne Edwards's—SWE HAM
Donna Edwards's—VA HAM

Potato and Leek Soup with Virginia Bacon and Sage

Serves 8–10

  4 thick slices Edwards bacon, diced
  4 tablespoons unsalted butter or margarine
1–½ pounds leeks (white part only), sliced thin and washed
  1 large onion, diced
2½–3 pounds baking potatoes, peeled and diced
  3 quarts rich chicken stock
  ½ teaspoon dried sage or 1 teaspoon minced fresh sage
  Salt and freshly ground white pepper to taste

In a heavy skillet, cook bacon until crisp. Transfer bacon bits to a plate and set aside. Pour bacon fat into a heavy soup pot, add butter, and heat over medium heat until butter has melted. Add leeks and onions. Cover, reduce heat, and cook for 30 minutes, stirring occasionally.

Add potatoes and stir over medium heat for 5 minutes. Then add chicken stock and bring to a boil. Reduce heat, partially cover, and simmer for another 30 minutes, or until potatoes are very tender.

Remove soup from heat. Using a slotted spoon, transfer solids from the pot into a food processor. (You may have to do this in several batches.) Add about 1 cup of soup liquid and puree until smooth. Stir pureed vegetables back into liquid. Return pot to low heat and add sage, salt, and pepper. Keep soup at a simmer while you heat reserved bacon bits in a toaster oven or nonstick skillet. Crumble some over each soup bowl just before serving.

Wine: Dry Creek Vineyard Sauvignon Blanc (Sonoma County)

Stuffed Mushrooms with Virginia Ham and Herbs

When you have lots of fresh herbs, think of this dish. It's a great appetizer, but it also makes a terrific accompaniment to a grilled chop.

12 large cultivated mushroom caps
4 tablespoons unsalted butter, or
  more if necessary
2 teaspoons dark soy sauce
3 ounces Wigwam ham, finely minced
1 shallot, finely minced
1 clove garlic, finely minced
1 tablespoon finely minced fresh
  parsley
1 tablespoon pine nuts
⅓ cup fine, dry bread crumbs
1 teaspoon fresh thyme
1 tablespoon finely minced fresh
  chives
½ teaspoon freshly ground white
  pepper
½ cup Sauvignon Blanc wine

Chopped fresh parsley and chives
for garnish

Chive flowers and thyme flowers
for garnish (optional)

Butter a baking dish that is just large enough to hold the mushroom caps and set aside.

Peel mushroom caps, remove stems, and set aside. Finely chop mushroom peelings and stems.

Preheat oven to 425°.

Melt butter in a medium-sized skillet. Add chopped mushroom mixture and soy sauce, toss, then cover and sauté for 1 minute. Add ham, shallot, and garlic and continue to sauté, uncovered, until vegetables are tender. Add parsley and pine nuts and cook for 2 minutes more. Stir in bread crumbs and seasonings. If mixture is too dry, add a bit more butter.

Fill reserved mushroom caps with stuffing mixture; arrange stuffed caps in the prepared baking dish and pour wine around them. Bake for 30 minutes. Garnish with chopped parsley, chives, and herb flowers, if desired.

Wine: Schramsberg Vineyards Blanc de Noirs (Napa Valley)

Our Home Fries

This is one of Linda's favorite dishes. The smoky bacon, the partially browned potatoes, and the crisp onions all meld together into a heavenly mélange. This is comfort food at its best.

Serves 8

3 thick strips Edwards bacon, diced
3 pounds white baking potatoes,
  peeled
  Approximately ½ cup oil, or more
  if necessary
2 Spanish or Vidalia onions (about 1
  pound), sliced
¼ cup minced fresh parsley
1 tablespoon minced fresh sage
  Kosher salt and freshly ground
  black pepper to taste

Over medium heat, sauté bacon in a 10–12-inch cast-iron skillet. Meanwhile, slice potatoes in a food processor fitted with a 4 mm blade and set aside. Using a slotted spoon, transfer bacon to a plate and reserve.

Add enough oil to the skillet so that it comes ⅛ inch up the side of the pan. Add potatoes and toss until potatoes are coated. Cover and cook over medium-low heat for 20 minutes. Add more oil if skillet becomes dry.

Add onions and toss so that onions are evenly distributed. If potatoes are somewhat tender, cover and cook for another 5 minutes. If not, cover and cook until they are, about 10 minutes.

Uncover skillet and turn heat up to medium-high. When bottom layer of potatoes is browned, turn potatoes with a spatula and brown on the other side. Turn several times so that most of the potatoes brown. The onions will darken as well. Toss browned vegetables with herbs, reserved bacon bits, and seasonings.

Virginia Surf and Turf

Sam Edwards sent us to the nearby Surry Restaurant, in Surry, Virginia, for their version of Surf and Turf—crab cakes and ham. We couldn't resist adding the recipe to our repertoire. Serve with cornbread or biscuits.

Serves 4

> 8 soft-shell crabs
> 2–3 cups milk
> ½ cup finely ground unsalted roasted peanuts
> ½ cup fine, dry bread crumbs
>   Salt and freshly ground black pepper to taste
> ½ cup unsalted margarine
> ½ cup butter
> 2 tablespoons fresh lemon juice
> 4 drops Tabasco
> 1 tablespoon minced fresh parsley
> 8 thin slices Wigwam ham

Clean crabs by removing lungs, eyes, and intestines (or ask your fish merchant to do this for you right before you buy the crabs). First, lift up sides of upper shell and remove gills. Place crab on a wooden board and, using a sharp knife, cut off head immediately behind eyes. Use a butter knife to scrape out the lungs and intestines through this opening. Rinse well under running water. Then turn crab over and pull open the "apron," or turned-under tail, and cut it off with a sharp knife or scissors. Soak crabs in the milk for at least 1 hour.

Combine peanuts and crumbs in a shallow bowl. Add salt and pepper to taste. Remove crabs from milk and shake off excess. Coat with nut mixture and set aside on a rack.

Melt margarine in a cast-iron skillet and heat until smoking. Fry crabs shell side down for 1–2 minutes, or until golden; turn and fry on other side for an additional minute. Drain crabs on paper towels, pour margarine from skillet, and add butter. Quickly melt butter, then add lemon juice, Tabasco, parsley, and a few grindings of pepper.

Arrange 2 slices of ham in the center of each serving plate. Place 2 crabs on top of each plate, pour lemon butter over crabs, and serve.

Wine: Justin Vineyards Chardonnay (Paso Robles)

Poultry and
Feathered Game

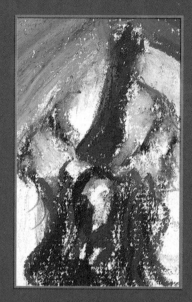

A. M. "Buddy" Lindeman, Jr., and David Lindeman

Buddy's Natural Chickens

250 South 123 Bypass

Seguin, Texas 78155

(512) 379-8782

*T*his part of Texas, around Gonzales County, is very good chicken country. Land is plentiful. The soil is well suited to the growing of feed. Water is abundant. And since so much water is needed for chicken processing—five gallons per bird—the unusually good drainage properties of the land around Gonzales make it ideal for processing plants.

The area has been so good, in fact, that it is the site of a huge operation owned by Tyson Poultry in neighboring Guadalupe County, one of the country's largest chicken companies. But while Tyson's plant generally processes more than 120,000 birds a day, Buddy's Natural Chickens only does 22,000 birds in a month.

There have now been three generations of Lindemans in the chicken business, all in this area of Texas. Buddy Lindeman is a big, burly man with gray hair, glasses, and a "gimme" hat. He's a Texas A&M man—an Aggie, as they're called in Texas. Buddy always wanted his own company. His years as a chicken man led him to believe that he could raise a better-tasting chicken by improving the feed, giving the birds more space, and avoiding antibiotics and hormones. And so Buddy began his business. He was processing the chickens in such an old plant, however, that he ended up with many damaged and parts-missing, or Grade B, chickens. The financial reality was that he could go broke before the business even took hold, since Grade B chickens have to be sold for a lower price than Grade A chickens, even though they cost the same to raise. Buddy's son, David, realized that a new plant was the solution to their quality-control problem. That's when he joined his dad in the operation while continuing his already established career in construction.

Buddy and David have scattered their farms around the county to protect against the possibility that a disease might wipe out the entire operation. The one-day-old chicks that they buy—a cross between Hubbard males and Indian River females—are taken to these various farms to be raised in well-ventilated houses. The Lindemans will only buy chicks from brooder hens that have not been given antibiotics. Since their chickens are fed no medications, they simply wash the facility with a solution of what Buddy calls "mother Clorox" if there is an outbreak of a virus or some other disease.

While most commercial operators allocate 0.7 square foot of space per bird, Buddy and David allow 1.75 to 2 square feet, and are even planning to increase that in the near future. Their birds move more, which makes them healthier. Proper ventilation of the hen houses is also a high priority. Chicks have air sacs in their wings and body cavities for the dispersal of body heat. In close, tight quarters with little ventilation, the ammonia given off by urine will build up in the air and infect the birds' air sacs. Although the one-day-old chicks are vaccinated against air sac disease and against leukosis, a serious disease of the nervous system, an outbreak of either could kill the chicks. On the other hand, treatment would render the chicks "unnatural." Buddy and David have discovered, however, that their careful approach, plus added ventilation, makes their chicks less susceptible to most kinds of diseases. Buddy and David do have a slightly higher mortality rate, 8 to 10 percent, than the 3 to 5 percent maintained by the chicken giants. For Buddy, it is an acceptable penalty. But he still works on making it lower.

Buddy gave us a copy of a USDA sample assay of tissue from one of his chickens. It was tested for sulfas, antibiotics, DDT, and other undesirable substances, and the report showed it to be a totally clean bird. He was very proud of it. This kind of testing is done constantly.

Buddy is proud of the feed formula he has developed. While organically grown grain would be prohibitively costly, Buddy is still very particular about what he does buy and from whom. His ration is a custom blend of soy, milo, plant oil, and natural vitamins and minerals. He is not using corn because, he told us, "It's just too hard to get clean corn here." No animal fat is given to the chicks. Buddy adds brewers' yeast as a vitamin supplement, which, along with the plant oils, contributes to the high cost of the feed.

He does not give the birds any growth stimulants, so the chicks are two days behind most commercially grown chicks in terms of weight gain. In addition, the feed conversion is a little less efficient for natural chickens. Most commercial growers will get a pound of chicken for 1.95 pounds of feed. Buddy gets a pound of chicken for 2.3 to 2.5 pounds of feed, so it takes extra days of feeding to achieve the desired weight. Ultimately, he goes to market with whole birds that retail at around $2 to $2.12 per pound. "Commercial chicken," said Buddy, "has no flavor. Our chicken has a real fowl flavor. Ours is like old-time chicken."

Buddy does not believe that birds should be raised and processed in the same venue, because the high traffic increases the disease hazard. So while he did not want to build the plant at one of his many growing sites, he remains very close to all of them at his new plant, in an industrial park in the city of Gonzales. The town government was helpful and encouraging, and it had the water they needed and the sewage capacity to handle their effluent.

At present, 7,500 birds per week are processed in Buddy's plant, which has the capacity to process 9,000 per day. The Lindemans have forty employees in all of their facilities. By comparison, Tyson has six hundred employees in their plant.

The Lindemans' facility is relatively un-automated. Their system allows for processing various sizes of birds, from 1½ pounds for a small chicken to perhaps 10 pounds for a turkey. The birds are stunned, bled, dipped in relatively hot water to defeather them, and then hand-eviscerated. (Natural chickens do not have to be scalded in order to whiten—a common practice in the chicken business.) Then the birds are placed in vats of ice water. Because Lindeman birds are not as fat, they don't pick up as much moisture as most commercially processed chicken: producers are allowed chickens that have as much as 12 percent water, but Buddy's contain a maximum of only 4 percent. Hand drawing allows the worker to rinse his tools between every bird, which is an important protection against contamination. The birds are delivered fresh and ice-packed, 24 to 48 hours after processing.

The Lindemans' principal customers are health-food stores, specialty-food markets, and gourmet meat departments of larger chain stores. Meanwhile, the Lindemans are also hoping to raise Cornish hens and are considering the many requests that they raise turkeys. As he speculated about the big bird, Buddy told us the old story of turkeys drowning themselves in rainwater by holding their open mouths up to the sky as the rain pours down. "I figure," he said, "that if they're that stupid I don't need them."

Buffalo Wings with Blue Cheese Dip

We always thought this recipe was terrific, but then our editor, Barbara Williams, sent us a message: "Ahem! Everyone knows that REAL buffalo wings can only be made with Durkee's Red Hot. Substitute ½–¾ cup of Red Hot for the Tabasco and vinegar." Not bad, Barbara! Either way it turns out that the wings are terrific!

Serves 2

DIP

- ½ cup plain yogurt
- ½ cup sour cream
- 4 ounces blue cheese, crumbled
- ½ teaspoon salt
- Juice of half a lemon
- ½ teaspoon freshly ground white pepper
- 1 tablespoon red wine vinegar

- 20 chicken wings
- ½ cup unsalted butter, melted
- 3 tablespoons Tabasco, or more to taste
- 1 tablespoon red wine vinegar
- 2–4 cups vegetable oil
- Salt to taste

- 3 stalks celery, trimmed and cut into sticks
- 3 carrots, peeled and cut into sticks

Combine dip ingredients in the bowl of a food processor fitted with the metal blade and blend until smooth. Scoop into a serving bowl, cover tightly with plastic wrap, and chill.

Remove tips from chicken wings and discard or save for stock. Separate drumstick from wing and place all pieces in a large, shallow baking dish.

Combine butter, Tabasco, and vinegar in a small skillet and heat over medium heat until butter is melted. Stir well. Pour half the mixture over the uncooked wings and set the other half aside. Let wings marinate for at least 30 minutes.

Pour enough oil to allow for deep frying into a wok or frying pan. Heat until smoking. When oil is hot enough to brown a cube of bread quickly, add marinated chicken. Fry for 6 minutes, or until golden brown on all sides.

Remove chicken from oil and place on paper towels to drain. Quickly reheat remaining half of butter mixture. Arrange chicken wings on a serving platter and pour hot butter mixture over them. Sprinkle with salt.

Serve with celery, carrots, and blue cheese dip on the side.

Wine: Piper Sonoma Sparkling Wine Brut (Sonoma County)

Perfect Roast Chicken

Serves 2

- 1 lemon, thinly sliced
- 2 medium onions, chopped
- 3 tablespoons minced fresh parsley
- 2 tablespoons minced fresh chives
- 1 3½–4-pound chicken
- 1 tablespoon olive oil
- Salt and freshly ground black pepper to taste

1 lemon, cut in half
1½ cups rich chicken stock
2 tablespoons unsalted butter
    (optional)

Preheat oven to 350°.

Combine sliced lemon with half the chopped onions, 1 tablespoon parsley, and 1 tablespoon chives. Blend well and stuff this mixture into the cavity of the chicken. Truss the chicken lightly by placing the middle of a piece of butcher's twine under the tail, crossing it over the body, and looping it around the drumsticks, around the sides, and between the first and second joint of the wing, which you have bent back to make a "catch" for the twine. Tie the twine on the underside.

Rub bird with olive oil, salt, and pepper. Put it in a large cast-iron skillet or on a rack in a roasting pan. Scatter the remaining onions around the pan. Squeeze the lemon halves over the chicken and put them in the pan too. Roast the chicken for 1¼ hours, basting with the stock about three times. Raise temperature to 400° and roast for 15 more minutes. Remove chicken from oven and let stand in warm place for 10 minutes before carving.

To make a delicious gravy, place roasting pan over high heat and scrape up browned bits. Swirl in a bit of butter if you wish and add remaining herbs.

Wine: Edna Valley Vineyard Chardonnay (Edna Valley)

Three-Generation Chicken Fricassee

As a child, Linda used to beg Grandma Weller to make this for her—it was always served on a bed of mashed potatoes. Then Linda's sons, Rob and Andy, began to ask Linda's mother, Gert LeVine, to make it for them. We can't wait to serve it to our grandchildren.

Serves 6

2 tablespoons hot paprika
1 teaspoon freshly ground black pepper
1 teaspoon salt
1½ 3-pound frying chickens
2 tablespoons vegetable oil
2 cloves garlic, minced
1 large onion, minced

MEATBALLS
1 pound ground veal
1 teaspoon kosher salt
1 teaspoon freshly ground black pepper
1 clove garlic, minced
2 tablespoons minced fresh herbs, such as parsley, oregano, sage, or thyme
1 small onion, minced
½ cup soft fresh breadcrumbs
1 jumbo egg

GRAVY
2 cups rich chicken stock
¼ cup vegetable oil
¼ cup unbleached flour

1 tablespoon minced fresh parsley

Combine paprika, pepper, and salt in a large bowl. Cut chicken into 6 breast pieces, 3 thighs, 3 drumsticks, 3 wings, and 3 drumettes. Add chicken pieces to seasonings and toss well. Let stand for 1 hour, then heat oil in a large skillet over medium heat. Add garlic and onions and sauté for 2 minutes. Add chicken and sauté until golden on all sides. Cover, reduce heat, and cook for 30 minutes.

Preheat oven to 500°.

While chicken is cooking, prepare meatballs: Combine all meatball ingredients in the bowl of an electric mixer and mix until light and fluffy. Form mixture into small balls and place them on a large baking sheet that has shallow sides. Roast balls until browned, about 10 minutes. When the chicken is done, stir into the pan with the cooked chicken.

To make the gravy, heat the chicken stock in a small saucepan. At the same time, heat the oil in a cast-iron skillet. Whisk the flour into the oil and heat over medium-high heat, whisking constantly, until the mixture is a rich, dark brown. Slowly stir this roux into the hot stock. Cook the gravy for 10 minutes, simmering briskly.

Add the gravy to the chicken and meatballs. Cook over medium heat for another 30 minutes, stirring occasionally. Skim off any fat that rises to the surface. Taste and adjust seasonings. Sprinkle with the parsley and serve.

Wine: Pine Ridge Winery Merlot (Napa Valley) or *Kalin Cellars Chardonnay* (Sonoma County)

Lemon-Mustard and Hazelnut Chicken Breasts

We think that the combination of lemon and mustard really enhances the natural flavor of chicken without dominating it.

Serves 4

    6 tablespoons Dijon mustard
      Juice of 2 large lemons
    20 drops Tabasco
     1 cup finely chopped hazelnuts
    ⅔ cup fine, dry bread crumbs
     1 tablespoon minced fresh tarragon
     1 tablespoon minced fresh parsley
     1 tablespoon minced fresh chives
     1 teaspoon kosher salt
     1 teaspoon freshly ground white
       pepper
     4 boneless chicken breasts, split and
       skinned
    ½ cup unsalted margarine, melted

      Chopped fresh tarragon and lemon
      slices for garnish

In a flat soup plate, combine mustard, lemon juice, and Tabasco. Whisk thoroughly. In another soup plate, combine nuts, crumbs, herbs, salt, and pepper.

Coat each breast with the mustard mixture, then dredge in the hazelnut mixture. Melt half the margarine in a large nonstick skillet. When margarine is sizzling, add the chicken breasts. Sauté for 5–6 minutes, or until golden. Add remaining margarine as needed. Turn and sauté about 5 minutes on the other side. Garnish with fresh tarragon and lemon slices.

Wine: Stony Hill Vineyard Chardonnay (Napa Valley)

James D. Reichardt

Reichardt Duck Farm

3770 Middle Two Rock Road

Petaluma, California 94952

(707) 762-6314

How did the first Peking ducks get to this country? While there are probably many variations on the legend, we sure like the story as we learned it from Jim Reichardt of Reichardt Duck Farm in Petaluma, California.

Sometime in the 1870s, a dozen live white Chinese Peking ducks mysteriously disappeared from a clipper ship in San Francisco. A few weeks later, two dozen ducks, after a trip around Cape Horn, were delivered to a farmer in New York. The now-famous Long Island duck industry grew from that delivery. The dozen left in San Francisco were the founders of the line now being bred in Petaluma.

Otto H. Reichardt, Sr., bought a flock of those ducks right after the turn of the century and started raising them in San Francisco. Then as now, his customers were the restaurants and markets of Chinatown. Otto, Jr., like his grandson Jim, grew up with ducks. And for a while, as his grandson would do, he left the business. He became a violinist, studied at Berkeley and Columbia, played in great orchestras, and was a high school music teacher. But the business needed him and the family needed him, so he put aside the fiddle and picked up the ducks.

The farm produces over a million ducks a year, and 90 percent of them still go to Chinatowns in Oakland and San Francisco. At any given moment, there are as many as 15,000 hens laying eggs. There are, on the average, five female ducks per drake, which means that 3,000 male ducks roam through the yard and keep the flow of fertilized eggs coming.

The females begin laying at six months and continue for about a year. So when a pen's production starts to slip at the eighteen-month mark, those birds become a very famous duck sausage, and a new group of breeders are brought in. This brood stock is carefully chosen from from the hatchlings for size, configuration, and activity.

The eggs are gathered every morning and screened for cleanliness. Dirty eggs don't hatch as well, so they are washed, packaged, and sold to those who swear that no chicken egg tastes as good as a duck egg. A judgment is made as to how many ducks will need to go to market in two and a half months, and the appropriate number of eggs go into the incubator. For about 28 days, they are kept at the correct temperature and moved periodically to simulate the movement they would experience if they were under a mother duck. After hatching, the ducklings go into a warm, moist, light room, where they start to eat.

The food they receive is basically pelletized corn, as organic or natural as the Reichardts can find. The food contains no hormones, antibiotics, or growth stimulants. While the Reichardts would like to buy certified organic feed, the cost would be prohibitive. They use 24,000 bales of hay every year to keep the birds clean and out of the muck. And the birds are not routinely inoculated.

As the ducks grow, they are moved into larger buildings with concrete paddocks, where they move about as they please and eat and drink whenever they want. Then, at 45 days, when they are between 4½ and 5 pounds in weight, they are humanely slaughtered.

No adrenaline-producing truck ride is necessary. They are killed quickly, suspended on a conveyor, given an initial plucking, dipped in wax, cooled, stripped of wax and feathers, and then eviscerated carefully by hand. All of this takes place in the presence of a USDA inspector.

Just minutes after the process starts, it ends when the ducks are plunged into a 32° ice bath, which puts them into total biological inactivity. The chilled ducks are then packed in boxes for shipment. They go out complete with their heads and feet, which is the way the Buddhist Chinese want them—to heaven in one piece.

Jim says he expects every duck to be consumed within one week after slaughter.

Is this a natural operation? Jim says it is. But he points out a paradox: he does not use antibiotics and does not inoculate his birds, but he is obliged to keep them in a controlled environment on wire mesh for the first few days. And that, he says, is not natural, but he wants to keep the birds warm for the first week or so, "just like their mommies would. Then they roam around inside and outside.

"We try to keep the raising process as natural as possible," said Jim, underscoring the complexities of labeling. "Mostly natural, but a little bit unnatural."

On the wall of the office are a number of extraordinary menus. They are for the Reichardts' series of "double duck dinners," which they started in the mid-1980s. They work with the Duxoup Wine Works (pronounce that duck soup, and it's for real) and the Bay Wolf Restaurant in Oakland to plan multicourse duck dinners accompanied by wines from Duxoup (and Duckhorn).

The Reichardt Duck Farm is about as big as you can get and still keep all functions under one management and in one place. What the Reichardt family raises on their farm, unfortunately for those of us who don't live there, is sold, cooked, and eaten in California. To expand would be to lose control, and perhaps lose quality. And Jim and his partners want to keep things just as they are.

So someday when you are in California and hungry, go into a restaurant and see if there is a Petaluma duck on the menu. If there is, it will be from the Reichardt Duck Farm and it will be the best duck you have ever eaten.

Bay Wolf's Crisp Roast Duck with Grapefruit, Black Pepper, Spinach, and Endive

Michael Wild, one of the owners of the Oakland, California, restaurant Bay Wolf, is an absolute duck fanatic, so one can always count on having some wonderful duck dishes there. This would be delicious with Wild Rice with Pecans (page 102), made with Manitok wild rice.

Serves 4–6

> Peel of one grapefruit, cut in fine julienne strips
> 3 tablespoons sugar
> 2 teaspoons salt
> 2 teaspoons freshly ground black pepper
> 2 teaspoons dried thyme or 2 sprigs fresh thyme
> 6 bay leaves
> 2 fresh ducks, 3½–4½ pounds each, cleaned, with excess fat trimmed, at room temperature
> 1 head garlic, cut in half
> ½ onion, cut in half
> 1 lemon, cut in half
> 1 cup Dark Brown Duck Glaze (page 294)

> 1 cup dry white wine
> Juice of 1 grapefruit
> 2 bunches spinach (about 1 pound), washed, blanched, cooled, and squeezed dry
> 2 heads Belgian endive, cut into julienne strips
> Sections of 2 grapefruits, pith removed

Bring 3 cups water to boil in a small saucepan. Add grapefruit peel and blanch for 1 minute, then drain. Combine peel with sugar in the same saucepan and cook over medium-low heat until sugar is absorbed by peel, 4–5 minutes. Transfer peel to a plate and spread out to dry.

Preheat oven to 450°. Combine salt, ½ teaspoon pepper, thyme, and bay leaves in a small dish. Place half this mixture inside each duck cavity, then add half a head of garlic, an onion quarter, and a lemon half to each cavity. Thoroughly prick skin with a fork. Place ducks on racks in roasting pans and cover pan bottoms with boiling water. Roast ducks in preheated oven for 1 hour and 15 minutes, pricking skin every 15 minutes. Add water as necessary to keep pan bottom covered.

When ducks are done, remove from oven and let rest 15–30 minutes in a warm place while you make the sauce. Skim 2 table-spoons of fat from the bottom of the pan and set aside.

Combine duck glaze, wine, and grape-fruit juice in a small saucepan. Cook over medium heat until mixture is syrupy. Lower heat and keep warm.

Quickly heat reserved duck fat in a large skillet over medium heat. Add spinach and endive. Toss until vegetables are heated through. Season with a bit of salt and pep-per. Add grapefruit sections and 1½ tea-spoons pepper to sauce.

Remove duck breasts from bone and slice on the diagonal. Remove thigh and drumstick in one piece. Divide spinach and endive mixture among four heated serving plates. Fan breast meat along one side of each plate and add thigh and drumstick. Nap with sauce and garnish with reserved candied grapefruit peel.

Wine: Carneros Creek Winery Pinot Noir (Carneros)

Dark Brown Duck Stock or Glaze

Save those carcasses when you bone duck breasts so that you can make this stock. To make a duck glaze, reduce it even further—to 1 cup.

    2 duck carcasses, broken into pieces
      Giblets from 2 ducks
    1 large onion, quartered
    3 carrots, scrubbed and cut into
      chunks
    1 parsnip, scrubbed and cut into
      chunks
    1 turnip, scrubbed and cut into
      chunks
    2 celery stalks
    1 bay leaf
    2 sprigs thyme
    1 whole clove
   10 black peppercorns, bruised

Preheat oven to 450°.

Place duck carcasses and giblets in a large roasting pan. Place pan in a preheated oven and roast for 30 minutes, turning frequent-ly. Add onion, carrots, parsnip, and turnip and continue roasting until everything is dark brown. This may take up to 1 hour.

Transfer browned duck pieces and veg-etables from the roasting pan to a large stockpot. Cover with cold water and bring to a boil over high heat. Remove scum as it forms, replacing any discarded liquid with fresh warm water. When scum no longer forms, add remaining ingredients and sim-mer, partially covered, for 3 hours.

Strain liquid through a double layer of cheesecloth into a large saucepan. Briskly simmer stock until reduced to 3–4 cups. Chill and remove fat before using. This stock freezes very well.

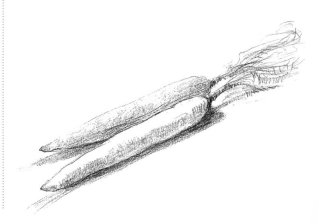

Duck Stew with Olives

This is a wonderful wintertime dish. It is especially good with Rosemary Mashed Potato Cakes (page 63) and a simple stir-fry of vegetables.

Serves 6–8

> 2 ducks, 3½–4½ pounds each, quartered and trimmed of excess fat

MARINADE
> 3 carrots, sliced
> ¾ pound onions, thinly sliced
> 2 bay leaves
> 3 sprigs fresh thyme
> 4 sprigs fresh parsley
> 1 tablespoon black peppercorns, bruised
> 2 tablespoons red wine vinegar
> 750 ml. R. H. Phillips Night Harvest or Côtes du Rhône wine
> ¾ cup unbleached flour
> 4 tablespoons unsalted margarine
> 2 cups Dark Brown Duck Stock (page 294)
> 16–24 fresh pearl onions
> 3 carrots, cut into 1-inch pieces
> Salt and freshly ground black pepper to taste
> ½–¾ cup pitted oil-cured black olives

> Minced fresh parsley and chives for garnish

Place ducks in a large glass or ceramic bowl. Add sliced carrots and onions, 1 bay leaf, 2 sprigs thyme, and remaining marinade ingredients. Cover with plastic wrap and marinate in the refrigerator for 24 hours. Remove duck meat, reserving marinade, and pat dry.

Dredge duck pieces in ½ cup flour and set aside on a rack. Heat margarine in a large cast-iron Dutch oven. When hot, completely brown duck pieces on both sides. Drain skillet, reserving ¼ cup of fat. Set duck meat aside.

Strain reserved marinade through cheese-cloth and discard solids. Then return reserved fat to Dutch oven and combine with remaining ¼ cup of flour. Whisk over medium heat until mixture is dark brown. Slowly add 2 cups of the strained marinade. Whisk well for 2 minutes. Then add duck stock, whisking well. Add duck meat, pearl onions, carrot pieces, remaining bay leaf and thyme, salt, pepper, and olives. Cover and simmer for 1½ hours, or until duck is very tender.

Transfer duck pieces to a plate and keep warm. Return pot and sauce to burner and heat over medium heat until simmering. Skim fat and scum off the surface of the stew as it forms; this process can take up to 30 minutes. Return duck pieces to degreased sauce for a few minutes to heat through.

Just before serving, garnish with parsley and chives.

Wine: Hess Collection Cabernet Sauvignon (Napa Valley)

Sticky Rice–Stuffed Duck

Kathy King used to make this for us when she lived in Cleveland. Dr. King is a respected neonatologist, and she is also skilled in preparing the cuisine of her native China. This is our version of her Cantonese dish. Have your butcher bone the duck from the inside for you; otherwise, refer to Ken Hom's book *Chinese Technique*.

1 5–6-pound duck, left whole but boned
4 tablespoons dark soy sauce
1 tablespoon dry sherry
2 tablespoons sugar
2 teaspoons plus 1 tablespoon dark sesame oil
3 cups sticky rice (see Note)
½ pound spicy smoked sausage, out of the casing
2 tablespoons minced fresh ginger
2 cloves garlic, minced
6 scallions, trimmed and diced (white part only)
1 ounce dried shiitake mushrooms, soaked in boiling water for 20 minutes, then stemmed and diced
3 tablespoons minced cilantro
1 tablespoon vegetable oil, or more if necessary
3½ cups rich chicken stock
1 cup fresh peas
2 tablespoons oyster sauce
1 tablespoon rice wine
2 teaspoons freshly ground black pepper

Bunches of fresh cilantro for garnish

Note: Sticky rice is a round, short-grained rice available in Oriental markets, where it might be called sweet rice.

Dry the duck with a clean kitchen towel and place it in a large glass or ceramic dish. Combine 1 tablespoon soy sauce, the sherry, 1 tablespoon sugar, and 2 teaspoons sesame oil in a small bowl and blend well. Rub this marinade all over duck, inside and out. Cover dish with plastic wrap and refrigerate for 24 hours, turning duck several times.

Meanwhile, place sticky rice in a colander and rinse several times. Then place the rice in a mixing bowl and cover with cold water. Let soak for at least 12 hours, then drain and rinse.

Bring duck to room temperature.

Heat a wok until hot, then add sausage meat and cook, stirring, until pink color is gone. (Add some vegetable oil if necessary.) Then add ginger, garlic, scallions, and mushrooms. Toss over medium-high heat for a minute, then transfer mixture to a large mixing bowl. Stir in cilantro.

Add more vegetable oil to the wok and heat again. Add drained rice and toss to coat well. Then add stock and cook over high heat about 10–20 minutes, stirring often, until stock is absorbed.

Add rice, peas, remaining soy sauce and sugar, 1 tablespoon sesame oil, oyster sauce, rice wine, and pepper to the sausage mixture. Blend well. When mixture is cool, stuff this into the duck cavity. Skewer both openings and tie with string, or sew both openings closed.

Preheat oven to 450°. Rub duck with any remaining marinade and place, back side up, on a rack in a roasting pan. Roast 30 minutes and turn breast side up, then roast an additional 20 minutes. Lower heat to 350° and roast for 20 minutes more.

Remove duck from oven and let rest at least 10 minutes before slicing. Garnish serving platter with cilantro.

Wine: Duckhorn Vineyards Merlot (Napa Valley)

Ted and Molly Bartlett

Silver Creek Farm

P.O. Box 254

7097 Allyn Road

Hiram, Ohio 44234

(216) 562-4381

*I*n 1985, Ted and Molly Bartlett bought Silver Creek Farm, 123 acres that are only about an hour to downtown Cleveland, where Ted teaches philosophy and biomedical ethics. "It's good that things worked out this way," said Ted. "We didn't realize how hard it would be to really make a living from the farm!"

"We backed into organics," added Molly, a potter and former student of Russian studies at Yale. "We didn't want to spray with anything we couldn't say. What we were looking for was quality; the more we read, the more we realized this was the way to go."

When they bought it, the farm had some apple orchards and blueberries. There were acres that were good for pastureland and others that looked good for produce. There were several barns as well. Little by little, the Bartletts have become diversified: guinea fowl, turkeys, and chickens are the most recent, and most important, additions.

"Guinea fowl are really tough to raise," Molly said. "You need to have very large covered caged areas for them, because they fly." Because they are so active, it takes them twice as long as chickens to reach their market weight of about 2½ to 3 pounds. "So they're really expensive to raise," Ted added. "And they make an awful noise, like a rusty gate." Another problem is the market. There's nothing delicate about a guinea fowl; the flavor is rich and lusty, and that's why many gourmets love them, but they are a hard sell in most Ohio restaurants.

Turkeys, on the other hand, are growing in popularity. Molly Bartlett is the only person who told us that she actually likes raising them. "I find them interesting," she said. "When the harvest is done we turn the turkeys out in the field. They follow us around like puppies. They are terribly curious—not smart, but curious. Especially the bronze ones."

The bronze turkeys are quite handsome. "They're the turkeys we all drew in school when we were young," Molly said. They develop beautiful feathers as they mature. "I think they have a much richer flavor than the standard white turkey," she added. When plucked, however, the turkeys retain little dark dots all over the skin, so nervous cooks might not like them. But cooking makes the dots disappear, and the taste is fabulous. The Bartletts also raise a large number of white turkeys. The white turkeys grow at a faster rate than the bronze, partly because they don't move around as much. "But they're not nearly as much fun," said Molly.

The Bartletts buy their turkey chicks at one day old. As soon as they are big enough, they go into spacious pens near the farmhouse. The pens are located in a spot where the Bartletts have raised tomatoes in the past, so tomatoes keep growing back naturally every spring. By the time the chicks are ready to go outside, the tomatoes are ripe. The birds pig out for days on tomatoes, eating the whole plant right down to the roots. Otherwise, their diet is a noncertified organic mix the Bartletts buy from a friend, along with some of their own corn. "Because we don't use any hormones or growth supplements, our turkeys will not get bigger than about 23 pounds," said Molly. In addition, the turkeys are kept free of antibiotics.

The Bartletts' chicken production is up to about 1,000 birds a year. "We're trying to see if there is really a market here for certified organic poultry," Ted said. "If so, our friend will get his feed certified, and we'll line up a federally inspected slaughterhouse." At the moment, according to Ohio law, they can do their own slaughtering as long as they sell directly to the consumer and limit their poultry production to its current level. This has worked well for them to this point, but as they build their market they will have to increase their quantities. "The chickens are easy," Molly said. "They pay our bills, not the zucchini." The birds are Cor-

nish Cross, a sturdy white-feathered chicken that is raised on the ground. "They hardly move about," said Molly. "They don't want to eat the grasses outside, and they don't want to range." They're fed and watered three times a day, are given no medication, and are ready for market in 7 to 7½ weeks.

There is a waiting list for the Bartletts' poultry. "People who were raised in Europe come out here regularly for their birds. And they bring their children or grandchildren. We just worry about getting away from farm sales," Molly said. "If we expand and sell through retail outlets, people will lose the 'farm connection.' "

Another strong product for the Bartletts is lamb. Grazed on (uncertified) organic pastures and supplemented with (uncertified) organically grown grain, the lamb also has the potential for becoming a significant source of income if the flock is increased. At the moment, three handsome rams service fifty breeding ewes.

Besides several acres of blueberries, the Bartletts also grow 25 acres of extraordinary vegetables—corn, zucchini, pattypan squash, multiple varieties of yellow squash, heirloom tomato varieties that taste the way tomatoes should, garlic, leeks, broccoli, cauliflower, and cabbage. Their baby lettuces, mustards, and kales are wonderful. And their forest-grown shiitake mushrooms are spectacular. Everything grows in raised beds using drip irrigation, an efficient system that delivers water directly to the base of the plants. "We're really lucky that we have three terrific wells here, so water isn't a problem," said Molly.

As each year passes, the farm becomes stronger. Ted and Molly get to know it better and learn more about their capabilities. Without farmers' markets in the area, they use the mail to sell their products. A nifty newsletter goes out regularly to even one-time visitors or casual acquaintances. "You have to learn to think quickly," said Molly. "The weather changes so often, and you just have to adjust to it. When you're organic you really have to be creative and resourceful, since you can't just use a spray to solve your problems."

Linda's Turkey

Thanks to Craig Claiborne, we learned that roasting a turkey in a hot oven, as opposed to a warm one, is the best way to get a really moist bird. It makes a mess, for sure, but it also results in a better taste and texture. This recipe will not work well with self-basting turkeys.

    1   17–30-pound turkey
        Salt and freshly ground black
        pepper to taste
    2   recipes Cornbread Stuffing
        (page 302)
        Olive oil
        Garlic powder
    1   large onion, unpeeled, cut in half
    2   carrots
    2   cups rich chicken stock
        Thanksgiving Gravy (page 302)

Calculate roasting time by multiplying 11 minutes by the weight in pounds of the unstuffed bird.

Preheat oven to 450°.

Pat the turkey dry with a clean kitchen towel. Lightly season cavities with salt and pepper and stuff with the dressing. Skewer cavities shut. Rub bird with some olive oil and lightly season with salt, pepper, and garlic powder. Truss turkey and place in a roasting pan. Add onion and carrots and roast, uncovered, for 45 minutes.

Reduce heat to 400° and baste with some of the chicken stock. Turn roasting pan so it sits lengthwise, not horizontally, in the oven. Loosely cover turkey with some foil if it is getting too brown. Return pan to oven for remaining cooking time, basting with chicken stock at least three times more and turning pan at least once again.

When turkey is done, transfer bird to a carving board. Let rest in a warm place for 20 minutes. If you wish, check bird with an instant-read thermometer. It should read about 160°. Remember that the bird will continue cooking while it is resting.

Skim fat from drippings in pan and discard onion and carrots. Place pan over medium heat, add Thanksgiving gravy, and cook, scraping very well to loosen all the particles at the bottom. When mixture comes to a boil, whisk well and remove from heat. Taste and adjust seasonings. Carve bird and serve with gravy and stuffing on the side.

Wine: Saintsbury Pinot Noir (Carneros) or *Cuvaison Chardonnay "Reserve"* (Napa Valley)

Thanksgiving Gravy

Our friends Lydie and Wayne Marshall often join us for Thanksgiving. Seeing that we always make our gravy in a skillet, Lydie suggested adding the liquid slowly, over a long period of time. The long cooking assures that there is no strong taste of flour. The gravy keeps very nicely; it also freezes well.

Makes about 3 quarts

STOCK

    4 sets of turkey giblets
    4 turkey necks
    2 carrots, scrubbed
    1 large onion, studded with 1 whole clove
    1 bay leaf
    4 sprigs fresh parsley
    6 black peppercorns, bruised
    2 sprigs fresh thyme or ½ teaspoon dried thyme

    ½ cup vegetable oil
    ⅔ cup unbleached flour
    1½ cups Cabernet Sauvignon or Zinfandel wine

Combine giblets, necks, and 3½ quarts water in a 5-quart soup pot. Bring to a boil, reduce heat, and simmer briskly for 30 minutes. Remove any scum that forms on the surface. Add remaining stock ingredients and continue to simmer briskly for 4 hours. Remove giblets and reserve. Strain stock, discarding solids, and measure; there should be 10 cups. If there is more, continue simmering until liquid is reduced to desired quantity. When there is the right amount, keep the stock warm while you prepare the rest of the recipe.

In a 10-inch cast-iron skillet, heat the oil, then add flour and whisk over medium heat until flour is a very dark brown. Reduce heat and add the wine. Whisk thoroughly until mixture is smooth and well blended. Add 1 cup of warm stock, whisking until very smooth.

Slowly, over 2 hours, add the remaining stock, which should be kept warm during the entire process. Cook mixture over very low heat, whisking frequently. As a skin forms on the surface, remove it. When all the stock is incorporated, add sliced giblets and set aside until you are ready to add it to the roasting pan (see page 301).

Cornbread Stuffing

We have to credit Paul Prudhomme for influencing the way we handle dried zesty spices, especially in this cornbread stuffing. And his use of evaporated milk with the cornbread gives it a certain something that was missing in our earlier efforts. This dressing is enough for 6 Cornish hens or two roasting chickens. We double it for the Thanksgiving turkey.

Makes 5–6 cups

    3 teaspoons kosher salt
    2 teaspoons freshly ground white pepper
    2 teaspoons freshly ground black pepper
    1 teaspoon cayenne pepper, or less to taste

1 teaspoon onion powder
2 teaspoons minced fresh oregano
1 teaspoon minced fresh thyme
3 tablespoons minced fresh basil
    (preferably Greek)
2 bay leaves
½ cup finely chopped onion
½ cup finely chopped scallions
    (including some green)
½ cup finely chopped fresh parsley
¾ cup finely chopped red bell pepper
1 small fresh hot chile pepper, seeded
    and minced
1 tablespoon finely minced garlic
½ cup unsalted butter or margarine
1 cup rich chicken stock
1 tablespoon Tabasco, or less to taste
1 loaf Country Cornbread (page 80)
1 cup evaporated milk
3 jumbo eggs, beaten

Combine salt, three ground peppers, onion powder, oregano, thyme, basil, and bay leaves and set aside. Combine onion, scallions, parsley, bell pepper, chile, and garlic in another bowl and set aside.

Melt butter in a large skillet over medium heat. Add the seasonings and sauté for two minutes. Add onion mixture and continue to sauté, stirring constantly, for 5 minutes. Do not brown onions. Then add stock and Tabasco. Stir well and cook for 5 more minutes. Remove pan from heat. Crumble cornbread into the skillet and mix well.

Add evaporated milk and eggs and stir mixture thoroughly. Return skillet to burner and cook over low heat, stirring often, for 2 minutes. Remove bay leaves and discard. Let dressing cool before stuffing the birds.

Turkey Tenderloins and Warm New Potatoes

Just as with chicken breasts, each half of turkey breast has a long finger-shaped strip of meat (with neither skin nor fat) that hangs from the underside, near the bone. This piece is called the tenderloin.

Serves 4

MARINADE
    Juice of 1 lime
    1 shallot, finely minced
    2 tablespoons red wine vinegar
    ¼ cup vegetable oil
    1 tablespoon minced cilantro

    8 turkey tenderloins, about 4 ounces
        each

DRESSING
    4 tablespoons red wine vinegar, or
        more if desired
    1 teaspoon Dijon mustard
    ⅓ cup extra-virgin olive oil
        Salt and freshly ground black
        pepper to taste

    16 small red or Yukon Gold potatoes,
        washed but unpeeled
    4–6 cups baby lettuces and mustard
        greens, washed and well drained
    1 red bell pepper, cut into julienne
        strips
    4 thin slices red onion, separated into
        rings
    1 tablespoon walnut oil, or more if
        desired

        Minced cilantro for garnish

Combine marinade ingredients in a small bowl and whisk until emulsified. Arrange turkey tenderloins in a glass dish, coat with marinade, and let stand for 1 hour. It is not necessary to refrigerate.

Combine dressing ingredients in a small bowl and whisk very well. Set aside. Place potatoes in a saucepan, cover with water, bring to a boil, and cook until tender, about 20 minutes. Drain, slice, and place in a mixing bowl. Pour all but 3 tablespoons of dressing over potatoes and toss.

To assemble the dish, spray a clean grill with Pam and heat it to medium high (a large cast-iron skillet brushed with vegetable oil may also be used). Drain tenderloins, reserving marinade. Bring reserved marinade to a boil, covered, and boil for 5 minutes. Grill the tenderloins over hot coals for about 1 minute on each side. Remove from grill and baste with marinade.

Combine remaining ingredients, add reserved dressing, and toss well. Add a bit more walnut oil and vinegar if desired to coat the greens. Distribute greens and potatoes among four dinner plates. Slice tenderloins on a slight angle and arrange attractively to one side. Add a few more grindings of pepper and sprinkle with cilantro.

Wine: Sanford Winery Sauvignon Blanc (Santa Barbara County)

Pat Hall

Rainbow Ridge Farm

200175 Rhoda Avenue

Welch, Minnesota 55809

(612) 437-7837

At Rainbow Ridge, the farmer is a woman. Not such a shock in today's society, perhaps, but a career choice that was fairly unusual for women of Pat Hall's generation. For many years, Pat worked as a biologist while raising her family. In 1980, life took a real turn when Pat's husband, Bob, a research scientist, accepted a job in Minnesota. The move from urban New Jersey gave them an opportunity to buy a patch of land less than an hour southeast of Minneapolis.

"We thought it would be nice to have a hobby farm," said Pat. "It would be a great retirement place where Bob and I could work together someday." Maybe it would be a U-pick farm.

The first year they planted 125 apple trees, including many antique varieties. "These were Bob's babies, but I dug 125 holes," she said. "It wasn't much fun. And then, of course, it takes years for the trees to bear fruit. Besides, in trying out so many different varieties, we later realized that we didn't plant enough of any one variety to make U-pick feasible." Pat then decided to do a U-pick vegetable garden. Pat planted 2,000 broccoli plants on her hands and knees. Much to her disappointment, however, there wasn't much interest in pick-it-yourself vegetables.

One day, Bob called home from his research lab. Some colleagues had been chatting about strawberries. Why not do U-pick strawberries? Bob modified a used two-row corn planter, and with son Eric on a sled on one side and daughter Kim on the other, Pat and the children planted 21,000 strawberry plants. By 1991, they had 4½ acres of strawberries and an acre of Half-high blueberries, a dwarf variety that is easy to pick. The berries were large, juicy, and delicious. Rainbow Ridge Farm had found its calling. Or at least part of it.

Pat follows the principles of integrated pest management in her fields. In recent years, concern over chemical insecticides, herbicides, fungicides, and other agricultural chemicals has led more and more contemporary farmers to turn to IPM. Knowledge is the key to success. The farmer must anticipate when and where specific pests are likely to appear and plan ways to control them. IPM techniques include the encouragement of predator insects, trapping or hand-picking harmful insects, crop rotation, and the careful use of organic sprays.

Once the berries were established, someone decided it would be fun to have a few ducks and geese running around. Besides, they'd take care of the weeds in the berry patch. Little did anyone realize they'd take care of the berries as well. But the Halls kept them anyway. They were, at least, a good source of natural fertilizer for the berries.

But what started out as a lark ended up being a pain. When goslings were hatched in the spring, the geese weren't very good mothers, and the ducks were recruited to raise them. The ducks and the geese nested in a little valley behind the house, and since the Halls don't have a pond, all of the birds' water had to be brought down to them by hand. "Romance goes out with lugging water through the snow," the farmer told us.

"But we were learning," she said. "Geese need water to clean their eyes and nostrils as well as for drinking. They need water deep enough to accomplish this, so first we tried pans, but they would get into them and splash out the water. So we turned to pails that were deeper and not as big in diameter. On several occasions we found a drowned goose caught in the pail head down, apparently not having the sense to tip the pail over to get out." So now Pat provides the geese with large puddles. She added, "Geese are also hard to handle. If you move them by their legs, you hurt their hips. And when you have to move a lot of them quickly, they need to be carried by their necks—while their flapping wings beat your thighs black and blue."

When the supply of birds exceeded the family's needs, Pat went to market. She learned that while the marketplace is filled with ducks, free-range geese are not difficult to peddle. She took some to Byerly's, a nationally known upscale Minneapolis market chain. The buyer was impressed with the quality of the birds. If they could be processed in a state-inspected or federally inspected facility, he told her, Byerly's would be a good customer.

That's all Pat Hall needed for motivation. She and Bob bought an old horse barn and pasture adjacent to their strawberry patches. The costs of equipment and personnel for breeding her own goslings would have been high, so she decided to buy goslings at one day old. Those born on May 6 will have just the right number of weeks of growing time before she brings them to market. "It's hard to find the perfect hatchery," Pat commented. "There aren't many around that can get me 800 of the White Emdens I prefer, so if I get some Emdens mixed with Toulouse it's okay."

The barn was ingeniously converted into warming pens for the goslings. The first year, Pat used electric lights for heat. Then, with a power failure, she lost 125 birds. Now she has four small gas brooders, special round hanging heaters, that keep the goslings warm. As the birds grow and become crowded, the pens are opened so the geese move freely about the barn. When the weather is nice and the birds no longer need the heat from the brooders or the shelter of the barn, they go outside. She uses electric fencing to rotate them from pasture to pasture for feeding. And in the heat of summer there are lots of shaded areas around the barn. When the heat gets intense, Pat runs sprinklers for them.

The birds get a fatty soy starter ration for four to five weeks; then they go to a standard grower ration of grain until they reach ten weeks. They are allowed to pasture as soon as they can go outside in the spring, but it doesn't become a main part of their diet until after ten weeks, when they cease being food-efficient. When they deplete the pasture oats and alfalfa, Pat gets whatever she can that is green, chops it, and feeds it to them. They range freely all day and are confined to the pen at night until a month before Thanksgiving. At that point, the birds are penned all day so that they are immobile enough to fatten.

Pat has found geese fairly simple to raise. She gives them no antibiotics, and after a vitamin supplement the first week, they need no medication. The main health problem is from hardware disease. "Geese will eat anything," she said. "So if someone drops a nail or a wire, a goose will eat it and never quite plump up the way it should."

Processing the geese was a bigger challenge than raising them. To find the state-inspected or federally inspected processing plant she needed in order to sell to Byerly's, she at first had to go hundreds of miles away, near North Dakota. But she was unhappy with the results. With the assistance of a federal compliance officer, she developed a creative solution. After obtaining a wholesaler's license, she could then lease a whole processing facility and its staff for only the length of time it takes to process her birds before both Thanksgiving and Christmas. Pat, or her representative, could supervise everything. Since she sells the birds fresh, a quarter of her crop is processed for the first holiday; the bulk are done before Christmas.

When she became the primary goose raiser for Byerly's, her flock doubled in size; then, with the addition of other markets, it went to 500. When she became the sole supplier to Lund's, another upscale Twin-Cities chain, the flock grew to 800. And she still sells direct to the consumer as well. "I send out postcard reminders to people. They know that we sell on a first-come, first-serve basis, so they're prompt with orders," Pat said.

In addition, the berry patches continue to do well; people like to come to pick because the berries are so good and the Halls so nice. There are delicious jams and preserves for sale, along with wonderful honey.

Pat has never been happier, even though some people are still unaccustomed to the farmer being the wife, not the husband. She still bristles at the recollection of being told to have her husband sponsor young Kimberly when she needed a pre-age-sixteen "farm driver's" license; her mother was not an acceptable sponsor. Needless to say, Pat clarified that issue quickly.

Though still far from retirement, Bob Hall loves the farm and helps when he can. Unfortunately, no one has much time to give his apple trees the attention they need. So the best they do is bear enough fruit for an infrequent pie and maybe some to stuff the occasional goose. And when the last delivery is made, and they can finally think about Christmas dinner, the Halls happily put a big prime rib into the oven and take a nap while it is roasting.

Our Favorite Goose

While we have been willing to experiment with turkey stuffing from Thanksgiving to Thanksgiving, we are totally committed to our dried fruit stuffing for the Christmas goose. You need two ovens if you're serving twelve.

Serves 12

    1 cup coarsely diced dried apricots
    1 cup coarsely diced dried peaches
    ½ cup golden raisins
    ½ cup coarsely diced dried pears
    ½ cup Muscat raisins

    ½ cup diced dried dates
    1 cup diced figs
    ½ cup dried pitted cherries
    2 whole cloves
750 ml. Zinfandel wine, or more if
      necessary
    2 cups applejack
    1 fresh apple, peeled, cored, and diced
    1 fresh pear, peeled, cored, and diced
    1 large navel orange, peeled,
      sectioned, and diced
    2 teaspoons freshly ground white
      pepper
    1 teaspoon salt
    2 teaspoons ground cardamom

1½ cups cooked wild rice
2 fresh geese, about 10 pounds each
Salt and freshly ground black
pepper to taste
2 cups chopped onion
2 cups chopped celery
4 teaspoons minced fresh thyme
4 teaspoons minced fresh sage
Port Wine Goose Gravy (below)
1 teaspoon bruised dried juniper
berries (optional)
1 teaspoon dried tarragon

Four days before serving, combine first 11 ingredients in a large ceramic bowl. Cover and allow to marinate at room temperature for 96 hours. Stir once each day. Add more wine if it becomes absorbed by the fruits. Drain marinated fruits, reserving liquid. Add apple, pear, orange, pepper, salt, cardamom, and rice. Blend well.

Preheat two ovens to 450°.

Stuff both goose cavities with fruit mixture and skewer them closed. Rub birds with salt and pepper. Place each bird in a large roasting pan and divide the onion, celery, thyme, and sage between the pans. Add 1 cup water to each pan. Place geese in ovens and reduce temperature to 400°. Roast each goose for 10 minutes per pound, draining fat several times during the roasting.

When geese are done, remove from pans and let rest in a warm place for at least 10 minutes before carving. Drain fat from roasting pans; then pour some of the reserved fruit marinade in each pan. Place pans over high heat and bring to a boil, scraping loose all of the particles that have adhered to the bottom of the pans. Pour contents of both pans into the gravy, which has been keeping warm in a saucepan. Add juniper berries and increase heat. When mixture comes to a boil, remove from heat and whisk well. Add lots of pepper and the dried tarragon.

Remove stuffing from cavities and transfer to a warmed casserole. Carve bird and serve with stuffing and gravy on the side.

Wine: Ridge "Geyserville" Zinfandel (Sonoma County)

Port Wine Goose Gravy

To make this sauce for roasted duck, substitute duck giblets and necks for those of the geese and use Zinfandel instead of the port.

Makes about 1½ quarts

2 goose giblets
2 goose necks
½ pound chicken bones
2 carrots, scrubbed
1 large onion, studded with 1 clove
1 bay leaf
4 sprigs fresh parsley
6 black peppercorns, bruised
2 sprigs fresh thyme, or ½ teaspoon
dried thyme
¼ cup vegetable oil
½ cup unbleached flour
1¼ cups Dow's Boardroom port wine

Combine giblets, necks, chicken bones, and 2 quarts water in a 3-quart pot. Bring to a boil, reduce heat, and simmer briskly for 30 minutes. Remove any scum that forms on the surface. Add carrots, onion, bay leaf, parsley, peppercorns, and thyme and continue to simmer briskly for 4 hours. Remove giblets and reserve. Strain stock, discarding solids, and measure; there should about be 6 cups. If there is more, continue simmering until liquid is reduced to desired quantity. When you have the right amount, keep stock warm while you proceed.

In a large cast-iron skillet, heat the oil, then add the flour and whisk over medium heat until mixture is a very dark brown. Reduce heat and add the port. Whisk thoroughly until mixture is smooth and well blended. Add 1 cup of stock, whisking until very smooth. Slowly, over the next hour, add the remaining stock, which should be kept warm during the entire process. Cook mixture over very low heat, whisking frequently. As a skin forms on the surface, remove it. When all the stock is incorporated, add sliced giblets and set aside. Keep warm until you are ready to add it to the juices from the roasting pan (see page 310).

Pat Hall's Roast Goose

Serves 6

> 1 10-pound goose
> Salt
> Herb and Chestnut Stuffing
> (page 111)
> Freshly ground black pepper to taste
> 1 cup boiling water
> Michigan Dried-Cherry and
> Zinfandel Sauce (page 399)

Preheat oven to 325°. Trim bird of any excess fat. Lightly salt cavity, then fill with stuffing. Skewer the opening closed. Generously salt and pepper bird. Prick skin all over with a sharp fondue fork or thin skewer, especially in very fatty areas. Place goose breast side up on a rack in roasting pan and roast in preheated oven for 3½ hours. Pour off fat from the pan, baste with ¼ cup of the cherry sauce, and roast for another 30–40 minutes. Let goose stand in a warm place for 15 minutes before carving. Serve with the remaining sauce and stuffing on the side.

Wine: Ravenswood "Old Vine" Zinfandel (Sonoma County)

Strawberry Soup

At Rainbow Farm, long before the geese are grown the strawberries are harvested. This is a great way to enjoy them.

Serves 6–8

> 1 quart fresh strawberries, hulled
> 2 cups freshly squeezed orange juice
> ¼ teaspoon cinnamon
> ¼ teaspoon freshly grated nutmeg
> 2 tablespoons honey
> 1 tablespoon balsamic vinegar
> 1 tablespoon cassis
> ⅔ cup club soda, or more if necessary
>
> Thinly sliced fresh strawberries, raspberries, blueberries, peaches, and plums for garnish
>
> Fresh fruit sorbet and fresh mint leaves for garnish

Combine all ingredients except club soda and garnishes in the bowl of a food processor and pulse until mixture is well puréed. Transfer mixture into a bowl and chill. Just before serving, stir in enough club soda to make a thick soup.

Ladle fruit soup into shallow soup plates. Garnish with little clusters of fruits, a small scoop of fruit sorbet, and mint leaves.

Rudy and Theodora Pluschke

3518 County Line Road
Marengo, Illinois 60152
(815) 597-4061

Rudy and Theodora Pluschke live in a ninety-year-old farmhouse in Marengo, Illinois, 65 miles northwest of Chicago. On their 11 acres they raise free-range pheasants, birds so good that they are used by the region's best restaurants.

The house is warm, solid, and fresh. It contains some wonderful pieces of stained glass, all of which have been created by Teddy, whose talented hands have made everything from lamps to massive church windows. "Stained glass," she told us, "is my way of having something that is mine. It is also my way of staying sane when the feathers are flying."

On the day of our visit, we saw some empty bird cages in the kitchen and an incubator so small that we knew it couldn't be for the pheasants. Rudy took us upstairs, where the entire second floor is given over to Australian finches and canaries. The rooms are full of branches and nesting boxes nailed to the walls. There are hundreds of them, spectacular little creatures, cousins of the Galápagos finches that gave Charles Darwin the breakthrough clue to the origin of species.

Rudy, it turns out, is one of the world's leading specialists in the propagation of these beautiful cage birds; he has been raising them for more than twenty-five years. And it was his expertise in this field that would lead him and Teddy to Marengo and another kind of bird.

Rudy left Prussia in 1965 and came to Chicago, where he did interior decorating; later he moved to nearby Antioch, where he met Teddy, a senior systems engineer for Quaker Oats. Somehow, she managed to be a successful stained-glass designer and artist at the same time. They were married in 1984.

While Rudy did well in the decorating business, he longed to go back to working on the land. Teddy was also ready for a change. So with a vague notion that they might use Rudy's understanding of birds to raise pheasants, they started looking for a farm. In late 1984, they found their little place in Marengo and moved in.

It was quite run-down, but the buildings were basically sound. They borrowed a large sum of money and Rudy started to refurbish the dairy barn. Despite what they knew was very careful planning, before Rudy had gotten halfway through the first stage the money was gone. By the time they finished converting the entire barn and an adjoining building into more hatchery and brooder space, they again had to refinance their farm. They were so busy with the building of the operation and the challenges of raising the birds that there was no sales plan in place.

Rudy placed some ads in hunting magazines, offering birds to hunting clubs. Eventually he got orders from clubs in South Dakota, Wyoming, and Minnesota. He had 5,000 birds and sold them all, but he had to deliver them himself—not a winning proposition. The following year, the clubs did not reorder, because their old source came through. Rudy had 8,000 birds and no market.

At just about that time, when the intrepid pheasant farmers were in the slough of despond, the *Chicago Tribune* ran an article on pheasants as gourmet food. Although Rudy and Teddy immediately began to contact local wholesalers and butchers, sales failed to improve. Then Teddy thought to call the fabled Chicago chef Louis Szathmary of the Bakery, whom she had met during her Quaker Oats days.

"He gave us a pep talk, some pointers, and most important, the names of chefs and restaurants to contact," Teddy told us. "My sister, Wilda, designed our logo, using a pheasant that we raised our first year. Then she and I wrote our brochure, which Rudy hand-carried to nearly every restaurant in town."

Rudy continued the narrative. "From the Ritz Carlton, we got an order for twelve birds each week. That encouraged me to call on the Tremont Hotel, where I had done a big decorating job a few years earlier. And the Tremont's John Carey gave us a standing order for six birds a week."

So for the next several months Rudy was delivering eighteen birds per week, a long trip for very little. Catch, transport, slaughter, chill, pack, and deliver. And come home with barely enough to pay for the gasoline. Ultimately, they sold the 8,000 birds and found themselves with a burgeoning market that increased every year. In 1990, the first year that Rudy did not have to supplement their income by decorating, the Pluschkes sold 20,000 birds. Chefs continue to rave about the birds and now know that they can count on him. They sell to about fifty restaurants, and now have a retail shop at the farm. Today, the birds are sold live, fresh, frozen, and smoked.

Rudy regrets that he cannot call his birds natural or organic. He medicates twice during the first six weeks of the birds' lives, until their own immune systems kick in—allowable under basic organic guidelines but not "natural." He uses 12 tons of soybeans, corn, minerals, vitamins, and grit every week. He buys carefully, but he says using certified organically grown feed would double the cost of raising his birds. The ration is unsupplemented with hormones, however, and Rudy's pheasants do qualify as free-range.

The Pluschkes hatch about 2,000 chicks at a time. The chicks are kept in a small warm room for one week; then they are moved to a larger warm room with a dim red light that keeps them from pecking at one another. When they are four weeks old, they begin to get some access to the outside. At six weeks, they are fitted with beak clips that inhibit fighting and are put into the large pens. Rudy plants the pens with sorghum and weeds and the birds grow up and live in luxuriant vegetation.

They raise three kinds of wild ring-necked pheasants: the Chinese ringneck, the buff, and the black. All three are gorgeous birds with vividly colored plumage, preferred by the hunting clubs. Most chefs, however, opt for the white hybrid pheasant; while not a pretty bird, it is noted for having more meat on its breast and for its overall juiciness when cooked.

"The white," Rudy told us, "is also a terrific bird for smoking."

Teddy said that one of Chicago's finest chefs, Cliff Pleau, of the Mayfair Regent Hotel's Le Ciel Bleu, was coming out to the farm the next day with his two assistants and their spouses. They were going to prepare an entire six-course dinner and all she would have to do is supply the pheasants. She worried that her kitchen wouldn't be adequate for these professionals.

"Why," she asked, "would this chef come all the way out here to make dinner for us?"

We know the answer.

Rudy's Roasted Pheasant

When we visited with Rudy and Theodora Pluschke for lunch, this was the way they prepared our pheasant.

Serves 2

1 Chinese ringneck pheasant (about 2½–3 pounds), dressed, cleaned, and plucked
Salt and freshly ground black pepper to taste
4 ounces dried apricots
4 ounces dried pitted prunes
10 dried juniper berries, crushed
6 slices smoked bacon
1 cup sour cream

Preheat oven to 325°.

Remove giblets from pheasant and set aside. Lightly season the cavity of the bird with salt and pepper, then stuff with apricots and prunes. Place stuffed bird breast side up in a roasting pan. Sprinkle with salt, pepper, and juniper berries. Wrap legs and wings with bacon. Arrange more bacon across breast of bird.

Pour in enough water to cover the bottom of the pan, cover, and roast for 1½–2 hours. Transfer bird to a platter and keep warm. Whisk sour cream into the pan juices and heat over low heat until sauce is warm. Slice breast meat and serve with leg, thigh, and some stuffing and sauce on the side.

Wine: Williams & Selyems "Richioli Vineyard" Pinot Noir (Sonoma County)

Braised Pheasant with Cabbage and Applejack

Serves 2

    4 tablespoons unsalted butter
    1 large onion, thinly sliced
    1 Savoy cabbage (about 1 pound), cored and finely shredded
    2 tart apples, peeled, cored, and thinly sliced
    ¼ cup applejack
      Freshly ground black pepper to taste
    1 pheasant (about 2½ pounds), dressed, cleaned, and plucked
      Kosher salt to taste
    1 tablespoon Dijon mustard
    ⅓ cup unbleached flour
  2–3 tablespoons olive oil

    1 tart apple, quartered
    1 small onion, quartered
    1 bay leaf
   10 dried juniper berries, crushed
    4 slices smoked bacon, cut in half
    ¼ cup rich chicken or pheasant stock
    ½ cup sour cream

      Fresh herbs for garnish

Preheat oven to 325°.

Melt butter in a large skillet. Add onion, reduce heat to low, and cover with a sheet of wax paper pressed directly on the onions. Sweat onions for 5 minutes, then discard wax paper and add cabbage. Toss, then cover and cook over low heat for 5 minutes. Add apples, applejack, and pepper; cover and cook for 5 more minutes. Set aside.

Remove giblets from pheasant and freeze for later use in stock. Remove liver and set aside. Wipe bird dry with paper towel, then season cavity with some salt and pepper. Lightly brush with Dijon mustard, then dredge in flour. Also dredge the liver in flour.

Heat olive oil in a 5½-quart cast-iron Dutch oven until hot, then sear bird on all sides; bird should be lightly brown. Sauté liver as well. Remove bird from pot and rub cavity with salt and pepper. Then stuff with quartered apple and onion and bay leaf. Discard any remaining olive oil in Dutch oven. Chop the liver.

Spoon cabbage mixture into Dutch oven and add chopped liver. Place pheasant on cabbage bed breast side up. Sprinkle bird and cabbage with crushed juniper berries. Wrap each leg with some bacon and arrange remaining bacon strips over the breast. Add stock, cover tightly, and roast for 1½–2 hours. Baste several times, allowing some of the cabbage to cling to the pheasant.

Test bird by piercing the thigh with a sharp skewer; bird is done when the juices run clear and leg moves easily in the socket. Remove pheasant from pot and let it rest in a warm place for 5 minutes. Place pot with cabbage mixture over medium heat and add sour cream; simmer until hot (do not let it boil), then stir in accumulated pan juices from the resting bird. Taste and adjust seasonings.

Cut the bird in half and serve on a bed of cabbage, or remove breast from bone, slice on the diagonal, and arrange breast slices, cut leg, and thigh section with the cabbage mixture. Either way, discard stuffing mixture. Spoon any pot liquid over bird and garnish with fresh herbs.

Wine: Cuvaison Winery Merlot (Napa Valley) or *Burgess Cellars Chardonnay "Triere Vineyard"* (Napa Valley)

Smoked Pheasant and Virginia Ham with Mushroom Pasta

Serves 4–6

    1 smoked pheasant, about 2½ pounds
    3 cups heavy cream
    4 tablespoons unsalted margarine or butter
    2 teaspoons minced garlic
    4 ounces thinly sliced fresh shiitake mushrooms
    2 tablespoons Madeira wine
    ¼ cup minced shallots
    1 tablespoon fresh tarragon
    6 ounces smoked Virginia ham, cut into julienne strips
    ¾ cup shelled fresh peas, blanched
    1 teaspoon freshly ground white pepper
    1 pound Gary Thomas's Wild Mushroom Pasta (page 325), made into fettuccine
    1 cup grated dry Jack (see pages 139–141) or aged sheep's-milk cheese
    1 tablespoon minced fresh chives

Carve meat from pheasant, slice into bite-sized pieces, and set aside.

Pour cream into a 3-quart saucepan and simmer until liquid is reduced by half.

Meanwhile, melt margarine or butter in a large skillet over medium-low heat. Add garlic and stir for 1 minute. Add mushrooms and Madeira, toss, cover, and simmer for 5 minutes to release mushroom juices. Remove lid, add shallots and tarragon, and sauté, uncovered, until mushrooms and shallots are tender. Add to reduced cream and stir.

Add pheasant meat, ham, peas, and pepper to saucepan with cream mixture. Stir over low heat until hot.

In a large stock pot, bring 6 quarts of salted water to a rolling boil. Quickly cook fettuccine until just *al dente,* about 2 minutes. Drain well and toss with sauce. Divide pasta among heated serving plates. Sprinkle generously with cheese, then with chives.

Wine: Saint Gregory Chardonnay (Mendocino County) or *Caymus Vineyards "Conundrum"* (Napa Valley)

Special Flavors

Jack and Heidi Czarnecki

Joe's Restaurant
450 South Seventh Street
Reading, Pennsylvania 19602
(215) 372-6794

*I*t is only slight hyperbole to say that the current culinary fascination with edible wild mushrooms began at Joe's Restaurant in Reading, Pennsylvania. True, our European immigrant ancestors had for centuries combed the woods for mushrooms. But the Czarneckis, father and son, lifted mycology to new heights a few decades ago, their mushroom cookery catching the attention of such writers as James Beard, Craig Claiborne, and Calvin Trillin. Words like "cèpes," "chanterelles," and "morels" started appearing on restaurant menus. People came to realize that mushrooms weren't all just white buttons cultivated in Pennsylvania cellars.

Jack's grandfather, Joe, founded the restaurant in 1916 as a workingmen's bar. He, too, was a devoted mushroom forager who prided himself on the hearty soup he served, made from mushrooms gathered in area forests. His son Joe continued the business, focusing more and more on food as the years passed. It became the place for mushroom lovers to eat. "We would spend every spare minute out in the woods," said Jack. "I can remember coming home with bushel baskets of mushrooms. Then my mother would spend the evening canning whatever we found. That way my father would still have wild mushrooms in the off seasons."

Jack and his wife, Heidi, joined the business in 1974 after their graduation from the University of California at Davis. They served their "internship" in the restaurant, and took it over in 1978. It was around that time that Joe's Restaurant was "discovered" by national food writers.

Demand was increasing for mushrooms that had rich flavors and aromas. And soon growers answered the call. Within half a dozen years, an industry for the cultivation of exotic mushrooms had come into existence. You could find shiitakes and oysters in the better supermarkets and restaurants. Even the Campbell Soup Company got into the business of cultivating shiitakes. Today, exotic mushrooms are a substantial industry.

"I hate to see wild mushroom written on someone's menu," said Jack, "when it's a shiitake. That's a cultivated exotic, not a wild mushroom." As a responsible mycologist, Jack is careful about the distinction. After all, people need to know that cultivated exotics will never replace the real thing.

"It's gratifying," said Jack, "that exotic mushroom consumption is not a fad, and it is steadily increasing." Mushroom clubs are still strong and popular. "Also," he said, "there is a small but steady increase in consumption of all foraged food." And very sophisticated chefs around the country now seek out foragers to provide them with such things as fiddlehead ferns, chokecherries, and gooseberries.

The problem now is that just when we have come to expect wild mushrooms in season, their availability is diminishing. "I really worry about acid rain around here," said Jack. "Mushrooms are very sensitive to the pH of the forest floor; and we're struggling to find things that used to be there in abundance. If the mushrooms aren't there when the conditions are right, you just have to worry."

The forest now ceases to support mushroom growth after a period of time. In pine forests, the boletus type of mushroom disappears after five years and the tricholoma variety after fifteen, even though there are millions of miles of mycelia (seeds) under the forest floor.

Proper harvesting techniques are important. "We'd never use rakes," said Jack. "You cut wild mushrooms with a knife. And you protect the ground around them. It's when people harvest with rakes that they destroy the mycelia." But there is a big problem these days, especially in the forests of the Pacific Northwest. There are companies there that are harvesting with rakes; some are actually using bulldozers. They then ship the mushrooms to Canada for processing and to Europe for packaging. And then the product is imported back in this country as European wild mushrooms.

This is happening, in part, because European countries are protecting their forests by limiting foraging. In Italy, you now must have a permit to hunt for porcini. Since the demand is outstripping supply, there are even morels sold as "French morels" that are harvested in northern India and smoked over dung fires to preserve them.

In some areas, people are using the wild mushroom as a cash crop. Many have no idea what they have. "It's a wonder that there aren't more poisonings," said Jack. Luckily, chefs are generally very careful about what they buy and from whom.

Most of us will probably live our entire lives without tasting a honey mushroom or a parasol mushroom. But if you've ever tasted fresh morels right out of the woods, or smelled golden chanterelles in the forager's sack, or eaten freshly picked cèpes in France, then you know why people flock to Joe's Restaurant. And if you come at the right time, Jack might have some *Amanita caesaria,* a mushroom that has a red-orange cap with yellow gills. "I'll sauté them in butter, which will become red from the mushrooms. They're fabulous," he said. "And I'll whisper about them into someone's ear. You save those for someone who really appreciates them."

The Czarnecki family still scours the woods each week. Now they are joined by another generation. Jack and Heidi have three children, Sonia, Christopher, and Stefan. Besides helping in the restaurant on weekends and vacations, each is already a well-trained mycologist. They all worry, however, about the state of their forests. "What we need," Jack said, "is an offshore hurricane. Not a big one, but one that brings clean rain here for about three days. That's perfect for the mushrooms."

Rich Wild and Shiitake Mushroom Sauce

This sauce is simply splendid with veal and duck. When we are enjoying the results of our forager friend John Pollack's labor, we add fresh Hen-of-the-Woods mushrooms.

Makes about 2 cups

> 2 cups Dark Brown Duck Stock (page 294)
> 2 ounces dried wild mushrooms, such as cèpes (porcini)
> 6 tablespoons unsalted margarine
> ¼ cup minced shallots
> 8–10 ounces fresh shiitake mushrooms, thinly sliced
> 2 teaspoons soy sauce
> 1½ cups Cabernet Sauvignon or Syrah wine
> Salt and freshly ground black pepper to taste
> 4 tablespoons unsalted butter, cut into small pieces
> ¼ cup combined minced fresh parsley and chives

Pour stock into a small saucepan and bring to a boil. Add dried mushrooms, stir well, and remove from heat. Allow mushrooms to soak for 30 minutes. Remove mushrooms with a slotted spoon, squeeze from them any remaining liquid, and chop. Pass stock through a coffee filter or cheesecloth to remove any lingering sand and set aside.

Melt margarine in a large skillet over medium-low heat. Add shallots, fresh mushrooms, chopped dried mushrooms, and soy sauce. Stir and cover. Cook for 5 minutes, shaking the pan several times. Uncover, stir, and continue to cook over low heat until mushrooms are tender.

Combine strained mushroom liquid with wine in a heavy saucepan and bring to a boil over high heat. Reduce heat to medium and simmer briskly to reduce liquid to 1½ cups. Add sautéed mushroom mixture, salt, and pepper. Whisk in butter a bit at a time. Stir in parsley and chives and serve.

Jack Czarnecki's Low-Heat Mushroom-Sautéeing Method

Long, slow cooking sweats the water out of mushrooms, concentrating the flavors. It's a simple way to prepare wild mushrooms, and the results are outstanding when the mushrooms are served alone or over pastry shells, toast, or pasta. We thank Jack for showing us how to do this right.

Serves 2–4

> 3 tablespoons unsalted butter
> ½ cup sliced or chopped onion
> 8 ounces sliced or whole fresh mushrooms, such as portobello or shiitake
> ½ teaspoon salt
> ½ teaspoon sugar
> 1 teaspoon soy sauce

Melt butter in skillet over medium heat. Add onion and sauté for 1 minute. Add mushrooms and continue to sauté for another minute. Reduce heat and cook until mushrooms begin to give up their liquid. Mushrooms will become submerged in liquid, but slowly increase the heat until liquid comes to a light boil and water begins evaporating. Continue to cook until almost all water has evaporated. Add salt, sugar, and soy sauce.

Wine for pasta: Chateau St. Jean Chardonnay (Sonoma County) or Babcock Vineyards Gewürztraminer (Santa Barbara County)

Gary Thomas's Wild Mushroom Pasta

Cleveland's Gary Thomas, a handsome young chef-turned-pasta-entrepreneur, makes extraordinary pastas in his Ohio City Pasta Shop. This is one of his very best. Gary reminds us that "humidity, the temperature of your kitchen, egg sizes, and flavorings all affect your pasta, so be patient and don't be afraid to make a mistake."

Makes 1¼ pounds; serves 4

> 3 ounces dried wild mushrooms, such as cèpes (porcini)
> ¾ cup boiling water
> 3 large eggs, beaten
> 2¼ cups unbleached flour, or more if necessary

In a small bowl, soak mushrooms in boiling water for 30 minutes. Remove mushrooms, reserving liquid, and squeeze them as dry as possible. Put mushroom liquid into a small saucepan and simmer over medium-low heat until reduced to 2–3 tablespoons. Let cool, then mince rehydrated mushrooms. Add liquid and mushrooms to eggs and blend.

Place flour in the bowl of a food processor fitted with the metal blade. Add egg mixture and pulse until dough becomes grainy and can easily be pressed together with your hand. Turn mixture out on a floured work surface and knead by hand until smooth. Add drops of water if dough is too dry or dust with flour if dough feels too wet.

Using a pasta machine to knead and roll dough, begin by dividing it into balls of about ⅓–½-cup amounts. While working one portion, keep remaining portions covered with a clean kitchen towel. Set pasta machine rollers to their widest setting. Flatten first portion with your hands on a lightly floured surface and feed it through the rollers. Fold it in thirds, as you would a letter. Feed it through the rollers again. Flouring as needed, folding as described, and turning in 45-degree rotations, repeat this rolling (kneading) process for a total of ten times.

Then reduce setting one number at a time and roll strip of pasta thinner and thinner, dusting lightly with flour as needed. You do not fold the pasta strip during this process. For ravioli, roll to within one setting of the thinnest and proceed to fill pasta immediately. For all other pastas, roll as thin as possible and allow the pasta to dry on kitchen towels for 15 minutes before you proceed to cut the pasta.

After the pasta is cut, let it dry on a pasta rack. Or dust it very well with cornmeal, coil it in bunches, and freeze until needed.

Farfel with Shiitake Mushrooms

This is yet another dish that goes back to Linda's childhood and her beloved Grandma Weller. In those days, this wonderful grated egg-noodle dish was probably as common as baked potatoes; it was also prepared fairly simply, without exotic mushrooms. We have gussied this up over the years, but it is still easy to make. When possible, we will prepare this with hen-of-the-woods mushrooms in place of shiitake. We love doing it for large groups because it can be prepared ahead and finished at the last minute. If you are not worrying about cholesterol, make this with duck fat for a truly fabulous flavor.

Serves 8–10

- ½ cup unsalted butter or margarine, or ¼ cup butter and ¼ cup chicken or duck fat
- 1 large onion (about 10 ounces), finely chopped
- 6–8 ounces fresh shiitake mushrooms, thinly sliced
- 14 ounces kosher farfel (available in the pasta section of most markets)
- 8–10 cups rich chicken stock, heated to simmering
  Salt and freshly ground black pepper to taste
- ¼ cup minced fresh parsley

Melt butter in a large, heavy-bottomed 3-quart sauté pan. Add onion and mushrooms; sauté over medium heat until vegetables are tender. With a slotted spoon, transfer vegetables to a small bowl and set aside.

Add farfel to sauté pan and stir over medium heat for 2 or 3 minutes. Add 2 cups of stock, reduce heat, and simmer very slowly until liquid is nearly absorbed. Add 2 more cups of stock and continue simmering until that is absorbed. Repeat this process until farfel is tender, about 45 minutes–1 hour.

Preheat oven to 375°. Add reserved mushroom mixture to farfel, season, and stir in parsley. Spoon mixture into a buttered 3-quart baking dish. If mixture seems too dry, add more stock. Bake, uncovered, for 45 minutes.

Paul E. Stamets

Fungi Perfecti
P.O. Box 7634
Olympia, Washington 98507
(206) 426-9292

"Grow the King Stropharia mushroom," Paul Stamets exhorts in his catalogue. "These giant mushrooms can weigh as much as five pounds. Giant burgundy-colored mushrooms will emerge in your backyard. They are delicious when cut like steaks and barbecued and basted with teriyaki sauce on a grill. They have been known to stop cars—causing pandemonium throughout the suburbs of America. With your active participation, your neighborhood could be next."

What he means is that if you have the right environment, Paul's company, Fungi Perfecti, has anything else that you might need to grow mushrooms. From his 17-acre farm, he offers kits for the propagation of shiitake, pearl oyster, golden oyster (esteemed for its nutty flavor), enokitake, lion's mane (valued for its beautiful icicle-like clusters), reishi (prized for its medicinal properties), conifer coral, chicken-of-the-woods, fairy ring, shaggy mane, and the mushroom that is certain to make a mushroom lover's heart skip a beat, the morel. In addition, Fungi Perfecti sells the mushrooms themselves as well as helpful and fanciful literature about them.

If you are lucky enough to encounter mushrooms in the wild, it is because you are in the right place at the right time after a period of months in which conditions have been just right. In recent years, mycologists—botanists with a special interest in fungi—have learned a great deal about what those conditions are. Paul Stamets, who has a degree in microbiology, is one of those pioneering mycologists.

Gourmet PUGET SOUND EXOTIC Delicious

Kamilche Point MUSHROOMS Washington

He understands the complex process and has cultivated dozens of kinds of mushrooms in his laboratory.

First he scrubs, as though preparing for surgery. Then, in his sterile workroom, he selects a mushroom that he would like to duplicate. It will be the best specimen he has. He takes a tiny bit of its tissue and places it on a sterile petri dish. In a few days it will have started to reproduce, ultimately yielding mushrooms exactly like the one from which the specimen was taken. He has cloned it.

To explain cloning, Paul told us to think about poker. "You can take spores from a mushroom and start them in the dish. But the spores will be like a random hand. All different. It's not likely to win for you. But if you clone from the tissue of a superior specimen, there is nothing random. You have dealt yourself four aces."

There are times, when he is happy with the strain of mushrooms that he is working with, that he will use spores to start the process. Either way, in a few days, in the temperature- and humidity-controlled room, the first stage in the mushroom's life cycle, the spider-web–like mycelium, appears. Once he is sure that the mycelium is uncontaminated, he puts it into a jar filled with sterilized grain or sawdust. In time, the mycelium spreads throughout this medium. This charged mixture becomes what mycologists call spawn. It is used to inoculate other jars of similar media or can be used directly on bulk media such as straw or wood. In some cases, wooden dowels are inoculated and pounded into holes drilled into logs of an appropriate wood. If conditions are otherwise right, mushrooms grow.

Fungi Perfecti offers a wide variety of mushroom kits. Many, for indoor use, are inoculated blocks, bags, or racks of the growing medium. Stamets gets shiitakes from his indoor wood chip blocks in just three or four weeks, while the backyard hobbyist who grows mushrooms on logs might have to wait for as long as a year and a half for the harvest.

Around Fungi Perfecti, there seem to be mushrooms growing everywhere. There are racks of logs laden with shiitakes under the trees. There are little speckled mushrooms growing out of brown patches on the lawn. Morels stand in fireplace ash that has been scattered under the trees. There are special buildings, airy and light, that are filled with rack after rack of the specially prepared blocks of media from which mushrooms grow in startling profusion. There seems not to be room on the surface of the blocks for all of the mushrooms that want to grow there.

Paul Stamets feels that his approach makes it possible to have any variety of mushroom on demand, thereby enabling him to save some species from extinction while simultaneously making them available to a wider market. And perhaps even more important, Paul believes, a ready supply of cultivated woodland mushrooms will reduce the impact of foragers who threaten this important element in the ecology of the forest.

Jimmy Schmidt's Chicken Linguine with Morels and Tarragon

There is something so perfect about the combination of morels, cream, and tarragon. In Detroit, The Rattlesnake Club's Jimmy Schmidt adds a few more ingredients to make a superlative pasta meal.

Serves 4

   1 2½- to 3-pound chicken

   2 tablespoons unsalted butter
   2 tablespoons chopped shallots
   3 cups fresh morels, stems trimmed
  ½ cup dry white wine
1¼ cups heavy cream
     Salt and coarsely ground black pepper to taste
   2 tablespoons fresh tarragon
   2 tablespoons chopped fresh chives
   1 pound linguine
  ¼ cup grated Pecorino Romano cheese
  ¼ cup grated Parmesan cheese

Preheat oven to 400°. Place chicken on a rack in roasting pan. Place pan on shelf in lower half of oven and roast until golden brown, about 1¼ hours. Remove, let cool, and pull all meat from carcass. Dice meat into ½-inch pieces and set aside.

In a large skillet over high heat, combine butter, shallots, and mushrooms. Sauté, stirring often, until mixture is browned, about 5 minutes. Add wine and cook until liquid is reduced by half, about 3 minutes. Add cream and cook until mixture is thick enough to coat the back of a spoon, about 10 minutes. Stir in chicken and lower heat. Season with salt and pepper; add tarragon and chives. Keep warm over low heat.

In a large pot of boiling water, cook pasta until *al dente,* about 1½ minutes for fresh pasta. Drain and rinse with warm water, then drain again. Add pasta to sauce mixture in skillet and toss until evenly coated.

Distribute among four heated serving plates and top with cheeses.

Wine: Sanford Winery Chardonnay (Santa Barbara County)

Sautéed Shiitakes with Chicken Livers

This dish goes back to Linda's youth, only in those days it was made with cultivated button mushrooms; add mashed potatoes, she's in heaven. If you find yourselves with golden chanterelles, by all means use them instead of shiitakes for a very special treat.

Serves 2

½ cup unsalted butter or margarine
2 large shallots, finely minced
1 large clove garlic, finely minced
6 ounces fresh shiitake mushrooms, thinly sliced
½ cup unbleached flour
1 teaspoon kosher salt
1 teaspoon freshly ground black pepper
¾ pound fresh chicken livers, lobes separated and trimmed
2 tablespoons Cognac
⅔ cup rich chicken stock
⅓ cup shelled fresh peas
2 teaspoons minced fresh tarragon
1 tablespoon minced fresh chives

In a cast-iron skillet, melt half the butter over medium heat. Add shallots, garlic, and mushrooms. Sauté, covered, for 5 minutes, stirring from time to time. Uncover and sauté until vegetables are tender. Pour mixture into a small dish and reserve.

Combine flour, salt, and pepper in a small dish and blend. Melt remaining butter in skillet over medium-high heat. Dredge livers in flour mixture and quickly sauté until light brown, about 3 minutes per side. Add Cognac and stock and scrape the pan well to loosen any particles that have adhered to the bottom. Return mushroom mixture to pan and add peas. Cook over medium-high heat for about 2 minutes. Sauce should be slightly thickened. Sprinkle with tarragon and chives and add more salt and pepper to taste.

Wine: Henry Winery "Estate" Pinot Noir (Umpqua Valley, Oregon)

Mushroom Lasagna

This is a wonderful dish that is well worth the time it takes to prepare it, especially if you make it a day ahead. It makes a fantastic vegetarian dinner.

Serves 10

1½ ounces dried cèpes (porcini)
1½ ounces dried morels
4 cups boiling water
1 pound fresh cremini mushrooms
1 pound fresh shiitake mushrooms
1 pound assorted fresh wild mushrooms, such as chanterelles, cèpes, or morels
¾ cup unsalted butter
1 dried red chile, crumbled
2 large sweet onions, minced
  Salt and freshly ground black pepper to taste
2 large cloves garlic, minced
1 tablespoon fresh lemon juice
1 teaspoon dried thyme
½ cup unbleached flour
2 cups milk, or more if necessary
1 cup heavy cream
4 ounces creamy blue cheese, such as Hubbardston blue or Gorgonzola
3 ounces mascarpone cheese
4 ounces grated dry Jack cheese (see pages 139–141) or pecorino
1 pound Gary Thomas's Wild Mushroom Pasta (page 325), cut to lasagna size
2 ounces grated Parmesan or aged dry goat cheese

2 tablespoons unsalted butter for garnish

⅓ cup fine, dry bread crumbs for garnish

Combine dried mushrooms and boiling water in a bowl and soak for at least 30 minutes. Remove mushrooms and reserve. Pour liquid through a coffee filter or cheesecloth to remove any lingering dirt and set aside.

Thinly slice cremini mushrooms. Discard shiitake stems and slice caps thinly. Trim and slice assorted wild mushrooms, then combine all fresh mushrooms in a bowl. Melt 2 tablespoons of the butter in a large skillet. Add half of the fresh mushroom mixture, the dried chile, and half of the onion. Sprinkle with salt and pepper. Cover and cook over medium-low heat, stirring often, until mushrooms are tender, about 5 minutes. Transfer mushrooms and onions to a mixing bowl with a slotted spoon. Drain pan juices into a measuring cup, then melt 2 more tablespoons of butter and repeat the process with the remaining fresh mushrooms and onions.

Finally, melt 2 more tablespoons of butter and cook the reserved dried mushrooms and the garlic, partially covered, for about 10 minutes, or until mushrooms are fairly tender. Add to the other mushrooms, adjust seasonings, and add lemon juice and thyme. Toss well and set aside.

Melt remaining butter in a heavy saucepan. Add flour and whisk well over low heat for 2 minutes. Add milk and cream and stir over medium heat until mixture is very thick. Stir in blue cheese, marscarpone, and dry Jack. Cook over low heat for 10 minutes. Slowly add reserved dried-mushroom liquid. If mixture needs more thinning, skim fat off surface of reserved mushroom-cooking liquid and whisk that into sauce. The sauce should be very thick but runny enough to coat the pasta. If needed, thin with more milk.

Bring a large pot of salted water to boil. Add lasagna and cook for 2–3 minutes. Drain and plunge into cold water to stop cooking. Drain again.

Butter a 9×12 baking dish and arrange a third of the pasta across the bottom. Spoon half the mushroom mixture over the pasta. Then ladle ⅓ of the cream sauce over that. Arrange another layer of pasta and repeat the process. Top with remaining pasta and remaining sauce. Distribute Parmesan cheese over the entire surface.

Preheat oven to 375°. Melt 2 tablespoons butter in a small skillet and add bread crumbs. Toss over medium heat for 2 minutes. Sprinkle lasagna with buttered bread crumbs and bake for 45 minutes. Let rest for 5 minutes before cutting and serving.

Wine: Floreal (Flora Springs)

Shiitake and Wild Mushroom Bread Pudding

Savory bread puddings? With venison or grilled chicken, what could be better? If you can get fresh cèpes (porcini) or any other robust mushrooms, use them instead of dried.

Serves 6–10

> 5 cups Challah pieces (page 70)
> 2 cups half-and-half, or more if necessary

> 1 cup heavy cream
> 4 jumbo eggs, beaten
> 4 tablespoons butter
> 1 shallot, minced
> 1–2 ounces dried porcini, reconstituted and chopped
> 5 ounces fresh shiitake mushroom caps, thinly sliced
> 2 teaspoons plus 1 scant tablespoon minced fresh tarragon
> 1 stalk celery, finely diced
> 1 small onion, finely diced
> Salt and freshly ground black pepper to taste

Place bread in large bowl. Combine with half-and-half, cream, and eggs. Blend well and let stand 1 hour. Mixture should be very creamy, so add a bit more half-and-half if too dry.

In a medium skillet, melt butter over medium heat. Add shallot and mushrooms, stir, and cover. Cook over medium-low heat for 5 minutes, stirring several times. Remove cover, sprinkle with 2 teaspoons tarragon, and sauté until liquid is mostly evaporated. When cool, combine with bread mixture. Add celery, onion, remaining tarragon, salt, and pepper. Blend well. Spoon into a buttered 2-quart baking dish and let stand another hour.

Preheat oven to 400°. Bake pudding in preheated oven for 45 minutes. Remove from the oven and serve.

Kevin Doyle

Forest Mushrooms

P.O. Box 93

St. Joseph, Minnesota 56374

(612) 363-7956

There is a strange machine in Kevin Doyle's barn. It is a blue-and-orange box, 6 feet high and 10 feet long. Two big stainless-steel chimneys vent it to the outside. There is a hatch that seals it tightly, and some dials, gauges, levers, and valves. It pasteurizes wheat straw, several hundred pound at time. It is the only device of its type in the United States.

Wheat straw is not an uncommon commodity in this part of central Minnesota, and Kevin can get all he wants of it. But before he can put it to use, he has to load a batch of it into the machine. He adds a little hot water and closes the hatch. Naturally occurring bacteria start to work. As the mixture ferments, the temperature gradually elevates to 140–145° Fahrenheit, destroying most of the bacteria that caused the fermentation in the first place and, along with it, molds, spores, and microscopic organisms.

This pasteurized straw becomes the medium for the cultivation of one of the most coveted and delicate of all mushrooms—*Pleurotus ostreatus,* the oyster mushroom. And this machine from Holland is at the heart of Kevin's operation. He discovered it while researching mushroom technology in Europe. Kevin prefers fermentation to steam pasteurization, with its higher heat. The fermentation process creates a resistance to a recontamination of the straw by green mold.

At nearby St. Johns University in Collegeville, Minnesota, Kevin had majored in Natural Science with an emphasis on botany. Mushrooms were not really

on his mind then. But in the early 1980s, he and some friends decided to explore the possibilities of growing exotic mushrooms commercially. In March of 1985, they started research in Kevin's kitchen. By fall, they were growing small quantities of shiitake and oyster mushrooms in the basement. They decided that they should concentrate on one or the other.

"We chose the oyster because it looked easier," Kevin told us with a laugh. "But little did we know the problems we would have starting up!" Actually, the shiitake need more space. They require more start-up capital and more time to produce a crop. They grow on logs or blocks of sterilized sawdust, which are more expensive than pasteurized straw. But the oyster mushrooms turned out to be more "finicky" than the shiitake. They were unpredictable and required more care. But although they had troubles in getting the oyster mushroom project under way, Kevin feels they did the right thing. "They are great to eat," he added, "and not many people were growing them."

The partners formed a corporation and bought an old pig farm that had been idle for years. They set up their operation in a shed and started going to market with oyster mushrooms in late 1986. The next year, Kevin and his wife, Wendy, bought out the partners, and for the next two years the two of them gave the farm every moment they had.

The operation quickly outgrew the little pig shed, so a new building was put up, and then another. Kevin expects to produce 6,000 pounds per week eventually, nearly twelve times the weekly average of the company's first successful year.

On his farm Kevin provides what he calls the "fruiting environment." He buys the spawn, the medium that carries the first stages of the mushroom's life, from skilled growers who specialize in producing it. These growers sterilize millet or some other grain, and then inject it with mushroom spores that are germinated in a petri dish. After a few days, the next stage of growth, what looks like a spider web or a mold, covers the grain. It is at this stage when Kevin takes over and mixes it with the pasteurized straw.

This mixture, now impregnated and ready to grow, is packed into sixty long plastic bags, each 3 feet long and 10 inches in diameter. These are taken to the spawn room, where they hang from racks for three weeks at 75°. By the end of this time, "pins" start to distend the plastic. These are the mushrooms. At this point the bags are taken to the fruiting room, where they are cut—3- to 4-inch slashes are made at 1-inch intervals over the entire surface. They are again suspended from racks, and after a few days at 60 to 65°, the first mushrooms are ready for picking.

Each bag typically sprouts three or four times over a five-week period before its energy is spent and it is sold to amateur gardeners as compost or mulch. "The only problem is the plastic bag," said Kevin. "Maybe we'll experiment with biodegradable plastic, the kind with cornstarch in it. But we're worried that the mushrooms will consume the bag, too, and everything will fall to the floor."

For the foreseeable future, Forest Mushrooms will grow oyster mushrooms only. Kevin sells all he can grow. But he has established relationships with growers of other kinds of mushrooms—such as shiitake, cremini, and enokitake—and with foragers who provide him with fresh morels. He sorts and packages these other mushrooms and distributes them to his customers along with his own oyster mushrooms.

We asked Kevin to tell us his very favorite way to eat *Pleurotus ostreatus.* It was akin to asking him to name his favorite child. "With eggs," he said. "Sautéed with minced garlic and chopped onion in two parts butter and one part vegetable oil. But then there is nothing like a cream of oyster mushroom soup. And salads. They are great sliced right into your tossed salad. And . . ." He could have gone on all afternoon.

Cream of Oyster Mushroom Soup

Serves 4–6

    6 tablespoons unsalted butter or
      margarine
    ½ cup finely minced onion
    12 ounces fresh oyster mushrooms,
      thinly sliced
    1 sprig thyme
    1 teaspoon kosher salt
    ½ teaspoon freshly ground white
      pepper
    3 tablespoons sifted unbleached flour
    2 cups rich chicken stock
    2 cups heavy cream
      Fresh chives for garnish

Melt butter in heavy-bottomed pot. Add onion, mushrooms, thyme, and salt; stir and cover with wax paper placed directly on the vegetables. Cook over low heat until onions are transparent and mushrooms are tender, about 6 minutes. Remove paper and thyme. Sprinkle with pepper and flour and stir to blend. Over medium heat, slowly stir in stock, then cream. Simmer briskly for 5 minutes. Adjust seasonings, garnish with chives, and serve.

Wine: Carmenet Vineyard "Cyril Chavez Vineyard" French Columbard (Sonoma County)

Omelet with Oyster Mushrooms

Serves 2

    4 jumbo eggs
    2 tablespoons milk
    ½ teaspoon kosher salt
    4 tablespoons unsalted butter or
      margarine
    1 shallot, finely minced
    4 ounces oyster mushrooms, thinly
      sliced
    1 teaspoon minced fresh tarragon
    1 teaspoon freshly ground white
      pepper
    ½ cup chopped steamed spinach

Combine eggs, milk, and salt in a mixing bowl and whisk vigorously. Set aside.

In a well-seasoned 9-inch omelet pan, melt butter over low heat. Add shallots and cook for 1 minute. Add mushrooms, tarragon, and pepper; sauté until tender, about 4 minutes. Sprinkle lightly with salt and toss with spinach. Cover with egg mixure and cook over medium-high heat, shaking pan back and forth until omelet is set.

Wine: Chappellet Vineyard Chenin Blanc (Napa Valley)

Shaw's Crab House Sautéed Salmon with Oyster Mushroom Sauce

Shaw's chef Yves Roubaud grew up in Marseilles. But while he may have been raised on Mediterranean fish, he has a remarkble talent for bringing out the best in the extraordinary salmon of our Pacific Northwest. We love this combination of meaty salmon with oyster mushrooms.

Serves 4

Mushroom Sauce
     2 tablespoons olive oil
     1 pound oyster mushrooms, trimmed
     2 tablespoons minced shallots
     1 teaspoon minced garlic
     1 cup R. H. Phillips Night Harvest
        Sauvignon Blanc wine
     1 quart clam juice
     1 tablespoon fresh thyme
     1 tablespoon cornstarch
        Salt and freshly ground black
        pepper to taste

     2 tablespoons vegetable oil
     4 8-ounce salmon fillets
     1 cup flour

        Bunches of fresh thyme and lemon
        wedges for garnish

Heat olive oil in skillet over medium heat. Add mushrooms and sauté for a minute or two. Add shallots, garlic, and wine. Cook until wine is almost completely evaporated. Add clam juice and thyme. Cook for 15–20 minutes, until mushrooms are very tender. Combine cornstarch with 3 tablespoons water and mix very well. Add to sauce a bit at a time, until sauce reaches the desired consistency. Season with salt and pepper; keep warm.

Heat vegetable oil in skillet until hot. Dredge salmon in flour and shake to remove excess. Sauté salmon 4 minutes over medium-high heat; turn and sauté on the other side for an additional 4 minutes.

Place fillets on heated serving plates. Cover fillets with mushroom sauce and garnish with bunches of fresh thyme and lemon wedges.

Wine: Swanson Vineyards Chardonnay (Napa Valley)

Oyster Mushrooms and Yellow Squash

This dish is so simple but so delicious—especially when you can pick an appropriate variety of squash, such as pattypan, right out of the garden. It's a good accompaniment to grilled fish or chicken.

Serves 4

     2 tablespoons olive oil or unsalted
        margarine
    12 ounces yellow squash, cut in ⅓-inch
        slices
   3–4 ounces fresh oyster mushrooms
     1 large shallot, finely minced
     ¼ cup chopped mixed borage flowers,
        fennel fronds, flat-leaf parsley, and
        tarragon
     ¼ cup low-fat sour cream
        Kosher salt and freshly ground
        black pepper to taste
     1 tablespoon minced fresh chives

Heat oil in a nonstick skillet over medium heat. Add squash, mushrooms, and shallot. Toss until squash is coated with oil, cover, and reduce heat. Cook, stirring from time to time, until squash is just tender, about 8 minutes. Add herbs, sour cream, salt, and pepper. Blend well and cook until just heated through. Sprinkle with chives and serve.

Sally LaPlace

Break-a-Heart Ranch

2450 Blucher Valley Road

Sebastopol, California 95472

(707) 823-8046

Break-a-Heart Ranch is 5 rich hillside acres in a high-density agricultural area of Sebastopol, California. A flower and vegetable garden, really, it is the domain of Sally LaPlace. To the south, up the ridge, there's a stand of woods—a mixture of oak, bay, and redwood. To the east, there's a stand of fragrant eucalyptus. The lay of this land, this valley, creates a microclimate that virtually precludes frost, even in winter, so while things grow slowly, they grow steadily and heartily.

"It's a cook's garden," said Sally LaPlace. "Chef-quality. Everything is chef-quality."

In fact, most of Sally's customers are chefs. "They want fresh, they want clean, they want regionally grown vegetables and flowers." In the great dining rooms, there have always been elegant arrangements of flowers, fresh and fragrant. But in recent years, the creative cooks of this country and France have explored flowers as ingredients. Many, perhaps even most, flowers are edible. Some add not just color to a dish but a dimension of flavor and aroma as well. When Sally LaPlace and her partner, Anthony Minichiello, bought their farm in 1983, Sally knew there were chefs in the neighborhood who were looking for flowers.

Sally packs her edible flowers 50 to 75 per box and markets 100 boxes a week.

Violets, with a sweet, perfumy flavor, are perfect for ice cream as well as for a garnish. Borage flowers, redolent of cucumber, can be made into sorbet to garnish a cold summer soup. Nasturtiums, flowers with a sweet and peppery flavor and big round leaves, taste almost hot in a salad. Colorful scented geranium petals add visual interest, with scent and flavor to match. Lavender flowers can top a scoop of honeyed ice cream or float atop a summer blueberry soup. Fuchsia makes a beautiful punctuation to any dish. The flowers of the pineapple sage add a hint of both flavors to a soup or salad dressing. Johnny jump-ups, pansies, flowers from virtually every herb, roses, and even some marigolds—Sally said she had just been trying to count the different varieties of edible flowers she had raised in the past year and couldn't remember them all.

And then there is Sally's signature product, one for which she has a registered trademark: Petal Confetti, an extraordinary garnish of color, taste, and texture and an amalgam of petals from all different kinds of flowers. Sally likes to scatter the confetti on white cheesecake or on a white plate around food. Sometimes she scatters it across the entire tabletop for a festive occasion.

For a while, all she grew were the flowers. But she couldn't keep away from vegetables, since the soil is rich and loamy and everything grows easily here. To get things started and to protect the tender, she has two small greenhouses filled with young plants, which are soon to be going outside to join a surprising number of delicate lettuces already growing in the garden. She raises all kinds of specialty tomatoes—yellow and red peach tomatoes, purple tomatoes, wrinkled Casbah tomatoes—purple cauliflower, green garlic, yellow and green Annelino tomatoes (small and crescent-shaped, with a rich Romano flavor), purple Brussels sprouts, sweet red cherry peppers, and red beard onions. A color is usually part of their names. Color always seems to be a consideration in the choices Sally makes for her vegetable garden.

Sally LaPlace was born in Texas. She was a hairdresser in the San Francisco Bay area and Lake Tahoe for nearly twenty years before she and Tony moved down to Sonoma County. He is a contractor who remodels and rebuilds houses. Their own beautiful home is always in "aesthetic transition." Sally nodded affec-

tionately as Tony described his work, glad that he does what he does, because, she said, "I bury my money," "plowing" it back into the ranch.

Sally LaPlace is determinedly organic. Certified, even. A sign on her gate proclaims it. She even raises ladybugs in her greenhouse, little beetles that make a beeline to the nearest aphid infestation.

As we stand in the barnyard talking, we are surrounded by Sally's pets: Boris, a big Polish rooster with a crazy haircut; two Muscovy ducks; four very loud Chinese geese, purchased to eat the weeds but retired to the barnyard after it was discovered that they liked radicchio and frisée better; three little Call Ducks, Lauren, Betty, and Honey; and an assortment of hens. No candidates for the cooking pot here. Their contribution to their keep? Just the eggs. A hundred quail come by to scavenge in the yard. And at the top of the ridge, above the 9-foot deer fence, two dozen buzzards are riding the thermals.

Susan Cavitch's Lemon Verbena and Mango Sorbet

Susan is Linda's dear cousin and also one of the best cooks we know.

Makes 1 quart

- ¾ cup sugar
- 2 ripe mangoes, peeled and pitted
- 1 tablespoon fresh lime juice
- 2 tablespoons chopped fresh lemon verbena

Combine sugar and ¾ cup water in a small saucepan and simmer over medium-low heat until sugar is completely dissolved. Cool, then refrigerate 2 hours, or until very cold.

Place mangoes in a food processor fitted with the metal blade and purée. Then force puree through a sieve into a mixing bowl. Add chilled syrup and remaining ingredients and mix well. Freeze in an ice-cream maker according to manufacturer's directions.

Chicken Valdrôme

This grew out of our dear friend Lydie Marshall's recipe for chicken and turnips. In her honor, we have named this for the village in Haute Provence where the Marshalls have a charming retreat. This is one of our most popular dishes. Serve with a crusty bread for mopping the sauce up and for spreading with the creamy garlic.

Serves 4–6

1 teaspoon minced fresh rosemary
1 teaspoon minced fresh sage
1 teaspoon minced fresh thyme
1 teaspoon minced fresh lavender flowers
1 tablespoon minced fresh parsley
2 tablespoons unsalted butter or margarine
2 tablespoons extra-virgin olive oil
3 1-pound chicken breasts, split and patted dry
6 small turnips, scrubbed, trimmed and cut in half
6 small white onions, cut in half
6 small thin-skinned potatoes, scrubbed and cut in half
3 carrots, scrubbed, trimmed, and cut in chunks
1–2 heads garlic, unpeeled and separated into cloves
Kosher salt and freshly ground black pepper to taste

Sprigs of fresh rosemary, thyme, sage, and parsley and edible flowers, such as scented geranium petals and herb flowers, for garnish

Combine rosemary, sage, thyme, lavender, and parsley. Mix well and set aside. In a large cast-iron or stamped-steel skillet that has a tight-fitting lid, combine butter and olive oil and heat over medium heat.

When butter mixture is hot, add chicken breasts and brown on both sides. When breasts are evenly browned, remove from pan and transfer to a plate.

Add turnips, onions, potatoes, and carrots and stir over medium-high heat for several minutes. Remove skillet from heat.

Place chicken breasts over vegetables. Sprinkle with herb mixture, garlic cloves, salt, and pepper.

Cover skillet tightly, place over very low heat, and cook for 50 minutes, or until chicken and vegetables are tender.

To serve, distribute chicken, vegetables, and garlic cloves among heated serving plates. Spoon some of the pan juices over the chicken and garnish with herbs and flowers.

Wine: Cline Cellars "Oakley Cuvee"
(Contra Costa County)

Susan Cavitch's Lavender Ice Cream

When we visited Sally LaPlace, we were enchanted with her fragrant lavender. We quickly asked Susan to create a lavender ice cream for us. We think this is outstanding.

Makes 1 quart

- 1 cantaloupe
- 4 large egg yolks
- 2 cups heavy cream
- ¾ cup milk
- ½ cup sugar
- ½ teaspoon vanilla extract
- 1½ tablespoons chopped lavender leaves

Candied or fresh lavender flowers for garnish

Cut cantaloupe in half and scoop out and discard the seeds. Carefully scoop out all of the flesh and discard the rind. Put flesh in the bowl of a food processor fitted with the metal blade and purée. Transfer puree to a colander fitted over a large bowl and allow puree to drain. Reserve ½ cup of drained liquid and store pulp and any remaining liquid for another use.

Place egg yolks in a small mixing bowl and beat lightly. Combine cream, milk, and sugar in a heavy saucepan. Stir over medium heat until sugar is dissolved. Gradually temper egg yolks by adding a cup of the hot cream mixture to the beaten eggs, whisking continuously. Then, still whisking, pour tempered eggs into the saucepan. Add vanilla and lavender leaves and cook over medium-low heat, whisking frequently, until mixture forms a custard that will coat the back of a spoon. Remove from heat and let stand until completely cooled.

Add reserved cantaloupe liquid to cooled custard, whisking thoroughly. Strain and discard lavender. Freeze in ice-cream maker according to manufacturer's directions and garnish with flowers.

Susan's Rose-Scented Geranium and Pear Preserves

Whether it's on a really good piece of toast, on a yummy muffin, or served as a garnish to some roast chicken, this is exquisitely original.

Makes 8 8-ounce jars

- 2 lemons
- 5½ pounds ripe seckel or anjou pears, peeled, cored, and coarsely chopped
- 5 cups sugar
- ¾ cup rose-scented geranium leaves, firmly packed
- 8 nicely formed rose-scented geranium leaves

Peel lemons in as large parings as possible and place it in large mixing bowl. Squeeze juice from lemons and add to bowl. Add pears and sugar and mix thoroughly. Cover bowl and refrigerate at least 8 hours, stirring well several times.

In a large, heavy saucepan, combine pear mixture with packed geranium leaves. Over medium heat, slowly bring mixture to a boil. Reduce heat to low and simmer until liquids form a very heavy syrup. This will take between 2 and 4 hours, depending on your stove and the ripeness of the pears.

Remove from heat and discard lemon peel and geranium leaves. Pour preserves into 8 hot, sterilized jars. Force 1 attractive fresh leaf into each jar with a sterile implement and seal with paraffin.

Our Pesto

Pesto is at its best when made with right-from-the-garden herbs. We make gobs of pesto every summer and spoon portions of it into small plastic baggies. These get put into heavier bags, which are tucked into the freezer for winter. We like to make several kinds of pesto. Sometimes we use pine nuts, sometimes walnuts. Sometimes we use Parmesan cheese, sometimes Romano. When we have it, we'll use Ig Vella's extra-aged Jack (see pages 139–141) or Sally Jackson's aged sheep's-milk cheese.

Makes 1–1 ¼ cups

> 2 cups tightly packed fresh basil
> ½ cup tightly packed fresh flat-leaf parsley
> 2 very large cloves garlic
> Scant ¾ cup grated Parmesan cheese
> 1 teaspoon finely ground black pepper
> 4 tablespoons unsalted butter, softened
> ⅓ cup pine nuts
> ½ cup extra-virgin olive oil

Combine basil, parsley, garlic, Parmesan, pepper, and butter in the bowl of a food processor fitted with the metal blade. Pulse until mixture is puréed. Add nuts and pulse again several times. Then, with motor running, gradually add olive oil in a thin stream until mixture becomes pastelike in consistency.

Arthur and Anne Berndt

Maverick Sugarbush
Box 99
Sharon, Vermont 05065
(802) 763-8680

When Arthur and Anne Berndt decided to leave their family-counseling practice in Norwich, Vermont, they were determined to become more actively involved in caring for Vermont's precious natural resources. They were also certain that whatever new enterprise they might develop would have to involve the land and would have to be environmentally sound.

Then they discovered a 400-acre sugarbush (a sugar maple forest) in Sharon, Vermont. The land was spectacular, the sugarbush was known to produce delicious syrup, and it came with Blaine Moore. Blaine had been the property manager for the previous owner, and he and his family had sugared on the land for generations. He knew the forest intimately, was an expert syrup maker, and understood the Berndts' environmental concerns. It was a match made in heaven.

The Berndts own 400 acres of sugarbush and lease another 150 acres of maple forest from neighbors. Maverick's maple trees are in a bowl-like depression in a mountainside that slopes down toward the sugarhouse. The trees are reached by Jeep or on foot in good weather, and snowshoes or snowmobiles in winter. But like most Vermont sugarbushes, this one is experiencing problems—especially obvious in autumn. Large stands of trees actually look stressed, their leaves dull and lifeless. Other sections of the forest have trees with brown leaves, which in turn have peculiar holes, indicating the presence of the maple leaf cutter. Arthur feels that the real problem is acid rain and other pollutants, which make the trees susceptible to insect damage and cause a general decline in health. But the Berndts will not spray the trees with pesticides—rather, they try to strengthen the forest itself by fertilization and by utilizing innovative forestry practices.

"We take our responsibility as stewards of the land seriously and give back some of what we take out," they say in their information sheet. "You must manage your forest wisely," said Arthur. "Doing nothing doesn't make you organic."

The Berndts *are* actively managing their forest, and they are doing it naturally. They use a helicopter to fertilize the forest with an organic fertilizer of natural potassium sulfate, hi-mag dolomitic limestone, and phosphate. Besides adding nutritional elements, Arthur and Anne feel that this practice helps activate the forest's natural composting processes by increasing the pH. When the soil is too acidic, often from acid rain, the breakdown of natural organic matter is slowed down, limiting the flow of nutrients.

They also selectively thin the forest to eliminate trees that compete for light and room with the syrup trees. But after removing the marketable timber from downed trees, most sugarbush folk simply leave the tops and limbs in disarray in the forest because there is little economic reason to do otherwise. Arthur and Anne don't want to leave the forest floor a mess, nor do they want to burn the wood and add smoke to the environment, so they have the remnants cut into logs and trucked away for pulp. "It's all part of being responsible," said Anne.

In addition, when Arthur and Anne first bought the property, they decided that instead of subscribing to the common practice of placing two or more taps on each tree they would be conservative and place only one tap on each tree. Thus they have gone from 18,000 taps in their sugarbush to 13,000. Maverick's sap is not collected in buckets, as many of us may envision. Rather, a flexible pipeline runs from each tree through the forest and down the mountainside to stainless-steel collection tanks near the sugarhouse. Most sugarmakers support pipeline by wrapping steel cable around the trees. These wires often cut into the trees and can cause serious damage. Maverick uses wooden blocks to cushion the tree from the cables that support the pipeline.

Since the Berndts purchased the sugarbush in 1988, Maverick has been as meticulous in its production practices as it has been in its forest management. Sap and syrup do not come in contact with lead in any part of the process. (Traditionally, in this industry, the cooking pans and storage tanks are often lead-soldered.) Maverick uses a unique five-stage filtering and clarifying system during processing. The sap is pumped from one tank to another, filtered, and passed through the delicate membranes of reverse osmosis machines that remove 75 percent of the water from the sap. The use of reverse osmosis reduces the boiling time for the sap to a fraction of the time traditionally needed. The less cooking the sap undergoes, the better the chance for realizing a lighter-colored (higher-grade) syrup. The sap is then cooked in a large stainless-steel pan, and the foam that collects during this process is removed by adding an organic defoaming agent. (The Berndts believe the agent they use is cleaner and healthier than lard, the traditional defoamer.)

Regulations for the production of maple syrup vary from state to state. Vermont's standards are among the most stringent in the country. Paraformaldehyde tablets, put into the tap holes in order to keep the holes fresh and the syrup color light, have been banned in Vermont because they further stress the trees by retarding the healing process. The density of syrup is measured on the Brix Scale: Vermont requires a density of 66.9, while the USDA requires only 66.5 and Canada only 66. As a result, Vermont's syrup is thicker, and thus has more flavor and a smoother, silkier texture.

Maple syrup is graded according to color, not flavor, and the grading standards vary from state to state, too. In Vermont, syrup falls into four different categories: Grade A light amber (also known as Fancy); Grade A medium amber (formerly known as Vermont Grade A); Grade A dark amber (formerly Vermont Grade B); and Grade B (formerly Vermont Grade C). The lighter the color, the more delicate the flavor. The flavor of syrup varies widely from one sugarbush to another. Maverick's flavor is unusually delicious. It has a delightfully rich maple taste, with complex round and mellow flavors. And typical of most Vermont syrups, it is thick on the tongue.

"It takes 35 to 45 gallons of sap to make a gallon of syrup, depending on the sugar content of the sap," Arthur said. "The first sap of the season is always the lightest and clearest, so it requires the least boiling." It is the most likely candidate for Fancy grade.

Fancy is the most difficult syrup to make. "The light color and flavor depend upon the trees themselves," Arthur added, "as well as on the temperature outside when the sap is running. The grade of syrup one makes is highly dependent upon Mother Nature from year to year, and how each sugarmaker processes the sap."

The syrup is stored in 30-gallon drums for as short a time as possible, since it tends to darken in storage, although the flavor does not change. The Berndts do not use plastic for storage because it imparts a flavor to the syrup. They sell the syrup in superior-quality metal containers and advise the consumer to decant their syrup into glass for long-term home storage.

Their efforts are paying off. The stunning orange, black, and lavender label, with its stylized redwing blackbird (the heralder of Vermont's springtime), makes their containers especially striking on store shelves. Anne and Arthur Berndt are selling all the syrup they can make, and they're having fun doing it.

Arthur's great-great-grandfather was Samuel Maverick of Texas, after whom the company was named. He might be surprised to find his kin hurtling up the mountainside in a wreck of a Jeep instead of on the back of a horse. But he'd sure be proud to know that they are maverick sugarmakers.

Pumpkin Chiffon Pie in Meringue Shell

This has been Linda's son Andy's favorite Thanksgiving dessert since 1966.

Makes 1 10-inch pie

CRUST

    4 jumbo egg whites, at room
      temperature
    Pinch salt
    ¾ cup superfine sugar
    ½ teaspoon fresh lemon juice

FILLING

    2 ¼-ounce envelopes unflavored
      gelatin
    2 tablespoons dark rum
    ¼ cup fresh orange juice
    4 jumbo eggs
    3 cups fresh pumpkin puree (see
      Heavenly Pumpkin Cheesecake,
      page 49)
    1 cup dark brown sugar, firmly
      packed
    ½ cup maple syrup
    ¾ cup evaporated milk
    ½ teaspoon freshly grated nutmeg
    1 teaspoon ground ginger
    ¼ teaspoon ground cloves
    1 teaspoon cinnamon
    1 teaspoon ground cardamom
    Zest of 1 orange, minced
    Pinch salt
    2½ cups Crème Fraîche (page 350)
    ¼ cup confectioners' sugar

Candied ginger or candied violets
for garnish

Preheat oven to 300°. Butter and flour a 10-inch Pyrex pie plate and set aside.

To make pie crust, combine egg whites and salt in the bowl of an electric mixer fitted with the beater. Beat on high speed until foamy, then very, very slowly add sugar. Beat until mixture is stiff and shiny. Add lemon juice and beat a few seconds. Spoon ¾ of the mixture into the prepared pie plate and spread it thickly over the bottom and all the way up the sides. Spoon remaining meringue in large adjoining mounds all the way around perimeter of plate. Bake in preheated oven for 50 minutes. Let cool.

To make the filling, combine gelatin, rum, and juice in a small bowl and let stand. Separate eggs; beat yolks in a small bowl. Place egg whites in another bowl and let stand at room temperature.

In a heavy 3-quart saucepan, combine pumpkin, brown sugar, maple syrup, milk, spices, and orange zest. Simmer over very low heat, stirring constantly, until mixture is hot.

Gradually temper the yolks by adding some of the hot mixture to them, a little at a time, until yolks are quite warm. Then pour the tempered eggs into the saucepan and continue to cook over very low heat, stirring constantly, until the mixture is very thick and custard-like. Then add the gelatin mixture and stir over low heat until gelatin is dissolved. Remove saucepan from heat and cool until mixture thickens. If you are in a hurry, set saucepan over ice bath. Stir often to cool.

Beat egg whites with a pinch of salt until soft peaks are formed. Gently fold egg whites into pumpkin mixture and chill for about 1 hour. The mixture should be cold but not set.

Place crème fraîche in a chilled mixing bowl, and using chilled beaters, whip it, gradually adding the confectioners' sugar. When stiff, gently fold half of the crème fraîche into the pumpkin mixture. Then spoon into prepared pie shell. Either spread remaining crème fraîche over surface of pie or pipe it decoratively around the edge. Decorate with candied ginger or candied violets and chill until set.

Crème Fraîche

Makes 2 cups

> 2 cups heavy cream
> 6 tablespoons buttermilk

In a small bowl, combine ingredients and mix well. Let stand at room temperature, loosely covered, for 12 hours. Then cover tightly and refrigerate. Crème fraîche will usually keep for several weeks.

Wonderful Winter-Squash and Black Walnut Bread

Butternut, Hubbard, Dumpling, Sugar Pumpkin, Red Kuri, Delicata—all are good for this dish. Bake the squash in a 425° oven until tender, then purée. Baking is better than boiling, because it causes the natural sugars to caramelize, giving a better flavor to the flesh.

Makes 2 loaves

> 2 cups whole-wheat pastry flour (available in health-food stores or from Arrowhead Mills, page 67)
> 2 cups unbleached flour
> 2 tablespoons baking powder
> 2 teaspoons baking soda
> 1 teaspoon salt
> 1 teaspoon cinnamon
> ½ teaspoon freshly grated nutmeg
> 1 teaspoon ground ginger
> 1 cup chopped black walnuts
> 4 jumbo eggs
> 1 cup brown sugar, firmly packed
> ½ cup maple syrup
> 2 cups cooked and pureed winter squash
> ½ cup unsalted butter or margarine, melted
> ½ cup buttermilk

Preheat oven to 350°.

Grease two 9¼×4¼ loaf pans and set aside.

Sift dry ingredients and spices together into a large bowl. Add walnuts and toss gently to coat them with the flour. Set aside.

In another bowl, beat eggs until fluffy, then add brown sugar and maple syrup and blend well. Add the squash puree and whisk until evenly mixed. Add butter and buttermilk and blend again.

Pour squash mixture over dry ingredients. Mix gently until blended. Do not overmix. Pour batter into prepared pans and bake in preheated oven for 1 hour. Bread is done when a cake tester inserted into the center comes out clean. Loaves should be brown on top and sides should be pulled away from pan. Let stand on racks for 10 minutes, then turn loaves out of the pan to finish cooling.

Cherry Pie Fit for a Queen

For all lovers of maple syrup, Tapawingo's Pete Peterson has outdone himself with this dessert. The pastry is splendid, the filling superb, and ah, the maple meringue!

Makes 1 10-inch pie

CRUST

    1 cup unbleached flour
    ½ cup whole-wheat pastry flour (available in health-food stores or from Arrowhead Mills, page 67)
    2 ounces blanched slivered almonds, toasted and finely ground
    ½ teaspoon cinnamon
    ½ cup unsalted butter, chilled and cut into cubes
    3 tablespoons maple syrup
    1 large egg yolk
    Scant teaspoon grated lemon zest

FILLING

    4 cups (2 pounds) fresh tart cherries, pitted, with juice reserved
    2 tablespoons quick-cooking tapioca
    2 tablespoons cornstarch
    ¾ cup maple syrup
    ½ teaspoon cinnamon
    1 tablespoon fresh lemon juice

    1 teaspoon grated lemon zest

TOPPING

    1 cup maple syrup
    4 large egg whites, at room temperature
    1 teaspoon fresh lemon juice
    1 teaspoon vanilla extract

First, make the crust: In the bowl of a food processor fitted with the metal blade, combine flours, almonds, cinnamon, and butter. Pulse until mixture resembles coarse meal. Add 3 tablespoons syrup, egg yolk, and lemon zest; pulse again until mixture just starts to form a mass. Remove from bowl, form into a flat disk, wrap in plastic wrap, and chill for 30 minutes.

Preheat oven to 375°.

Roll dough between sheets of parchment paper into a circle large enough to cover bottom and sides of a 10-inch pie plate. (Nut dough is fragile and cannot be rolled much thinner than 3/16- to ¼-inch thickness.) Place dough in pie plate and flute the edges. Chill for 15 minutes. Cover crust with parchment and fill with baking beans. Bake in preheated oven for 10 minutes, remove parchment and beans, and bake for an additional 7–10 minutes, or until crust crisps and browns. Transfer to a rack to cool.

Meanwhile, make the filling: Combine cherries, cherry juice, tapioca, cornstarch, ¾ cup syrup, and cinnamon in an enamel saucepan. Let sit for about 15 minutes, until the cherries have released more juices and the tapioca has softened. Place pan over medium heat and slowly bring to a boil, stirring occasionally. Cook until filling has thickened and tapioca is clear, being careful not to break up cherries. Remove from heat and stir in lemon juice and zest. Pour into baked pastry shell.

Preheat oven to 400°.

To make the topping, place 1 cup maple syrup in a small saucepan. Bring to a boil and cook until syrup reaches the soft-ball stage, about 238° on a candy thermometer. Meanwhile, beat egg whites until soft peaks form. Immediately pour syrup in a thread-like stream into the egg whites and beat until meringue is firm and shiny, about 2 or 3 more minutes. Fold in lemon juice and vanilla. Spoon meringue into a large pastry bag with a large star-shaped tip. Pipe towering, generous mounds of meringue onto the cherry filling, one mound for each slice. Place pie on a cookie sheet and bake in preheated oven for 5–7 minutes, or until ridges in meringue are nicely browned. Let pie return to room temperature before serving.

Maple Ginger Crème Brûlée

The extraordinary texture of this dessert will be worth the effort to find a good dairy. If you have access to direct-from-the-dairy heavy cream that has not been overly pasteurized, you can eliminate the step of baking the custard in a water bath and instead chill the strained custards in the refrigerator for 6 hours.

Serves 8

3 cups heavy cream, not
   ultrapasteurized
1-inch knob fresh ginger
9 jumbo egg yolks
3 tablespoons superfine sugar
1 tablespoon maple syrup
½ cup plus 3 tablespoons maple sugar
½ cup dark brown sugar, firmly
   packed

Candied violets for garnish

Pour cream into a heavy-bottomed saucepan. Puncture ginger in several places with a fork and add to cream. Place saucepan over medium-low heat until cream is scalded, then remove from heat.

Preheat oven to 300°.

In a medium mixing bowl, combine egg yolks, superfine sugar, maple syrup, and 3 tablespoons of the maple sugar. Beat vigorously until light and creamy. Gradually add scalded cream, beating constantly. Return mixture to saucepan and stir over low heat until a very, very thick custard is formed. Remove ginger and pour through a strainer into eight shallow 4-ounce heatproof dishes. Place dishes in a larger baking dish, add boiling water until it comes halfway up the sides of the cups, and bake for 25 minutes. Remove desserts from water bath, cool, then chill.

Place broiler rack at the highest level and preheat broiler. Arrange dishes on a cookie sheet that has sides. Combine remaining maple sugar with brown sugar in a small bowl. Spoon mixture into a fine strainer and stir over each dish so that a fine sprinkling evenly covers the surface of each custard. Pack ice cubes around dishes, then place pan under hot broiler just until sugar melts, less than 1 minute. Quickly remove from broiler and chill until very cold. Garnish with a candied violet before serving.

Wine: Shenandoah Vineyards Orange Muscat (Shenandoah Valley, California)

Robert Dean Bialic

Willoughby Hills, Ohio

and John Root

A. I. Root Company

P.O. Box 706

Medina, Ohio 44258

(216) 725-6677

*R*obert Dean Bialic is not easily excited. And yet one day when we visited, he was practically jumping up and down in his kitchen. "We may get black locust honey," he cried. The hives were in position and the unseasonable May warmth and moisture had created a perfect bloom.

Rob Bialic is a beekeeper, an apiarist. Actually, by profession he is a master lithographer, but he has always been a student of arcane disciplines. For nearly a decade his leisure hours have been consumed by a fascination with the honeybee, notwithstanding the fact that he is allergic to their sting and carries an antidote in a syringe when he is working with them.

Friends and family enjoy the fruits of the labor of Rob Bialic's bees. ("R. D. Bee says 'Eat your honey' " reads the label on his package.) Because he is our son-in-law, we are particularly blessed—we have received some of his black locust honey, something that makes a simple breakfast biscuit soar to greatness.

Ask a beekeeper to speak of his art and craft and you are likely to learn more than you bargained for. Ask Rob Bialic and you will get a lecture on the pantheon of apiarial greats and have bee books and magazines thrust upon you.

In actual fact, his recent marriage to Fred's daughter, a historian at the University of Texas, has taken Rob Bialic away from his hives. (He tends them by making hurried trips back to Ohio.) But he reminded us that the center of the bee-keeping universe is in Medina, Ohio, at the offices and factory of The A. I. Root Company. It is from there that five generations of Roots have purveyed bee lore, understanding, and paraphernalia to the beekeepers of the world.

John Root, generation four, is the president. In his handsome office, in the house that his great-grandfather A. I. Root built back in the 1870s, there is a marvelous porcelain sculpture of a beekeeper assembling a hive. The remarkable thing about the sculpture is that it could as well portray an apiarist of A.I.'s day as a contemporary of A.I.'s great-great-grandson, Brad. Beekeeping, it seems, really hasn't changed much in the past hundred years.

"It's the principle of bee space and the Langstroth hive that make modern beekeeping possible," said John. L. L. Langstroth was a congregational minister who, in the middle of the last century, devised a hive with removable frames. The idea was for the bees to build a honeycomb within the frames, structures resembling vertical drawers that could be inserted in the hive. When the frames were full, they could be removed easily. But he discovered that if he left less than ¼ inch between the frames in the hive, the bees would fill the space with propolis, a tree resin. On the other hand, if he gave them more than ⅜ of an inch, they would build honeycomb not just within the removable frames but between them as well. So Langstroth settled on a hive with "bee space" in between the frames—that is, a space between ¼ and ⅜ of an inch wide. That meant the bees would construct neither propolis nor honeycomb, and the frames full of honey could then easily be lifted out of the hive without destroying or damaging the honeycombs and wasting honey.

But while L.L. made the workable hive, credit A.I. with perfecting it and carrying word of it to the world. A. I. Root was a jeweler in the little agricultural town of Medina, about 30 miles southwest of Cleveland. One day in 1865, he encountered a swarm of bees in the public square. Another man came by, lured the bees into a box, and gave them to A.I., who had not the vaguest idea of what to do with them. The next day he rode into Cleveland on the pretext of doing business. Instead, he bought a book by L.L. and within days found himself hooked on bees.

After a couple of years of trial and error, A.I. was gathering a lot of honey in an era before cane and beet sugar were readily available, so he had a ready market for his product. But very few beekeepers knew anything about the movable-frame hive. And most farmers felt it just wasn't worth the effort. A.I. made some improvements on L.L.'s hive and started building them in his shop, then used his marketing skills to get them into the hands of other beekeepers.

A.I. started the magazine *Gleanings in Bee Culture,* using its pages to answer the letters he received from apiarists across the country. Founded in 1872, and now edited by Kim Flottum, it is the ultimate publication for all lovers of bees and their honey.

Beekeeping has had its ups and downs. Before easy access to cheap granulated sugar, prior to World War I, Americans ate 6 to 8 pounds of honey per capita. But between the wars, commercial honey wasn't readily available. Its manufacture was mainly left to the hobbyist. There was another spurt of availability during the Second World War, when cane sugar was again in short supply, and sales went back up yet again during the "back to nature" movement of the mid-1960s. Nowadays, with the founding of the National Honey Board, honey tends to be marketed as a specialty luxury item.

But Rob Bialic or Kim Flottum or John Root or anyone else who is serious about bees will tell you that these are not the best of times. Start with insecticides. While we are not spreading chemical agents that have the savagery of the sprays of the 1960s, there is still enough poison around to kill off entire colonies of foraging honeybees.

In addition, there are fewer floral sources for the bees to take advantage of. Sweet clover, for example, is rarely used to make hay these days. And there is relatively little space on farms for such non-income-producing plants, with farmers planting from fence line to fence line. Wild animals die from destruction of habitat, and so do honeybees.

Furthermore, tracheal mites and varroa mites have gotten out of hand. These diminutive pests have destroyed billions of bees in tens of thousands of colonies. Fortunately, the tracheal mites yield to menthol, a natural product that seems not to hurt bees, and a variety of agents are being developed which it is hoped might help control varroa mites. There is also the hope that selective breeding might develop new strains of bees that will be mite-resistant.

Chalkbrood, a mold, American foulbrood, and European foulbrood have to be caught and dealt with quickly. These diseases devastate the bees when they are in the larval and pupal states. Time was when you would burn an infected hive. But now tetracycline is being used effectively. And there is also the threat of the Africanized bees. Between 25 and 40 percent of the honeybees in the United States have been killed in the past three or four years because of these problems.

But great honey, well handled, is a treasure worth preserving. And the 140,000 beekeepers of the United States, including John Root and Rob Bialic, understand that.

Kim Flottum has tasted and rated hundreds of honeys. He loves honey tastings where a lot of different floral sources are represented. But he says he has to reserve his highest rating for one honey, one that almost none of us has ever tasted. Sourwood—his only perfect ten.

If we haven't had sourwood, at least we've had Rob Bialic's black locust, which has to be at least second-best. And if he was right on that spring day in Ohio, when he jumped for joy in his kitchen, we may get some more.

Grandma Weller's Lekach

Linda's Grandma Weller always made this honey cake to have as a dessert following the Rosh Hashanah (New Year) meal, since honey—to ensure a sweet new year—was an integral part of the holiday table. It often appears in our home, regardless of the occasion, since it brings back many happy memories. Sweetened whipped cream blended with a tablespoon of sour cream is also a wonderful garnish.

Makes 1 9-inch cake

- 2½ teaspoons vegetable oil
- 3 cups unbleached flour
- 1 teaspoon baking powder
- 1 teaspoon baking soda
- 1¼ teaspoons ground cloves
- 1 teaspoon cinnamon
- 2 teaspoons ground ginger
- 1 cup sugar
- 3 jumbo eggs
- 1 cup honey
- ¾ cup very strong brewed coffee

  Freshly made Simple Applesauce (page 414) for garnish

Place oven rack in the center of the oven and preheat oven to 350°.

Using 1 teaspoon of the vegetable oil, coat the sides of a 9-inch springform tube pan, line the bottom of the pan with parchment, and oil the parchment as well.

Combine flour, baking powder, soda, and spices and sift three times. Set aside.

Combine remaining 1½ teaspoons oil, sugar, eggs, and honey in the bowl of an electric mixer fitted with the paddle. At medium speed, cream these ingredients together for at least 2 minutes. Add flour mixture in thirds, alternating with the coffee. Scrape sides of bowl after each addition.

Pour batter into prepared pan and bake for 1 hour, or until a cake tester comes out clean.

Cool cake on a rack, then release sides and peel off parchment. Garnish with freshly made applesauce.

Paul Minnillo's Honey Chocolate Ice Cream

Thanks to Paul Minnillo, Clevelanders can enjoy superlative food at the Baricelli Inn. This dessert is one of his best.

Makes about 1 quart

>   2 cups half-and-half
>   2 cups heavy cream
>   ½ pound semisweet chocolate, chopped
>   12 large egg yolks
>   1 cup honey

Combine half-and-half, cream, and chocolate in a heavy-bottomed saucepan. Cook over medium heat until chocolate has melted.

Meanwhile, place egg yolks in a medium-sized bowl and whisk thoroughly. Slowly whisk in honey. Then, very gradually, whisk chocolate mixture into bowl. Pour combined mixture back into saucepan.

Place pan over low heat. Stir constantly with a spatula, being careful not to let yolks curdle. When mixture coats the back of a wooden spoon, remove pan from heat.

Chill custard, then freeze in a commercial ice-cream maker according to manufacturer's instructions.

A. I. Root Airline Honey Ladyfingers

This wonderfully fragrant recipe is from the A. I. Root Company's charming 1915 cookbook, which was written to showcase the company's Airline brand honey. These cookies are a perfect accompaniment to a dish of homemade ice cream or a simple dish of berries.

Makes 2 dozen

>   4 cups flour
>   ½ teaspoon baking powder
>   ½ teaspoon baking soda
>   1 teaspoon salt
>   ½ cup unsalted butter, melted
>   1 cup honey
>   2 large eggs, beaten
>   Approximately 1 cup sugar

Preheat oven to 425°.

Sift the flour, baking powder, soda, and salt together into a mixing bowl. Combine butter and honey and add to dry ingredients along with eggs. Mix well. Lightly flour a large surface and roll dough to a thickness of about ½ inch. Cut into 3-by-1-inch strips. Roll strips into cylinders, roll cylinders in sugar, and place on a nonstick cookie sheet. Bake in preheated oven until golden, about 10–12 minutes. Cool on a rack.

Susan's Chocolate Sorbet

Put an ice-cream machine in the hands of Susan Cavitch and she comes up with one treat after another. Chocolate sorbet was no great shakes until this version. This will meet with enthusiastic approval from all chocoholics.

Makes about 1 quart

>   ½ cup honey
>   9 ounces bittersweet chocolate, coarsely chopped
>   2 tablespoons Truffles chocolate liqueur

Combine 3 cups water and the honey in a small saucepan and place over medium-low heat until honey is dissolved. Remove from heat, then stir in chocolate. Continue stirring until chocolate is thoroughly incorporated. Cool mixture completely, then add liqueur and blend.

Freeze in an ice-cream maker according to manufacturer's instructions.

A. I. Root Airline Honey Shortcake

Another charming recipe from the 1915 cookbook. The biscuit alone is fairly plain; add the honey topping and berries and you have a different and delicious dessert.

Serves 6–8

> 4 cups unbleached flour
> ½ teaspoon baking powder
> 1 teaspoon baking soda
>   Pinch salt
> 1 tablespoon lard
> 1 teaspoon unsalted butter
> 2 cups buttermilk
> 2 cups heavy cream
> ¼ cup confectioners' sugar
> 1 cup honey
> 1 egg white
> 1 tablespoon fresh lemon juice
> 2 cups fresh blackberries or
>   raspberries
> 1 cup whipped cream
> ½ cup chopped macadamia nuts

Preheat oven to 450°.
    Lightly oil an 8×8 cake pan.

Sift flour, baking powder, soda, and salt into a large bowl. Cut in lard and butter until mixture is evenly blended. Add buttermilk and blend thoroughly. Pat dough into cake pan and bake until done, about 20 minutes. Remove from oven and turn out on a rack to cool.

Whip the cream with the sugar. Then whip honey with the egg white and lemon juice. Spread top of shortcake with honey whip, then cover with cream mixture, then the berries. Finally, top with plain whipped cream, sprinkle evenly with nuts, and serve.

Wine: Joseph Phelps Vineyards Semillon and Sauvignon Blanc "Delice"
(Napa Valley)

Berry Farmers and Orchardists

Anthony Maskal

Sunrise Farm

5022 Forty-fourth Street

Tacoma, Washington 98443

(206) 922-9809

"*I*f I died tomorrow," says Anthony Maskal, "I'd have no regrets about my work. I pushed the envelope."

Anthony Maskal is a forester who left his profession because of the direction it had taken. He felt that forestry had become a pawn of the loggers and the bureaucrats, and that forest management practices were so bad that they were certain to produce an environmental tragedy. After giving up his work in the beautiful forests of the Northwest, he turned to teaching, got an M.A., and spent nearly two decades in the classroom. But the concerns that led him to give up his chosen career stayed with him. He became an expert on environmental issues and got involved in the movement.

Then, in the late 1970s, he put his expertise in the botany of woody plants back to work. He bought a blueberry farm in Puyallup. The bushes, it turned out, were planted the same year he was born.

His land lies in a gorgeous valley to the south and east of Seattle, on the road to Mt. Rainier, although you rarely get to see it, so foggy and wet is the region. In the 1880s, it was the main hops-growing region in the United States, supplying the magic herb that enriched the beers of the West Coast. But the hops beetle put an end to that by 1893.

It then became a region for general agriculture, a place where prosperous

farmers raised happy children who they hoped would follow in their footsteps. But not many did. Often, when a farmer retired or died, his land would fall into disuse. Eventually, great stretches of the rich valley stood fallow. It seemed a pity to Tony Maskal. And that was what led him out of the classroom and onto the farm. He now has 60 acres of high-bush blueberries and has 10 more of orchard and garden, land that had been well treated and had not been poisoned by bad farming practices.

Tony Maskal is determinedly organic. When he sprays, as he sometimes must, the agent is organic. In winter he uses fish oil, which is effective against certain insects and also has some nutritive value for the plants. He remembers an outbreak of what is called mummy berry in the late 1970s. It was destroying half the crop in Washington and Oregon some years, and the usual fungicides weren't helping. Tony became involved in getting permission to use an unproven organic fungicide from Canada. It was called Funginex, and it broke the mummy-berry cycle. Now if he finds a patch of disease in the bushes his approach is to pick and destroy. It is cheaper and safer to hire a picker to excise the bad patch than it is to do a wholesale spraying. And he lives with the birds. No traps, no poisons, no scarecrows, just a plastic netting that he stretches out over his bushes.

Tony dates his passion for clean farming from his high school days. He remembers that when he was growing up many of his friends' parents had died early. Tony began to think about the agricultural chemicals he had watched them spread about the fields with no thought as to the hazards they might pose. He is sure they were killed by the very agents that were supposed to make them better, more productive farmers.

Somewhere on the farm there are a couple of tractors. One is from 1958 and the other was built in 1971. They are both Holders with two-cycle engines, originally used in vineyards. Tony bought them cheap and fixed them up. And he never had a payment to make on either of them.

"That's the secret to small farming," said Tony. "Very important when you start small and dumb. Pinch to the point of penury."

The rest of the work is done by hand. One hundred miles of rows between the bushes are hoed by hand. Half a million pounds of berries are picked by hand—picked into ventilated trays, not into buckets. Tony is currently growing about five varieties of berries so they don't all ripen at the same time. There are people picking all summer long, and at the end of the season 70,000 bushes are pruned by hand. At 8 minutes per bush, that is 560,000 minutes, or nearly 1,200 eight-hour days. At the peak of the season, he may have as many as two hundred workers on the properties he leases. He believes his is the largest organic hand-picking operation in the country.

Tony feels that organic farmers experiment more. That's why he is working with the strawberries now. Recently, he got 5,000 pounds of berries from one half-acre patch. "Because we made love to it," he said. He has so many berries that part of his job is to eat 5 pounds a day from early June to the middle of September.

He loves the Cambodian farmers who work for him. "Wonderful people," he said, "who understand my kind of agriculture." He admires their energy and intelligence. He would like to see them take over some of the farms in the valley and raise their children on the land as farmers did generations ago. Tony also is investing in the education of some of the children. His hope is that they might someday rejoin their parents on the land and be a part of a new tradition.

Tony's office is in a corner of a large warehouse building. There is packaging, freezing, processing, and cooking equipment scattered about. And strangely, a wrecked airplane, warped and bent. The airplane is what is left of an earlier hobby. It came to grief in a farm field, but its pilot, the blueberry man, was not badly hurt. And the other equipment is testimony to Tony Maskal's belief in value added.

"If you are going to be financially successful, you have to add something to the product at the farm," he said. "Either greater identifiable quality or packaging. Or turn your berries into syrup, jam, or jelly." He loves selling his berries from farm stands. He has developed markets all over the country and beyond—his fresh berries fly regularly to Boston and New York. And those that he can't sell fresh he freezes and packages for his institutional customers.

Tony is also involved in the development of new strains of berries. He is always experimenting, growing, tasting, and testing. Already he is researching other varieties of strawberries.

When we left this passionate environmentalist, we realized that he is still the teacher. Perhaps his greatest pleasure in life is in demonstrating that the organic approach works.

We asked him what he is going to do next. "I'm thinking about trying out my newest batch of blueberry preserves," he said. "I'm pushing the blueberry preserve envelope."

On July 5, 1991, Tony Maskal and his brother, Nick, were killed in an airplane crash. They were flying to Oregon to go hunting. Another brother, Tom, lately retired from the military, is working to organize the affairs of the farm. It is too soon to know if it can continue to operate as it did. But it is not too soon to know that Tony's work, his pushing of the envelope, was an effort of national importance, worth study and emulation.

Jacques Williams's Blueberry Tart with Almond Cream

Jacques Williams is the talented husband of our editor, Barbara. During his stint with New York's fabled David Bouley, Jacques often combined Bouley's almond cream with fruits. When we asked Jacques to make some desserts for us, this was his first creation. Jacques's almond pastry is terrific, but it is somewhat challenging to handle. He keeps his hands floured, but even so he often has to piece sides and bottom together. Not to worry—it binds together beautifully in the baking.

Makes 1 9-inch tart

- 7½ ounces blanched slivered almonds
- 4 large eggs
- 1 tablespoon Sauternes wine
- 1 cup plus 2 tablespoons sugar
- 1 cup unsalted butter, softened
- 6 ounces unbleached flour
- 1 pint fresh blueberries

- 1 pint vanilla ice cream and sprigs of fresh mint for garnish

In the bowl of a food processor fitted with the metal blade, grind the almonds to an extremely fine powder. Measure 1 cup almond meal into a small bowl and set aside. Transfer the remaining almond meal to the bowl of an electric mixer fitted with the paddle and add 2 eggs, the Sauternes, and ½ cup plus 1 tablespoon of the sugar. Beat at low speed until evenly blended. Add half the butter and beat again until smooth. With mixer still running, gradually add the flour until fully incorporated. Form dough into a ball, wrap in plastic wrap, and freeze for at least 1 hour, or until dough is well chilled.

Meanwhile, place remaining butter in the bowl of an electric mixer fitted with the paddle and add all but 1 teaspoon of remaining sugar; beat until creamy. With the mixer still running, add reserved almond meal and beat thoroughly; add 2 eggs and beat until mixture is smooth. Set aside to rest.

When pastry dough is completely chilled, lightly butter a 9-inch tart, or quiche, pan with a removable bottom (an ordinary pie plate will do in a pinch). Lightly flour a cool surface and gently roll the dough to a thickness of ⅛ inch. Keeping your hands lightly floured, carefully line prepared pan with dough, gently piecing dough where it breaks or tears. Trim edges.

Spoon almond cream into prepared crust and gently press half the blueberries evenly into it. Place tart in the freezer for 1 hour.

Preheat oven to 375°.

Bake tart for 45 minutes, or until center is set and top is golden brown. Remove tart from oven and let cool on a rack.

While tart is baking, place remaining berries in a small saucepan with 1 tablespoon water and 1 teaspoon sugar. Simmer over medium heat until berries are very soft, about 20–30 minutes. Purée cooked berries in the bowl of a food processor fitted with the metal blade. Then force puree through a strainer to remove skin and seeds.

Serve wedges of tart garnished with blueberry sauce, a small scoop of vanilla ice cream, and mint sprigs.

Blueberry Catsup

This freezes nicely, and it tastes wonderful served with any kind of poultry, especially smoked. We also like it with ham, and it's terrific when served on a grilled burger.

Makes 3 ½ cups

> 2 tablespoons vegetable oil
> 1 large clove garlic, thinly sliced

1 tablespoon minced fresh ginger
5 ounces minced onion
1 cup peeled, seeded, and chopped
   fresh tomato
2 large purple plums, pitted and
   chopped
   Zest of 1 lemon, cut into julienne
   strips
2 pints fresh blueberries
1 tablespoon fresh lemon juice
¼ cup dark brown sugar, firmly
   packed
1 tablespoon blackberry, blueberry,
   or raspberry vinegar
1 teaspoon ground cardamom
1 teaspoon ground coriander
1¼ teaspoons cinnamon
¼ teaspoon ground cloves
1 teaspoon salt
1 teaspoon freshly ground mixed
   white, green, red, and black
   peppercorns
1 dried chile pepper, crumbled

Heat oil in a heavy-bottomed saucepan. Add garlic and ginger and cook over low heat for two minutes. Add onion and cook until transparent, stirring often. Add remaining ingredients and stir well. Increase heat and cook over medium heat until mixture begins to simmer. Reduce heat and keep simmering for 30 minutes, then remove from heat.

Allow blueberry mixture to cool slightly, then purée in a food processor. Return puree to saucepan and bring to a brisk simmer. Cook mixture until thick, about 1 hour. Cool. It will keep for several weeks stored in a tightly closed jar in the refrigerator.

Blueberry Plum Cobbler

We like cobblers in our family. When the prune plums and blueberries appear in the market at the same time, this is a must. If there are fresh figs available, we also add them. And to gild the lily, Fred likes to garnish this with some Wonderful Cinnamon Ice Cream (page 118).

Serves 8–10

⅔ cup plus 2 tablespoons maple sugar
1 cup granulated sugar
2 teaspoons grated lemon zest
1 teaspoon cinnamon
½ teaspoon freshly grated nutmeg
2 cups unbleached flour
6 cups pitted fresh prune plums,
   sliced
2 cups fresh blueberries
4 diced fresh figs, if available
1 tablespoon fresh lemon juice
2 teaspoons baking powder
½ teaspoon salt
½ cup unsalted butter, softened
1 jumbo egg plus one jumbo egg
   yolk, lightly beaten

Preheat oven to 375°.

Combine ⅔ cup maple sugar with ½ cup granulated sugar, zest, cinnamon, nutmeg, and ¼ cup of flour. Add fruit and lemon juice and toss lightly. Place in a well-buttered 3-quart baking dish and set aside.

Combine the remaining granulated sugar and flour with baking powder and salt. Using your fingers or a fork, blend in the butter until the mixture looks like coarse cornmeal. Pour in the eggs and yolk and mix just until mixture holds together. It will be coarse and lumpy. Distribute this dough over the fruit. Sprinkle cobbler with remaining maple sugar. Bake in the preheated oven for about 35 minutes, or until top is browned and crusty and fruit is bubbling. Serve warm.

Gert LeVine's Blueberry Pie

Linda grew up on this pie. She still thinks it may be her favorite dessert, but as leftovers, it can taste even better at breakfast.

Makes 1 10-inch 2-crust pie

    1 recipe Pie Crust (page 416)
    1½ quarts fresh blueberries
    ⅓ cup granulated sugar
    2 tablespoons unbleached flour
    2 tablespoons fresh lemon juice
    2 teaspoons ground cardamom
    1 tablespoon milk
    1 rounded tablespoon superfine sugar
    1 tablespoon butter

Preheat oven to 425°.

Place oven rack in upper third of oven. Arrange one 12-inch circle of pie-crust dough in a 10-inch pie plate.

Combine berries, sugar, flour, lemon juice, and cardamom in a large bowl. Mix carefully but thoroughly and gently spoon berries into lined plate, mounding a bit in the middle.

Cut decorative vents in the other 12-inch circle of pie-crust dough and carefully fit it over the top of the berries. Trim edges of crust to extend 1½ inches beyond rim. Roll edges toward center and flute. Rub surface with milk, sprinkle with superfine sugar, and dot with butter. Bake pie for 15 minutes; then reduce heat to 400° and bake 30 minutes more, or until top is golden brown.

Remove from oven and let cool on a rack.

Norman and Dolores DeLucia

DeLucia's Berry Farm

96 Willow Avenue

Little Compton, Rhode Island 02837

(401) 635-2698

Give Norman and Dolores DeLucia a field of berry bushes and they are in Nirvana. From late June to the first frost, from dawn to dusk, Dolores's straw hat, with its orange flowers, can be seen bobbing up and down the rows of berry bushes that fill 4 of the 6 acres of former pastureland behind their Rhode Island home. The land is flat, backed by a small forest and surrounded by a typical New England stone wall. Sakonnet Bay runs along the shore, 3 or 4 miles to the west, and the farm is not far from Sakonnet Point, where the bay empties into Rhode Island Sound and the Atlantic Ocean. Unfortunately, this beautiful setting is highly vulnerable to Atlantic hurricanes.

The berry business was an accident. Their first spring, in the mid-1970s, Norm decided he wanted a small garden, so he went out with his shovel to dig one. Before he could do much, his farmer neighbor offered to do the work by tractor. While Norm was pleased to accept this offer, he felt it necessary to make the garden worth the tractor's capabilities. In a matter of moments the project grew from a small kitchen garden to half an acre.

The nascent farmer was in business, planting a huge variety of vegetables. "We had never done this before," Dolores said, "and we had a great crop."

Flushed with success, the very next season they were ready to accept a gift of fifty strawberry plants from the tractor owner, who had purchased too many plants for himself. "It seemed like a good thing for our two daughters," said Norm. "We figured that they could sell strawberries from a roadside stand and learn about private enterprise." Instead, Dolores and Norm learned about hard work.

"We had far more berries than we could either use or sell," said Norm. So he approached a local farm stand. The owner was delighted to buy the excess berries. In fact, he was so pleased with the quality of the DeLucias' berries that he asked if they would grow raspberries for him in the future.

Norm figured that raspberries would be a snap. So he bought 500 bushes, all the same variety. The next season was a real bear. That's when Norm realized just how many berries are produced by that many bushes. Also, all of the berries ripened within the same period of time, so they all needed picking at the same time. And the supply far exceeded the demand at the local farm stand, let alone at their own roadside stand.

When the supply was too great to be absorbed locally, Norm took berries into Providence, to the produce market there. His berries were never refused by the top broker. "He really trained us," said Norm. "That's how we learned about the absolute perfect time to pick." That was also how they learned to control their yields by knowing when to prune and when not to prune.

It wasn't long before the berry bug really got them. "We were given a gift of some fruit trees," said Norm. "And there were some currant bushes included in the package." And then there were blueberries. "Eventually we decided that we were too old for strawberries. We wanted berries we could pick standing up; no more bending," said Dolores.

The blueberries, planted in 1980, took a decade to reach maturity. The DeLucias grow close to a dozen varieties—some ripen early, some late, some are very sweet and others are wonderfully tart. Some are small and some are large and plump. All are grown near the back of the field, protected from birds by netting.

There are also numerous varieties of large, plump blackberries on the DeLucia farm, along with red currants and gooseberries. "These are the ones that restaurants love since they're so uncommon," Dolores commented. There are also a few exotic plants, including tayberry and wild Chinese raspberry.

Many of the raspberries are propagated by the DeLucias themselves. Brandywine is a very purple raspberry with a rich winelike flavor. It's highly perishable, but the flavor is extraordinary. And it is a big, round berry that looks terrific in tarts. "It's important to diversify," said Norman. "If we have a hard winter, the summer berries are iffy, but the fall crop will be terrific. If there is a mild winter, the  summer crop is usually outstanding." They stopped growing golden raspberries because they were so very perishable. "They had to be sprayed for everything," Norm said. "When there is that much spray on a berry, there just cannot be a good flavor."

Before the foliage appears, Norm sprays with liquid lime sulfa, an organic spray that prevents cane disease. The DeLucias try to grow without any pesticides and herbicides. Parts of the fields are completely organic. But in certain areas, the Japanese beetle seems to evade all efforts at capture, so Norm will use a very mild spray just in the rows where the Japanese beetles have reduced the leaves to lace.

The roadside stand is now back near the field, enabling Dolores to tend it from where she works. Norm leaves for work in Providence at 6 A.M., and every morning in season, Dolores dons her floppy hat, grabs a portable phone, turns on the driveway bell that alerts her to arriving customers, and goes to the berries at dawn. She spends her days picking. "I just love it," she said. "I don't want a radio to interfere with the birds. There are little rabbits that romp nearby, and chipmunks, too. And I pick until my feet get tired." Norm gets home most afternoons about four. He does whatever chores there are while Dolores is still picking. Then, at dusk, the pair begin deliveries. "I go along to keep him awake," said Dolores. At some point the two grab a quick dinner before falling asleep.

Besides selling to area roadside markets, the DeLucias also have top bakeries and restaurants among their clientele. In addition, they have developed a line of extraordinary jams and jellies. All summer they freeze berries and fruit, and after the first frost, when the berrying is finished, they rent a commercial kitchen and Dolores goes to work. DeLucia gooseberry marmalade and raspberry, blueberry, and blackberry jams are exceptionally wonderful. They sell all they can make.

"I have two full-time jobs," Norm said. "Eventually I'll retire and do only one of them. Every time I plant another bush I am a bit closer to retirement. Then I can do this full-time." And he added that their work has enabled them to save money in several ways. "Besides the added income from the berries," he said, "is the fact that Dolores is too busy and too tired to visit the malls."

Dolores's Gooseberry Jam

One can order some of Dolores's superlative jams and preserves directly from their farm. But if you are fortunate enough to have your own gooseberries, you'll want to make the jam this way.

Makes 4 pints

> 4 pints fresh gooseberries
> 7 cups granulated sugar

Remove stem-and-blossom end from berries. Combine berries with 3 cups water in a large saucepan and bring to boil. Lower heat and simmer until berries are soft. Add sugar and stir over low heat until sugar is dissolved, then bring to a boil. Boil, stirring occasionally, until temperature reaches 221° on a candy thermometer.

Pour into sterile pint-size jars and seal. Process 20 minutes in a hot-water bath. Remove and allow to cool.

Linzertorte

This is a recipe that was given to Linda in 1960 by her sons' great-aunt, Frieda Doeppler. It goes back many generations in Tante Frieda's family. This linzertorte differs from most other recipes in that it has chocolate in it. It is a heavy pastry but one that keeps well, freezes well, and is delicious. Serve this in thin slices, since it is so rich. It is fabulous when made with Dolores DeLucia's preserves.

Makes 2 9-inch tortes

1 cup unsalted butter, softened
1 cup plus 2 tablespoons granulated
   sugar
2 jumbo eggs
4 cups unbleached flour
3 teaspoons cinnamon
1 teaspoon ground cloves
2 ounces unsweetened chocolate,
   melted
½ pound finely chopped almonds
1 jigger (3 tablespoons) whiskey
16 ounces high-quality raspberry
   preserves

Whipped Crème Fraîche (page 350)
sweetened with confectioners' sugar
for garnish

Combine butter and sugar in the bowl of an electric mixer fitted with the paddle and cream thoroughly. Then, with motor running, add the eggs one at a time and mix well. Still with motor running, slowly add 2 cups of the flour, then add the spices, chocolate, almonds, and whiskey. With mixer at low speed, gradually add the remaining flour. Scrape sides of bowl and mix again.

Gather dough into a ball and divide into two even chunks. Cut a wedge off each chunk, wrap the wedges in plastic, and chill. Line 2 9-inch quiche or tart pans having removable bottoms with the two large chunks of dough by pressing evenly to cover the bottoms and sides. Then fill with raspberry preserves.

Preheat oven to 350°.

Dust work surface with flour and roll one chilled wedge of dough into a fairly thin sheet. Slice into thin strips. This dough will break easily, so handle with care. We use a long bread knife or spatula to facili-

tate handling, but don't worry if you have to piece things together. Arrange strips in an attractive lattice pattern on top of one of the tortes. Repeat for the second torte.

Bake tortes in preheated oven for 30 minutes. Let cool on racks.

Blueberry and Blackberry Gratin

This is a versatile dessert. Besides being able to mix and match the berry varieties and combine them with other fruits, such as sliced peaches or pitted cherries, one can also simply combine them with the sabayon in a beautiful goblet, garnish with a mint leaf, and serve. The sabayon is fun to make, once you get the hang of it. While you can use a double boiler, there is nothing more perfect for this dessert than a rounded copper zabaglione pot, which doesn't have cracks and corners to inhibit the whisk.

Serves 6

1 pint fresh blackberries
1 pint fresh blueberries
¼ cup sugar
½ teaspoon vanilla extract
1 teaspoon grated lemon zest
8 jumbo egg yolks
1 cup Johannisberg Riesling "Late
   Harvest" wine
Freshly grated nutmeg

Fresh mint leaves for garnish

Wash and drain berries and distribute among 6 small ovenproof gratin dishes. Preheat broiler.

In a tall 3-quart saucepan that is narrow enough to support a zabaglione pot, or in the bottom half of a double boiler, add water to a point *just* below the upper pot. Bring the water to a boil, then lower heat to a simmer. The top pot should not actually touch the water.

In the zabaglione pot itself, or in the top half of a double boiler, before putting the top pot over the water, combine sugar, vanilla, lemon zest, and egg yolks. Whisk until mixture is thick and light in color. Place pot over simmering water and gradually add wine, beating in a rapid folding motion with a balloon whisk until the mixture swells in volume and becomes an airy and creamy custard. About the time your arm is ready to fall off, the sabayon is ready. Pour it over the berries. Sprinkle with some nutmeg and place under preheated broiler until top is browned, about 1–2 minutes. Place a few fresh mint leaves on each dish and serve.

Wine: Joseph Phelps Vineyards Johannisberg Riesling "Late Harvest" (Napa Valley)

Raspberry Hazelnut Crisp

Be creative with this. It would be equally wonderful made with blackberries or blueberries. Or you might even try mixing in some currants or gooseberries. While this is fine served at room temperature, we usually serve it slightly warm with whipped cream or ice cream.

Serves 10

FILLING
- 6 cups fresh raspberries
- 1¼ cups chopped hazelnuts
- ⅔ cup dried currants
- ½ cup dark brown sugar, firmly packed

- ⅓ cup maple sugar
- 1 teaspoon ground allspice
- ¼ teaspoon mace
- 1 tablespoon cinnamon
- 1 teaspoon freshly grated nutmeg
- Zest of 1 lemon, finely minced

TOPPING
- ¾ cup dark brown sugar, firmly packed
- ¾ cup maple sugar
- 1½ cups rolled oats (not instant)
- 1¾ cup unbleached flour
- 1 cup unsalted butter, cut into pieces
- 2 jumbo eggs
- ⅓ cup finely chopped hazelnuts
- 1 tablespoon granulated sugar
- ½ teaspoon freshly grated nutmeg

Preheat oven to 375°.

Butter a 3-quart ceramic baking dish.

Combine all the filling ingredients and mix very gently. Distribute evenly in the baking dish.

To make the topping, combine ¾ cup brown sugar, ¾ cup maple sugar, oats, flour, and butter in the bowl of a food processor fitted with the metal blade. Pulse until mixture is the texture of coarse cornmeal. Add eggs and process for 10 seconds. Distribute mixture evenly over filling and sprinkle with chopped hazelnuts. Combine sugar and ½ teaspoon nutmeg, then sprinkle over the topping. Bake in preheated oven for 40 minutes, or until topping is nicely browned. Remove from oven and cool on rack.

Wine: Eberle Winery Muscat Canelli (Paso Robles)

Shelly and Bob Berryman

Twin Springs Farm

1744 Heidegger Road

Rice, Washington 99167

(509) 738-2095

The 80 acres of Twin Springs Farm are high on a mountainside overlooking Washington's Lake Roosevelt and the mountains beyond. Rice is a tiny place near Kettle Falls in the northeast corner of the state, just about as far as you can be from Seattle and still be in Washington. And very far from the Casbah in Morocco, where Shelly and Bob Berryman first met in the late 1960s!

Bob is passionate about agricultural practices, good and bad. Their current farm is in a region that had been filled with apple and peach orchards before the Grand Coulee Dam project. But the orchards were flooded, creating the enormous Lake Roosevelt and leaving little room for fruit-tree cultivation. The higher elevation of the Berryman farm means a slightly shorter growing season, but it also means that the trees usually don't bud until after the last heavy frost.

Besides cherries, peaches, nectarines, some summer apples, and plums, the Berrymans also raise strawberries, tomatoes, peppers, and squash. These latter plants are protected by plastic for the early part of their growing season. "In fact, plastic makes us the main tomato grower in the area—about twenty-eight hundred plants," said Bob. They grow for taste and firmness, raising bush varieties so that there is no staking necessary. Most are sold at the local farmers' market.

The Berrymans' cherries are gorgeous and delicious. They grow Bings, Vans, Black Republicans, and Montmorency. The Black Republicans are small and

super-sweet. They're used as a pollinator. The Montmorency are quite tart, making them a popular pie cherry. They also grow a small amount of Rainiers, the large yellow cherry that has a beautiful red blush.

A nonorganically raised cherry tree will yield about 400 pounds of cherries; the organic farmer gets between 300 and 350 pounds. Some cherries are lost to disease, others are discarded because of bird picks. Following the practices of integrated pest management means that the farmer is picking off lots of bad bugs and adding lots of good ones, but he still has problems.

"I lose about twenty percent of my crop to the birds," Bob mourns. "The big guys use a propane cannon, but that's obnoxious, so I try all kinds of alternatives. We fill a weather balloon with helium and anchor it to a tree, then we tie a hawk-shaped kite to the balloon. I even trade cherries for the helium. Many of the birds do stay away." He told us that he didn't mind so much the beautiful cedar waxwings, but the robins . . . "The problem wasn't so bad for a while, 'cause the hillside above us burned. But now the vegetation is growing back and the birds love it. So they come in droves."

There is also a big problem with deer and bear. "We put a huge deer fence around the place. That generally did the trick. But a huge black bear, about 400 pounds, got under the fence and ate many of the Italian prunes. We could tell by his claw marks on the tree trunks. Another time he dug under the fence and got into the beehives. He ate all the honey and just stretched out and went to sleep— he was so stuffed he didn't even move when Shelly went near him. Now we have electric fencing around the beehives."

Bob works with a broker and plans his planting according to market demands and the exigencies of the weather. A very rainy spring wiped out the delicata squash planting, so he turned everything under and planted corn. Butternut, spaghetti, buttercup, and acorn squashes all survived; he'll ship off about 34,000 pounds to the broker. Heat and sun are not plentiful in Rice, yet big, juicy Benton strawberries need heat and sun to show their finest qualities. When the weather is right, their rich flavor makes them popular with people in the area, who are happy to come and pick their own berries. The smaller, squatter Shukson is firmer and less sweet than the Benton. Its slightly longer season makes it popular with the farmer; it is also a bit less fragile.

We walked the orchards with Bob. He showed us how he'll have to thin the peaches a bit to get a better fruit; he'll do the same with the nectarines. The whole apricot crop was marked by ill-timed hail. That's fruit that will go to the cannery, not to the markets.

Bob has no regrets about his choice to farm organically, but sometimes he wonders if he should still be farming at all. He grew up on a farm in Indiana; his grandparents had been farmers, too. He worries about the government's lack of concern for major environmental issues. He has not lost his social consciousness and is frustrated that life is so terribly hard for today's farmers. In fact, he drives an area school bus in order to supplement his income a bit.

At the end of our visit, we feasted on ripened berries and early cherries. We reveled in the gorgeous view, the sounds of silence that one enjoys high on a mountainside, away from men and machines. And as we carefully drove down the dirt road, a huge coyote ran across our path, its healthy coat glistening in the emerging sunshine.

Summer Peaches Poached in Zinfandel

These taste best if prepared a day or two ahead.

Serves 6

    6 ripe peaches
750 ml. red Zinfandel wine
    1 cup sugar
    1 cinnamon stick
    3 cloves
    1 teaspoon ground cardamom
    1 slice fresh ginger

    Crème Anglaise (page 119), fresh mint leaves, and fuchsia petals for garnish

Skin the peaches by filling a small saucepan with water, bringing it to a boil, and plunging the peaches into the boiling water for 2 minutes. Cool quickly and peel. Then cut peaches in half and discard stone.

Combine wine, sugar, and spices in a 2-quart saucepan, preferably one that is wide and shallow.

Bring the mixture to a boil and lower the heat a bit. Add the peaches, which you may have to do in two batches. Poach over medium heat for about 5 minutes, then turn peaches over and poach 5 minutes on the other side.

Remove peaches with a slotted spoon and let drain on a rack, flat side down.

Return the poaching liquid to a boil and cook over high heat until reduced by half.

It should be somewhat syrupy. Remove from heat and cool.

Arrange peaches in a shallow dish, pour syrup over them, wrap tightly in plastic wrap, and chill in refrigerator.

Just before serving, spoon several tablespoons of Crème Anglaise onto each serving plate (we like to use attractive shallow soup plates). Then arrange the peach halves on the cream. Spoon a bit of the syrup over the peaches. Garnish with mint leaves and fuchsia petals.

Tropical Cheesecake

This is a wonderful way to use those luscious fresh peaches we see every summer. But when winter comes, don't despair. Make this with some of the mangos and papayas that find their way into our fruit markets during cooler months.

Serves 10

CRUST
    1 cup rusk crumbs
    ¾ cup finely chopped macadamia nuts
    ½ cup unsalted butter, melted
    ½ teaspoon freshly grated nutmeg
    ½ teaspoon ground ginger
    ⅓ cup superfine sugar
    1 teaspoon finely minced lime zest

FILLING
    1 pound cream cheese
    ⅔ cup superfine sugar
    1 teaspoon ground ginger
    1 teaspoon ground coriander

1 teaspoon ground cardamom
1 tablespoon rum, preferably dark
   Myers's
4 jumbo eggs
1 cup puree of fresh peeled peaches,
   papaya, or mango
1 tablespoon fresh lime juice

TOPPING
2 cups sour cream
2 tablespoons rum, preferably dark
   Myers's
¼ cup superfine sugar

Fresh mint leaves and slices of fresh
fruit for garnish
½ cup finely chopped macadamia
nuts for garnish

Preheat oven to 375°.

Combine all the crust ingredients in a small mixing bowl and blend well. Press evenly and firmly in the bottom and halfway up the sides of a very well-buttered 9-inch springform pan. Chill 15 minutes in the freezer, then bake in the preheated oven for 10 minutes. Remove from oven and cool.

To make the filling, combine cream cheese, ⅔ cup superfine sugar, 1 teaspoon ginger, coriander, cardamom, and rum in the bowl of an electric mixer fitted with the paddle and beat until smooth. Then, with the motor running, add the eggs one at a time. Beat on high speed for 3 minutes. Then fold fruit puree and lime juice into the mixture and blend well. Pour the filling into the crust and bake 1 hour.

When cake is baked, remove it from the oven and place on a rack. Increase the oven heat to 450°. Combine all the topping ingredients in a small mixing bowl and blend well.

Spread topping evenly over cake, return it to the oven, and bake for 5 minutes. Turn heat off, leave oven door open, and cool cake in oven 1 hour. Then transfer cake immediately to the refrigerator until thoroughly cooled.

Garnish with mint leaves, slices of fresh fruit, and nuts.

Chocolate Cherry Torte

NOVA is an artists' service organization in the Cleveland area with which we have had a long association. At their annual benefit the dessert is a truly decadent chocolate buffet, served with champagne. This cake was created for that event and has been served there for almost ten years. It is simply splendid with fresh, pitted cherries, but since cherries have such a short season, in winter we look for frozen cherries or jars of good-quality cherries packed in syrup.

Makes 1 9-inch torte

¼ cup fine amaretti crumbs
1 tablespoon granulated sugar
2 jumbo eggs
1 cup superfine sugar
1 tablespoon kirsch
½ cup unsalted butter, melted
1 teaspoon vanilla extract
5 tablespoons Dutch cocoa powder
½ cup unbleached flour
1½ teaspoons baking powder
½ cup finely chopped almonds
2 cups pitted sweet cherries
⅓ cup plus 1 tablespoon
   confectioners' sugar
1 cup Crème Fraîche (see page 350)
10 candied violets for garnish

Place oven rack in upper half of oven and preheat oven to 325°.

Butter a 9-inch springform pan. Combine crumbs and granulated sugar, then turn mixture into the pan and shake well so that bottom and sides are evenly coated. Shake out excess and set pan aside.

Place eggs and superfine sugar in the bowl of an electric mixer; beat until mixture is very thick. Add kirsch. Then, with motor on low, stir in butter, vanilla, and cocoa. Remove bowl from mixer.

Combine flour and baking powder in a small bowl. Carefully fold flour mixture into batter, then gently add almonds.

Distribute cherries evenly in prepared pan, then pour batter over them and firmly smooth cake with a rubber spatula.

Bake in preheated oven for about 50 minutes, or until cake feels firm to the touch. Remove cake from oven and place it on a rack for 10 minutes. Run a sharp knife around outer edge of the cake to loosen it from the pan, then release spring. Let cake cool completely, then invert it and remove bottom of pan. Carefully turn cake once more.

Just before serving, sift ⅓ cup confec-tioner's sugar evenly over the top of the cake. Whip crème fraîche with remaining tablespoon confectioners' sugar until soft peaks form. Distribute 10 generous dollops of cream evenly around edge of cake, then place one violet on each.

Heavenly Strawberry Sauce

This is especially wonderful when made with organically grown strawberries. We use this sauce for Imperial Crème Caramel (page 113), and it is also superlative on homemade ice cream.

Makes 4 cups

- 1 quart fresh strawberries, hulled and sliced
- 1 10-ounce package frozen raspberries, defrosted
- ½ cup superfine sugar
  Juice of half a lemon
- 2 tablespoons crème de cassis liqueur
- ⅓ cup dark brown sugar, firmly packed

Divide fresh berries between two bowls. Mash the berries in one bowl quite thoroughly and set both bowls aside.

Combine frozen berries, superfine sugar, lemon juice, and liqueur in a saucepan and simmer briskly over medium heat for 10 minutes. Remove from heat and force through a strainer into the bowl of mashed strawberries. Discard seeds remaining in strainer. Add brown sugar to this mixture and mix well. Fold in reserved whole berries and serve.

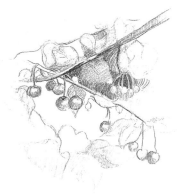

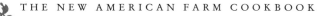

Ronald and Ruth Waltenspiel

Timber Crest Farms
4791 Dry Creek Road
Healdsburg, California 95448
(707) 433-8251

Ronald and Ruth Waltenspiel bought their farm in 1957. Ronald was the kind of farmer, according to his wife, who could do anything, deal with any problem with a pair of pliers and a piece of wire. As they worked with their crops, they found that the less they did to make them better, the better they turned out to be. But when they grew fine pears and sold them to a commercial drier, their pears turned out no better than those of less careful growers. That's why they leapt at the opportunity to buy drying equipment when a retiring neighbor offered it to them for a song. It also enabled them to experiment, to work out new product ideas.

Ruth and Ronald found that processing their own fruit gave them more control over quality and generated "more electricity." It was exciting to manage the driers, the packaging equipment, and the sales. And there was no difficulty in establishing a solid market for their high-quality organically grown and processed dried Bartlett pears, Blenheim apricots, French prunes, dates, Golden Delicious apples, and Muir peaches. They say that today theirs is a "tree-to-table" farm operation.

It was early in the 1980s that the Waltenspiels realized that dried tomatoes were being imported in large quantities from Italy. Ruth and Ronald had almost forgotten the sun-dried tomatoes brought to them by their Italian neighbors in Dry Creek Valley in exchange for homemade wine back in the 1950s. It had not escaped the notice of Ronald Waltenspiel that the price people paid for this delicacy was startlingly high, $12 a jar, and people were buying enthusiastically. At the time Ruth bought her first jar of sun-dried tomatoes, she immediately thought of drying the tomatoes herself as well. After all, California's long growing season makes it possible to have two delicious tomato crops each year.

It took a little trial and error to learn how to do it. Ronald remembers his horror at finding a whole day's work had turned gray with mold overnight and had to go to the compost heap. And he also found out why that jar of Italian sun-dried tomatoes costs so much. It takes 17 pounds of fresh tomatoes to make 1 pound of dried tomatoes. (He had been used to drying apricots, peaches, and pears, for which the ratio is something like 6 to 1.)

The Waltenspiels, it turned out, had made a good business decision. They dried the tomatoes, packed them simply in cellophane bags, and easily sold all they could produce. But the Italian product they had admired was packed in olive oil, and the Waltenspiels wanted to do that, too. The demand was so great, however, that it was three years before they had enough tomatoes to do something other than just ship them out in bags.

At the ranch (the people around Healdsburg in Sonoma County call places like this a ranch rather than a farm, and the farmer is called a rancher) the Sunday-go-to-meeting clothes give way to denim and flannel. But when we first saw Ronald, he was dressed like a well-to-do cowboy who had come to the big city; in a fine western twill suit, a string tie, good boots, and a pearl-gray ten-gallon hat, he surely stood out in the big food-show crowd. Tall in any riggings, he looked like Gary Cooper, and was as taciturn.

Ruth and Ronald's office is on one

side of a large paved quadrangle. Around it are a huge cold storage area, a retail store, parking space for big trucks, a shed covering the pallets and boxes of fruit, and an enormous processing line for the preparation, sorting, grading, and drying of the products. Orchards fill the horizon behind the drying shed. Fifty people work the farm and the plant, and at harvestime there will be as many as two hundred on the payroll.

An organic farm operation with two hundred employees? How could it be, when most such places are small and marginal? Because at Timber Crest the Waltenspiels cultivate 350 acres.

"This works," says Ronald Waltenspiel, "because organic is a better way."

Today the Waltenspiels test-market new ideas by asking first, "Does Ronald like it?" When he puts a bowl of it on a table in the office, does the staff eat it, and if so, how quickly? If it's there very long, it's pronounced a bad idea. Their success flows from the fact that their marketing decisions have frequently been correct.

They do buy some fruit, and not all of it is organically grown, but all must meet Ronald's strict standards. They have always refrained from using sulfur dioxide as a preservative on their dried apricots. In fact, no fumigation of any kind is ever employed. Instead, they have opted for the more expensive technique of refrigerated storage. With the success of their sun-dried tomatoes, there is now an even broader audience for their complete range of totally organic products.

"Farming is a great teacher," said Ronald. "One time recently the weather ruined our grapes, which we were going to sell to Gallo. That was thirty thousand dollars we could have used that we didn't get." So the Waltenspiels keep their farm as financially sound as possible, reinvesting everything back into the operation in order to withstand such losses. And they diversify to be better able to deal with lean years.

"And never forget," said Ronald, "that you don't have a crop until you have a crop in the box."

Apricot Cranberry Bread

Makes 2 loaves

>   1½ cups unbleached flour
>   1 cup whole-wheat pastry flour
>   (available in health-food stores or
>   from Arrowhead Mills, page 67)
>   1¼ cups rolled oats (not instant)
>   1 tablespoon baking powder
>   1 teaspoon ground allspice
>   1 tablespoon ground cardamom
>   1½ cups unsalted butter, softened
>   1 cup granulated sugar
>   ½ cup light brown sugar, firmly
>   packed
>   3 jumbo eggs
>   2 cups chopped fresh cranberries
>   1½ cups chopped dried apricots
>   Zest of 1 orange, finely minced
>   1½ cups milk
>   ½ cup fresh orange juice
>   ¼ cup sour cream

Preheat oven to 375°.

Thoroughly oil two 9¼x5¼ loaf pans.

Combine flours, oats, baking powder, and spices in a mixing bowl. Set aside.

In the bowl of an electric mixer fitted with the paddle, cream butter with sugars. Beat in eggs, one at a time, scraping sides of bowl. Mix in cranberries, apricots, and orange zest. Then add milk, juice, and sour cream and blend. Finally, add flour mixture and mix just until blended.

Pour batter into prepared pans and bake until a cake tester inserted into the center comes out dry, about 50–60 minutes. Cool on rack for 5 minutes before removing from pans.

Aunt Teenie's Crescents

This recipe goes back to Linda's Aunt Teenie Kay in Pittsfield, Massachusetts.

Makes about 4 dozen

>   1 tablespoon active dry yeast
>   ¼ cup warm water
>   1 cup unsalted butter
>   1 cup heavy cream
>   3 egg yolks
>   4 cups unbleached flour
>   1⅓ cups sugar
>   2 tablespoons cinnamon
>   2 cups fruit preserves
>   1 cup finely chopped pecans or
>   walnuts
>   ½ cup finely chopped dried apricots
>   ½ cup raisins
>   2 jumbo egg whites, beaten to soft
>   peaks

Combine yeast and water in a small bowl, mix, and set aside. Melt butter, remove from heat, and whisk in heavy cream. When mixture is no longer hot (but still warm), pour into the bowl of an electric mixer fitted with the paddle; add yeast mixture and egg yolks. Add flour and ⅓ cup of sugar. Mix well, scrape sides, and mix again. Cover bowl with plastic wrap and place in refrigerator overnight.

Remove bowl from refrigerator and let stand at room temperature for 1 hour. Divide dough into 6 parts. Combine remaining sugar and cinnamon; set aside.

Preheat oven to 350°.

On a lightly floured surface, roll the first piece of dough in a circle about 12 inches in diameter and ⅛ inch thick. Spread with about ⅙ of the preserves, then sprinkle with cinnamon-sugar mixture, nuts, apricots, and raisins. Slice circle into 8 pie-shaped wedges and roll each wedge from the wide end to the center. Gently bend the roll into a crescent shape and place each crescent on an ungreased cookie sheet. Brush top with some egg white and sprinkle with some cinnamon-sugar. Repeat with remaining dough.

Bake in preheated oven until nicely brown, about 20–25 minutes. Place crescents on rack to cool. Store in a tightly sealed container.

Apple and Dried Fruit Cobbler

This wonderfully fragrant dessert is influenced by Pete Peterson, of Tapawingo, in Ellsworth, Michigan. It is best made with a variety of antique cooking apples.

Makes 8–10 servings

> 6 cups peeled and chopped tart apples (about 24 pieces per apple)
> Juice of 1 lemon
> 1 cup dark brown sugar, firmly packed
> ¾ cup granulated sugar
> 2 teaspoons grated lemon zest
> 2 teaspoons ground ginger
> 2 teaspoons ground cardamom
> 1 teaspoon cinnamon
> ½ teaspoon freshly grated nutmeg
> 1 cup diced dried apricots
> ½ cup golden raisins
> ¼ cup diced dates
> ¼ cup muscat raisins
> ¼ cup Calvados or applejack
> 2 cups unbleached flour

> 2 tablespoons cornstarch
> 2 teaspoons baking powder
> ½ teaspoon salt
> ½ cup unsalted butter
> 1 egg plus one egg yolk, lightly beaten
> 2 tablespoons granulated sugar mixed with 1 teaspoon cinnamon

Preheat oven to 375°.

Carefully butter a 3-quart casserole or deep oval baking dish.

Combine apples and lemon juice in a large bowl and toss well. Add brown sugar, ¼ cup granulated sugar, lemon zest, spices, dried fruits, Calvados, ¼ cup of flour, and cornstarch. Toss thoroughly.

Combine the remaining sugar and flour with baking powder and salt. Using a pastry blender, your fingers, or a fork, blend in the butter until the mixture looks like coarse cornmeal. Pour in the beaten eggs and mix just until mixture holds together. Dough will be coarse and lumpy. Distribute this dough evenly over the fruit. Sprinkle the cobbler with sugar and cinnamon mixture, then bake in the preheated oven for about 50 minutes, or until top is nicely browned and crusty and juices are bubbling. Serve warm.

Wine: Pine Ridge Chenin Blanc "Late Harvest" (Napa Valley)

Plum Pudding with Hard Sauce

We make this right after Thanksgiving for the holidays to come. And when we serve it at the end of Christmas dinner, Fred marches into the darkened room with the flaming pudding in all of its glory. Stem ginger, sweetened and preserved in syrup, is available from gourmet shops.

Serves 14

1 cup golden raisins
1 cup finely chopped dried apricots
4 ounces chopped candied fruits
8 ounces chopped glacé cherries
½ cup chopped figs
¾ cup chopped dates
¾ cup Myers's dark rum or Armagnac
¼ cup chopped candied orange peel
2 tablespoons chopped stem ginger
½ cup chopped black walnuts
½ pound beef suet, finely minced
4 jumbo egg yolks, beaten
¼ cup dark brown sugar, firmly packed
1 cup stale ladyfinger crumbs
⅓ cup whole-wheat pastry flour (available in health-food stores or from Arrowhead Mills, page 67), sifted
1 teaspoon ground ginger
1 teaspoon freshly grated nutmeg
1 teaspoon cinnamon
½ teaspoon ground cloves
½ teaspoon mace
⅓ cup heavy cream
5 jumbo egg whites, beaten stiff but not dry
Approximately 1½ cups Myers's dark rum or Armagnac

HARD SAUCE
2 cups unsalted butter, softened
3–4 cups confectioners' sugar
3 tablespoons Myers's dark rum or Armagnac

Sprig of holly for garnish

Combine raisins, apricots, candied fruits, glacé cherries, figs, dates, and rum in large bowl and mix well. Let marinate overnight at room temperature.

The next day, thoroughly butter an 8-cup mold or bowl and set aside. Add orange peel, stem ginger, walnuts, suet, egg yolks, and brown sugar to marinated dried fruit. Blend well. Add crumbs, flour, spices, and cream. Blend again. Fold in egg whites. Pour into prepared 8-cup mold and cover tightly. If you are not using a plum-pudding mold that has a tight-fitting lid, wrap container tightly in plastic wrap, then in foil.

Prepare a soup pot for steaming by placing a metal bowl in it upside down to form a platform for pudding. Fill pot with enough water to make steam but not enough to reach pudding. Place wrapped pudding bowl on inverted bowl and steam, covered, for 3½ hours, then cool.

Store covered pudding in refrigerator for at least 3 weeks. Moisten each week with approximately ⅓ cup rum. To serve, bring to room temperature, then steam as above for an hour.

To make hard sauce, cream butter in bowl of electric mixer fitted with the paddle. Gradually add sugar until mixture is thick and creamy. Beat in rum and spoon into serving bowl.

Unmold plum pudding on serving platter and put holly sprig in center. Heat ½ cup rum in saucepan, pour over pudding, and ignite. Serve with hard sauce on the side.

Dick Keim

Natural Choice

7177 Brockton Avenue

Riverside, California 92506

(714) 369-9484

*I*n downtown Riverside, California, stand what are said to be the first two navel orange trees to be planted in California, brought to Riverside back in 1890. They used to be out on a farm, but now the farm has been swallowed up by development. They still produce fruit, even though they are old and gnarled. The joke in the city is that it takes two full-time professors from U.C. Riverside to keep the trees alive.

Riverside is the branch of the University of California system for students of citrus. Davis is for grapes, Riverside is for oranges and grapefruit. If you need help keeping old orange trees alive, Riverside's agricultural gerontologists will be able to fill the bill.

Dick Keim acknowledges that truth, although he himself went to Cal Poly. He is not a professor, but he could be. He is a leader of the organic citrus growers of California. And he feels if you just keep the soil around the trees healthy and alive, the trees will be healthy too, and live as long as those two antiques in the middle of downtown Riverside.

In Orange County, you could pick a fresh ripe orange any day of the year, although every year there are fewer than there were before, with more and more groves being swept away by development. The main varieties are navels, in winter, and Valencias, which ripen throughout the spring and summer months. Sometimes you'll see blood oranges and mandarins. And white and red grapefruit, tangerines, lemons, and tangelos.

You can't tell the organic groves from the conventional as you drive by. They look the same. The trees everywhere are neatly coiffed; Dick Keim keeps his trees about 15 to 16 feet high. "We give them a butch haircut about every third year, and we take a little off the sides as well," he said. "It makes for easier picking and allows much more sunlight to bathe the leaves and set the growing fruit." But the conventional groves are pruned the same way.

There are two ways to tell the groves apart. "On an organic ranch," Dick said, "you would find soil that is alive with microscopic plant and animal life." He explains how transactions of all kinds are under way on and below the surface. Bacteria, molds, protozoa, and animals of a higher level—worms, insects, their larvae, spiders—deal with one another in ways that yield a balance ideal for the trees. You would not find this riot of life in the soil of the conventional orchard floor.

The other way to differentiate is to taste the fruit. "I am convinced," said Dick Keim, "that the organic ecosystem yields better flavor."

The conventional orchardist has two major enemies: insects and weeds. He blasts them both with chemicals. And when he needs to fertilize, the answer is again in the chemical tank.

The organic orchardist faces the same problems, but his solutions are different. With organically derived insecticides, there is no schedule; you spray when you really need to, rarely more often than once a year, and only after a careful study of the ecosystem.

Dick explained that "you need to envision your property as a space station with its own ecosystem and hang in there in spite of the people around you who won't do it or don't want to do it."

"We like groves that are isolated," he said. "We like weeds all around so that there is a place for insects to develop. This way you'll get a balance. You may not have to bring in beneficial insects. They will be there naturally." Dick does buy Decollate snails, however, which kill the European brown snails, a voracious enemy of the fruit trees. And he bands his trees with a strip of copper, which also discourages the brown snails.

Chemicals are often thought of as the engine that runs California agriculture. But in 1921, a Ventura County "pest control district" pioneered what is called integrated pest management, or IPM. The experiment has shown that with an organic approach, using organic sprays and beneficial insects, costs of pest control can be reduced $150 to $200 per acre to as low as $22, with no penalty in yield. The economics of this approach have not been lost on growers. Thousands of farmers who have not applied for organic certification still find it helpful to use some aspect of this organic approach for insect management.

Dick controls his weeds by mowing and cultivation. If they leap ahead of the mower, he will sometimes disk them under. Green manure. He fertilizes with composted chicken and steer manure, and for a quick blast of nitrogen, blood meal. His groves also get a topical application of foliar micronutrients derived from seaweed.

Dick Keim grew up farming. The family ranch was in the Coachella Valley, about 75 miles east of Riverside. Dick went to ag school in the early 1950s, when the new order for American agriculture was being promulgated by universities and chemical companies. Everything would be easier, everything would be better, productivity would soar, things would last longer and sell better. In fact, when Dick came out of college, in the 1950s, his first job was selling agricultural chemicals. But eventually he began to wonder about the long-term impact of the chemicals he had sold and was using. What would they do to the ground water, the microecosystems of the soil, or the fruit itself? In the early to mid-1980s, well before the alar apple scare, when alar was sprayed on apples and an entire season's worth of West Coast apples was thrown away, Dick and several other growers in the region began growing organically. Most of the acreage he works with has been certified, and more and more citrus is being grown organically every year.

"We must be completely credible," he said. "Certification must be impeccable. We have a technician whose sole job is to monitor the quality of our suppliers."

In 1987, Dick and two partners set up a packing facility to specialize in packing the organic fruit being grown in the area. "We had to figure out a way to get our fruit to stand out at the retail level," he said. "If we are asking for a fifty percent premium, how do we identify our oranges?" Typically, organic citrus was shipped in net bags, as was the second-rate conventional fruit. Dick and his partner devised a machine that would print a well-promoted logo on each piece of top-quality fruit. And they now ship their best oranges in boxes.

Dick's other marketing emphasis is freshness. Every extra day of tree ripening will make the fruit tastier. He and the growers he works with pick as late as possible and then put heavy emphasis on getting the fruit to market as quickly as possible. Their system allows them to deliver tasty fruit throughout the United States, Canada, and even Europe and Japan.

If you call Dick Keim someday, you may not be able to hear him. After he leaves the packinghouse, checks the groves, and comes home, he is greeted by a cacophony. He is a fancier of rare caged birds and breeds them in his house. Finches, cockatiels, exotic parrots, and a dozen other varieties occupy his leisure, and take his mind, if only briefly, off the challenges of leading a revolution.

Scallop Seviche

Serves 6 as an appetizer

- 1 pound bay scallops
- 2 medium tomatoes, peeled, seeded, and diced
- 1 small jalapeño pepper, seeded and minced
- ½ red bell pepper, finely minced
- ½ cup minced Spanish onion
- Juice of 3 limes
- ¼ cup extra-virgin olive oil
- Salt and freshly ground white pepper to taste
- 1 tablespoon minced cilantro
- 1 tablespoon minced fresh parsley
- 1 tablespoon minced fresh chives
- 1 avocado

3 cups baby lettuces tossed with 2 tablespoons walnut oil for garnish
Fresh herbs and edible flowers for garnish

Combine all the ingredients except avocado in a large glass or ceramic bowl. Refrigerate, stirring from time to time, for at least 2 hours but not more than 4. Just before serving, peel, seed, and dice avocado and add to seviche. Divide dressed greens among 6 large serving plates and distribute seviche evenly over them. Garnish with fresh herbs and flowers.

Wine: Sterling Vineyards Sauvignon Blanc (Napa Valley)

Gary Thomas's Shrimp with Lemon Fettuccine and Tequila-Cilantro Beurre Blanc

Serves 2

PASTA
        2 lemons
        2 large eggs
    1½ cups unbleached flour, or more if necessary

SAUCE
    ¼ cup white wine
    ½ cup tequila
        1 clove garlic, minced
        1 shallot, minced
    2–3 ounces unsalted butter, cut into pieces
    12 cooked shrimp
    ¼ cup minced cilantro

        Thin slices of lemon and bunches of cilantro for garnish

Finely mince the zest from the lemons and squeeze and reserve juice. Place eggs in small bowl and beat well, then combine with lemon zest and juice.

Place flour in the bowl of a food processor fitted with the metal blade. Add egg mixture and pulse just until dough becomes grainy and can be easily pressed together with your hand. Turn out on a table and finish kneading with your hands until dough is completely smooth and elastic. Add drops of water if dough is dry, or dust with flour if dough is too wet.

Using a pasta machine to knead and roll dough, begin by dividing it into balls of about ⅓–½-cup amounts. While working one portion, keep remaining portions covered with a clean kitchen towel. Set pasta machine rollers to their widest setting. Flatten first portion with your hands on a lightly floured surface and feed it through the rollers. Fold it in thirds, as you would a letter. Feed it through the rollers again. Flouring as needed, folding as described, and turning in 45-degree rotations, repeat this rolling (kneading) process for a total of 10 times.

Then reduce setting one number at a time and roll strip of pasta thinner and thinner, dusting lightly with flour as needed. You do not fold the pasta strip during this process. Roll as thin as possible and allow the pasta to dry on towels for 15 minutes before you cut it.

After the pasta is cut, let it dry on a pasta rack. Or dust it very well with cornmeal, coil it in bunches, and freeze until needed.

To make the sauce, pour wine and tequila into a saucepan and cook over moderate heat. Add garlic and shallot. Simmer until mixture is reduced to ¼ cup. Lower heat to very low and slowly whisk in butter pieces, one at a time (as one melts, add the next), whisking constantly. Meanwhile, have 4 quarts salted water for pasta coming to a rolling boil. Add 8 ounces of pasta and cook about 2 minutes. While pasta is cooking, add shrimp and cilantro to sauce.

Drain pasta, toss with sauce, and serve on heated plates. Garnish with lemon slices and cilantro.

Freeze remaining fettuccine (recipe makes about 12 ounces of pasta).

Wine: Ferrari-Carano Fumé Blanc (Sonoma County)

Orange and Jícama Salad with Red Onion and Lime

This really refreshing salad is terrific with everything spicy hot.

Serves 4–6

    1 pound jícama, peeled and cut into
      matchstick-sized julienne strips
    2 navel oranges, peeled, quartered,
      and thinly sliced
      Juice of 1–2 limes
    4 ounces red onion, sliced into thin
      rings
      Freshly ground black pepper to
      taste

In a ceramic bowl, combine ingredients, mix well, and cover. Marinate at least several hours in refrigerator. Adjust lime juice and pepper before serving.

Orange Surprise Fool

Serves 8

    2 cups pureed melon, such as
      cantaloupe or honeydew
    2 cups pureed poached pear
    ½ cup maple sugar or light brown
      sugar, firmly packed
      Zest of 1 lemon
    ½ teaspoon freshly grated nutmeg
    ½ teaspoon ground ginger
    1 teaspoon ground cardamom
    2 cups lowfat vanilla yogurt
    2 cups chopped, peeled, and seeded
      oranges
    ½ cup chopped macadamia nuts

    Mint leaves for garnish

In a large mixing bowl, combine fruit purees with sugar, lemon, and spices. Blend thoroughly. Add yogurt and blend again. In each of 8 parfait glasses, spoon a dollop of yogurt mixture, then a layer of oranges, another dollop of yogurt, another layer of oranges, and top with a final layer of yogurt mixture. Chill well. Sprinkle with nuts and garnish with mint leaves before serving.

Wine: Bonny Doon "Vin du Glacier" Gewürztraminer (California)

Ken and Julie Kamp

Good Nature Farm Market

US 31 North and Cresswell Road

Kewadin, Michigan 49648

(616) 264-6868

One damp fall afternoon as we drove down US Highway 31, heading for the Traverse City, Michigan, airport, an unusually handsome roadside sign caught our attention. Good Nature Farm Market, it read. It did what a good sign is supposed to do; it made us slow down and drive in. Inside, we found out that the sign was the work of Julie Kamp, one of the market's owners. She was making cider in a press behind the stand. We talked with her awhile, sipping some of her extraordinary cider through a straw.

At one point a green John Deere tractor chugged noisily past. "It's my husband," she said.

Months later, on a gorgeous spring morning, we drove by again. This time, Julie was behind the counter putting together a little sign announcing that she had avocado and ham sandwiches for sale.

Again, the green John Deere tractor rumbled by. "It's my husband," she said. "And yes, he's still on the tractor."

This time, however, we met him. Ken Kamp had, in fact, been on the tractor all night. Under powerful lights, he had been spraying his cherry trees. It had been the wettest, hottest May in history and his crop was at risk. Brown rot, a fungus, and bacterial canker were a clear and present danger, threatening 850,000 pounds of cherries. So although he doesn't like to do it, he sprayed.

"I've been sprayed a lot," Ken said. "I got sprayed by an airplane once. And one time a guy sprayed my car as I drove by. Spraying makes me nervous. I just don't like to mess with stuff that could kill me." So Ken Kamp chooses the most benign agent that he can get for the job at hand. He likes sprays that degrade quickly. He is willing to pay more for a safer, more forgiving product. He will not spray on a schedule. He tries to use agents that are target-specific. He will try to find an insecticide that will get the bad bugs and leave the beneficial insects—predatory mites, for example—unharmed. And he sprays at night, when there is less heat and less wind and fewer people around.

"With this farm," he said, "everything is ad hoc. Nothing gets anything unless it really needs it. I'd really rather not spray at all."

In the state of Michigan, it is virtually impossible for a commercial farmer or orchardist to be organic. Agricultural authorities have vast power to confiscate crops, or at least deny them a market, if they suspect that they haven't been properly protected by the farmer with his armamentarium of chemicals.

But in spite of regulations, the Kamps have discovered that there is still room for discretion. Ken and Julie own 329 acres, huge by Midwest orchard standards. "Ken reads the orchards every day," Julie told us. "He knows every tree, and he knows when something is going wrong."

Ken smiled. "Farming has its insecurities," he said. Since he doesn't apply chemicals routinely, a lot rides on his judgment. If he does not spray exactly when he should, he stands to lose part of a crop. If he sprays when he doesn't have to, he has wasted a lot of money. In fact, one of the reasons it is worth his while to "read the orchards" every day is that in the past five years he has been able to cut his spraying costs—for herbicides, fungicides, insecticides, and antibacterial agents—from $40,000 to just over $15,000. "But," he said, "it's a tough gamble."

It's easy to make a mistake. One year, 300,000 pounds of cherries were ruined when they absorbed too much moisture too early and split open. "I might have saved them with vaporguard," he said, a sugar-based spray that retards osmosis and keeps cherries from drawing in moisture through their skins.

Under ideal circumstances, the Kamps could get a million pounds of cherries from their orchards. But at the time of our visit, a late-spring freeze had already caused them to lower their estimate by 150,000 pounds. Seagulls sometimes glide in from the lake and partake of early cherries. The crows are a threat, too. Sometimes, propane cannons and other noisemakers will have an effect on the thieving magpies and robins. But the Kamps worry until all the cherries are harvested and put into pies.

Part of their strategy is to put more emphasis on the farm market, to sell as much as possible directly to the customers. Also, the Kamps emphasize variety. A recent census showed that there were over 100 varieties of fruit trees on the property, including 33 kinds of cherries, 32 types of apples, and assorted plums, apricots, pears, and peaches. Some patches have recently been given over to strawberries, and rhubarb, blueberries, and raspberries are in the planning stages.

At the peak of the picking season, the orchard needs, in addition to the family, at least twenty other workers. And in the spring, as many as 10 million bees are on the payroll. A Michigan beekeeper deploys eighty-five hives in the orchards, at $25 per hive, for purposes of pollination. "Not enough bees around here these days to do the job," said Ken. "Too many people spray insecticides while the bees are out during the daylight hours.

"Well, I've got weeds to chop," he said. He finishes a Coke, his reward for working all night. Then he is back on the John Deere. The spray rig has been replaced with the mowing machine, and he heads off down a row of trees, cutting the high grass and the ragweed and probably reading the orchard yet one more time.

Tapawingo's Tart Cherry Chutney

We visit Ellsworth, Michigan, at the end of every spring and fall in order to have two dinners at Tapawingo. One fall, chef Pete Peterson was preparing to close for a month's vacation and we had the fun of helping to eat up some of the treasures left in the refrigerator. (His refrigerator is more fun than Aunt Tillie's attic!) We've been asking for this recipe ever since. Thanks, Pete. We especially love it with poultry and game.

Makes about 1 quart

> 4 pounds tart fresh cherries, pitted
> 2 red or green bell peppers, seeded and chopped
> 2 jalapeño peppers, seeded and minced
> 3 cloves garlic, minced
> ½ cup cider vinegar
> 1 cup molasses
> 2 tablespoons green peppercorns
> 2 bay leaves
> 8 whole cloves
> 1 teaspoon cinnamon
> 1 teaspoon freshly grated nutmeg
> 1 teaspoon salt
> ½ teaspoon freshly ground black pepper

Combine all the ingredients in an enamel saucepan and cook over medium-low heat until liquids begin to bubble. Reduce heat to low and cook, uncovered, for about 1 hour, until the mixture has darkened and is the consistency of jam. If mixture seems too dry, add a small amount of water. Discard bay leaves. This will keep for weeks in the refrigerator.

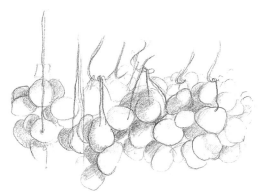

Michigan Dried-Cherry Zinfandel Sauce

Finally, dried cherries have become easier to obtain all over the country and they are really fun to use. We can even find them in our supermarket these days. Sometimes we use this as a dessert sauce, sometimes on grilled duck or venison. Sometimes, too, we make it with dried blueberries; then we use crème de cassis instead of Kijafa.

Makes 2 cups

> 3 cups red Zinfandel wine
> ½ cup Kijafa wine
> 1 cup dried cherries
> 1 cinnamon stick
> 2 whole cloves
> ½ teaspoon freshly grated nutmeg
> 1 cup sugar
> 1 tablespoon fresh orange juice

Combine all the ingredients except orange juice in a heavy-bottomed saucepan and bring to a boil. Reduce heat and simmer briskly. Continue to cook until the liquids reduce and the mixture begins to thicken, about 1 hour. When mixture has thickened, remove from heat. Stir in orange juice and serve.

Tapawingo's Peach and Pecan Crumble

While we're not usually in northern Michigan during peach season, we know that Pete Peterson's dessert will be especially delicious when made with peaches right off the Kamps' trees.

Serves 6–8

- ⅓ cup light brown sugar, firmly packed
- 2 tablespoons unbleached flour
- ¼ teaspoon freshly grated nutmeg, or more to taste
- 2 tablespoons fresh lemon juice
- 3 pounds ripe peaches, peeled, pitted, and sliced

TOPPING
- 1½ cups unbleached flour
- Approximately 1 cup granulated sugar, depending on sweetness of peaches
- Pinch salt
- ¾ cup cold unsalted butter, cut into ½-inch cubes
- 2 cups chopped pecans

- Heavy cream, whipped cream, or ice cream for garnish

Lightly butter a 9-inch-square baking pan. Preheat oven to 375°.

In a large bowl, combine brown sugar, 2 tablespoons flour, and nutmeg. Add lemon juice and peaches, toss, and pour into prepared baking pan.

To make topping, combine 1½ cups flour, granulated sugar, salt, and butter.

Using your fingers, quickly blend mixture until it resembles coarse crumbs. Mix in chopped pecans and spread topping evenly over peach mixture. Bake crumble in preheated oven for 30 minutes, or until juices are bubbling and top is golden. Garnish with cream or ice cream.

Wine: Long Vineyards Johannisberg Riesling "Botrytis" (Napa Valley)

Harvest-Time Upside-Down Pear Cake

This cake is wonderful with any variety of pear, but we especially enjoy making it with Seckel and Anjou.

Makes 1 10-inch cake

SAUCE
- 4 large fresh pears, peeled, cored, and cut into pieces
- ¼ cup granulated sugar

TOPPING
- ¾ cup dark brown sugar, firmly packed
- 5 tablespoons unsalted butter, melted
- ¼ cup chopped pecans
- 2 large fresh pears, peeled, cored, and sliced into 16 slices each

CAKE
- 3 cups unbleached flour
- 2 teaspoons baking soda
- ½ teaspoon baking powder
- ½ teaspoon salt
- 1 teaspoon ground ginger
- 1 teaspoon cinnamon

1 teaspoon ground cardamom
½ teaspoon freshly grated nutmeg
½ teaspoon ground allspice
½ cup honey
½ cup apple cider
½ cup corn oil
⅔ cup dark brown sugar, firmly packed
3 jumbo eggs
½ cup golden raisins
½ cup chopped pecans

Whipped cream or Caramel Sauce (recipe follows) for garnish

To make sauce, combine pears, sugar, and 2 tablespoons water in a saucepan, cover, and simmer until tender but not mushy—about 15 minutes. Set aside.

Lightly oil a 10-inch Bundt pan.

Preheat oven to 350°.

To make topping, combine the ¾ cup brown sugar, butter, and pecans in a small bowl and blend well. Evenly distribute this mixture over the bottom of the Bundt pan. Then arrange the pear slices in a circle over the nut mixture and press in firmly.

To prepare the cake, sift dry ingredients together into a medium bowl and set aside. Combine honey and cider in a small bowl and set aside.

Cream the oil and ⅔ cup brown sugar in the bowl of an electric mixer. With the motor on medium, add the eggs one at a time, beating well after each addition. Then gradually add flour mixture alternately with honey mixture. Do not overbeat. Blend in raisins and pecans, then add the pear sauce.

Pour batter into the prepared pan and bake in preheated oven for 50 minutes. Test by inserting a cake tester. This cake may bake as long as 1 hour and 10 minutes, depending upon how juicy the pears are.

When done, remove pan from oven and place on a rack for 30 minutes, then invert cake on the rack and finish cooling. Serve with whipped cream or caramel sauce.

Wine: Hidden Cellars Winery Johannisberg Riesling "Late Harvest" (Potter Valley)

Caramel Sauce

This has been our favorite dessert sauce for many years. It's great over ice cream, as well as pooled under cakes and tarts.

1¾ cups Crème Fraîche (page 350)
1¼ cups superfine sugar
½ cup milk

Heat crème fraîche to just below the boiling point.

In a small saucepan, slowly heat and stir sugar over medium heat until it has melted and turned a beautiful golden brown. Remove from heat and pour in half of the warm crème fraîche. Return to low heat and stir until caramel is well blended with the crème fraîche.

Once mixture is blended, remove from heat and whisk in remaining crème fraîche. Let cool.

Just before serving, heat milk in a small saucepan. Pour caramel into top of double boiler. Over simmering water, heat caramel and gradually add warm milk until proper sauce density is achieved.

Fragrant Coffee Cake

Linda can never resist playing with even the most successful of recipes. The dough for this cake goes back to her childhood and was made by her mother, Gert LeVine. The addition of the fruit is Linda's. Her cousin Susan Cavitch has also substituted 8 Granny Smith apples for the 16 apricots. It would also be delicious with 4 cups of pitted fresh cherries.

Makes 2 9-inch cakes

>   2 tablespoons active dry yeast
>   4 ounces warm water
>   5 cups unbleached flour
>   1 cup sugar
>   ½ teaspoon salt
>   1 cup milk
>   ½ cup unsalted butter
>   2 tablespoons sour cream, at room temperature

FILLING

>   16 apricots, peeled, pitted, and cut into pieces (peel by dipping in boiling water)
>   1 cup sugar
>   1 cup raisins
>   1 tablespoon cinnamon
>   ¼ teaspoon freshly grated nutmeg
>   ½ cup unsalted butter, melted

Warm oven to 200°.

Combine yeast and water in a small bowl, mix, and set in a warm place to proof (bubble). Combine flour, sugar, and salt in a mixing bowl; place in the warmed oven to heat.

Combine milk and butter in a saucepan. Place over low heat until butter has melted, then set aside.

Add proofed yeast to warmed flour mixture and mix well. Add sour cream to warmed milk mixture, then mix thoroughly with flour mixture. Cover bowl with a clean kitchen towel and let stand for 2 hours in a very warm place. Beat dough thoroughly with a wooden spoon and let rise for 2 more hours.

To make filling, combine apricots, ¼ cup sugar, and 2 tablespoons water in a saucepan. Cook over medium heat until apricots are tender. Drain any liquid and combine apricots with raisins. Set aside.

Thoroughly butter 2 9-inch springform pans. Divide dough into four portions. Cover the bottom of each pan with a portion of dough. Combine cinnamon and nutmeg with remaining ¾ cup sugar.

Generously butter surface of first layer of dough with a pastry brush. Divide fruit filling between the two pans and spread evenly. Sprinkle each pan thoroughly with ¼ of the sugar-and-spice mixture. Then cover each pan with remaining dough. Butter liberally again and sprinkle with remaining sugar mixture. Cover pans and let rise for 1½ hours.

Preheat oven to 375°.

Bake cakes for about 30 minutes, or until nicely browned and a tester inserted into the middle of a cake comes out dry.

Let cakes cool for 10 minutes on racks, then remove cakes from pans and continue cooling. These freeze well.

Bob and Jane Willard

Ela Orchard

Box 127

Rochester, Wisconsin 53167

(414) 534-2545

"We're not especially fun or exciting," Bob Willard said to us on the telephone, "but you are welcome to visit." Ela Orchard is just west of the tiny Wisconsin village of Rochester, about an hour's drive from Milwaukee and two hours from Chicago, where we had first met Bob at the Best of the Midwest Market. Something attracted us to his stand there—perhaps the apples, antique varieties not often seen. We took the little flyer that told of the farm's approach to orcharding.

Both Bob and his wife, Jane, are graduates of small but prestigious and challenging liberal arts colleges—Bob from Oberlin, in Ohio, and Jane from Carleton, in Minnesota. After graduation in 1970, Bob came back to the farm as he had throughout his youth to pick apples for the summer. Then he took a professional job in Kentucky. But he came back for a second summer of picking. Then he decided to put in a full season. And after that experience, he concluded that the life on the farm was what he loved.

Jane finished her work at Carleton in 1979, an English literature major, and through some friends found a summer job picking apples on the Ela Orchard. She met Bob, who by then, with his cousin Edwin Ela, had taken over ownership and management of the farm. Bob's grandfather had originally planted the trees in the 1920s. Then the orchard was taken over by two of his children, Mary and Ben—Bob's aunt and uncle. When they retired, Bob and his cousin took over.

Bob and Edwin thus became third-generation orchardists. It is axiomatic that the first generation plants, the second generation nurtures, and the third replants. Most of what Bob and Edwin's grandparents planted more than sixty-five years ago has now run its course. "Age does not affect the quality of the fruit," said Bob, "it affects the quantity." The original trees were big, the kind that develop great broad canopies; the kind you must climb to pick or to prune. When they are that large, you start to worry about the shade of the canopy inhibiting the growth and ripening of the apples. Bob and Edwin have been putting in the newer dwarf and semi-dwarf varieties. They are not necessarily better, and they won't live as long, but they are much quicker to yield, easier to manage, and more resistant to pests, an important consideration for a farmer working to be as organic as possible.

There are 22 acres of apple trees now producing 33 different varieties, many of them antique. Liveland Raspberry, Tolman Sweet, Charlemoff, Wolf River, Seek No Further, Black Willow Twig—these old-time varieties will remain a part of the orchard as Bob and Edwin graft cuttings from the old trees onto dwarf root stock.

Bob apologizes for what he calls the summer jumble in the big cool barn and shed. He has a small cider press, but because it is such a time-consuming enterprise, he rarely presses more than 500 gallons in a week. Some Ela apples are sold through specialty-food stores in Madison and some at the famous Dane County Market on the capitol grounds. But most of them are sold from the barn to people who come every year to buy.

"There is a capacity for communication and understanding between the farmer and the customer," said Bob. "The customers want to know about the apples. I can sell apples with hail pits to my customers because they understand that hail doesn't hurt the taste. I couldn't sell those apples at a supermarket."

The farm is well equipped and clearly successful. Bob reads and studies about IPM and LISA, integrated pest management and low-input sustainable agriculture. There are monitors in the orchards to track moisture and temperature trends and to help him make spraying decisions. And on the trees, something decidedly low-tech—apple maggot balls, red sticky spheres that attract harmful flies and bog them down in sweet mucilage. This careful management has paid off in many ways. Because there are acres of woodland nearby, there are enough bees for pollination without having to import hives.

In one of the fields, there are some sheep and lambs grazing around a '36 Ford that one of the cousins hopes someday to rebuild. And in another paddock, there are some goats. Bob grows hay for them and uses their manure in the orchard. "We like their milk and children love to feed them apples in the fall," he told us.

There is a rich body of often elegant writing about orcharding that goes back to the earliest times in this country. Since the growing of fruit trees has always been a slow and deliberate process, it was frequently felt that only the contemplative and philosophical could thrive at it. It used to be a calling for the wealthy, since it might be twelve to fifteen years after a planting before there was fruit for the market, not the kind of venture to excite an entrepreneur. But the proposition was set forth by educated gentleman orchardists that contemplating the trees, caring for them, and plucking their fruit were ennobling activities that enhanced the quality of life. And it was felt that children who grew up among the trees would be healthier, happier, and morally and ethically sound.

We asked Jane about her role in the operation. She works as every farmer works—on whatever needs to be done, although the children take much of her time. But whenever she can, she told us, she writes. Her short stories are occasionally published in *Harper's* magazine. And she is now at work on a new novel. It has been in progress for two and a half years, she tells us. But the lifestyle on the farm, the rhythms of the seasons, and the longer cycle of planting, growing, and picking, have made her content with her pace. "It's just a part of my life," she said.

Only after we had talked for a while did we learn that she had already published an earlier novel. She was too modest to say much about it and reluctant to mention its title. It is called *The Book of Ruth* and was written under the name Jane Hamilton. This powerful work won for her in 1989 the PEN/Ernest Hemingway Foundation Award for the best first novel of the year. She smiles shyly when she is reminded that few books are ever accorded such a high honor.

Bob has a brother who is an ornithologist, another who is a neurophysiologist, and a sister who is a teacher in Boston. Bob almost certainly would have been out there in academia, too, but for that summer after college when he came back to the orchard one last time to pick apples. Jane makes us lemonade. We sit on her porch looking at the old stone silo across the way and the windmill that no longer has to pump water but still clatters in the breeze.

For the writer-farmer and for the farmer-philosopher, thought, time, and toil have yielded sweet fruit.

Apple Noodle Pudding

This is a delicious dish for a brunch buffet. It is also good cold. It's a dish that goes back to Linda's childhood, when it would be served to break the Yom Kippur fast.

Serves 10–12

- 6 tart cooking apples, peeled, cored, and sliced
- 1 tablespoon fresh lemon juice
- 2 cups apple cider
- ½ cup maple sugar
- 1 cup raisins
- 2–3 tablespoons applejack
- 1 pound cottage cheese
- 1 cup sour cream
- ½ cup superfine sugar
- 1 teaspoon freshly grated nutmeg
- ½ cup unsalted butter, melted
- 6 jumbo eggs, beaten
- 1 pound wide egg noodles, cooked, drained, and cooled
- ⅓ cup granulated sugar
- 2 tablespoons cinnamon

Preheat oven to 350°.

Thoroughly butter a 9x12 baking dish and set aside.

Combine apples, lemon juice, and cider in a small saucepan. Bring to a boil and reduce heat; simmer 5 minutes. Drain apples thoroughly, reserving cider (the cooled boiling liquid makes a refreshing beverage), and place in a small bowl with maple sugar. Mix well and set aside.

Combine raisins and applejack in a small dish and set aside.

In a large mixing bowl, blend cottage cheese and sour cream. Add superfine sugar, nutmeg, butter, and eggs. Blend thoroughly. Fold in apples, raisin mixture, and noodles. Blend well and pour into prepared baking dish. Combine granulated sugar and cinnamon and sprinkle evenly over noodles. Bake in prepared oven for 1½ hours. Let stand 5 minutes before serving.

Wine: Wagner Vineyards Ravat "Ice Wine" (New York Finger Lakes)

Freddie's Famous Phyllo Tart

This is one of Fred's great *tours de force* and is especially wonderful with a mixture of antique apples. Fred prefers to see this accompanied by both whipped Crème Fraîche (page 350) and Wonderful Cinnamon Ice Cream (page 118).

Serves 10–12

- ½ cup raisins
- ¼ cup Grand Marnier or Cointreau liqueur
- 4–5 pounds mixed cooking apples, peeled, cored, and thinly sliced
- ½ cup granulated sugar
- ⅓ cup dark brown sugar, firmly packed
- 1 teaspoon ground ginger
- 1 teaspoon cinnamon
- ½ teaspoon ground cloves
- ½ teaspoon freshly grated nutmeg
- ¼ cup cornstarch
- ½ cup blanched slivered almonds or chopped pecans
- 1 cup unsalted butter, melted
- 1 pound frozen phyllo pastry dough, defrosted

Confectioners' sugar for garnish

Combine raisins with liqueur in a small bowl and allow to marinate for at least 30 minutes.

In a large bowl, combine the apples, sugars, spices, cornstarch, and nuts. Toss well. Add raisin mixture and blend well.

Preheat oven to 350°. Brush the surface of a 12-inch pizza pan with some of the butter. Cover dough with a slightly damp clean kitchen towel to keep it from drying out.

Working quickly, lay one sheet of dough across the pan so that one end covers the center of the pan and the other end hangs over the edge. Brush generously with butter. Working clockwise, layer and butter remaining sheets of phyllo so that a circle of dough is formed. When there are only 4 sheets left, set 2 aside and cover with a damp towel. Fold remaining sheets in half, butter well, and place these in the middle of the pan as a final base for the filling.

Pile the filling into the middle of the prepared pan. Then quickly bring the phyllo leaves over the top to cover, buttering the top of each leaf as you flip it over. Generously butter the whole tart.

Cut the 2 remaining sheets of phyllo into 1-inch strips. Roll some of these strips into curls and gently tie some into knots. Toss all of these on the top of the tart and pour remaining butter evenly over the top.

Bake in preheated oven for an hour, watching to make certain tart doesn't burn during the last half hour. If it gets too brown, reduce heat slightly.

Transfer pan to a rack and let cool for 10 minutes, then carefully remove tart from the pan and continue cooling on the rack. Dust with confectioners' sugar and serve at room temperature.

Wine: Chateau St. Jean Johannisberg Riesling "Late Harvest" (Sonoma County)

Baked Apples with Filberts and Fruit Chutney

Serves 6

> 6 large baking apples, preferably Wolf River
> Juice of 1 lemon combined with 1½ quarts water
> 1 cup granulated sugar
> ⅓ cup applejack
> ¾ cup apple cider
> ½ cup chopped skinned filberts
> 4 ounces combined dried apricots, raisins, dates, and figs, chopped
> 1 tablespoon brown sugar, firmly packed
> ½–1 teaspoon freshly grated nutmeg
> ½ teaspoon ground ginger
> 1 cup heavy cream, warmed (optional)

Carefully core the apples without going all the way through the bottom. Then pare away a decorative strip of skin around the middle. Place the prepared apples in the bowl of lemon water and set aside.

Preheat oven to 425°.

Combine granulated sugar and applejack in a small, heavy saucepan and cook over medium heat until sugar is dissolved and mixture begins to turn golden. Carefully add ½ cup of cider and stir well. Allow syrup to simmer about 5 minutes, then set aside. While syrup is cooking, place filberts in a small pan and brown them in the oven. This should take about 10 minutes.

Combine browned filberts and dried fruits in a small mixing bowl. Add 2 tablespoons of cider syrup, remaining cider, brown sugar, grated nutmeg to taste, and ginger. Mix well.

Drain apples thoroughly, pack hollowed cores with fruit mixture, and arrange stuffed apples in a baking dish that is just large enough to hold them. Pour remaining cider syrup around the apples and then bake in the preheated oven, basting several times, for 30 minutes, or until tender. Remove baking dish from oven and allow apples to cool. Serve each apple in a bowl, surrounded by some of the syrup. It is also nice to pour some warmed heavy cream over the top of each apple.

Kenneth Weston

Harvey Weston's Antique Orchards
19760 West National Avenue
New Berlin, Wisconsin 53146
(414) 679-1784

Kenneth Weston, algebraist, mathematics professor, and farmer, and his sister, Genevieve, retired teacher, serve as curators of what may be one of America's finest museums. The collection of antiques, begun with an order dated October 12, 1938, contains about a hundred different specimens, many of which can be traced back to our country's early history. A tour introduces names like Pink Pearl, Yellow Transparent, Ashmeads Kernel, and Jacobson Strawberry. Today, this 16-acre apple orchard begun by Kenneth and Genevieve's parents more than fifty years ago is still enjoyed by Harvey and Alice Weston, now in their nineties, who oversee things from the white farmhouse on the edge of the orchard.

Alice Weston's father, William Markwardt, bought the farm in the early 1930s. It had a nice house, a barn built in 1901, and a large shed. While there were a few apple trees in the orchard, there was plenty of room for more. When Alice ordered her first trees, she paid $4.50 each for such varieties as Winter Banana, Grimes Golden, Willow Twig, and Wilson Red June. Those first trees represented the beginning of a lifetime passion for collecting. For decades, she pored over farm catalogues and books, researching historic varieties of apples and instilling her children with an extraordinary passion for the fruit.

The first orchard is filled with full-size apple trees—the kind that one needs to pick from ladders. Contemporary orchardists work with dwarf and semi-dwarf trees, which are more easily managed than the big, old-fashioned ones. They have a higher yield per acre, but they are also more fragile. While the Westons chose to pass on the dwarf varieties, in recent times they have been planting semi-dwarfs.

"I'm just not sure how long-lived they will be," Kenneth told us. "While a full-sized tree can live close to a hundred years, a dwarf might last for only twenty. With luck," he continued, "a carefully managed semi-dwarf tree will last for forty years or more."

The trees are raised as naturally as possible. "Genevieve and I use cow manure, compost, and some topsoil for fertilizer. And we use as few chemicals as possible," he said. They keep the high grasses closely cut, but they leave the clippings to form a kind of natural mulch.

"We are trying to work toward using no chemicals at all, because some spray chemicals are so hazardous to apply," Kenneth continued, "but organic sprays for these orchards have not yet reached a state of dependability." Because so many neighboring orchards are infected with scab, the Westons cannot avoid spraying against it. Before there were other orchards around, their father sprayed arsenate of lead and sulfur. A neighbor used whitewash. But on the other hand, the Westons find that spray hazards to bees are so minimal here that there is no need to bring in more bees for pollination.

Deer are a problem with saplings. Without some protective fencing, the deer nibble off the tops, slowing growth if not destroying the tree. Woodchucks, raccoons, and pheasants don't seem to bother anything. And there is also very little damage from mice, who are known to eat a band around a tree, severely weakening it.

While the birds seem to leave the apples alone, Kenneth and Genevieve complain mightily about them when it comes to the nearly ripe Queen Anne and rainbow cherries. As we walked the orchards we came upon some newly naked trees with only a few ripening berries hanging in solitary splendor. "We've tried almost everything to scare the birds away," Kenneth told us with great frustration. "We even tried a large plastic snake. But that thing," he went on, "only scared my sister. In fact, the damn birds sat on it while their friends picked the trees clean." Because

their area has become well populated, they can no longer use acetylene cannons to scare the birds away. The Westons plan to baffle a noisemaker to prevent disturbing the nearby neighbors.

We learned that apples are not native to this country; all of the Westons' wonderful varieties have roots in the other countries. The White Winter Calville was grown by Louis XIII at his garden in Orléans. This apple contains twice as much vitamin C as an orange. The Spitzenberg was brought here before the Revolution. Thomas Jefferson loved this apple, with its bright red-orange skin, small gray spots, and crisp yellow flesh. There are records of an order he placed in 1790.

Indeed, the orchards are filled with names and lore that correspond to American history. Alice Weston's passion for historic apples has outgrown the first orchard. And so the Westons acquired more land and planted a second orchard in the early 1970s. These trees are all semi-dwarf.

"While we usually buy one-year-old nursery stock," Kenneth commented, "I do like to try my hand at cleft grafting." A bunch of branches—or whips, as they are known—are sharpened, the cambium layers are matched to the roots, and the two parts are sealed together with wax. Kenneth was quick to admit, however, that Wally Marks, a mechanical engineer friend of his, was far more successful than he in this endeavor. In fact, Wally's grafting skills are responsible for the inclusion of twenty additional antique varieties in the orchard. But Kenneth proudly pointed out several trees that his father saved by radical resectioning and grafting.

Today all the orchard work is done by Kenneth and Genevieve. The picking is done by the whole family; rarely do they hire any help. The high work is done by Kenneth from a kind of cherry-picking platform that he attaches to a tractor. He does his trimming this way as well.

Weston apples are prized for their intense flavor. Like the winemakers of France, who boast of their *terroir,* Kenneth Weston is also convinced that climate and soil are the chief makers of good fruit. "I can often taste an apple," he told us, "and tell you where it's from. There is nothing better than Wisconsin apples. Here there's lots of limestone in the soil; add our climate and you get a special richness of flavor." Apples are very sensitive to weather changes, he suggested. "Most people know that an apple's stage of ripeness when it's picked will influence its flavor, but a heavy storm will influence it too."

Some apples—like Jonathans, King Davids, and Black Gilli Flowers—have a better texture if picked a bit early, before they are completely ripe. Otherwise, they tend to get water core, which causes a deterioration of texture and a browning of the centers. Yet other apples, like the Macoun, will have little flavor if picked early—left too long, though, they fall off the tree and bruise.

Some of the Westons' trees are more than eighty years old. Kenneth told us that the old varieties are prone to fire blight, a virus that kills parts of the tree at a time. "Some older varieties don't store well, and some tend to be ugly. But, oh, what flavor!"

An old Maidenblush tree is one of Alice Weston's early plantings. This apple, one of America's oldest, has flat cheeks with a reddish hue on a yellow background. The old tree died, but before they got around to removing the stump, two new limbs came out. Today it is producing luscious summer apples. "A miracle tree," Kenneth suggested. "It's funny about apple trees," he told us. "They start to die on the sides, but then there's new growth from the bottom."

Kenneth knows the orchard intimately and can identify most of the trees by their shape and bark. His descriptions of their fruits are often poetic. The Pink Pearl is a fall apple. It is a fragrant cream-and-pale-green fruit that has a delicate crimson blush to the cheek. "Its bright pink flesh makes a splendid picture," he said, "but it's also a delicious eating apple, and it leaks like a tomato when you bite it." Yellow Transparent is another variety that ripens in the summer (in addition to Red Bird). The yellow fruit makes a fragrant and creamy applesauce. The Melba trees go back to Alice Weston's first order. Kenneth mused, "These are beautiful oblong-shaped apples, they're white with pink cheeks; the ones you get today don't look the same and they are not as good. Ashmead's Kernel is a variety that goes back more than two hundred years; it's one our finest eating apples."

There's a very old Beacon tree, one of the early summer apples. "That's one my father grafted many years ago," he told us. It's a crisp, tart apple. About another, he commented, "Jonathan crossed with Arkansas Black is the kind of apple that brings tears to your eyes. The apple is so dark a red, it's almost black; its yellow flesh is crisp and richly flavored." The Twenty-ounce Pippin is a very big apple. It is greenish in color, with a rough, knobby skin. "A few students who sometimes help us pick love these," Kenneth said. "It's a great eating apple."

There are apples with names like Hubbardston Nonesuch (a great nineteenth-century Massachusetts apple), Chenango Strawberry (from Chenango County, New York), and Westfield Seek-No-Further (pre-Revolutionary Westfield, Massachusetts). Each has different flavor characteristics, each has a unique history. The Chenango, also known as Sheepsnose, is a very fragrant apple that has a whitish-green skin with red stripes and a pink blush. Pick it just a bit late and it is dull and tasteless. "People buy them just to have a bowlful in the living room. They are better than flowers," Curator Weston said.

Some of the apples are still sold from a simple market in the old barn. But every Friday they carefully pick just for the Dane County market in Madison on Saturday. "We don't polish the apples," said Kenneth's wife, Isabelle, "because we don't want to remove the natural wax coating."

Kenneth told us that in springtime, when the orchard is in bloom, it's like a gorgeous flower garden. And then, as we passed a particular tree, he commented, "This is a Thompson King; it's an ugly green apple with brown stripes. But," he continued, "it's incredibly juicy and sweet. In fact, it is so wonderful that you know you want to die with one in your mouth."

Simple Applesauce

We can't get Pink Pearl apples in Cleveland, but Linda dreams about making applesauce from them. Do seek out orchards in your area so that you can experiment with different varieties and different combinations. And remember that applesauce freezes like a dream.

Makes about 2 quarts

    6 pounds cooking apples, stemmed and quartered

Approximately 3 tablespoons granulated sugar, or more or less to taste
Freshly grated nutmeg to taste

Cut each apple quarter in half. In a large, heavy-bottomed pot, combine apples and ½ cup water (the amount given is not a mistake). Add sugar, cover, and cook over very low heat until apples are very tender, about 20 minutes. Uncover and let stand until cool. Pass cooked apples through a food mill. Taste and adjust seasonings.

Apple Horns

The better the flour, the better the pastry.
The better the apples, the better the Horns.

Makes 3 dozen

PASTRY

> 3 cups unbleached flour
> 4 cups whole-wheat pastry flour
> (available in health-food stores or
> from Arrowhead Mills, page 67)
> ¼ cup superfine sugar
> Pinch of salt
> 1 cup shortening
> 1¼ cups ice-cold apple cider
> ¼ cup buttermilk

FILLING

> 6 cups peeled, cored, and chopped
> mixed cooking apples
> 2 tablespoons apple cider
> 1 teaspoon cinnamon
> ½ teaspoon ground ginger
> ½ teaspoon ground allspice
> ½ teaspoon freshly grated nutmeg
> ¼ teaspoon ground cloves
> 1 cup chopped dried apricots
> 1 cup chopped pecans
> ⅔ cup blueberry or wildflower honey

TOPPING

> ½ cup unsalted butter, melted
> 1 jumbo egg beaten with 1 tablespoon
> water
> ½ cup sugar mixed with 1 teaspoon
> cinnamon

To make the pastry, sift flours, sugar, and salt into a large mixing bowl. Add shortening and cut with a pastry blender until mixture is the texture of cornmeal. Add liquids and quickly mix with a fork until dough forms a ball. Set aside while you prepare the filling.

Combine apples, cider, and spices in a heavy saucepan and cook over medium heat until apples begin to soften, about 5 minutes. Add apricots, pecans, and honey and cook until mixture is thick and syrupy. Set aside to cool.

Preheat oven to 375°. Divide dough into quarters. Lightly flour work surface and roll each dough quarter into a 12-inch circle. Cut into 8 wedges and brush each with melted butter.

Place a spoonful of filling at the top of each wedge and roll toward the narrow end. Pinch sides together to seal, then prick top with a fork. Brush each pastry with egg wash and sprinkle with sugar mixture. Repeat steps with remaining dough. Bake on nonstick cookie sheets in preheated oven until golden brown, about 30 minutes. Transfer with a spatula to a wire rack to cool.

Almost Mother's Apple Pie

For Linda, this may be the most important recipe in this book. Some of her best food memories date back to her childhood, when every autumn her mother, Gert LeVine, would make heavenly apple pies. This recipe is our variation on Gert's pie. It is at its absolute best, however, when made with a variety of antique cooking apples. While Fred likes it best with some ice cream, Linda and her son Andy think pie is best served plain for breakfast.

Makes 1 10-inch 2-crust pie

1 recipe Pie Crust (recipe follows)
4¼ pounds mixed cooking apples
   Juice of 2 lemons
½ cup raisins
¼ cup flour
½ cup granulated sugar
¼ cup dark brown sugar, firmly
   packed
1½ teaspoons cinnamon
2 teaspoons ground ginger
1 teaspoon ground cardamom
½ teaspoon freshly grated nutmeg
3 tablespoons unsalted butter or
   margarine
1 tablespoon milk
1 tablespoon mixed cinnamon and
   sugar

Place rack in the upper third of oven and preheat oven to 450°. Arrange one 12-inch circle of pie-crust dough in a 10-inch Pyrex pie plate. Keep top crust dough chilled until ready to use.

Peel and core apples. Cut each apple into 16 slices and put into a large mixing bowl. Toss with lemon juice. Add raisins, flour, sugars, and spices. Mix thoroughly to coat apple slices evenly. Gently fill prepared pie plate with apple mixture. This will make a very full and tall pie. Dot apple mixture with 2 tablespoons butter.

Carefully cut decorative vents into the top crust and set it over apple mixture. Trim edges evenly, roll edges together toward the pie's center, and pinch all the way around in an attractive scallop pattern. Brush top crust with milk and sprinkle with half the cinnamon-sugar mixture.

Bake in preheated oven for 15 minutes. Lower oven temperature to 375° and bake

for another 40 minutes, or until pie is golden brown. Check apples for tenderness by gently piercing them through one of the vents with a bamboo skewer. Then rub crust with remaining butter and sprinkle with remaining cinnamon-sugar. Reduce heat to 350° and, if apples are tender, bake just another 5 minutes, or until crust is a darker brown. If apples are not really tender, bake another 10–15 minutes. Through the Pyrex plate, you'll see that even the bottom crust has become golden. Remove pie from oven and let it cool on a rack. Serve warm or at room temperature.

Pie Crust

The recipe for this pie crust was part of Linda's "trousseau" when she married back in 1960.

Makes 2 crusts for a 10-inch pie

2 cups unbleached flour
1¼ teaspoons sugar
¼ teaspoon salt
5 ounces Crisco shortening
3–6 tablespoons very cold milk

Sift dry ingredients together into a shallow mixing bowl. (We always use a wooden one.) Using a pastry cutter, cut shortening into dry ingredients until mixture is the texture of coarse meal. Sprinkle with 2 tablespoons of the cold milk and, using a large-tined fork, lightly blend mixture together. Sprinkle with more milk, a tablespoon at a time, and quickly blend until mixture forms a ball. Do not add too much milk, or the dough will become gooey.

Gently pat dough into a smooth ball, wrap with plastic, and chill at least 1 hour.

Divide dough in half. Lightly flour your work surface, or use a pastry cloth or wax paper. Roll each half of dough into a 12-inch circle and fit into pie plate as instructed in recipe.

If you are making a single crust shell, flute edges, place parchment paper into unbaked shell and fill with dried beans or pie weights. Bake at 425° for 15 minutes. Remove pie shell from oven and place on baking rack. Remove parchment and weights from shell and cool until needed. If pie shell is to be totally baked before using, bake with weights for 15 minutes, remove them, and continue baking the shell until it is golden. Then cool.

Remaining dough can be stored in refrigerator or freezer.

Apple Cranberry Conserve

While this conserve is marvelous to give as a gift at holiday time, it also freezes beautifully. We serve it with Thanksgiving turkey and Christmas goose.

Makes 3 quarts

  ½ cup golden raisins
  ½ cup chopped dried apricots
  ½ cup dried currants
  ⅓ cup Cointreau liqueur
  1 cup crème de cassis liqueur
  ½ cup red wine vinegar
  1½ cups dark brown sugar, firmly packed
  1½ teaspoons curry powder
  1 tablespoon grated fresh ginger
  ½ teaspoon ground cloves
  ½ teaspoon ground allspice
  ½ teaspoon freshly grated nutmeg
  1 teaspoon cinnamon
  1 teaspoon ground cardamom
  1 lemon, peel finely zested and fruit coarsely chopped
  1 lime, peel finely zested and fruit coarsely chopped
  2 oranges, peel finely zested and fruit coarsely chopped
  8 cups fresh cranberries
  6 ounces honey
  ½ cup chopped pecans
  3 large tart cooking apples, peeled, cored, and chopped

Combine raisins, apricots, currants, and Cointreau in a small bowl and set aside.

In a large, heavy saucepan, combine 1 cup water, crème de cassis, vinegar, sugar, and spices. Blend, bring to a boil, and stir until sugar is dissolved. Add citrus zests and simmer briskly 5 minutes.

Add citrus fruits; continue to simmer 5 minutes more. Then add marinated dried fruits and 3 cups of the cranberries. Simmer for 30 minutes.

Add 3 more cups of the cranberries and the honey; simmer 10 minutes. Then add remaining cranberries, pecans, and apples. Cook 15 minutes more. Remove from heat, cool, and chill.

Index